*After the Fact*

# *After the Fact*

## THE ART OF HISTORICAL DETECTION

### SIXTH EDITION
### Volume II

James West Davidson

Mark Hamilton Lytle
*Bard College*

The McGraw·Hill Companies

Mc Graw Hill

Connect
Learn
Succeed™

Published by McGraw-Hill, an imprint of The McGraw-Hill Companies, Inc., 1221 Avenue of the Americas, New York, NY 10020. Copyright © 2010, 2005, 2000, 1992. All rights reserved. No part of this publication may be reproduced or distributed in any form or by any means, or stored in a database or retrieval system, without the prior written consent of The McGraw-Hill Companies, Inc., including, but not limited to, in any network or other electronic storage or transmission, or broadcast for distance learning.

This book is printed on acid-free paper

3 4 5 6 7 8 9 0 DOC/DOC 0

ISBN: 978-0-07-729269-0
MHID: 0-07-729269-3

Editor in Chief: *Michael Ryan*
Publisher: *Chris Freitag*
Sponsoring Editor: *Matthew Busbridge*
Marketing Manager: *Pam Cooper*
Developmental Editor: *Denise Wright*
Managing Editor: *Nicole Bridge*
Production Editor: *David Blatty*
Manuscript Editor: *Andrea McCarrick*
Design Manager and Cover Designer:
Photo Research: *Sarah Evertson*
Production Supervisor: *Rich DeVitto*
Composition: *10.5/12 Janson by Laserwords*
Printing: *45# New Era Matte Plus, R.R. Donnelley & Sons*

Cover Image: © Jean Shifrin/America 24-7/Getty Images

Credits: The credits section for this book begins on page 449 and is considered an extension of the copyright page.

**Library of Congress Cataloging-in-Publication Data**

Davidson, James West.
  After the fact : the art of historical detection / James West Davidson, Mark Lytle.—6th ed.
    p. cm.
  Includes bibliographical references and index.
  ISBN-13: 978-0-07-729268-3 (v. 1 : acid-free paper)
  ISBN-10: 0-07-729268-5 (v. 1 : acid-free paper)
  1. United States—Historiography. 2. United States—History. I. Lytle, Mark H. II. Title.
  E175.D38 2009
  973—dc22                                                                    2009029656

The Internet addresses listed in the text were accurate at the time of publication. The inclusion of a Web site does not indicate an endorsement by the authors or McGraw-Hill, and McGraw-Hill does not guarantee the accuracy of the information presented at these sites.

www.mhhe.com

# *About the Authors*

JAMES WEST DAVIDSON received his PhD from Yale University. A historian who has pursued a full-time writing career, he is the author of numerous books, among them *The Logic of Millennial Thought: Eighteenth-Century New England* and *Great Heart: The History of a Labrador Adventure* (with John Rugge). He is coeditor, with Michael Stoff, of the Oxford New Narratives in American History, in which his own most recent book appears, *"They Say": Ida B. Wells and the Reconstruction of Race.*

MARK H. LYTLE, a PhD from Yale University, is Professor of History and Chair of the Environmental Studies Program at Bard College. He has served two years as Mary Ball Washington Professor of American History at University College Dublin, in Ireland. His publications include *The Origins of the Iranian-American Alliance, 1941–1953, America's Uncivil Wars: The Sixties Era from Elvis to the Fall of Richard Nixon,* and most recently, *The Gentle Subversive: Rachel Carson, Silent Spring, and the Rise of the Environmental Movement.* He recently coedited a joint issue of the journals *Diplomatic History* and *Environmental History* dedicated to the field of environmental diplomacy.

# Contents

# *Preface*

We began this book more than a quarter century ago with an introduction—still there, if you turn the page—which compares the process of doing history to deciphering the tales hidden in the tree rings of a newly felled hemlock. The dust jacket to the first edition even included an authors' photo of the two of us in front of such a stump, looking very young, very hirsute, and vaguely disreputable. (This was the 1970s, by way of historical context.)

The sixth edition finds us quantitatively less hirsute, but the book certainly has gained foliage, having accumulated nearly as much of a history as the old hemlock in our introduction. The first edition of *After the Fact* contained thirteen chapters; the recent fifth edition boasted seventeen, not counting an additional three chapters that have been retired over the years. History may be the past, but its writing moves ahead. We decided that for this edition, we needed to focus on pruning and shaping as well as adding and revising.

We went over each of the existing chapters with an eye to streamlining the narrative, making it more accessible, and eliminating unnecessary detail, without compromising our portrayal of the often messy process of historical detection. The result is that most chapters are shorter and, we believe, more engaging and readable. As in previous editions, we have added two new chapters, as well as rewritten an old one, but the total number remains at seventeen. They progress in chronological order through American history.

"Contact," our new Chapter 1, uses the De Soto expedition of 1539–1543 to examine the difficulties of reconstructing the contested ground of first contact, and the need to take a broader ecological perspective. The progress made by archaeologists over the past few decades allows us to see better some of the remarkable transformations sparked by the De Soto *entrada*, as well as the meeting of Europeans and first Americans more generally. This chapter replaces our previous essay on ecological history, "The Invisible Pioneers." While the new chapter incorporates some material from the original chapter, it also demonstrates how new scholarship has turned other parts of the story nearly upside down.

"Sitting-In," our new Chapter 15, uses the early years of the civil rights struggle to examine how and why broad social movements emerge when and where they do. The lunch-counter demonstrations at Greensboro in 1960 appeared to be a spontaneous event, which then spread like wildfire. Why did the sit-ins in Greensboro trigger this outburst of activism when earlier demonstrations did not? Was Greensboro really spontaneous, as many observers and historians first thought? And does the response to it support the notion that discontinuity rather than continuity defines the process of change over time?

"The Madness of John Brown," Chapter 7, still asks the same question: "Was John Brown insane?" But it employs dynamic psychology rather than psychoanalytic theory to reach a similar conclusion. In times of political upheaval "it's hard to tell who's mad."

Finally, we have included a new feature periodically throughout the text, "Past and Present." In it we make connections between the topics on which we practice detective work from the past with present-day issues or themes worthy of further examination.

Besides streamlining and adding new material, we have made our interactive Web site the place where ancillary materials are now available. The Primary Source Investigator (PSI), previously supplied on CD-ROM, is redesigned and now online. There you will find additional documents and images, as well as chapters from previous editions, including "The 'Noble Savage' and the Artist's Canvas," "Huey Generis," "Instant Watergate," and "The Body in Question." The Research and Writing Center, also found on PSI, will assist students in a range of skills, from time management to conducting their own research and producing quality papers.

Meantime, we owe thanks to those who helped with revisions to this edition. For reviews of this book and for assistance on one or both of our new chapters, we would like to thank Amelia Dees-Killette, Coastal Carolina Community College; Andrew Eugene Barnes, Arizona State University; Angela M. Payne, University of Arkansas; Angela T. Thompson, East Carolina University; Ann F. Ramenofsky, University of New Mexico; Carmen V. Harris, University of South Carolina-Upstate; Kenneth Millen-Penn, Fairmont State University; Mario A. Perez, Crafton Hills College; Marlon Mowdy, Hampton Archaeological Museum State Park, Wilson, Arkansas; Martin B. Cohen (retired), George Mason University; Nancy Mitchell, North Carolina State University; Natalie Graham, University of Florida; Raymond Nathan Wilson, University of Tulsa; W. Frederick Limp, University of Arkansas.

We also have benefited from the assistance of the editorial team at McGraw-Hill, including Nicole Bridge and Denise Wright. As always, we appreciate the enthusiasm of our readers and are pleased to receive any advice, corrections, or comments on this new edition.

# Introduction

This book began as an attempt to bring more life to the reading and learning of history. As practicing historians, we have been troubled by a growing disinterest in or even animosity toward the study of the past. How is it that when we and other historians have found so much that excites curiosity, other people find history irrelevant and boring? Perhaps, we thought, if lay readers and students understood better how historians go about their work—how they examine evidence, how they pose questions, and how they reach answers—history would engage them as it does us.

As often happens, it took a mundane event to focus and clarify our preoccupations. One day while working on another project, we went outside to watch a neighboring farmer cut down a large old hemlock that had become diseased. As his saw cut deeper into the tree, we joked that it had now bit into history as far back as the Depression. *"Depression?"* grunted our friend. "I thought you fellas were historians. I'm deep enough now so's Hoover wasn't even a gleam in his father's eye."

With the tree down, the three of us examined the stump. Our woodcutter surprised us with what he saw.

"Here's when my folks moved into this place," he said, pointing to a ring. "1922."

"How do you know without counting the rings?" we asked.

"Oh, *well*," he said, as if the answer were obvious. "Look at the core, here. The rings are all bunched up tight. I bet there's sixty or seventy—and all within a couple inches. Those came when the place was still forest. Then, you notice, the rings start getting fatter all of a sudden. That's when my dad cleared behind the house—in '22—and the tree started getting a lot more light. And look further out, here—see how the rings set together again for a couple years? That's from loopers."

"Loopers?" we asked cautiously.

"Sure—*loopers*. You know. The ones with only front legs and back." His hand imitated a looping, hopping crawl across the log. "Inchworms. They damn near killed the tree. That was sometime after the war—'49 or '50." As his fingers traced back and forth among the concentric circles, he spoke of other events from years gone by. Before we returned home, we had learned a good deal about past doings in the area.

Now it occurs to us that our neighbor had a pretty good knack for putting together history. The evidence of the past, like the tree rings, comes easily enough to hand. But we still need to be taught how to see it, read it, and explain it before it can be turned into a story. Even more to the point, the explanations and interpretations *behind* the story often turn out to be as interesting as the story itself. After all, the fascination in our neighbor's account came from the way he traced his tale out of those silent tree rings.

Unfortunately, most readers first encounter history in schoolbooks, and these omit the explanations and interpretations—the detective work, if you will. Textbooks, by their nature, seek to summarize knowledge. They have little space for looking at how that knowledge was gained. Yet the challenge of doing history, not just reading it, is what attracts so many historians. Couldn't some of that challenge be communicated in a concrete way? That was our first goal.

We also felt that the writing of history has suffered in recent years because some historians have been overly eager to convert their discipline into an unadulterated social science. Undeniably, history would lose much of its claim to contemporary relevance without the methods and theories it has borrowed from anthropology, psychology, political science, economics, sociology, and other fields. Indeed, such theories make an important contribution to these pages. Yet history is rooted in the narrative tradition. As much as it seeks to generalize from past events, as do the sciences, it also remains dedicated to capturing the uniqueness of a situation. When historians neglect the literary aspect of their discipline—when they forget that good history begins with a good story—they risk losing that wider audience that all great historians have addressed. They end up, sadly, talking to themselves.

Our second goal, then, was to discuss the methods of American historians in a way that would give proper due to both the humanistic and scientific sides of history. In taking this approach, we have tried to examine many of the methodologies that allow historians to unearth new evidence or to shed new light on old issues. At the same time, we selected topics that we felt were inherently interesting as stories.

Thus our book employs what might be called an apprentice approach to history rather than the synthetic approach of textbooks. A textbook strives to be comprehensive and broad. It presents its findings in as rational and programmatic a manner as possible. By contrast, apprentices learn through a much less formal process; they learn their profession from artisans who take their daily trade as it comes through the front door. A customer orders a pewter pot? Very well, the artisan proceeds to fashion the pot and in doing so shows the apprentice how to pour the mold. A client needs some engraving done? Then the apprentice receives a first lesson in etching. The apprentice method of teaching communicates a broad range of knowledge over the long run by focusing on specific situations.

So also this book. Our discussion of methods is set in the context of specific problems historians have encountered over the years. In piecing the individual stories together, we try to pause as an artisan might and point out problems of evidence, historical perspective, or logical inference. Sometimes we focus on problems that all historians must face, whatever their subjects. These problems include such matters as the selection of evidence, historical perspective, the analysis of a document, and the use of broader historical theory. In other cases, we explore problems that are not encountered by all historians but are characteristic of specific historical fields; these include the use of photographic evidence, questions of psychohistory, problems encountered analyzing oral interviews, the value of decision-making models in political history, and so on. In each case, we have tried to provide the reader with a sense of vicarious participation—the savor of doing history as well as of reading it.

Given our approach, the ultimate success of this book can be best measured in functional terms—how well it works for the apprentices and artisans. We hope that the artisans, our fellow historians, will find the volume's implicit as well as explicit definitions of good history worth considering. In choosing our examples, we have naturally gravitated toward the work of those historians we most respect. At the same time, we have drawn upon our own original research in many of the topics discussed; we hope those findings also may be of use to scholars.

As for the apprentices, we admit to being only modest proselytizers. We recognize that of all the people who read this book, only a few will go on to become professional historians. We do hope, however, that even casual readers will come to appreciate the complexity and excitement that go into the study of the past. History is not something that is simply brought out of the archives, dusted off, and displayed as "the way things really were." It is a painstaking construction, held together only with the help of assumptions, hypotheses, and inferences. Readers of history who push dutifully onward, unaware of all the backstage work, miss the essence of the discipline. They miss the opportunity to question and to judge their reading critically. Most of all, they miss the chance to learn how enjoyable it can be to go out and do a bit of digging themselves.

# After the Fact

# The Strange Death of Silas Deane

*The rumors floating around London pointed to suicide. But "what really happened" to Silas Deane could not be discovered unless historians rejected the notion that they were merely couriers between the past and present.*

The writing of history is one of the most familiar ways of organizing human knowledge. And yet, if familiarity has not always bred contempt, it has at least encouraged a good deal of misunderstanding. All of us meet history at a tender age when tales of the past easily blend with heroic myths of the culture. In Golden Books, Abe Lincoln looms every bit as large as Paul Bunyan, while George Washington's cherry tree gets chopped down yearly with almost as much ritual as St. Nick's Christmas tree goes up. Despite this long familiarity, or perhaps because of it, most students absorb the required facts about the past without any real conception of what history is. Even worse, most think they do know what it is and never get around to discovering what they missed.

"History is what happened in the past." That statement is the everyday view of the matter. It supposes that historians must return to the past through the surviving records and bring it back to the present to display as "what really happened." The everyday view recognizes that this task is often difficult. But historians are said to succeed if they bring back the facts without distorting them or forcing a new perspective on them. In effect, historians are seen as couriers between the past and present. Like all good messengers, they are expected simply to deliver their information without adding to it.

This everyday view of history is profoundly misleading. In order to demonstrate how it is misleading, we would like to examine in detail an event that "happened in the past"—the death of Silas Deane. Deane does not appear in most American history texts, and rightly so. He served as a distinctly second-rank diplomat for the United States during the years of the American Revolution. Yet the story of Deane's death is an excellent example of an event that cannot be understood merely by transporting it, courier-like, to the present. In short, it illustrates the important difference between "what happened in the past" and what history really is.

## AN UNTIMELY DEATH

Silas Deane's career began with one of those rags-to-riches stories so much appreciated in American folklore. In fact, Deane might have made a lasting place for himself in the history texts, except that his career ended with an equally dramatic riches-to-rags story.

He began life as the son of a humble blacksmith in Groton, Connecticut. The blacksmith had aspirations for his boy and sent him to Yale College, where Silas was quick to take advantage of his opportunities. After studying law, Deane opened a practice near Hartford; he then continued his climb up the social ladder by marrying a well-to-do widow, whose inheritance included the business of her late husband, a merchant. Conveniently, Deane became a merchant. After his first wife died, he married the granddaughter of a former governor of Connecticut.

Not content to remain a prospering businessman, Deane entered politics. He served on Connecticut's Committee of Correspondence and later as a delegate to the first and second Continental Congresses, where he attracted the attention of prominent leaders, including Benjamin Franklin, Robert Morris, and John Jay. In 1776 Congress sent Deane to France as the first American to represent the united colonies abroad. His mission was to purchase badly needed military supplies for the Revolutionary cause. A few months later, Benjamin Franklin and Arthur Lee joined him in an attempt to arrange a formal treaty of alliance with France. The American commissioners concluded the alliance in March 1778.

Deane worked hard to progress from the son of a blacksmith all the way to Minister Plenipotentiary from the United States to the Court of France. Most observers described him as ambitious: someone who thoroughly enjoyed fame, honor, and wealth. "You know his ambition—" wrote John Adams to one correspondent, "his desire of making a Fortune. . . . You also know his Art and Enterprise. Such Characters are often useful, altho always to be carefully watched and contracted, specially in such a government as ours." One man in particular suspected Deane enough to watch him: Arthur Lee, the third member of the American mission. Lee accused Deane of taking unfair advantage of his official position to make a private fortune—as much as £50,000, some said. Deane stoutly denied the accusations, and Congress engaged in a heated debate over his conduct. In 1778 it voted to recall its Minister Plenipotentiary, although none of the charges had been conclusively proved.

Deane embroiled himself in further controversy in 1781, having written friends to recommend that America sue for peace and patch up the quarrel with England. His letters were intercepted, and copies of them turned up in

*J. Deane.*

*Drawn from the life by Du Simitier in Philadelphia.*      *Engraved by B. L. Prevost at Paris.*

**"You know his ambition**—his desire of making a Fortune. . . . You also know his Art and Enterprise. Such Characters are often useful, altho always to be carefully watched and contracted, specially in such a government as ours."—John Adams on Silas Deane.

a New York Tory newspaper just after Cornwallis surrendered to Washington at Yorktown. For Deane, the timing could not have been worse. With American victory complete, anyone advocating that the United States rejoin Britain was considered as much a traitor as Benedict Arnold. So Deane suddenly found himself adrift. He could not return to America, for no one would have him. Nor could he go to England without confirming his reputation as a traitor. And he could not stay in France, where he had injudiciously accused Louis XVI of aiding the Americans for purely selfish reasons. Rejected on all sides, Deane took refuge in Flanders.

The next few years of his life were spent unhappily. Without friends and with little money, he continued in Flanders until 1783, when the controversy had died down enough for him to move to England. There he lived in obscurity, took to drink, and wound up boarding at the house of an unsavory prostitute. The only friend who remained faithful to him was Edward Bancroft, another Connecticut Yankee who, as a boy, had been Deane's pupil and later his personal secretary during the Paris negotiations for the alliance.

*The only friend who remained faithful was Edward Bancroft, a spy for the Americans who had known Deane in Paris.*

Although Bancroft's position as a secretary seemed innocent enough, members of the Continental Congress knew that Bancroft was also acting as a spy for the Americans, using his connections in England to secure information about the British ministry's war plans. With the war concluded, Bancroft was back in London. Out of kindness, he provided Deane with living money from time to time.

Finally, Deane decided he could no longer live in London and in 1789 booked passage on a ship sailing for the United States. When Thomas Jefferson heard the news, he wrote his friend James Madison: "Silas Deane is coming over to finish his days in America, not having one sou to subsist on elsewhere. He is a wretched monument of the consequences of a departure from right."

The rest of the sad story could be gotten from the obituaries. Deane boarded the *Boston Packet* in mid-September, and it sailed out of London down the Thames River to the Atlantic. A storm came up, however, and on September 19 the ship lost both its anchors and beat a course for safer shelter, to wait out the storm. On September 22, while walking the quarterdeck with the ship's captain, Deane suddenly "complain'd of a dizziness in his head, and an oppression at his stomach." The captain immediately put him to bed. Deane's condition worsened; twice he tried to say something, but no one was able to make out his words. A "drowsiness and insensibility continually incroached upon his faculties," and only four hours after the first signs of illness he breathed his last.

Such, in outline, was the rise and fall of the ambitious Silas Deane. The story itself seems pretty clear, although certainly people might interpret it in different ways. Thomas Jefferson thought Deane's unhappy career demonstrated "the consequences of a departure from right," whereas one English newspaper more sympathetically attributed his downfall to the mistake of "placing confidence in his [American] Compatriots, and doing them service before he had got his compensation, of which no well-bred Politician was before him ever guilty." Yet either way, the basic story remains the same— the same, that is, until the historian begins putting together a more complete account of Deane's life. Then some of the basic facts become clouded.

For example, a researcher familiar with the correspondence of Americans in Europe during 1789 would realize that a rumor had been making its way around London in the weeks following Deane's death. According to certain people, Deane had become depressed by his poverty, ill health, and low reputation, and consequently had committed suicide. John Cutting, a New England merchant and friend of Jefferson, mentioned the rumor that Deane "had predetermin'd to take a sufficient quantity of Laudanum [a form of opium] to ensure his dissolution" before the boat could sail for America. John Quincy Adams heard that "every probability" of the situation suggested Deane's death was "voluntary and self-administered." And Tom Paine, the famous pamphleteer, also reported the gossip: "Cutting told me he took poison."

At this point we face a substantial problem. Obviously, historians cannot rest content with the facts that come most easily to hand. They must search the odd corners of libraries and letter collections in order to put together a complete story. But how do historians know when their research is "complete"? How do they know to search one collection of letters rather than another? These questions point up the misconception at the heart of the everyday view of history. History is not "what happened in the past"; rather, it is the act of selecting, analyzing, and writing about the past. It is something that is done, that is constructed, rather than an inert body of data that lies scattered through the archives.

The distinction is important. It allows us to recognize the confusion in the question of whether a history of something is "complete." If history were merely "what happened in the past," there would never be a "complete" history of Silas Deane—or even a complete history of the last day of his life. The past holds an infinite number of facts about those last days, and they could never all be included in a historical account.

The truth is, no historian would want to include all the facts. Here, for example, is a list of items from the past that might form part of a history of Silas Deane. Which ones should be included?

> Deane is sent to Paris to help conclude a treaty of alliance.
> Arthur Lee accuses him of cheating his country to make a private profit.
> Deane writes letters that make him unpopular in America.
> He goes into exile and nearly starves.
> Helped out by a gentleman friend, he buys passage on a ship for America as his last chance to redeem himself.
> He takes ill and dies before the ship can leave; rumors suggest he may have committed suicide.

*    *    *

> Ben Franklin and Arthur Lee are members of the delegation to Paris.
> Edward Bancroft is Deane's private secretary and an American spy.
> Men who know Deane say he is talented but ambitious and ought to be watched.

*    *    *

> Before Deane leaves, he visits an American artist, John Trumbull.
> The *Boston Packet* is delayed for several days by a storm.
> On the last day of his life, Deane gets out of bed in the morning.

He puts on his clothes and buckles his shoes.
He eats breakfast.
When he takes ill, he tries to speak twice.
He is buried several days later.

Even this short list demonstrates the impossibility of including all the facts. For behind each one lie hundreds more. You might mention that Deane put on his clothes and ate breakfast, but consider also: What color were his clothes? When did he get up that morning? What did he have for breakfast? When did he leave the table? All these things "happened in the past," but only a comparatively small number of them can appear in a history of Silas Deane.

Readers may object that we are placing too much emphasis on this process of selection. Surely, a certain amount of good judgment will suggest which facts are important. Who needs to know what color Deane's clothes were or when he got up from the breakfast table?

Admittedly, this objection has some merit, as the list of facts about Deane demonstrates. The list is divided into three groups, roughly according to the way common sense might rank them in importance. The first group contains facts that every historian would be likely to include. The second group contains less important information, which could either be included or left out. (It might be useful, for instance, to know who Arthur Lee and Edward Bancroft were, but not essential.) The last group contains information that appears to be either too detailed or else unnecessary. Deane may have visited John Trumbull, but then he surely visited other people as well. Why include any of that? Knowing that the *Boston Packet* was delayed by a storm reveals little about Silas Deane. And readers will assume without being told that Deane rose in the morning, put on his clothes, and had breakfast.

But if common sense helps select evidence, it also produces a good deal of pedestrian history. The fact is, the straightforward account of Silas Deane we have just presented has actually managed to miss the most fascinating parts of the story.

Fortunately, one enterprising historian named Julian Boyd was not satisfied with the traditional account of the matter. He examined the known facts of Deane's career and put them together in ways that common sense had not suggested. Take, for example, two items on our list: (1) Deane was down on his luck and left in desperation for America; and (2) he visited John Trumbull. One fact is from the "important" items on the list and the other from items that seem incidental. How do they fit together?

To answer that, we have to know the source of information about the visit to Trumbull's, which is the letter from John Cutting informing Jefferson of Deane's rumored suicide.

A subscription had been made here chiefly by Americans to defray the expense of getting [Deane] out of this country. . . . Dr. Bancroft with great humanity and equal discretion undertook the management of the man and his business. Accordingly his passage was engaged, comfortable cloaths and stores for his voyage were laid in, and apparently without much reluctance he embarked. . . . I happen'd to see him a few days since at the lodging of Mr. Trumbull and thought I had never seen him look better.

We are now in a better position to see how our two items fit together. And as Julian Boyd has pointed out, they don't fit. According to the first, Deane was depressed, dejected, almost starving. According to the second, he had "never looked better." Alert historians begin to get nervous when they see contradictions like that, so they hunt around a little more. And Julian Boyd found, among the collection of papers published by the Connecticut and New York historical societies, that Deane had been writing letters of his own.

One went to his brother-in-law in America, who had agreed to help pay Deane's transportation over and to receive him when he arrived—something that nobody had been willing to do for years. Other letters reveal that Deane had plans for what he would do when he finally returned home. He had seen models in England of the new steam engines, which he hoped might operate gristmills in America. He had talked to friends about getting a canal built from Lake Champlain in New York to the St. Lawrence River in order to promote trade. As early as 1785 Deane had been at work drumming up support for his canal project. He had even laboriously

*Was Deane really depressed enough to commit suicide? Or looking forward to a chance to clear his name?*

calculated the cost of the canal's construction ("Suppose a labourer to dig and remove six feet deep and eight feet square in one day. . . . 2,933 days of labour will dig one mile in length, twenty feet wide and eight feet deep.") Obviously, Deane looked forward to a promising future.

Lastly, Deane appeared to believe that the controversy surrounding his French mission had finally died down. As he wrote an American friend,

> It is now almost ten years since I have solicited for an impartial inquiry [into the dispute over my conduct] . . . that justice might be done to my fortune and my character. . . . You can sufficiently imagine, without my attempting to describe, what I must have suffered on every account during so long a period of anxiety and distress. I hope that it is now drawing to a close.

Other letters went to George Washington and John Jay, reiterating Deane's innocence.

All this information makes the two items on our list even more puzzling. If Deane was depressed and discouraged, why was he so enthusiastic about coming back to build canals and gristmills? If he really believed that his time of "anxiety and distress" was "drawing to a close," why did he commit suicide? Of course, Deane might have been subject to dramatic shifts in mood.

Perhaps hope for the future alternated with despair about his chances for success. Perhaps a sudden fit of depression caused him to take his life.

But another piece of "unimportant" information, way down in the third group of our list, makes this hypothesis difficult to accept. After Deane's ship left London, it was delayed offshore for more than a week. Suppose Deane did decide to commit suicide by taking an overdose of laudanum. Where did he get the drug? Surely not by walking up to the ship's surgeon and asking for it. He must have purchased it in London, before he left. Yet he remained on shipboard for more than a week. If Deane bought the laudanum during a temporary "fit" of depression, why did he wait a week before taking it? And if his depression was not just a sudden fit, how do we explain the optimistic letters to America?

This close look at three apparently unrelated facts indicates that perhaps there is more to Deane's story than meets the eye. It would be well, then, to reserve judgment about our first reconstruction of Silas Deane's career and try to find as much information about the man as possible—whether or not it seems relevant at first. That means investigating not only Deane himself but also his friends and associates, such as Ben Franklin, Arthur Lee, and Edward Bancroft. Since it is impossible in this prologue to look closely at all of Deane's acquaintances, for purpose of example we will take only one: his friend Bancroft.

## SILAS DEANE'S FRIEND

Edward Bancroft was born in Westfield, Massachusetts, where his step-father presided over a respectable tavern, the Bunch of Grapes. Bancroft was a clever fellow, and his father soon apprenticed him to a physician. Like many boys before him, Edward did not fancy his position and so ran away to sea. Unlike many boys, he managed to make the most of his situation. His ship landed in Barbados, and there Bancroft signed on as the surgeon for a plantation in Surinam, also known as Guiana. The plantation owner, Paul Wentworth, liked the young man and let him use his private library for study. In addition, Bancroft met another doctor who taught him much about the area's exotic tropical plants and animals. When Bancroft returned to New England in 1766 and continued on to London the following year, he knew enough about Surinam's wildlife to publish a book entitled *An Essay on the Natural History of Guiana in South America.* It was well received by knowledgeable scholars and, among other things, established that an electric eel's shock was caused by electricity, a fact not previously recognized.

A young American bright enough to publish a book at age twenty-five and to experiment with electric eels attracted the attention of another electrical experimenter then in London, Ben Franklin. Franklin befriended Bancroft and introduced him to many influential colleagues, not only learned philosophers but also the politicians with whom Franklin worked as colonial agent for Pennsylvania. A second trip to Surinam produced more research on plants used in making color dyes, research so successful that Bancroft soon found himself elected to the prestigious Royal Society of Medicine. At the same time, Franklin led Bancroft into the political arena, both public and private. On the public side, Bancroft published a favorable review of Thomas Jefferson's pamphlet *A Summary View of the Rights of British America;* privately, he joined Franklin and other investors in an attempt to gain a charter for land along the banks of the Ohio River.

Up to this point we have been able to sketch Bancroft's career without once mentioning the name of Silas Deane. Common sense would suggest that the information about Bancroft's early travels, his scientific studies, his friends in Surinam, tell us little about Deane, and that the story ought to begin with a certain letter Bancroft received from Deane in June 1776. (Common sense is again wrong, but we must wait a little to discover why.)

The letter, which came to Bancroft in 1776, informed him that his old friend Silas Deane was coming to France as a merchant engaged in private business. Would Bancroft be interested in crossing over from England to meet Deane at Calais to catch up on news for old time's sake? An invitation like that would very likely have attracted Bancroft's curiosity. He did know Deane, who had been his teacher in 1758, but not very well. Why would Deane now write and suggest a meeting? Bancroft may have guessed the rest, or he may have known it from other contacts; in any case, he wrote his "old friend" that he would make all possible haste for Calais.

The truth of the matter, as we know, was that Deane had come to France to secure military supplies for the colonies. Franklin, who was back in Philadelphia, had suggested to Congress's Committee of Secret Correspondence that Deane contact Bancroft as a good source of information about British war plans. Bancroft could easily continue his friendship with English officials, because he did not have the reputation of being a hotheaded American patriot. So Deane met Bancroft at Calais in July, and the two concluded their arrangements. Bancroft would be Deane's "private secretary" when needed in Paris and a spy for the Americans when in England.

It turned out that Deane's arrangement worked well—perhaps a little too well. Legally, Deane was permitted to collect a commission on all the supplies he purchased for Congress, but he went beyond that. He and Bancroft used their official connections in France to conduct a highly profitable private trade of their own. Deane, for instance, sometimes sent ships from France without declaring whether they were loaded with private or public goods. Then if the ships arrived safely, he would declare that the cargo was private, his own. But if the English navy captured the goods on the high seas, he labeled it government merchandise and the public absorbed the loss.

Deane used Bancroft to take advantage of his official position in other ways. Both men speculated in the London insurance markets, which were the eighteenth-century equivalent of gambling parlors. Anyone who wished could take out "insurance" against a particular event that might happen in the future. An insurer, for example, might quote odds on the chances of France going to war with England within the year. The insured would pay whatever premium he wished, say £1,000, and if France did go to war and the odds had been five-to-one against it, the insured would receive £5,000. Wagers were made on almost any public event: which armies would win which battles, which politicians would fall from power, and even whether a particular lord would die before the year was out.

Obviously, someone who had access to inside information—someone who knew in advance, for instance, that France was going to war with England—could win a fortune. That was exactly what Bancroft and Deane decided to do. Deane was in charge of concluding the French alliance, and he knew that if he succeeded, Britain would be forced to declare war on France. Bancroft hurried across to London as soon as the treaty had been concluded and took out the proper insurance before the news went public. The profits shared by the two men from this and similar ventures amounted to approximately £10,000. Like most gamblers, however, Deane also lost wagers. In the end, he netted little for his troubles.

*Deane and Bancroft both made money from inside information, by gambling on the London insurance markets.*

Historians know these facts because they now have access to the papers of Deane, Bancroft, and others. Acquaintances of the two men lacked this advantage, but they suspected shady dealings anyway. Arthur Lee publicly accused Deane and Bancroft of playing the London insurance game. (Deane shot back that Lee was doing the same thing.) And the moralistic John Adams found Bancroft's conduct distasteful. Bancroft, according to Adams, was

> a meddler in stocks as well as reviews, and frequently went into the alley, and into the deepest and darkest retirements and recesses of the brokers and jobbers . . . and found amusement as well, perhaps, as profit, by listening to all the news and anecdotes, true or false, that were there whispered or more boldly pronounced. . . . This man had with him in France, a woman with whom he lives, and who by the French was called La Femme de Monsieur Bancroft. At tables he would season his foods with such enormous quantities of cayenne pepper which assisted by generous burgundy would set his tongue a running in the most licentious way both at table and after dinner.

Yet for all Bancroft's dubious habits, and for all the suspicions of men like Lee and Adams, there was one thing that almost no one at the time suspected, and that not even historians discovered until the records of certain British officials were opened to the public more than a century later. Edward Bancroft was a double agent.

At the end of July 1776, after he had arranged to be Deane's secretary, Bancroft returned to England and met with Paul Wentworth, his friend from Surinam, who was then working in London for Britain's intelligence organization. Immediately Wentworth realized how valuable Bancroft would be as a spy and introduced him to two secretaries of state. They in turn persuaded Bancroft to submit reports on the American negotiations in France. For his services, he received a lifetime pension of £200 a year—a figure the British were only too happy to pay for such good information. So quick was Bancroft's reporting that the secretaries of state knew about the American mission to France even before the United States Congress could confirm that Deane had arrived safely!

Eventually, Bancroft discovered that he could pass his information directly to the British ambassador at the French court. To do so, he wrote innocent letters on the subject of "gallantry" and signed them "B. Edwards." On the same paper would go another note written in invisible ink, to appear only when the letter was dipped in a special developer held by Lord Stormont, the British ambassador. Bancroft left his letters every Tuesday morning in a sealed bottle in a hole near the trunk of a tree on the south terrace of the Tuileries, the royal palace. Lord Stormont's secretary would put any return information near another tree on the same terrace. With this system in operation, Stormont could receive intelligence without having to wait for it to filter back from England.

Did any Americans suspect Bancroft of double-dealing? Arthur Lee once claimed he had evidence to charge Bancroft with treason, but he never produced it. In any case, Lee had a reputation for suspecting everybody of everything. Franklin, for his part, shared lodgings with Deane and Bancroft during their stays in Paris. He had reason to guess that someone close to the American mission was leaking secrets—especially when Lord Stormont and the British newspapers made embarrassingly accurate accusations about French aid. The French wished to keep their assistance secret in order to avoid war with England as long as possible, but of course Franklin knew America would fare better with France fighting, so he did little to stop the leaks. "If I was sure," he remarked, "that my valet de place was a spy, as he probably is, I think I should not discharge him for that, if in other respects I liked him." So the French would tell Franklin he really ought to guard his papers more closely, and Franklin would say yes, yes, he really would have to do something about that; and the secrets continued to leak. Perhaps Franklin suspected Deane and Bancroft of playing the London insurance markets, but there is no evidence that he knew Bancroft was a double agent.

What about Deane, who was closer to Bancroft than anyone else? We have no proof that he shared the double agent's secret, but his alliance with Bancroft in other intrigues tells against him. Furthermore, one published leak pointed to a source so close to the American commissioners that Franklin began to investigate. As Julian Boyd has pointed out, Deane immediately directed suspicion toward a man he knew perfectly well was not a spy. We can only conclude he did so to help throw suspicion away from Bancroft. Very likely, if Bancroft was willing to help Deane play his games with the London insurers, Deane was willing to assist Bancroft in his game with British intelligence.

**The Tuileries,** much as it appeared when Bancroft and Lord Stormont used the south terrace as a drop for their secret correspondence. The royal palace overlooks a magnificent formal garden that, as a modern observer has noted, "seems so large, so full of surprising hidden corners and unexpected stairways, that its strict ground plan—sixteen carefully spaced and shaped gardens of trees, separated by arrow-straight walks—is not immediately discernable."

Of the two, Bancroft seems to have made out better. While Deane suffered reproach and exile for his conduct, Bancroft returned to England still respected by both the Americans and the British. Not that he had been without narrow escapes. Some of the British ministry (the king especially) did not trust him, and he once came close to being hanged for treason when his superiors rightly suspected that he had associated with John the Painter, an unbalanced fanatic who tried to set England's navy ablaze. But Bancroft left for Paris at the first opportunity, waited until the storm blew over, and returned to London at the end of the war with his lifetime pension raised to £1,000 a year. At the time of Deane's death, he was doing more of his scientific experiments, in hopes that Parliament would grant him a profitable monopoly on a new process for making dyes.

## DEANE'S DEATH: A SECOND LOOK

So we finally arrive, the long way around, back where the story began: September 1789 and Deane's death. But now we have a much larger store of information out of which to construct a narrative. Since writing history involves the acts of analyzing and selecting, let us review the results of our investigation.

We know that Deane was indeed engaged in dubious private ventures, ventures Congress would have condemned as unethical. We also have reason to suspect that Deane knew Bancroft was a spy for the British. Combining that evidence with what we already know about Deane's death, we might theorize that Deane committed suicide because, underneath all his claims to innocence, he knew he was guilty as Congress charged. The additional evidence, in other words, reveals a possible new motive for Deane's suicide.

Yet this theory presents definite problems. In the first place, Deane never admitted any wrongdoing to anyone—not in all the letters he wrote, not in any of his surviving papers. That does not mean he was innocent, nor even that he believed himself innocent. But often it is easier for a person to lie to himself than to his friends. Perhaps Deane actually convinced himself that he was blameless, that he had a right to make a little extra money from his influential position, and that he did no more than anyone would in his situation. Certainly his personal papers point to that conclusion. And if Deane believed himself innocent—correctly or not—would he have any obvious motive for suicide? Furthermore, the theory does not explain the puzzle that started this investigation. If Deane felt guilty enough about his conduct to commit suicide, why did that guilt increase ten years after the fact? If he did feel suddenly guilty, why wait a week aboard ship before taking the fatal dose of laudanum? For that matter, why go up and chat with the captain when death was about to strike?

No, things still do not sit quite right, so we must question the theory. What proof do we have that Deane committed suicide? Rumors about London. Tom Paine heard it from Cutting, the merchant. And Cutting reports in his letter to Jefferson that Deane's suicide was "the suspicion of Dr. Bancroft." How do we know the circumstances of Deane's

*Since writing history involves the acts of analyzing and selecting, we need to review the results of our investigation.*

death? The captain made a report, but for some reason it was not preserved. The one account that did survive was written by Bancroft, at the request of a friend. Then there were the anonymous obituaries in the newspapers. Who wrote them? Very likely Bancroft composed at least one; certainly, he was known as Silas Deane's closest friend and would have been consulted by any interested parties. There are a lot of strings here, which, when pulled hard enough, all run back to the affable Dr. Bancroft. What do we know about his situation in 1789?

We know Bancroft is dependent on a pension of £1,000 a year, given him for his faithful service as a British spy. We know he is hoping Parliament will grant him a monopoly for making color dyes. Suddenly his old associate Deane, who has been leading a dissolute life in London, decides to return to America, vindicate himself to his former friends, and start a new life. Put yourself in Bancroft's place. Would you be just a little nervous about that idea? Here is a man down on his luck, now picking up and going to America to clear his reputation. What would Deane do to clear it? Tell everything he knew about his life in Paris? Submit his record books to Congress, as he had been asked to do so many years before? If Deane knew Bancroft was a double agent, would he say so? And if Deane's records mentioned the affair of John the Painter (as indeed they did), what would happen if knowledge of Bancroft's role in the plot reached England? Ten years earlier, Bancroft would have been hanged. True, the angry feelings of the war had faded, but even if he were spared death, would Parliament grant a monopoly on color dyes to a known traitor? Would Parliament continue the £1,000 pension? It was one thing to have Deane living in London, where Bancroft could watch him; it would be quite another to have him all the way across the Atlantic Ocean, ready to tell—who knows what?

Admit it: if you were Bancroft, wouldn't you be just a little nervous?

We are forced to consider, however reluctantly, that Deane was not expecting to die as he walked the deck of the *Boston Packet*. Yet if Bancroft did murder Deane, how? He was not aboard ship when death came and had not seen Deane for more than a week. That is a good alibi, but then, Bancroft was a clever man. We know (once again from the letters of John Cutting) that Bancroft was the person who "with great humanity and equal discretion undertook the management of the man and [the] business" of getting Deane ready to leave for America. Bancroft himself wrote Jefferson that he had been visiting Deane often "to assist him with advice, medicins, and money for his subsistence." If Deane were a laudanum addict, as Bancroft hinted to Cutting, might not the good doctor who helped with "medicins" also have procured the laudanum? And having done that, might he not easily slip some other deadly chemical into the mixture, knowing full well that Deane would not use it until he was on shipboard and safely off to America? That conclusion is only conjecture. We have no direct evidence to suggest that this scenario is what really happened.

But we do know one other fact for sure; and in light of our latest theory, it is an interesting one. Undeniably, Edward Bancroft was an expert on poisons.

He did not advertise that knowledge, of course; few people in London at the time of Deane's death would have been likely to remember the fact. But twenty years earlier, the historian may recall, Bancroft wrote a book on the natural history of Guiana. At that time he not only investigated electric eels and color dyes, but also the poisons of the area, particularly curare (or "Woorara" as Bancroft called it). He investigated it so well, in fact, that when he returned to England he brought samples of curare with him, which (he announced in the book) he had deposited with the publishers so that any gentleman of "unimpeachable" character might use the samples for scientific study.

Furthermore, Bancroft seemed to be a remarkably good observer not only of the poisons, but also of those who used them. His book described in ample detail the natives' ability to prepare poisons that, given in the smallest quantities, produce a very slow but inevitable death, particularly a composition which resembles wheat-flour, which they sometimes use to revenge past injuries, that have been long neglected, and are thought forgotten. On these occasions they always feign an insensibility of the injury which they intend to revenge, and even repay it with services and acts of friendship, until they have destroyed all distrust and apprehension of danger in the destined victim of the vengeance. When this is effected, they meet at some festival, and engage him to drink with them, drinking first themselves to obviate suspicion, and afterwards secretly dropping the poison, ready concealed under their nails, which are usually long, into the drink.

Twenty years later Bancroft was busy at work with the color dyes he had brought back from Surinam. Had he, by any chance, also held onto any of those poisons?

Unless new evidence comes to light, we will probably never know for sure. Historians are generally forced to deal with probabilities, not certainties, and we leave you to draw your own conclusions about the death of Silas Deane.

What does seem certain is that whatever "really happened" to Deane two hundred years ago cannot be determined today without the active participation of the historian. Being courier to the past is not enough. For better or worse, historians inescapably leave an imprint as they go about their business: asking interesting questions about apparently dull facts, seeing connections between subjects that had not seemed related before, shifting and rearranging evidence until it assumes a coherent pattern. The past is not history, only the raw materials of it. How those raw materials come to be fashioned and shaped is the central concern of this book.

## Additional Reading

The historian proposing the possibility of foul play on the *Boston Packet* is Julian Boyd. He makes his case in a series of three articles titled "Silas Deane: Death by a Kindly Teacher of Treason?" *William and Mary Quarterly*, 3d ser., 16 (1959): 165–187, 319–342, and 515–550. Edward Bancroft's role as double agent was not established conclusively until the 1890s. His connections to the British are spelled out in Paul L. Ford, *Edward Bancroft's Narrative of the Objects and Proceedings of Silas Deane* (Brooklyn, NY, 1891). Further background on Bancroft's youth may be gained, of course, from his lively *Essay on the Natural History of Guiana in South America* (London, 1769).

Boyd's case for murder has been questioned by William Stinchcombe in "A Note on Silas Deane's Death," *William and Mary Quarterly*, 3d ser., 32 (1975): 619–624. Stinchcombe has suggested that, contrary to Boyd's suggestion, Deane did not face any really hopeful prospects for success in America. If Deane continued to be down on his luck when he departed for America, then the suicide theory again becomes more probable. For a third opinion, consult D. K. Anderson and G. T. Anderson, "The Death of Silas Deane," *New England Quarterly* 62 (1984): 98–105. The Andersons surveyed several medical authorities and concluded that Deane may well have suffered from chronic tuberculosis and died from a stroke or some other acute attack.

CHAPTER 8

# The View from the Bottom Rail

*How can we know anything about newly freed slaves who left behind few written records? Oral evidence provides one answer.*

Thunder. From across the swamps and salt marshes of the Carolina coast came the distant, repetitive pounding. Thunder out of a clear blue sky. Down at the slave quarters, young Sam Mitchell heard the noise and wondered. In Beaufort, the nearby village, planter John Chaplin heard too, and dashed for his carriage. The drive back to his plantation was as quick as Chaplin could make it. Once home, he ordered his wife and children to pack; then he looked for his slaves. The flatboat must be made ready, he told them; the family was going to Charleston. He needed eight men at the oars. One of the slaves, Sam Mitchell's father, brought the news to his wife and son at the slave quarters. "You ain't gonna row no boat to Charleston," the wife snapped, "you go out dat back door and keep agoing." Young Sam was mystified by all the commotion. How could it thunder without a cloud in the sky? "Son, dat ain't no t'under," explained the mother, "dat Yankee come to gib you freedom."

The pounding of the guns came relatively quickly to Beaufort—November 1861, only seven months after the first hostilities at Fort Sumter. Yet it was only a matter of time before the thunder of freedom rolled across the rest of the South, from the bayous and deltas of Louisiana in 1862 to the farms around Richmond in 1865. As the guns of the Union spoke, thousands of Sam Mitchells experienced their own unforgettable moments. Freedom was coming to a nation of four million slaves.

To most slaves, the men in the blue coats were foreigners—and sometimes suspect. Many southern masters painted the prospect of northern invasion in lurid colors. Union soldiers, one Tennessee slave was told, "got long horns on their heads, and tushes [pointed teeth] in their mouths, and eyes sticking out like a cow! They're mean old things." A fearful Mississippi slave refused to come out of a tree until the Union soldier below her took off his cap and demonstrated he had no horns. Many slaves, however, scoffed at such tales. "We all hear 'bout dem Yankees," a Carolina slave told his overseer. "Folks

**This slave family** lived on a plantation at Beaufort, South Carolina, not far from the plantation where Sam Mitchell heard the thunder of northern guns in 1861. The photograph was taken after northern forces had occupied the Sea Islands area.

tell we they has horns and a tail. . . . Wen I see dem coming I shall run like all possess." But as soon as the overseer fled, leaving the plantation in the slaves' care, the tune changed: "Good-by, ole man, good-by. That's right. Skedaddle as fast as you kin. . . . We's gwine to run sure enough; but we knows the Yankees, an' we runs that way."

For some slaves, the bond of loyalty or the fear of alternatives led them to side with their masters. Faithful slaves hid valuable silver, persuaded Yankees that their departed masters were Union sympathizers, or pretended they had a contagious illness in order to scare off marauding soldiers. But in many cases, the conflict between loyalty and freedom caused anguish. A Georgia couple, both more than sixty years old, greeted Sherman's soldiers calmly and with apparent lack of interest. They seemed content to remain with their master instead of joining the slaves flocking along behind Union troops. As the soldiers prepared to leave, however, the old woman suddenly stood up, a "fierce, almost devilish" look in her eyes. "What you sit dar for?" she asked her husband vehemently. "You s'pose I wait sixty years for nutten? Don't yer see de door open? I'se follow my child; I not stay. Yes, anudder day I goes 'long wid dese people; yes, sar, I walks till I drop in my tracks."

Other slaves felt no hesitation about choosing freedom; indeed, they found it difficult to contain their joy. One woman, who overheard the news of emancipation just before she was to serve her master's dinner, asked to be excused to get water from a nearby spring. Once there, and out of sight, she allowed her feelings free rein.

> I jump up and scream, "Glory, glory hallelujah to Jesus! I'se free! I'se free! Glory to God, you come down an' free us; no big man could do it." An' I got sort o' scared, afeared somebody hear me, an' I takes another good look, an' fall on de goun' an' roll over, an' kiss de gound' fo' de Lord's sake, I's so full o' praise to Masser Jesus.

To newly freed slaves, it seemed the world had turned upside down. Rich and powerful masters were fleeing, while freed slaves were left with the run of the plantation. The situation was summed up by one black soldier who was surprised—and delighted—to find his former master among the prisoners he was guarding. "Hello, massa!" he said cheerfully, "bottom rail top dis time!"

## RECOVERING THE FREEDPEOPLE'S POINT OF VIEW

The freeing of four million black slaves ranks as one of the major events in American history. Yet the story has not been easy to tell. To understand the personal trials and triumphs of the newly liberated slaves, or "freedpeople" as they have come to be called,* historians must draw on the personal experiences of those at the center of the drama. They must recreate the freedpeople's point of view. But slaves had occupied the lowest level of America's social and economic scale. They sat, as the black soldier correctly noted, on the bottom rail of the fence. For several reasons, that social reality has made it more difficult to recover the freedpeople's point of view.

In the first place, most traditional histories suffered from a natural "top-rail" bias, writing primarily about members of the higher social classes. Histories cannot be written without primary-source material, and by and large, those on the top rails of society have produced the most records. Having been privileged to receive an education, members of the middle and upper classes are more apt to publish memoirs, keep diaries, or write letters. As leaders of society who make decisions, they are the subjects of official minutes and records.

At the other end of the social spectrum, ordinary folk lead lives that are less documented. While political leaders involve themselves in one momentous issue after another, the work of farmers and laborers is often repetitive

---

* White contemporaries of the newly freed slaves referred to them as *freedmen*. More recently, historians have preferred the gender-neutral term *freedpeople*, which we will use here except when quoting primary sources.

*Git away from dat dar fence while man or I'll make Old Abe's Gun smoke at you. I can hardly hold de ball back now.—De bottom rails on top now.*

*Point Lookout Md.*

**"Git away from dat dar fence white man** or I'll make Old Abe's Gun smoke at you. I can hardly hold de ball back now.—De bottom rails on top now." More than one former slave used the image of the "bottom rail on top" to define the transformation wrought by the Civil War. This watercolor sketch was made by a Confederate soldier being held prisoner by Union forces at Point Lookout, Maryland.

and appears to have little effect on the course of history. The decade of the 1970s, however, saw an increasing interest in the lives of ordinary people. In Chapter 2, for example, we saw that appreciating the social and economic position of the serving class was essential to understanding the volatile society of early Virginia. Similarly, in Chapter 3 we turned to the social tensions of ordinary farmers in order to explore the alliances behind the witchcraft controversy at Salem.

Reconstructing the perspective of enslaved African Americans has proved particularly challenging. Before the Civil War, slaves were not only discouraged from learning to read and write, southern legislatures passed slave codes that flatly forbade whites to teach them. The laws were not entirely effective. A few blacks employed as drivers on large plantations learned to read and correspond so that their absent masters might send them instructions. Some black preachers were also literate. Still, most reading remained a furtive affair, done out of sight of the master or other whites. During the war, a literate slave named Squires Jackson was eagerly scanning a newspaper for word of northern victories when his master unexpectedly entered the room and demanded to know what the slave was doing. The surprised reader deftly turned the newspaper upside down, put on a foolish grin, and said, "Confederates done won the war!" The master laughed and went about his business.

Even though most slaves never wrote letters, kept diaries, or left other written records, it might at first seem possible to learn about slave life from accounts written by white contemporaries. Any number of letters, books, travelers' accounts, and diaries survive, after all—full of descriptions of life under slavery and of the experiences of freedpeople after the war. Yet the question of perspective raises serious problems. The vantage point of white Americans observing slavery was emphatically not that of slaves who lived under the "peculiar institution."

Consider, first, the observations of those whites who associated most closely with black slaves: their masters. The relationship between master and slave was inherently unequal. Slaves could be whipped for trifling offenses; they could be sold or separated from their families and closest friends; even under "kind" masters, they were bound to labor as ordered if they wanted their ration of food and clothing. With slaves so dependent on the master's authority, they were hardly likely to reveal their true feelings; the dangerous consequences of doing so were too great.

*With slaves so dependent on the master's authority, they were hardly likely to reveal their true feelings to their owners*

In fact, we have already encountered an example in which a slave deceived his master: the case of Squires Jackson and his newspaper. Think for a moment about the source of that story. Even without a footnote to indicate where the information came from, readers of this chapter can deduce that it was left in the historical record by Jackson, not the planter. (The planter, after all, went away convinced Jackson could not read.) Imagine how different our impression would be if the only surviving record of the incident was the planter's diary. We might then be reading an entry something like the following:

> A humorous incident occurred today. While entering the woodshed to attend some business, I came upon my slave Squires. His eyes were fixed with intense interest upon an old copy of a newspaper he had come upon, which alarmed me some until I discovered the rascal was reading its contents upside down. "Why Squires," I said innocently. "What is the latest news?" He looked up at me with a big grin and said, "Massa, de 'Federates jes' won de war!" It made me laugh to see the darkey's simple confidence. I wish I could share his optimism.

This entry is fictional, but having Jackson's version of the story serves to cast suspicion on similar entries in real planters' diaries. One Louisiana slave owner, for instance, marveled that his field hands went on with their Christmas party apparently unaware that Yankee raiding parties had pillaged a nearby town. "We have been watching the negroes dancing for the last

**"They are having a merry time,** thoughtless creatures, they think not of the morrow." This scene of a Christmas party, similar to the one described by the Louisiana planter, appeared with an article written by a northern correspondent for *Frank Leslie's Illustrated Newspaper* in 1857. The picture, reflecting the popular stereotype of slaves as cheerful and ignorantly content with their lot, suggests that the social constraints of the times made it as difficult for southern African Americans to be completely candid with their northern liberators as it had been to be candid with their southern masters.

two hours. . . . They are having a merry time, thoughtless creatures, they think not of the morrow." It apparently never occurred to the planter that the "thoughtless" merriment may have been especially great because of the northern troops nearby.*

The harsh realities of the war forced many southerners to consider just how little they really knew about their slaves. Often, the very servants that masters deemed most loyal were the first to run off. Mary Chesnut, whose house was not far from Fort Sumter, sought in vain to penetrate the blank expressions of her slaves. "Not by one word or look can we detect any change in the demeanor of these Negro servants. . . . You could not tell that

---

* Readers who review the opening narrative of this chapter will discover that they have already encountered quite a few other examples of deception arising out of the social situations in which the actors found themselves. In fact, except for the black soldier's comment about the bottom rail being top, every example of white-black relationships cited in the opening section has some element of concealment or deception. It may be worth noting that we did not select the opening incidents with that fact in mind. The preponderance of deception was noted only when we reviewed the draft several days after it had been written.

they even hear the awful noise that is going on in the bay [at Fort Sumter], though it is dinning in their ears night and day. . . . Are they stolidly stupid, or wiser than we are, silent and strong, biding their time?"

It is tempting to suppose that white northerners who helped liberate slaves might have provided more accurate accounts of freedpeople's attitudes. But that assumption is dangerous. Although virtually all northern slaves had been freed by 1820, race prejudice remained strong. Antislavery forces often combined a strong dislike of slavery with an equally strong desire to keep the freedpeople out of the North. Most housing and transportation facilities were segregated there, so that whites and blacks had much less close social contact than in the South.

Thus, while some Union soldiers went out of their way to be kind to slaves they encountered, many looked upon African Americans with distaste or open hostility. More than a few Yankees believed they were fighting a war to save the Union, not to free the "cursed Nigger," as one recruit put it. White officers who commanded black regiments could be remarkably unsympathetic.

*Both northern and southern white accounts of black Americans need to be viewed with caution.*

"Any one listening to your shouting and singing can see how grotesquely ignorant you are," one officer lectured his troops, when they refused to accept less than the pay promised on enlistment. Even missionaries and other sympathetic northerners who came to occupied territory had preconceptions to overcome. "I saw some very low-looking women who answered very intelligently, contrary to my expectations," noted Philadelphia missionary Laura Towne. So we need to be cautious even when reviewing northern accounts.

Indeed, perceptive whites recognized that just as slaves had been dependent on their southern masters before the war, freedpeople found themselves similarly vulnerable to the new class of conquerors. "One of these blacks, fresh from slavery, will most adroitly tell you precisely what you want to hear," noted northerner Charles Nordhoff.

> To cross-examine such a creature is a task of the most delicate nature; if you chance to put a leading question he will answer to its spirit as closely as the compass needle answers to the magnetic pole. Ask if the enemy had fifty thousand men, and he will be sure that they had at least that many; express your belief that they had not five thousand, and he will laugh at the idea of their having more than forty-five hundred.

Samuel Gridley Howe, a wartime commissioner investigating the freedpeople's condition, saw the situation clearly. "The negro, like other men, naturally desires to live in the light of truth," he argued, "but he hides in the shadow of falsehood, more or less deeply, according as his safety or welfare seems to require it. Other things equal, the freer a people, the more truthful; and only the perfectly free and fearless are perfectly truthful."

Furthermore, northerners found it hard to imagine the freedpeople's point of view because the culture of southern African Americans was so unfamiliar. The first hurdle was simple communication, given the wide variety of accents and dialects spoken by northerners and southerners. Charles Nordhoff noted that often he had the feeling that he was "speaking with foreigners." The slaves' phrase "I go shum" puzzled him until he discovered it to be a contraction of "I'll go see about it." Another missionary was teaching his students "what various things were for, eyes, etc. He asked what ears were made for, and when they said, 'To yer with,' he could not understand them at all."

If black dialect was difficult to understand, black culture and religion could appear even more unfathomable. Although most slaves shared with northerners a belief in Christianity, black methods of worship shocked more than one staid Unitarian. After church meetings, slaves often participated in a singing and dancing session known as a "shout," in which the leader would sing out a line of song and the chorus would respond, dancing in rhythm to the music. As the night proceeded, the music became more vocal and the dancing more vigorous. One missionary noted, "It was the most hideous and at the same time the most pitiful sight I ever witnessed."

As sympathetic as many northerners wished to be, significant obstacles prevented them from fully appreciating the freedpeople's point of view. The nature of slave society and the persistence of prejudice made it virtually impossible for blacks and whites to deal with one another candidly.

## THE FREEDPEOPLE SPEAK

From the very beginning, however, some observers recognized the value of the former slaves' perspective. If few black people could write, their stories could be written down by others and made public. Oral testimony, transcribed by literate editors, would allow black Americans to speak out on issues that affected them most.

The tradition of oral evidence began even before the slaves were freed. Abolitionists recognized the value of firsthand testimony against the slave system. They took down and published the stories of fugitive slaves who escaped to the North. During the war, Congress also established the Freedman's Inquiry Commission, which collected information that might aid the government.

In the half century following Reconstruction, however, interest in preserving black history languished. An occasional journalist or historian interviewed former slaves. Educators at black schools, such as the Hampton Institute, published recollections. But most historians writing about Reconstruction ignored them, as well as the freedpeople's perspective in general. Instead they relied on white accounts, which painted a rather partial picture.

William A. Dunning, a historian at Columbia University, was perhaps the most influential advocate of the prevailing viewpoint. He painted the freedpeople as childish, happy-go-lucky creatures who failed to appreciate the responsibilities of their new status. "As the full meaning of [emancipation] was grasped by the freedmen," Dunning wrote, "great numbers of them abandoned their old homes, and, regardless of crops to be cultivated, stock to be cared for, or food to be provided, gave themselves up to testing their freedom. They wandered aimless but happy through the country." At the same time, Dunning claimed that southern whites had "devoted themselves with desperate energy to the procurement of what must sustain the life of both themselves and their former slaves." Such were the conclusions deduced without the aid of the freedpeople's perspectives.

Only in the twentieth century were systematic efforts made to question blacks about their experiences. Interest in the African American heritage rose markedly during the 1920s, spurred by the efforts of black scholars such as W. E. B. DuBois, Charles Johnson, and Carter Woodson, the editor and founder of the *Journal of Negro History*. Those scholars worked hard to overturn the stereotypes promoted by the Dunning school. Moreover, sociologists and anthropologists at American universities began to analyze southern culture, using the tools of the new social sciences. By the beginning of the 1930s, historians at Fisk University in Nashville and Southern University in Baton Rouge had instituted projects to collect oral evidence.

Ironically, the hard times of the Depression sparked the greatest single effort to gather oral testimony from the freedpeople. One of the many agencies chartered by the Roosevelt administration was the Federal Writers' Project (FWP). The project's primary goal was to compile and publish cultural guides to each of the forty-eight states, using unemployed writers and journalists. But under the direction of folklorist John Avery Lomax, the FWP also organized staffs in many states to interview former slaves.

*The hard times of the Depression sparked the greatest single effort to gather oral history from former slaves.*

Although Lomax's project placed greatest emphasis on collecting black folklore and songs, the FWP's directive to interviewers included a long list of historical questions that they were encouraged to ask. The following sampling gives an indication of the project's interests:

What work did you do in slavery days? Did you ever earn any money?
What did you eat and how was it cooked? Any possums? Rabbits? Fish?
Was there a jail for slaves? Did you ever see any slaves sold or auctioned off?
   How and for what causes were the slaves punished? Tell what you saw.
What do you remember about the war that brought you your freedom? When
   the Yankees came, what did they do or say?

The results of these interviews were remarkable. More than 2,300 were recorded and edited in state FWP offices and sent to Washington, assembled in 1941, and published in typescript. A facsimile edition, issued during the 1970s, takes up nineteen volumes. Supplementary materials, including hundreds of interviews never forwarded to Washington during the project's life, comprise another twenty-two volumes. Benjamin Botkin, the series' original editor, recognized the collection's importance. "These life histories, taken down as far as possible in the narrator's words, constitute an invaluable body of unconscious evidence or indirect source material," he noted. "For the first and last time, a large number of surviving slaves (many of whom have since died) have been permitted to tell their own story, in their own way."

Even Botkin, however, recognized that the narratives could not simply be taken at face value. Like all primary-source materials, they need to be viewed in terms of the context in which they originated. To begin with, even nineteen volumes packed with interviews constitute a small sampling of the original four million freedpeople. What sort of selection bias might exist? Geographic imbalance comes quickly to mind. Are the slave interviews drawn from a broad cross section of southern states? Counting the number of slaves interviewed from each state, we discover only 155 interviews from African Americans living in Virginia, Missouri, Maryland, Delaware, and Kentucky—about 6 percent of the total number of interviews published. Yet in 1860, 23 percent of the southern slave population lived in those states. Thus the upper South is underrepresented in the collection.

What about age? Because the interviews took place primarily between 1936 and 1938, former slaves were fairly old: fully two-thirds were more than eighty years of age. How sharp were the elderly informants' memories? The Civil War was already seventy years in the past. Common sense suggests that the further away from an event, the less detailed a person's memory is likely to be. In addition, age may have biased the type of recollections given. Historian John Blassingame has noted that the average life expectancy of a slave in 1850 was less than fifty years. Those who lived to a ripe old age might well have survived because they were treated better than the average slave. If so, their accounts would reflect some of the milder experiences of slaves.

*Are the interviews biased because they focus on those who survived slavery, rather than those who died from harsh treatment?*

Also, if those interviewed were predominantly old in 1936, they were predominantly young during the Civil War. Almost half (43 percent) were less than ten years old in 1865. Sixty-seven percent were under age fifteen, and 83 percent were under age twenty. Thus many interviewers remembered slavery as it would have been experienced by a child. If the conditions of bondage were relatively less harsh for a child than for an adult slave, once again the FWP narratives may be somewhat skewed toward an optimistic view of slavery. (On the other hand, it might be argued that because children are so impressionable, memories both good and bad might have been magnified.)

Distortions may be introduced into the slave narratives in ways more serious than sample bias. Interviewers, simply by choosing their questions, define the kinds of information a subject will volunteer. Even the most seemingly innocent questions are liable to influence the way a subject responds. Take, for example, the following questions:

> Where did you hear about this job opening?
> How did you hear about this job opening?
> So you saw our want ad for this job?

Each question is directed at the same information, yet each suggests to the subject a different response. The first version ("Where did you hear . . .") implies that the interviewer wants a specific, limited answer ("Down at the employment center."). The second question, by substituting "how" for "where," invites the subject to offer a longer response ("Well, I'd been looking around for a job for several weeks, and I was over at the employment office when . . ."). The final question signals that the interviewer wants only a yes or no confirmation to a question whose answer is believed to be already known.

Interviewers, in other words, constantly communicate to their subjects the kind of evidence they want, the length of the answers, and even the manner in which answers ought to be offered. If such cues influence routine conversations, they prove even more crucial when a subject as controversial as slavery is involved, and when relations between blacks and whites continue to be strained. In fact, the most important cue an interviewer was likely to have given was one presented before any conversation took place. Was the interviewer white or black? Interracial tensions remained sharp throughout the South during the 1930s. In hundreds of ways, black people were made aware that they were still considered inferior and that they were to remain within strictly segregated and subordinate bounds. From 1931 to 1935, more than seventy African Americans were lynched in the South, often for minor or nonexistent crimes. Black prisoners found themselves forced to negotiate grossly unfavorable labor contracts if they wished to be released. Sharecroppers and other poor farmers were constantly in debt to white property owners.

Matters of etiquette reflected the larger state of affairs. White southerners commonly addressed black adults by their first names, or as "boy," "auntie," or "uncle," regardless of the black person's status and even if the white person knew the black person's full name. Black people were required to address white people as "ma'am" or "mister." Such distinctions applied even on the telephone. If an African American placed a long-distance call for "Mr. Smith" in a neighboring town, the white operator would ask, "Is he colored?" The answer being yes, her reply would be, "Don't you say 'Mister' to me. He ain't 'Mister' to me." Conversely, an operator would refuse to place a call by a black caller who did not address her as "Ma'am."

Thus most African Americans were reticent about volunteering information to white FWP interviewers. "Lots of old slaves closes the door before they tell the truth about their days of slavery," noted one black Texan to an interviewer. "When the door is open, they tell how kind their masters was how rosy it all was." Samuel S. Taylor, a skilled black interviewer in Arkansas,

**"I've told you too much.** How come they want all this stuff from the
colored people anyway? Do you take any stories from the white people? . . .
They don't need me to tell it to them." This Georgia woman, like many of
the subjects interviewed for the Federal Writers' Project, was still living in
the 1930s on the plantation where she had grown up as a slave child. The
plantation was still owned by descendants of her former master. Under such
conditions, suspicion toward FWP interviewers was a predictable reaction,
even if the interviewer was black; doubly so if he or she was white and a
resident of the community.

found that he had to reassure informants that the information they were giving would not be used against them. "I've told you too much," one subject concluded. "How come they want all this stuff from the colored people anyway?

Do you take any stories from the white people? They know all about it. They know more about it than I do. They don't need me to tell it to them."

Often the whites who interviewed blacks lived in the same town and were long acquaintances. "I 'members when you was barefoot at de bottom," one black interviewee told his white (and balding) interviewer; "now I see you a set-tin' dere, gittin' bare at de top." Another black man revealed an even closer rela-tionship when he noted that his wife, Ellen, "'joy herself, have a good time nussin' [nursing] white folks chil-lun. Nussed you; she tell me 'bout it many time." In such circumstances, African Americans could hardly be expected to speak frankly. One older woman summed up the situation quite cheerfully. "Oh, I know your father en your granfather en all of dem. Bless Mercy, child, I don't want to tell you nothin' but what to please you."

*"I've told you too much. How come they want all this stuff from the colored people anyway? Do you take any stories from the white people?"*

The methods used to set down FWP interviews raise additional prob-lems. With only a few exceptions, voice recorders were not used. Instead, interviewers took written notes of their conversations, from which they later reconstructed their interviews. In the process, interviewers often edited their material. Sometimes changes were made simply to improve the flow, so that the interview did not jump jarringly from topic to topic. Other interviewers edited out material they believed to be irrelevant or objectionable.

Furthermore, no protocol existed for transcribing African American dia-lect. A few interviewers took great pains to render their accounts in cor-rect English, so that regional accents and dialect disappeared. ("Fo" became "for," "dem" became "them," and so forth.) But most interviewers tried to provide a flavor of black dialect, with wildly varying success. In some cases the end result sounded more like the stereotypical "darky dialect" popular with whites of the period. "I wuz comin' frum de back uv de stable," an interviewer might quote his subject as saying—a colloquial approach that, to some readers, might at first seem unobjectionable. Yet few of the same interviewers would have thought it necessary to render, with similar offbeat spelling, the accents of a white "southun plantuh," whose speech might seem equally exotic to an American from another region of the United States. For that matter, consider the spellings used in "I wuz comin' frum de back uv de stable." In fact, there is no difference in pronunciation between "was" and "wuz"; or "frum" and "from"; or "uv" and "of." In effect, those tran-scriptions are simply cultural markers conveying the unspoken message that, in the eyes of the interviewer, the speaker comes from a less cultured and less educated social class. Eventually, the FWP sent its interviewers a list of Approved Dialect Expressions: "dem," "dose," and "gwine" were among the permitted transcriptions; "wuz," "ovah," and "uv" were not allowed.

By understanding the difficulties of gathering oral evidence, researchers are able to proceed more carefully in evaluating the slave narrative collec-tion. Even so, readers new to this field may find it difficult to appreciate the varying responses that different interviewers might elicit. In order to bring the point home, it may be helpful to analyze material that we came across during our own research in the slave narrative collection. The interview below is with Susan Hamlin, a black woman who lived in Charleston, and we reprint it exactly as it appears in typescript.

### Interview with Ex-Slave

On July 6th, I interviewed Susan Hamlin, ex-slave, at 17 Henrietta street, Charleston, S. C. She was sitting just inside of the front door, on a step leading up to the porch, and upon hearing me inquire for her she assumed that I was from the Welfare office, from which she had received aid prior to its closing. I did not correct this impression, and at no time did she suspect that the object of my visit was to get the story of her experience as a slave. During our conversation she mentioned her age. "Why that's very interesting, Susan," I told her, "If you are that old you probably remember the Civil War and slavery days." "Yes, Ma'am, I been a slave myself," she said, and told me the following story:

"I kin remember some things like it was yesterday, but I is 104 years old now, and age is starting to get me, I can't remember everything like I use to. I getting old, old. You know I is old when I been a grown woman when the Civil War broke out. I was hired out then, to a Mr. McDonald, who lived on Atlantic Street, and I remembers when de first shot was fired, and the shells went right over de city. I got seven dollars a month for looking after children, not taking them out, you understand, just minding them. I did not got the money, Mausa got it." "Don't you think that was fair?" I asked. "If you were fed and clothed by him, shouldn't he be paid for your work?" "Course it been fair," she answered, "I belong to him and he got to get something to take care of me."

"My name before I was married was Susan Calder, but I married a man named Hamlin. I belonged to Mr. Edward Fuller, he was president of the First National Bank. He was a good man to his people till de Lord took him. Mr. Fuller got his slaves by marriage. He married Miss Mikell, a lady what lived on Edisto Island, who was a slave owner, and we lived on Edisto on a plantation. I don't remember de name cause when Mr. Fuller got to be president of de bank we come to Charleston to live. He sell out the plantation and say them (the slaves) that want to come to Charleston with him could come and them what wants to stay can stay on the island with his wife's people. We had our choice. Some is come and some is stay, but my ma and us children come with Mr. Fuller.

"We lived on St. Philip street. The house still there, good as ever. I go 'round there to see it all de time; the cistern still there too, where we used to sit 'round and drink the cold water, and eat, and talk and laugh. Mr. Fuller have lots of servants and the ones he didn't need hisself he hired out. The slaves had rooms in the back, the ones with children had two rooms and them that didn't have any children had one room, not to cook in but to sleep in. They all cooked and ate downstairs in the hall that they had for the colored people. I don't know about slavery but I know all the slavery I know about, the people was good to me. Mr. Fuller was a good man and his wife's people been grand people, all good to their slaves. Seem like Mr. Fuller just git his slaves so he could be good to dem. He made all the little colored chillen love him. If you don't believe they loved him what they all cry, and scream, and holler for when dey hear he dead? 'Oh, Mausa dead my Mausa dead, what I going to do, my Mausa dead.' Dey tell dem t'aint no use to cry, dat can't bring him back, but de chillen keep on crying. We used to call him Mausa Eddie but he named Mr. Edward Fuller, and he sure was a good man.

"A man come here about a month ago, say he from de Government, and dey send him to find out 'bout slavery. I give him most a book, and what he give me? A dime. He ask me all kind of questions. He ask me dis and he ask me dat, didn't de white people do dis and did dey do dat but Mr. Fuller was a good man, he was sure good to me and all his people, dey all like him, God bless him, he in de ground now but I ain't going to let nobody lie on him. You know he good when even the little chillen cry and holler when he dead. I tell you dey couldn't just fix us up any kind of way when we going to Sunday School. We had to be dressed nice, if you pass him and you ain't dress to suit him he send you right back and say tell your ma to see dat you dress right. Dey couldn't send you out in de cold barefoot neither. I 'member one day my ma want to send me wid some milk for her sister-in-law what lived 'round de corner. I fuss cause it cold and say 'how you going to send me out wid no shoe, and it cold?' Mausa hear how I talkin and turn he back and laugh, den he call to my ma to gone in de house and find shoe to put on my feet and don't let him see me barefoot again in cold weather.

> *"He ask me all kind of questions. He ask me dis and he ask me dat, didn't de white people do dis and did dey do dat but Mr. Fuller was a good man, he was sure good to me and all his people."*

"When de war start going good and de shell fly over Charleston he take all us up to Aiken for protection. Talk 'bout marching through Georgia, dey sure march through Aiken, soldiers was everywhere.

"My ma had six children, three boys and three girls, but I de only one left, all my white people and all de colored people gone, not a soul left but me. I ain't been sick in 25 years. I is near my church and I don't miss service any Sunday, night or morning. I kin walk wherever I please, I kin walk to de Battery if I want to. The Welfare use to help me but dey shut down now, I can't find out if dey going to open again or not. Miss (Mrs.) Buist and Miss Pringle, dey help me when I can go there but all my own dead."

"Were most of the masters kind?" I asked. "Well you know," she answered, "times den was just like dey is now, some was kind and some was mean; heaps of wickedness went on just de same as now. All my people was good people. I see some wickedness and I hear 'bout all kinds of t'ings but you don't know whether it was lie or not. Mr Fuller been a Christian man."

"Do you think it would have been better if the Negroes had never left Africa?" was the next question I asked. "No Ma'am, (emphatically) dem heathen didn't have no religion. I tell you how I t'ink it is. The Lord made t'ree nations, the white, the red and the black, and put dem in different places on de earth where dey was to stay. Dose black ignoramuses in Africa forgot God, and didn't have no religion and God blessed and prospered the white people dat did remember Him and sent dem to teach de black people even if dey have to grab dem and bring dem into bondage till dey learned some sense. The Indians forgot God and dey had to be taught better so dey land was taken away from dem. God sure bless and prosper de white people and He put de red and de black people under dem so dey could teach dem and bring dem into sense wid God. Dey had to get dere brains right, and honor God, and learn uprightness wid God cause ain't He make you, and ain't His Son redeem you and save you wid His Precious blood. You kin plan all de wickedness you want and pull hard as you choose but when the Lord mek up His mind you is to change, He can change you dat quick (snapping her fingers) and easy. You got to believe on Him if it tek bondage to bring you to your knees.

"You know I is got converted. I been in Big Bethel (church) on my knees praying under one of de preachers. I see a great, big, dark pack on my back, and it had me all bent over and my shoulders drawn down, all hunch up. I look up and I see de glory, I see a big beautiful light, a great light, and in de middle is de Sabior, hanging so (extending her arms) just like He died. Den I gone to praying good, and I can feel de sheckles (shackles) loose up and moving and de pack fall off. I don't know where it went to, I see de angels in de Heaven, and hear dem say 'Your sins are forgiven.' I scream and fell off so. (Swoon.) When I come to dey has laid me out straight and I know I is converted cause you can't see no such sight and go on like you is before. I know I is still a sinner but I believe in de power of God and I trust his Holy name. Den dey put me wid de seekers but I know I is already saved."

"Did they take good care of the slaves when their babies were born?" she was asked. "If you want chickens for fat (to fatten) you got to feed dem," she said with a smile, "and if you want people to work dey got to be strong, you got to feed dem and take care of dem too. If dey can't work it come out of your pocket. Lots of wickedness gone on in dem days, just as it do now, some good, some mean, black and white, it just dere nature, if dey good dey going to be kind to everybody, if dey mean dey going to be mean to everybody. Sometimes chillen was sold away from dey parents. De Mausa would come and say 'Where Jennie,' tell um to put clothes on dat baby, I want um. He sell de baby and de ma scream and holler, you know how dey carry on. Geneally (generally) dey sold it when de ma wasn't dere. Mr. Fuller didn't sell none of us, we stay wid our ma's till we grown, I stay wid my ma till she dead.

"You know I is mix blood, my grandfather bin a white man and my grandmother a mulatto. She been marry to a black so dat how I get fix like I is. I got both blood, so how I going to quarrel wid either side?"

SOURCE: Interview with Susan Hamlin, 17 Henrietta Street.

NOTE: Susan lives with a mulatto family of the better type. The name is Hamlin not Hamilton, and her name prior to her marriage was Calder not Collins. I paid particular

attention to this and had them spell the names for me. I would judge Susan to be in the late nineties but she is wonderfully well preserved. She now claims to be 104 years old.

From the beginning, the circumstances of this conversation arouse suspicion. The white interviewer, Jessie Butler, mentions that she allowed Hamlin to think she was from the welfare office. Evidently, Butler thought Hamlin would speak more freely if the real purpose of the visit was hidden. But surely the deception had the opposite effect. Hamlin, like most of the black people interviewed, was elderly, unable to work, and dependent on charity. If Butler appeared to be from the welfare office, Hamlin would likely have done whatever she could to ingratiate herself. Many black interviewees consistently assumed that their white interviewers had influence with the welfare office. "You through wid me now, boss? I sho' is glad of dat," concluded one subject. "Help all you kin to get me dat pension befo' I die and de Lord will bless you, honey. . . . Has you got a dime to give dis old nigger, boss?"

Furthermore, Butler's questioning was hardly subtle. When Hamlin noted that she had to give her master the money she made from looking after children, Butler asked, "Don't you think that was fair?" "Course it been fair," came the quick response. Hamlin knew very well what was expected, especially since Butler had already answered the question herself: "If you were fed and clothed by him, shouldn't he be paid for your work?"

Not surprisingly, then, the interview paints slavery in relatively mild colors. Hamlin describes in great detail how good her master was and how she had shoes in the winter. When asked whether most masters were kind, Hamlin appears eminently "fair"—"some was kind and some was mean." She admits hearing "all kinds of t'ings but you don't know whether it was lie or not." She does note that slave children could be sold away from parents and that black mothers protested; but she talks as if that were only to be expected ("de ma scream and holler, you know how dey carry on").

Equally flattering is the picture Hamlin paints of relations between the races. "Black ignoramuses" in Africa had forgotten about God, she explains, just as the Indians had; but "God sure bless and prosper de white people." So Africans and the Indians are placed under white supervision, "to get dere brains right, and honor God, and learn uprightness." Those were not exactly the words proslavery apologists would have used to describe the situation, but they were the same sentiments. Defenders of slavery constantly stressed that Europeans served as benevolent models leading Africans and Indians on the slow upward road to civilization.

All these aspects of the interview led us to be suspicious about its content. Moreover, several additional clues in the document puzzled us. Hamlin had mentioned a man who visited her "about a month ago, say he from de Government, and dey send him to find out 'bout slavery." Apparently her interview with Jessie Butler was the second she had given. Butler, for her part, made a fuss at the end of the transcript over the spelling of Hamlin's name ("I paid particular attention to this."). It was "Hamlin not Hamilton," and her maiden name was "Calder not Collins." The phrasing indicates that somewhere else Butler had seen Hamlin referred to as "Susan Hamilton." If someone had interviewed Hamlin earlier, we wondered, could Hamilton have been the name on that original report?

We found the answer when we continued on through the narrative collection. The interview following Butler's was conducted by a man named Augustus Ladson, with a slave named "Susan Hamilton." When compared with Jessie Butler's interview, Augustus Ladson's makes absorbing reading. Here it is, printed exactly as it appears in the collection:

### Ex-Slave 101 Years of Age

### Has Never Shaken Hands Since 1863

### Was on Knees Scrubbing when Freedom Gun Fired

I'm a hund'ed an' one years old now, son. De only one livin' in my crowd frum de days I wuz a slave. Mr. Fuller, my master, who was president of the Firs' National Bank, owned the fambly of us except my father. There were eight men an' women with five girls an' six boys workin' for him. Most o' them wus hired out. De house in which we stayed is still dere with de sisterns an' slave quarters. I always go to see de old home which is on St. Phillip Street.

My ma had t'ree boys an' t'ree girls who did well at their work. Hope Mikell, my eldest brodder, an' James wus de shoemaker. William Fuller, son of our Master, wus de bricklayer. Margurite an' Catharine wus de maids an' look as de children.

My pa b'long to a man on Edisto Island. Frum what he said, his master was very mean. Pa real name wus Adam Collins but he took his master' name; he wus de coachman. Pa did supin one day en his master whipped him. De next day which wus Monday, pa carry him 'bout four miles frum home in de woods an' give him de same 'mount of lickin' he wus given on Sunday. He tied him to a tree an' unhitched de horse so it couldn't git tie-up an' kill e self. Pa den gone to de landin' an' cetch a boat dat wus comin' to Charleston wood fa'm products. He (was) permitted by his master to go to town on errands, which helped him to go on de boat without bein' question'. W'en he got here he gone on de water-front an' ax for a job on a ship so he could git to de North. He got de job an' sail' wood de ship. Dey search de island up an' down for him wood houndogs en w'en it wus t'ought he wus drowned, 'cause dey track him to de river, did dey give up. One of his master' friend gone to New York en went in a store w'ere pas wus employed as a clerk. He reconize' pa is easy is pa reconize' him. He gone back home an' tell pa master who know den dat pa wusn't comin' back an' before he died he sign' papers dat pa wus free. Pa' ma wus dead an' he come down to bury her by de permission of his master' son who had promised no ha'm would come to him, but dey wus' fixin' plans to keep him, so he went to de Work House an' ax to be sold 'cause any slave could sell e self if e could git to de Work House. But it wus on record down dere so dey couldn't sell 'im an' told him his master' people couldn't hold him a slave.

People den use to do de same t'ings dey do now. Some marry an' some live together jus' like now. One t'ing, no minister nebber say in readin' de matrimony "let no man put asounder" 'cause a couple would be married tonight an' tomorrow one would be taken away en be sold. All slaves wus married in dere master house, in de livin' room where slaves an' dere missus an' mossa wus to witness de ceremony. Brides use to wear some of de finest dress an' if dey could afford it, have de best kind of furniture. Your master nor your missus objected to good t'ings.

I'll always 'member Clory, de washer. She wus very high-tempered. She was a mulatto with beautiful hair she could sit on; Clory didn't take foolishness frum anybody. One day our missus gone in de laundry an' find fault with de clothes. Clory didn't do a t'ing but pick her up bodily an' throw 'er out de door. Dey had to sen' fur a doctor 'cause she pregnant an' less than two hours de baby wus bo'n. Afta dat she begged to be sold fur she didn't [want] to kill missus, but our master ain't nebber want to sell his slaves. But dat didn't keep Clory frum gittin' a brutal whippin'. Dey whip' 'er until dere wusn't a

*"Our master ain't nebber want to sell his slaves. But dat didn't keep Clory frum gittin' a brutal whippin'. Dey whip' 'er until dere wusn't a white spot on her body. Dat wus de worst I ebber see a human bein' got such a beatin'. I t'ought she wus goin' to die."*

white spot on her body. Dat wus de worst I ebber see a human bein' got such a beatin'. I t'ought she wus goin' to die, but she got well an' didn't get any better but meaner until our master decide it wus bes' to rent her out. She willingly agree' since she wusn't 'round missus. She hated an' detest' both of them an' all de fambly.

W'en any slave wus whipped all de other slaves wus made to watch. I see women hung frum de ceilin' of buildin's an' whipped with only supin tied 'round her lower part of de body, until w'en dey wus taken down, dere wusn't breath in de body. I had some terribly bad experiences.

Yankees use to come t'rough de streets, especially de Big Market, huntin' those who want to go to de "free country" as dey call' it. Men an' women wus always missin' an' nobody could give 'count of dere disappearance. De men wus train' up North fur sojus.

De white race is so brazen. Dey come here an' run de Indians frum dere own lan', but dey couldn't make dem slaves 'cause dey wouldn't stan' for it. Indians use to git up in trees an' shoot dem with poison arrow. W'en dey couldn't make dem slaves den dey gone to Africa an' bring dere black brother an' sister. Dey say 'mong themselves, "we gwine mix dem up en make ourselves king. Dats d only way we'd git even with de Indians."

All time, night an' day, you could hear men an' women screamin' to de tip of dere voices as either ma, pa, sister, or brother wus take without any warnin' an' sell. Some time mother who had only one chile wus separated fur life. People wus always dyin' frum a broken heart.

One night a couple married an' de next mornin' de boss sell de wife. De gal ma got in in de street an' cursed de white woman fur all she could find. She said: "dat damn white, pale-face bastard sell my daughter who jus' married las' night," an' other t'ings. The white man tresten' her to call de police if she didn't stop, but de collud woman said: "hit me or call de police. I redder die dan to stan' dis any longer." De police took her to de Work House by de white woman orders an' what became of 'er, I never hear.

W'en de war began we wus taken to Aiken, South Ca'lina were we stay' until de Yankees come t'rough. We could see balls sailin' t'rough de air w'en Sherman wus comin'. Bumbs hit trees in our yard. W'en de freedom gun wus fired, I wus on my 'nees scrubbin'. Dey tell me I wus free but I didn't b'lieve it.

In de days of slavory woman wus jus' given time 'nough to deliver dere babies. Dey deliver de baby 'bout eight in de mornin' an' twelve had to be back to work.

I wus a member of Emmanuel African Methodist Episcopal Church for 67 years. Big Zion, across de street wus my church before den an' before Old Bethel w'en I lived on de other end of town.

Sence Lincoln shook hands with his assasin who at de same time shoot him, frum dat day I stop shakin' hands, even in de church, an' you know how long dat wus. I don't b'lieve in kissin' neider fur all carry dere meannesses. De Master wus betrayed by one of his bosom frien' with a kiss.

SOURCE: Interview with (Mrs.) Susan Hamilton, 17 Henrietta Street, who claims to be 101 years of age. She has never been sick for twenty years and walks as though just 40. She was hired out by her master for seven dollars a month which had to be given her master.

Susan Hamlin and Susan Hamilton are obviously one and the same, yet by the end of Ladson's interview, we are wondering if we have been listening to the same person! Kindness of the masters? We hear no tales about old Mr. Fuller, only vivid recollections of whippings so harsh "dere wusn't a white spot on her body." To Butler, Hamlin had mentioned only cruelties that she had heard about secondhand ("you don't know whether it was lie or not"); to Ladson, she recounts firsthand experiences ("I see women hung frum de ceilin' of buildin's an' whipped with only supin tied 'round her lower part of de body").

Happy family relations? Instead of tales about shoes in the winter, we hear of Hamlin's father, whipped so severely he rebels and flees. We hear of family separations, not downplayed with a "you know how dey carry on," but with all the bitterness of mothers whose children had been taken "without any warnin'." We hear of a couple married one night, then callously separated and sold the next day. In the Butler account, slave babies are fed well, treated nicely; in the Ladson account, the recollection is of mothers who were given only a few hours away from the fields in order to deliver their children.

Benevolent white paternalism? This time Hamlin's tale of three races draws a different moral. The white race is "brazen," running the Indians off

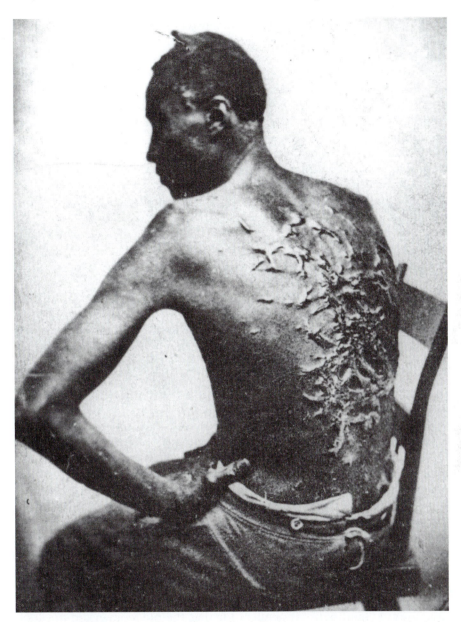

**"W'en any slave wus whipped** all de other slaves was made to watch. . . . I had some terribly bad experiences." The scars from whippings on this slave's back were recorded in 1863 by an unknown photographer traveling with the Union army.

their land. With a touch of admiration, she notes that the Indians "wouldn't stan' for" being made slaves. White motives are seen not as religious but as exploitative and vengeful: "Dey say 'mong themselves, 'we gwine mix dem

up en make ourselves king. Dats d only way we'd git even with de Indians.'"
The difference between the two interviews, both in tone and substance, is
astonishing.

How do we account for this difference? Nowhere in the South Carolina
narratives is the race of Augustus Ladson mentioned, but internal evidence
would indicate he is black. In a culture in which blacks usually addressed
whites respectfully with a "sir," "ma'am," or "boss," it seems doubtful that
Susan Hamlin would address a white man as "son" ("I'm a hund'ed an' one
years old now, son"). Furthermore, the content of the interview is just too
consistently critical of whites. Hamlin would never have remarked "De white
race is so brazen" if Ladson had been white, especially given the reticence
demonstrated in her interview with Butler. Nor would she have been so specific about the angry mother's curses ("damn white, pale-face bastard"). It
would be difficult to conceive of a more strikingly dramatic demonstration
of how an interviewer can affect the responses of a subject.

## FREEDOM AND DECEPTION

The slave narrative collection, then, is not the unfiltered perspective it first
appears to be. In fact, interviews like Susan Hamlin's seem to suggest that
the search for the "true" perspectives of the freedpeople is bound to end in
failure and frustration. We have seen, first, that information from planters
and other white sources must be treated with extreme skepticism and, second, that northern white sources deserve similar caution. Finally, it appears
that even the oral testimony of African Americans themselves must be questioned, given the circumstances under which much of it was gathered. It is as
if a detective discovered that all the clues so carefully pieced together were
hopelessly biased, leading the investigation down the wrong path.

The seriousness of the problem should not be underestimated. It is fundamental. We can try to ease out of the dilemma by noting that differing
degrees of bias exist—that some accounts are likely to be less deceptive
than others. Susan Hamlin's interview with Ladson, for instance, surely
portrays her feelings more accurately than the interview with Butler. But
does that mean we reject all of the Butler interview? Presumably, Susan
Hamlin's master did give her a pair of shoes one cold winter day. Are we to
assume, because of Ladson's interview, that the young child felt no grati-
tude toward "kind old" Mr. Fuller? Or that the old woman did not look
back on those years with some ambivalence? For all her life, both slave
and free, Susan Hamlin lived in a world where she was required to "feel"
one set of emotions when dealing with some people and a different set
when dealing with other people. Can we be confident that the emotions
she expressed to Ladson were her "real" feelings, while the ones to Jessie
Butler were her "false" feelings? How can we arrive at an objective conclusion about "real" feelings in any social situation in which such severe
strains existed?

Putting the question in this light offers at least a partial way out of the dilemma. If so many clues in the investigation are "biased"—that is, distorted by the social situation in which they are set—then the widespread nature of the distortion may serve as a key to understanding the situation. The evidence in the case is warped precisely because it reflects a distortion in the society itself. The elements of racism and slavery determined a culture in which personal relations were grounded in mistrust, creating a kind of economy of deception, in which slaves could survive only if they remained conscious of the need to adapt their feelings to the situation.

*The elements of racism and slavery determined a culture in which personal relations were grounded in mistrust, creating a kind of economy of deception.*

The deception was mutual—practiced by both sides on each other. Susan Hamlin was adapting the story of her past to the needs of the moment at the same time that Jessie Butler was letting Hamlin believe her to be a welfare agent. White masters painted lurid stories of Yankee devils with horns, while slaves, playing roles they were expected to play, rolled their eyes in fear until they could run straight for Union lines.

Given this logic, it would be tempting simply to turn old historical interpretations on their heads. Whereas William Dunning took most white primary sources at face value and saw only cheerful, childlike Sambos, an enlightened history would read the documents upside down, stripping away the camouflage to reveal slaves who, quite rationally, went about the daily business of "puttin' on ole massa." We have already seen abundant evidence that slaves did consciously deceive in order to protect themselves.

But simply to replace one set of feelings with another is to drastically underestimate the strains arising out of an economy of deception. The longer that masters and slaves were compelled to live false or inauthentic lives, the easier it must have been for them to mislead themselves as well as others. Where white and black people alike engaged in daily deception, some of it was inevitably directed inward, to preserve the fiction of living in a tolerable, normally functioning society.

When the war came, shattering that fiction, whites and blacks were exposed in vivid ways to the deception that had been so much a part of their lives. For white slaveholders, the revelation usually came when Union troops entered a region and slaves deserted the plantations in droves. Especially demoralizing was the flight of slaves whom planters had believed most loyal. "He was about my age and I had always treated him more as a companion than a slave," noted one planter of the first defector from his ranks. Mary Chesnut, the woman near Fort Sumter who had tried to penetrate the blank expressions of her slaves, discovered how impossible the task had been. "Jonathan, whom we trusted, betrayed us," she lamented, while "Claiborne, that black rascal who was suspected by all the world," faithfully protected the plantation.

Many slaveholders, when faced with the truth, refused to recognize the role that deception had played in their lives, thereby deceiving themselves further. "The poor negroes don't do us any harm except when they are put up to it," concluded one Georgia woman. A Richmond newspaper editor demanded that a slave who had denounced Jefferson Davis "be whipped every day until he confesses what white man put these notions in his head." Yet the war brought painful insight to others. "We were all laboring under a delusion," confessed one South Carolina planter. "I believed that these people were content, happy, and attached to their masters. But events and reflection have caused me to change these opinions. . . . If they were content, happy and attached to their masters, why did they desert him in the moment of his need and flock to an enemy, whom they did not know?"

For slaves, news of emancipation brought an entirely different reaction, but still one conditioned by the old habits. We have already seen how one old Georgia slave couple remained impassive as Sherman's troops passed through, until finally the wife could restrain herself no longer. Even the servant who eloquently praised freedom by a secluded brook remembered the need for caution: "I got sort o' scared, afeared somebody hear me, an' I takes another good look." Although emancipation promised a society founded on equal treatment, slaves could not help wondering whether the new order would fully replace the old. That transformation would occur only if freedpeople could forge relationships that were no longer based on the customs of deception nor rooted in the central fiction of slavery: that blacks were incapable of assuming a place in free society.

As historians came to recognize the value of the slave narrative collection, they drew upon its evidence, along with other primary sources, to discover how freedpeople sought to define their new freedoms, how they distanced themselves from the old habits of bondage. The taking of new names was one step. As slaves, African Americans often had no surnames, or they took the names of their masters. Equally demeaning, given names were often casually assigned by their owners. Cicero, Pompey, and other Latin or biblical names were bestowed in jest. And whether or not slaves had surnames, they were always addressed familiarly, by their given names. Such customs were part of the symbolic language of deception, promoting the illusion that black people were helpless dependents of the planter's family.

Thus freedpeople took for themselves new names, severing the symbolic tie with their old masters. "A heap of people say they was going to name their selves over," recalled one freedman. "They named their selves big names. . . . Some of the names was Abraham an' some called their selves Lincum. Any big name 'ceptin' their master's name. It was the fashion." Even former slaves who remained loyal to their masters recognized the significance of the change. "When you'all had de power you was good to me," an older freedman told his master, "an I'll protect you now. No niggers nor Yankees shall touch you. If you want anything, call for Sambo. I mean, call for Mr. Samuel—that's my name now."

Just as freedpeople took new names to symbolize their new status, so also many husbands and wives reaffirmed their marriages in formal ceremonies. Under slavery, family ties had been ignored through the convenient fiction that Africans were morally inferior. Black affections, the planters argued, were dominated by impulse and the physical desires of the moment. Such self-deception eased many a master's conscience when slave families were separated and sold. Similarly, many planters married slaves only informally, with a few words sufficing to join the couples. "Don't mean nuthin' less you say, 'What God done jined, cain't no man pull asunder,'" noted one Virginia freedman. "But dey never would say dat. Jus' say, 'Now you married.'" For reasons of human dignity, black couples moved to solemnize their marriage vows. There were practical reasons for an official ceremony, too: it might qualify families for military pensions or the division of lands that was widely rumored to be coming.

Equally symbolic for former slaves was the freedom to travel. Historian William Dunning recognized this fact but interpreted it from the viewpoint of his southern white sources as "aimless but happy" wandering. Richard Edwards, a preacher in Florida, explicitly described how important moving or traveling was:

> You ain't, none o' you, gwinter feel rale free till you shakes de dus' ob de Old Plantashun offen yore feet an' goes ter a new place whey you kin live out o' sight o' de gret house. So long ez de shadder ob de gret house falls acrost you, you ain't gwine ter feel lak no free man, an' you ain't gwine ter feel lak no free 'oman. You mus' all move—you mus' move clar away from de ole places what you knows, ter de new places what you don't know, whey you kin raise up yore head douten no fear o' Marse Dis ur Marse Tudder.

And so, in the spring and summer of 1865, southern roads were filled with black people, hiving off "like bees trying to find a setting place," as one former slave recalled. Most freedpeople remained near family and friends, merely leaving one plantation in search of work at another. But a sizable minority traveled farther, to settle in cities, move west, or try their fortunes at new occupations.

Many former slaves traveled in order to reunite families separated through previous sales. Freedpeople "had a passion, not so much for wandering, as for getting together," a Freedman's Bureau agent observed, "and every mother's son among them seemed to be in search of his mother; every mother in search of her children." Often, relatives had only scanty information; in other cases, so much time had passed that kin could hardly recognize each other, especially when young children had grown up separated from their parents.

*"Every mother's son among them seemed to be in search of his mother; every mother in search of her children."*

A change of name or location, the formalization of a marriage, a reunion with relatives—all these acts demonstrated that freedpeople wanted no part of the old constraints and deceptions of slavery. But as much as these acts defined black freedom, larger issues remained. How much would emancipation broaden economic avenues open to African Americans? Would freedom provide an opportunity to rise on the social ladder? Freedpeople looked anxiously for signs of change.

Perhaps the most commonly perceived avenue to success was through education. Slavery had been rationalized, in part, through the fiction that blacks were incapable of profiting from an education. Especially where masters had energetically prevented slaves from acquiring skills in reading, writing, and arithmetic, the hunger for learning was intense. When northerners occupied the Carolina Sea Islands during the war, Yankee plantation superintendents found that the most effective way to force unwilling laborers to work was to threaten to take away their schoolbooks. "The Negroes . . . will do anything for us, if we will only teach them," noted one missionary.

After the war, when the Freedman's Bureau sent hundreds of northern schoolteachers into the South, black students flocked enthusiastically to the makeshift schoolhouses. Often, classes could be held only at night, but the freedpeople were willing. "We work all day, but we'll come to you in the evening for learning," Georgia freedpeople told their teacher. Some white plantation owners discovered that if they wished to keep their field hands, they would have to provide a schoolhouse and teacher.

Important as education was, the freedpeople were preoccupied even more with their relation to the lands they had worked for so many years. The vast majority of slaves were field hands. The agricultural life was the one they had grown up with, and as freedpeople they wanted the chance to own and cultivate their own property. Independent ownership would lay to rest the lie that black people were incapable of managing their own affairs. But without land, the idea of freedom would be just another deception. "Gib us our own land and we take care of ourselves; but widout land, de ole massas can hire us or starve us, as dey please," noted one freedman. In the heady enthusiasm at the close of the war, many former slaves were convinced that the Union would divide up confiscated Confederate plantations. Each family, so the persistent rumor went, would receive forty acres and a mule. "This was no slight error, no trifling idea," reported one white observer, "but a fixed and earnest conviction as strong as any belief a man can ever have." Slaves had worked their masters' lands for so long without significant compensation, it seemed only fair that compensation should finally be made. Further, ever since southern planters had fled from invading Union troops, some black workers had been allowed to cultivate the abandoned fields.

The largest occupied region was the Sea Islands along the Carolina coast, where young Sam Mitchell first heard the northern guns. As early as March

**"My Lord, ma'am, what a great thing larning is!"** a freedman exclaimed to a white teacher. Many white people were surprised by the intensity of the ex-slaves' desire for an education. To say that the freedpeople were "anxious to learn" was not strong enough, one Virginia school official noted; "they are *crazy* to learn." These schoolboys were from South Carolina.

1863, freedpeople were purchasing confiscated lands from the government. Then in January 1865, after General William Sherman completed his devastating march to the sea, he extended the area open to confiscation. In his Special Field Order No. 15, Sherman decreed that a long strip of abandoned lands, stretching from Charleston on the north to Jacksonville on the south, would be reserved for the freedpeople. The lands would be subdivided into forty-acre tracts, which could be rented for a nominal fee. After three years, the freedpeople had the option to purchase the land outright.

Sherman's order was a tactical maneuver, designed to deal with the overwhelming problem of refugees in his path. But black workers widely perceived this order and other promises by northerners as a foretaste of Reconstruction policy. Consequently, when white planters returned to their plantations, they often found blacks who no longer bowed and tipped their hats. Thomas Pinckney of South Carolina, having called his former slaves together, asked them if they would continue to work for him. "O yes, we gwi wuk! we gwi wuk all right," came the angry response. "We gwi wuk fuh ourse'ves. We ain' gwi wuk fuh no white man." Pinckney asked where they would go to work—seeing as they had no land. "We ain't gwine nowhar," they replied defiantly. "We gwi wuk right here on de lan' whar we wuz bo'n an' whar belongs tuh us."

Despite the defiance, Pinckney prevailed, as did the vast majority of southern planters. Redistribution of southern lands was an idea supported only by more radical northerners. Thaddeus Stevens introduced a confiscation bill in Congress, but it was swamped by debate and never passed. President Johnson, whose conciliatory policies pleased southern planters, determined to settle the issue as quickly as possible. He summoned General O. O. Howard, head of the Freedman's Bureau, and instructed him to reach a solution "mutually satisfactory" to both blacks and planters. Howard, though sympathetic to the freedpeople, could not mistake the true meaning of the president's order.

Sadly the general returned to the Sea Islands in October and assembled a group of freedpeople on Edisto Island. The audience, suspecting the bad news, was restless and unruly. Howard tried vainly to speak and made "no progress" until a woman in the crowd began singing, "Nobody knows the trouble I've seen." The crowd joined, then was silent while Howard told them they must give up their lands. Bitter cries of "No! No!" came from the audience. "Why, General Howard, why do you take away our lands?" called one burly man. "You take them from us who have always been true, always true to the Government! You give them to our all-time enemies! That is not right!"

Reluctantly, and sometimes only after forcible resistance, African Americans lost the lands to returning planters. Whatever else freedom might mean, it was not to signify compensation for previous labor. In the years to come, Reconstruction would offer freedom of another sort, through the political process. By the beginning of 1866 the radicals in Congress had charted a plan that gave African Americans basic civil rights and political power. Yet even that avenue of opportunity was sealed off. In the decades that followed the first thunder of emancipation, black people would look back on their early experiences almost as if they were part of another, vanished world. The traditions of racial oppression and the daily deceptions that went with them were too strong to be thoroughly overturned by the war.

"I was right smart bit by de freedom bug for awhile," Charlie Davenport of Mississippi recalled.

> It sounded pow'ful nice to be tol: "You don't have to chop cotton no more. You can th'ow dat hoe down an' go fishin' whensoever de notion strikes you. An' you can roam 'roun' at night an' court gals jus' as you please. Aint no marster gwine a-say to you, 'Charlie, you's got to be back when de clock strikes nine.'"
> I was fool 'nough to b'lieve all dat kin' o' stuff.

Both perceptions—the first flush of the "freedom bug" as well as Davenport's later disillusionment—accurately reflect the black experience. Freedom had come to a nation of four million slaves, and it changed their lives in deep and important ways. But for many years after the war put an end to human bondage, too many freedpeople still had to settle for a view from the bottom rail.

# *Additional Reading*

Leon Litwack's superb *Been in the Storm So Long: The Aftermath of Slavery* (New York, 1979) was seminal in integrating evidence from the slave narratives into a reevaluation of the Reconstruction era. It serves as an excellent introduction to the freedpeople's experience after the war. Eric Foner's *Reconstruction: America's Unfinished Revolution* (New York, 1988) is the definitive survey of the period. Steven Hahn provides an even broader sweep in *A Nation Under Our Feet: Black Political Struggles in the Rural South from Slavery to the Great Migration* (Cambridge, MA, 2003). A selection of oral interviews from the Federal Writers' Project appears in Ira Berlin et al., *Remembering Slavery: African Americans Talk about Their Personal Experiences of Slavery and Freedom* (New York, 1998). The highlight of this collection is an audiocassette containing more than a dozen of the only known original recordings of former slaves. For the full collection of interviews, see George P. Rawick, *The American Slave: A Composite Autobiography*, 19 vols. and suppl. (Westport, CT, 1972–). Further analysis of the slave narratives may be found in John Blassingame, *Slave Testimony* (Baton Rouge, LA, 1977). Paul D. Escott, *Slavery Remembered: A Record of Twentieth-Century Slave Narratives* (Chapel Hill, NC, 1979), breaks down the percentage of interviews with field hands, house servants, and artisans; the occupations they took up as freedpeople; and the destinations of those who migrated. Heather Andrea Williams, *Self-Taught: African American Education in Slavery and Freedom* (Chapel Hill, NC, 2003), details the desire for learning.

# *Whose Oral History?*

During the 1930s, John Avery Lomax and his son Alan used state-of-the-art equipment to record the oral histories of former slaves on acetate disks. Their recorder was portable, but only barely: they had to load its 315 pounds into the trunk of a car. Given the cumbersome technology, most slave narratives were not recorded on audio disks. Still, the voices of twenty-three former slaves are available on CD from PaperlessArchives.com for those who wish to listen to them today.

Historians now face a different problem—too much material. Almost anyone can record recollections of the past. Through StoryCorps, for example, the Library of Congress and National Public Radio have created both permanent booths and mobile facilities where ordinary people can record their memories. But anyone with a digital voice recorder can undertake his or her own independent project. These devices, smaller than a pack of cigarettes,

have the capability of capturing well over 100 hours of material. Think what the Lomaxes could have done with such portable equipment.

Who, then, is a proper subject for an oral-history interview? The Federal Writers' Project chose slaves because the survivors were dying out. Now we are losing the recollections of those who experienced World War II and the Korean War. Quickly enough we will face the loss of veterans from Vietnam and the civil rights movement. Obviously, the older the subject being interviewed, the greater the chronological reach. A 90-year-old recalling his or her childhood can provide personal recollections of the 1920s, while memories passed along by *their* parents and grandparents might contain stories reaching back to the Civil War.

But oral history is equally useful in preserving recent experiences, to be recalled by family or historians decades from now. "Our parents forced us to read the Korean bible every night," recalled one Korean American in an oral history from the 1990s. "If we couldn't finish reading it, we sometimes had to stay up until two in the morning on school nights. . . . My younger sister, who's at Barnard College in New York, doesn't go to church now; she despises the dogma and sees the ideology as male chauvinist. Lately, I'm a little in line with her. I went to a Korean church here in L.A. for a while, but some of the things they said really bothered me. In the pulpit, the minister would say something about Hillary Clinton or make snide remarks about 'feminazis.'" Such contemporary stories bid fair to create a mosaic as engrossing as those recorded by the Lomaxes eight decades ago.

# CHAPTER 9
## The Mirror with a Memory

*Is a photograph true to nature itself, or is it possible to lie with a camera?*

Anyone walking around Manhattan will eventually become aware of Jacob Riis. A housing project and community center bear the name of this reformer who, at the end of the nineteenth century, fought against the evils of slums and tenements. Alexander Alland, a professional photographer, spent much of his life in the communities of New York where Riis once worked the crime beat as a journalist. Alland knew about Riis as a reformer, but nothing about his pioneering work as a photographer. In 1942, while browsing in a second-hand bookstore, he came across a used copy of *How the Other Half Lives*, in which Riis used photographs and halftone illustrations to support his message about the evil conditions of the city's slums. Those images revealed a world of homeless street urchins, crowded tenements, and urban poor struggling to survive. Alland wondered whether there were more of these photographs. He managed to locate Riis's youngest son, Roger William, and asked if he would look through the family's Long Island house to see if his father had left any of his photographic materials behind. A short time later a box arrived, in which Alland found 415 glass plate negatives, 326 slides, and 192 prints. This treasure trove would become the Jacob A. Riis Collection of the Museum of the City of New York.

What was the significance of the images Roger William Riis discovered in the family attic? Historians already had considerable evidence with which they could reconstruct Riis's life as a journalist and social reformer. He had written books about the slums of New York and an autobiography in which he recollected his life as an immigrant. Now evidence had surfaced that suggested he had made a major contribution to documentary photography as well. Historians were already familiar with the work of Lewis Hine, who, in the early twentieth century, captured images of child labor, immigrants, and urban workers; and of the Farm Security Administration photographers, who revealed the look of rural poverty and the Dust Bowl during the Great Depression.

In 1973 Alland published *Jacob A. Riis: Photographer and Citizen*, which included many photographs not seen in public since Riis used them in his lantern slide shows some ninety years earlier. The book suggested that Riis had importance as a photographer as well as a social reformer. The director of the Department of Photography at New York's Museum of Modern Art suggested that Riis had the photographer's intuitive sense of discovered images; he "knew the habits and habitat of photographer's luck," which framed his work. Riis may not have concerned himself with producing art, but he "was intuitively interested in problems of form without identifying these as artistic problems." In short, he believed that Riis, no matter how unintentionally, was an artist.

For the historian, certain evidence contradicts that claim. If photography was important to Riis, why did he hide his work in the attic without telling his family? A grandson asserted, "In his letters—I have read most of them—he never mentions a camera." In fact, in *The Making of an American*, Riis talks at length about his journalism and writing, yet he says little about his photographs. It was not even a pastime. "I had use for it," he explained, "and beyond that I never went." For him photography was a tool, not an avocation. All the same, Riis the photographer remains important to historians. His images provide an invaluable record of an urban world invisible to most middle-class Americans who, safe in their prosperous neighborhoods, ignored the presence of mass poverty in the rapidly growing cities of late-nineteenth-century America. The poor and their troubles were "out of sight" and hence "out of mind." What, then, can historians learn from this photographic record that more traditional written sources haven't already told them? Can they read Riis's photographs to learn more about life in the teeming cities of late-nineteenth-century America?

> "In his letters—I have read most of them—he never mentions a camera."

In the forty years following the Civil War, more than 24 million people flooded into American cities. While the population of the agricultural hinterlands doubled during these years, urban population increased by more than 700 percent. Sixteen cities could boast populations over 50,000 in 1860; by 1910 more than a hundred could make that claim. New York City alone grew by 2 million. Urban areas changed not only in size but also in ethnic composition. While many of the new city-dwellers had migrated from rural America, large numbers came from abroad. Most antebellum cities had been relatively homogeneous, with perhaps an enclave of Irish or German immigrants; the metropolises at the turn of the century were home to large groups of southern- as well as northern-European immigrants. Again, New York City provides a striking example. By 1900 it included the largest Jewish population of any city in the world, as many Irish as in Dublin, and more Italians and Poles than in any city outside Rome or Warsaw. Enclaves of Bohemians, Slavs, Lithuanians, Chinese, Scandinavians, and other nationalities added to the ethnic mix.

The quality of living in cities changed, too. As industry crowded into city centers, the wealthy and middle classes fled along newly constructed trolley and rail lines to the quiet of developing suburbs. Enterprising realtors either subdivided or replaced the mansions of the rich with tenements, in which a maximum number of people could be packed into a minimum of space. Crude sanitation transformed streets into breeding grounds for typhus, scarlet

*Disease a crowded citizs*

fever, cholera, and other epidemic diseases. Few tenement rooms had outside windows; less than 10 percent of all buildings had either indoor plumbing or running water.

The story of the urban poor and their struggle against the slum's cruel waste of lives is well known today—as it was even at the turn of the century—because several generations of social workers and muckrakers studied the slums firsthand and wrote indignantly about what they found. Not only did they collect statistics to document their general observations, but they compiled numerous case studies that described the collective experience in compelling stories about individuals. Jacob Riis was a leader in this endeavor. Few books have had as much impact on social policy as his landmark study of New York's Lower East Side, *How the Other Half Lives*. It was at once a shocking revelation of the conditions of slum life and a call for reform. As urban historian Sam Bass Warner concluded, "Before Riis there was no broad understanding of urban poverty that could lead to political action."

Riis had come to know firsthand the degrading conditions of urban life. In 1870, at the age of twenty-one, he joined the growing tide of emigrants who fled the poverty of the Scandinavian countryside for the opportunities offered in America. Riis was no starving peasant; in fact his father was a respected schoolmaster and his family comfortably middle class. But Jacob had little taste for book learning and preferred manual work as a carpenter. Unable to find a job in his hometown and rejected by his local sweetheart, he set out for the United States.

Once there, Riis retraced the pattern that millions of immigrants before him had followed. For three years he wandered in search of the promise of the new land. He built workers' shacks near Pittsburgh, trapped muskrats in upstate New York, sold furniture, did odd jobs, and occasionally returned to carpentry. In none of that work did he find either satisfaction or success. At one point, poverty reduced him to begging for crumbs outside New York City restaurants and spending nights in a police lodging house. His health failed. He lingered near death until the Danish consul in Philadelphia took him in. At times his situation grew so desperate and his frustration so intense that he contemplated suicide.

Riis, however, had a talent for self-promotion. Eventually he landed a job with a news association in New York and turned his talent to reporting. The direction of his career was determined in 1877, when he became the police reporter for the *New York Tribune*. He was well-suited for the job, his earlier wanderings having made him all too familiar with the seamy side of urban life. The police beat took him to headquarters near The Bend, what Riis referred to as the "foul core of New York's slums." Every day he collected the "news that means trouble to someone: the murders, fire, suicides, robberies, and all that sort that don't get into court." Over the course of a year, police dragnets collected some forty thousand indigents, who were carted off to the workhouses and asylums. And at night Riis shadowed the police to catch a

> *He collected the "news that means trouble to someone: the murders, fire, suicides, robberies, and all that sort that don't get into court."*

view of the neighborhood "off its guard." He began to visit immigrants in their homes, where he observed their continual struggle to preserve a measure of decency amidst disease and poverty.

As a *Tribune* reporter, Riis published exposé after exposé on wretched slum conditions. In so doing he followed the journalistic style of the day. Most reporters had adopted the strategies found in the Charles Dickens novels Riis had enjoyed as a boy, personifying social issues through the use of graphic detail and telling vignettes. Such concrete examples involved readers most directly with the squalor of city slums. The issue of female exploitation in sweatshops became the story of an old woman Riis discovered paralyzed by a stroke on her own doorstep. The plight of working children, who had neither education nor more than passing familiarity with the English language, was dramatized by the story of Pietro, the young Italian boy unable to keep awake at night school. Touching stories brought home the struggles of the poor better than general statistics. They also sold newspapers, because middle-class readers found these stories both disturbing and fascinating.

But Riis found the newspaper life frustrating. His stories may have been vivid, but apparently not vivid enough to shock anyone to action. For over four decades, New York authorities had made token efforts at slum clearance, but by 1890 the conditions about which Riis protested had grown steadily worse. The Lower East Side had a greater population density than any neighborhood in the world—335,000 people to one square mile of the tenth ward and as many as 1 person per square foot in the worst places.* New York's poor died at a rate much higher than cities elsewhere in the United States and Europe.

In frustration, Riis left the *Tribune* to give lectures and write *How the Other Half Lives.* He wanted to make a case for reform that even the most callous officials could not dismiss, and a full-length book accompanied by public talks was more likely to accomplish what a series of daily articles could not. The new format enabled Riis to weave his individual stories into a broader indictment of urban blight. It allowed him to buttress concrete stories with collections of statistics. And perhaps most important, it inspired him to provide documentary proof of a new sort—proof so vivid and dramatic that even the most compelling literary vignettes seemed weak by comparison. Riis sought to document urban conditions with the swiftly developing techniques of photography.

From his own experience and that of other urban reformers, Riis had learned that photographs could be powerful weapons to engage the public imagination. In 1876, over a decade before Riis would publish *How the Other Half Lives,* he bought a stereopticon, or "magic lantern," that projected pictures onto a screen. With it, he traveled around Brooklyn and Long Island, attracting audiences to his exhibitions of beautiful landscapes in which he mingled advertisements from local merchants. From that experience, he learned that pictures engaged the popular imagination in ways the spoken

---

* Those readers conjuring up a picture of slum-dwellers standing like sardines row on row, each with his or her own square foot, must remember that tenement space reached upward through several stories. The statistic refers to square footage of ground area, not square footage of actual floor space.

or written word could not. And from the experience of two English authors, John Thompson and Adolph Smith, he learned that photographs could be powerful weapons to arouse popular indignation. Thompson and Smith had included photographs in their 1877 book on London slums because, as they explained, "The unquestionable accuracy of this testimony will enable us to present true types of the London poor and shield us from accusations of either underrating or exaggerating individual peculiarities of appearance." For Riis their argument was a compelling one. If photographs accompanied *How the Other Half Lives*, no corrupt politician could dismiss its arguments as opinionated word-paintings spawned by the imagination of an overheated reformer. Photography indisputably showed life as it really was.

## "REALITY" AND PHOTOGRAPHIC EVIDENCE

From the moment in 1839 when the French pioneer of photography Louis-Jacques Daguerre announced his discovery of a process to fix images permanently on a copper plate, observers repeatedly remarked on the camera's capacity to record reality. More than anything else, the seeming objectivity of the new medium caught the popular imagination. The camera captured only those objects that appeared before the lens—nothing more, nothing less.

*The camera captured only those objects that appeared before the lens—nothing more, nothing less.*

So faithful was the camera that people often commented that the photographic image recorded the original with an exactness "equal to nature itself." Indeed, one of the attractions of the new medium was that it could accurately reveal the look of other parts of the United States and the world. Nineteenth-century Americans were hungry for visual images of unseen places. Few had ever seen the trans-Mississippi West, much less Europe or the South Pacific. Almost no one had access to pictures that satisfied curiosity about exotic lands or people. As a result, crowds flocked to the galleries of a painter such as Albert Bierstadt when he displayed his grand landscapes of the Rocky Mountains. Even Bierstadt's paintings, though, were colored by his romantic notions of the West, just as all artists' work reflects their own personal biases.

The new photography seemed to have no style—that was its promise. It recorded only what was before the camera. Reproductions were so faithful to the original that close observation with a magnifying glass often revealed details that had been invisible to the naked eye. The American writer and physician Oliver Wendell Holmes summed up the popular conception when he noted that the camera was even more than "the mirror of reality"; it was "the mirror with a memory."

Certainly, there was no denying the camera's unprecedented ability to record detail in a way that paintings could not. Yet from today's vantage point, it is easier to see the limits of the camera's seeming objectivity. Any modern amateur photographer will appreciate immediately how deceptive the camera's claim to mirroring reality can be. Merely to sight through the viewfinder reminds us that every photograph creates its own frame, including some objects and

**The cumbersome technology of early photography** restricted the use of photography largely to professionals. Field photographers had to take along darkrooms in which they prepared the photographic plates that went into a heavy box camera. The van pictured here was used by a photographer during the Crimean War. Matthew Brady and his assistants employed similar large wagons during the Civil War. They soon discovered, much to their chagrin, that such rolling darkrooms made uncomfortably obvious targets for enemy artillery and sharpshooters.

excluding others. The problem of selection of evidence, which is at the heart of the historian's task, remains of paramount importance in photography.

The situation becomes even more complex when we begin to make simple photographic adjustments once the frame has been selected. Far from recording every detail within the lens's reach, we immediately begin excluding details by turning the focusing ring: in choosing a closeup, background details blur; if aiming for a distant subject, it is the foreground that becomes hazy. The technical constraints of the camera thus limit what can be recorded. If we close down the aperture of the camera's lens (the circular hole that allows light to pass through the lens), the camera's depth of field is increased, bringing into focus a larger area within the path of the lens. On the other hand, photographers who wish to concentrate the viewer's attention on a central subject will eliminate cluttering details by decreasing the depth of field.

Of course, it may be argued with a good deal of justice that many, if not all, of these distorting capabilities of the camera are irrelevant when

*ets him apart*

discussing the work of Jacob Riis. Riis worked with neither a sophisticated camera nor a particularly extensive knowledge of photographic principles. His primary goals were not to record scenes aesthetically and artistically but to capture the subject matter before his camera. The niceties of art would have to wait.

Indeed, when Riis began his photographic efforts, he quickly discovered that the primitive nature of photography precluded too much attention to aesthetic details, especially in his line of work. In the 1880s taking pictures was no simple matter. Each step in the photographic process presented formidable obstacles. First, would-be photographers had to learn to prepare a light-sensitive chemical mixture and spread it evenly on the glass plates that served as photographic negatives. For work in the field, they had to take along a portable darkroom, usually a clumsy tent perched on a tripod. Here the negatives were taken from the cumbersome box camera and developed in chemical baths. Additional solutions were necessary to transfer the image from the plate to the final paper print. Such a process taxed the ingenuity and dedication of even the most avid practitioners.

*In the 1880s taking pictures was no simple matter.*

Fortunately, advances in chemistry, optics, and photographic technology gave birth to a new generation of equipment, the "detective camera." Wily photographers took to disguising cameras as doctors' satchels, briefcases, books, revolvers, and vest buttons—hence the nickname detective camera. To ease the burden of field photographers and make possible the candid shot, a number of companies had introduced small cameras about the size of a cigar box. Some carried as many as twelve photographic plates that could be used before the camera required reloading.

George Eastman simplified the process even further with his Kodak camera. Introduced to the public in 1888, the Kodak was more than an improved detective camera; it was the first model that replaced glass negatives with a photographic emulsion coated on paper rolls. For twenty-five dollars, an aspiring photographer could acquire the camera loaded with a hundred shots. Once the film had been exposed, the owner simply returned the camera to the dealer, who removed the spool in a darkroom and shipped it to Eastman's factory for processing. For an additional ten dollars, the dealer would reload the camera with new film. So successfully had Eastman reduced the burden on amateur photographers that his ads could boast, "You press the button, we do the rest."

But even the advances in photographic technology did not eliminate Riis's difficulties. To help him, he enlisted the assistance of several friends in the Health Department who also happened to be amateur photographers. Together they set out to catch their subjects unawares. That meant skulking around the Bend in the dead of night, with the normal photographic paraphernalia increased by bulky and primitive flash equipment. For a flash to work, a highly combustible powder was spread along a pan. The pan was then held up, and Riis exploded a blank cartridge from a revolver to ignite

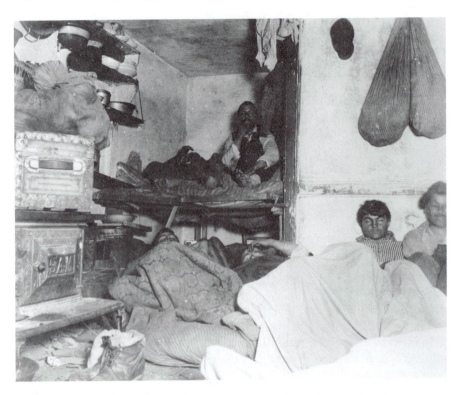

**Lodgers in a crowded Bayard Street tenement—**"Five Cents a Spot"

the powder. This photographic entourage sneaking about town after hours made a remarkable sight, as the *New York Sun* reported:

> Somnolent policemen on the street, denizens of the dives in their dens, tramps and bummers in their so-called lodgings, and all the people of the wild and wonderful variety of New York night life have in turn marvelled at and been frightened by the phenomenon. What they saw was three or four figures in the gloom, a ghostly tripod, some weird and uncanny movements, the blinding flash, and then they heard the patter of retreating footsteps and their mysterious visitors were gone before they could collect their scattered thoughts.

The results from using such finicky equipment were not always predictable. Sometimes the noise would awaken unsuspecting subjects and create a disturbance. On one particularly unfortunate occasion Riis had gone to "Blind Man's Alley" to photograph five sightless men and women living in a cramped attic room. Soon after his eyes cleared from the blinding flash, he saw flames climbing up the rags covering the walls. Fear gripped him as he envisioned the blaze sweeping through twelve rickety flights of stairs between the attic and safety. Fighting the impulse to flee, he beat out the

*"The dirt was so thick on the walls it smothered the fire."*

**In the original edition of** *How the Other Half Lives,* seventeen of the photographs appeared as blurry halftones and nineteen as artists' engravings, such as this rendering of the "Five Cents a Spot" photograph. A comparison of the two illustrations quickly demonstrates how much more graphically the photograph presented Riis's concerns. Riis continued to take photographs for other books he published, although it was not until well into the twentieth century that mass-reproduction techniques could begin to do justice to them.

flames with his coat and then rushed to the street seeking help. The first policeman who heard his story burst out laughing. "Why, don't you know that's the Dirty Spoon?" he responded. "It caught fire six times last winter, but it wouldn't burn. The dirt was so thick on the walls it smothered the fire."

Under such precarious circumstances, it might be argued that Riis's photography more closely mirrored reality precisely because it was artless, and that what it lacked in aesthetics it gained in documentary detail. On page 210, for example, we see a picture taken on one of Riis's night expeditions, of lodgers at one of the crowded "five cents a spot" tenements. The room itself, Riis informs us in *How the Other Half Lives,* is "not thirteen feet either way," in which "slept twelve men and women, two or three in bunks in a sort of alcove, the rest on the floor." The sleepy faces and supine bodies reflect the candid nature of the picture; indeed, Riis had followed a policeman who was raiding the room in order to drive the lodgers into the street. The glare of the flash, casting distinct shadows, reveals all of the crowding, dirt, and disorder. This photograph is no aesthetic triumph, perhaps, but it does reveal a wealth of details that prove most useful to the curious historian.

We notice, for instance, that the stove in the foreground is a traditional wood-burning model, with its fuel supply stacked underneath. Space in the apartment is so crowded that footlockers and bundles have been piled directly on top of the stove. (Have they been moved from their daytime resting places on the bunks? Or do these people carry their possessions onto the street during the day?) The dishes and kitchen utensils are piled high on shelves next to the stove. The bedding is well-used, dirty, and make-shift. Such details are nowhere near as faithfully recorded in the line drawing originally published in *How the Other Half Lives*.

Yet no matter how "artless" the photographs of Jacob Riis may be in terms of their aesthetic control of the medium, to assume they are bias-free seriously underestimates their interpretive content. However primitive a photographer Riis may have been, he still influenced the messages he presented through an appropriate selection of details. Even the most artless photographers make such interpretive choices in every snapshot they take.

Let us look, for example, at the most artless photographic observations of all: the ordinary family scrapbook found in most American homes. When George Eastman marketed his convenient pocket camera, he clearly recognized the wide appeal of his product. At long last the ordinary class of people, not just the rich and wellborn, could create for themselves a permanent documentary record of their doings. "A collection of these pictures may be made to furnish a pictorial history of life as it is lived by the owner," proclaimed one Kodak advertisement.

But while family albums provide a wide-ranging "pictorial history," they are still shaped by conventions every bit as stylized as the romantic conventions of Bierstadt or other artists with equally distinct styles. The albums are very much ceremonial history—birthdays, anniversaries, vacations. Life within their covers is a succession of proud achievements, celebrations, and uncommon moments. A father's retirement party may be covered, but probably not his routine day at the office. We see the sights at Disney World, not the long waits at the airport. Arguments, rivalries, and the tedium of the commonplace are missing.

If the artless photographers of family life unconsciously shape the records they leave behind, then we must expect those who self-consciously use photography to be even more interpretive with their materials. This manipulation is not a matter of knowing how to use Photoshop, but rather a desire to convey a coherent message through a photograph. Civil War photographer Matthew Brady wanted to capture the horrific carnage of the war. To achieve it, he did not hesitate to drag dead bodies to a scene in order to further the composition or the effect he desired.

But to point out such literal examples of the photographer's influence almost destroys the point by caricaturing it. A later generation of government

**"A collection of these pictures** may be made to furnish a pictorial history of life as it is lived by the owner." Following the dictum in the Kodak advertisement, these two men pose happily, one holding one of the new Kodak cameras while a friend uses another to record the scene. Like so many family album "candids," this shot follows the tradition of ceremonial history—proud achievements, celebrations, and uncommon moments. These men, dressed in their best, are tourists from Pennsylvania enjoying spring on the White House lawn in April 1889.

photographers, those who worked during the Great Depression of the 1930s, also viewed photographs as vehicles to convey their social messages. Few photographers were more dedicated to the ideal of documentary realism than Walker Evans, Dorothea Lange, Ben Shahn, and others who photographed tenant farmers and sharecroppers for the Farm Security Administration. Yet these photographers also brought to their work

preconceived notions about how poverty should look. As critic Susan Sontag has noted, they "would take dozens of frontal pictures of one of their

> *"In deciding how a picture should look . . . photographers are always imposing standards on their subjects."*

sharecropper subjects until satisfied
that they had gotten just the right look
on film—the precise expression on the
subject's face that supported their own
notions about poverty, light, dignity,
texture, exploitation, and geometry.
In deciding how a picture should look . . . photographers are always imposing standards on their subjects."

Thus any series of photographs—including those Jacob Riis took for his
books—must be analyzed in the same way a written narrative is. We can
appreciate the full import of the photographs only by establishing their
historical context. What messages are they meant to convey? What are the
premises—stated or unstated—that underlie the presentation of photographs? Ironically, in order to evaluate the messages in the Riis photographs,
we must supplement our knowledge of his perspectives on the city by turning to his writings.

## Images of the Other Half

Jacob Riis was an immigrant to America, like so many of those he wrote
about. He had tasted poverty and hardship. Yet in a curious way, Riis the
social reformer might best be understood as a tourist of the slums, wandering from tenement to tenement, camera in hand. To classify him as such is
to suggest that despite his immigrant background, he maintained a distance
between himself and his urban subjects.

In part, that distance can be explained by Riis's own background as an
immigrant. Despite his tribulations, he came from a middle-class family,
which made it easy to choose journalism as a career. As a boy, in fact, Riis
had helped his family prepare copy for a weekly newspaper. Once established in a job commensurate with his training, Riis found it easy to accomplish the goal of so many immigrants—to rise to middle-class dignity and
prosperity and to become, in the most respectable sense, not a newcomer
but an American.

Furthermore, because Riis emigrated from Denmark, his northern-
European background made it more difficult for him to empathize with the
immigrant cultures of southern and eastern Europe, increasingly the source
of new immigrants in the 1880s and 1890s. Like many native-born Americans, Riis found most of these immigrants' customs distasteful and doubted
whether they could successfully learn the traditional American virtues. He
often entertained his audiences with tales highlighting his subjects' inferior-
ity. There was Kwan Wing, a restaurant worker, who after a night of heavy
drinking and eating rice cakes had a dream that led him to a cache of silver coins in his basement. Kwan's discovery inspired some local business
leaders to form "Children of the Sun Mining Company." Its entrepreneurs

**"Photographing in High Places,"** Teton range 1872, by William Henry Jackson. A member of John Wesley Powell's earlier expedition down the Colorado River recalled the effort involved in handling the unwieldy photographic equipment: "The camera in its strong box was a heavy load to carry up the rocks, but it was nothing to the chemical and plate-holder box, which in turn was feather weight compared to the imitation hand organ which served as a darkroom." Mishaps along the way were not uncommon. "The silver bath had gotten out of order," reported one of Powell's party, "and the horse bearing the camera fell off a cliff and landed on top of the camera . . . with a result that need not be described."

promised to provide the public with the foods needed to discover their own hidden treasures. Such appeal to prejudices led historian Sam Warner to remark that Riis ascribed a "degree of opprobrium to each group directly proportional to the distance from Denmark."

Yet for all that, Riis retained a measure of sympathy and understanding for the poor. He did not work his way out of poverty only to find a quiet house far from the turmoil of the urban scene. He was unable to ignore the squalor that so evidently needed the attention of concerned Americans. Thus an ambivalence permeated Riis's writings. On the one hand, he sympathized with the plight of the poor and recognized how much they were the victims of their slum environment. "In the tenements all the elements make for evil," he wrote. He struggled to maintain a distinction between the "vicious" classes of beggars, tramps, and thieves and the working poor who made the slum their home because they had no other choice. On the other hand, Riis could not avoid using language that continuously dismissed whole classes of immigrants as inherently unable to adapt themselves to what he considered acceptable American behavior.

Of southern- and eastern-Mediterranean people, Riis was the least understanding. The "happy-go-lucky" Italians, he observed, were "content to live in a pig sty." Not only did they "come in at the bottom," but they also managed to stay there. They sought to reproduce the worst of life in Italy by flocking to slum tenements. When an Italian found better housing, "he soon reduced what he did find to his own level, if allowed to follow his natural bent." These affable and malleable souls "learned slowly, if at all." And then there was the passion for gambling and murder: "[The Italian's] soul is in the game from the moment the cards are on the table, and very frequently his knife is in it too before the game is ended." Such observations confirm our sense of Riis as a tourist in the slums, for he seemed only to have educated his prejudices without collecting objective information.

A second quality that strikes the reader of *How the Other Half Lives* is its tone of Christian moralism. Riis was no radical or socialist. He blamed the condition of the urban poor on the sins of individuals—greedy landlords, petty grafters, corrupt officials, the weak character of the poor, and popular indifference. Insensitive to the economic forces that had transformed cities, he never attempted a systematic analysis of urban conditions.

*Riis blamed the condition of the urban poor on the sins of individuals*

Instead, he appealed to moral regeneration as the means of overcoming evil and approvingly cited the plea of a philanthropic tenement builder: "How are these men and women to understand the love of God you speak of, when they see only the greed of men?" In his own ominous warning to his fellow New Yorkers, Riis struck an almost apocalyptic note: "When another generation shall have doubled the census of our city," he warned, "and to the vast army of workers, held captive by poverty, the very name of home shall be a bitter mockery, what will the harvest be?" If conditions worsened, the violence of labor strikes during the 1870s and 1880s might seem quite tame in comparison.

**Bohemian cigar makers** at work in their tenement

Given those predispositions, how do we interpret Riis's photographs? Like the arrangers of family albums, his personal interests dictated the kinds of photographs he included in his books. And as with the family albums, by being aware of these predispositions we can both understand Riis better by consciously examining his photographic messages and at the same time transcend the original intent of the pictures.

For example, Riis's Christian moralism led him to emphasize the need for stable families as a key to ameliorating slum conditions. Many American Protestants in his audience thought of the home and family as a haven from the bustle of the working world as well as a nursery of piety and good morals. Fathers could return at the end of the day to the warm, feminine environment in which their children were carefully nurtured. Thus the picture we have already examined of the "five cents a spot" lodging takes on added significance in light of these concerns. It is not simply the lack of cleanliness or space that would make such an apartment appalling to many viewers, but the corrosive effect of such conditions on family life. Yet this building was a family dwelling, for Riis heard a baby crying in the adjoining hall-room.

How could a family preserve any semblance of decency, Riis asked his readers, in a room occupied by twelve single men and women?

Let us turn from that photograph to the one on the previous page, which is more obviously a family portrait. The middle-class Protestant viewer of Riis's day would have found this picture shocking as well. The home was supposed to be a haven away from the harsh workaday world, yet here the factory has invaded the home. This small room of an immigrant Bohemian family is crowded with the tools and supplies needed to make a living. The business is apparently a family enterprise, since the husband, wife, and at least one child assist in the work. Although the young boy cannot keep his eyes off the camera, he continues to stretch tobacco leaves from the pile on his lap.

The room speaks of a rather single-minded focus on making a living. All the furnishings are used for cigar making, not for creature comforts or living after work. The only light comes from a small kerosene lamp and the indirect sunlight from two windows facing out on the wall of another building. Yet Riis had a stronger message for the picture to deliver. The text stresses the exploitation of Bohemians in New York, most of whom worked at cigar making in apartments owned by their employers, generally Polish Jewish immigrants.

It is interesting to contrast the portrait of the Bohemian family with a different family portrait, this one taken by another reforming photographer, but still often published in reprints of *How the Other Half Lives*.* Unlike the photograph of the cigar makers' lodging, the photograph on page 219 is a more formal family portrait. Very much aware of the camera's presence, everyone is looking directly at the lens. Perhaps the photographer could gain consent to intrude on their privacy only by agreeing to do a formal photograph. The children have been scrubbed and dressed in what appear to be their good clothes—the oldest son in his shirt and tie, his sister in a taffeta dress, and a younger girl in a frock. Unlike the "five cents a spot" lodging, where dishes were stacked one upon the other, here the family china is proudly displayed in the cabinet. Perhaps it was a valued possession carefully guarded on the journey from Europe.

Other details in the picture suggest that this family enjoyed a more pleasant environment than was seen in the previous photos. We notice on the left a gas stove, a relatively modern improvement in an age when coal and wood were still widely used for heating and cooking. Perhaps these people had found a room in a once-elegant home divided by the realtor into a multiple dwelling. Certain details suggest that may be the case. Few tenements would have had gas, much less built-in cupboards or the finished moldings around doors and windows. The window between the kitchen-bedroom and closet-bedroom indicates that the room may have once looked out on open space.

---

* The photographer is Jessie Tarbox Beals, and the picture was taken in 1910. Although not included in the original edition of *How the Other Half Lives*, it is among the photographs in the Riis Collection held by the Museum of the City of New York.

**Room in a tenement flat,** 1910

    By contrast, the picture communicates a sense of crowding. This image hardly seems an accident. Had the photographer wished to take only a family portrait, she could have clustered her subjects in the center of her lens. Instead, she placed them around the room so that the camera would catch all the details of their domestic circumstance. We see not just a family, but the conditions of their lives in an area far too small for their needs. Each space and almost all the furnishings are used for more than one purpose. The washtub just before the window and washboard behind it indicate that the kitchen doubles as a laundry room—and the tub was probably used for baths as well. The bed serves during the day as a sofa. To gain a measure of privacy, the parents have crowded their bed into a closet stuffed with family possessions. Seven people seem to share a room perhaps no more than 250 square feet in total. The children appear to range in age from one to twelve.

    This portrait, then, does not conform to the stereotype we would expect to find of urban immigrant slum-dwellers. In the first place, many immigrants came to America without families. Of those, a majority were young men who hoped to stay just long enough to accumulate a small savings with which to improve their family fortunes upon returning to Europe. On the other hand, immigrant families tended to be much larger than those of middle-class, native-born Americans. Rather than evoking a sympathetic response among an American audience, the picture might instead reinforce the widespread fear that prolific breeding among foreign elements threatened white Protestant domination of American society.

What, then, does the modern viewer derive from this family portrait? Overall, it seems to say that immigrants, like other Americans, prized family life. The father perches at the center almost literally holding his family together, though with a rather tenuous grip. The son with his tie appears to embody the family's hopes for a better future. His mother securely holds the baby in her arms. Each element, in fact, emphasizes the virtues of the domestic family as it was traditionally conceived in America. The picture, while sending a mixed message, conveys less a sense of terrible slum conditions than a sense of the middle-class aspirations among those forced to live in inadequate housing.

*Immigrants, like other Americans, prized family life.*

Does the fact that the picture is posed make it less useful as historical evidence? Not at all. Even when people perform for the camera, they communicate information about themselves. There is no hiding the difficulty of making a decent life for seven people in a small space. Nor can the viewer ignore the sense of pride of person and place, no matter how limited the resources. What remains uncertain, however, is what message the photographer meant to convey. The scene could serve equally well to arouse nativist prejudice or to extol the strength of family ties in the immigrant community. Both were concerns that Riis addressed in his writing and photographs.

Concern over the breakdown of family life drew Riis to children. They are among his most frequently photographed subjects. He shared the Victorian notion of childhood innocence and therefore understood that nothing could be more disturbing to his middle-class audience than scenes of homeless children, youth gangs, and "street arabs" sleeping in alleys, gutters, and empty stairways. At first glance, the three "street arabs" pictured on page 221 appear as if they might even be dead. A closer look suggests helpless innocence—children alone and unprotected as they sleep. Their ragged clothes and bare feet advertise poverty and the absence of parents to care for them. In each other, though, they seem to have extracted a small measure of warmth, belonging, and comfort. It would be almost impossible for any caring person to view the picture without empathy for its subjects and anger at a society that cares so little for its innocent creatures.

Riis hints at his sympathies through the location of the camera. He did not stand over the boys to shoot the picture from above. That angle would suggest visually the superiority of the photographer to his subjects. From ground level, however, observer and subject are on the same plane. We look at the boys, not down on them. And should we dismiss as accidental his

In that sense the photographic "mirror" is silvered on both sides, catching the reflections of its user as well as its subjects. The prints that emerge from the twilight of the darkroom must be read by historians as they do all evidence—appreciating messages that may be simple and obvious or complex and elusive. Once these evidentiary limits are appreciated and accepted, the historian can recognize the rueful justice in Oliver Wendell Holmes's definition of a photograph: an illusion with the "appearance of reality that cheats the senses with its seeming truth."

## Additional Reading

Readers wishing to examine more visual evidence from Jacob Riis's *How the Other Half Lives* should consult the Dover Publications edition (New York, 1971) of his book. It includes 100 photographs and several reproductions of line illustrations from the original version. Another edition of *How the Other Half Lives* (Cambridge, MA, 1970) has an excellent introduction by urban historian Sam Bass Warner but suffers because of a limited number of photos. A more comprehensive collection is Robert J. Doherty, ed., *The Complete Photographic Work of Jacob Riis* (New York, 1987). The Riis photographs are also available on microfiche from the International Archives of Photography (New York, 1981). Peter B. Hales, *Silver Cities: Photography of Urban America, 1839–1915* (Philadelphia, 1984), offers a persuasive interpretation of Riis's place in the tradition of urban photography and social reform.

Bonnie Yochelson and Daniel Czitrom, *Rediscovering Jacob Riis: Exposure Journalism and Photography in Turn of the Century New York* (New York, 2007), evaluate Riis both as a reformer and as a photographer. Riis's autobiographic account of his life is found in Roy Lubove, ed., *The Making of an American* (New York, 1966). An interesting but dated biography exists in Louise Ware, *Jacob A. Riis, Police Reporter* (New York, 1938); see also the more recent study by Edith P. Mayer, *"Not Charity But Justice": The Story of Jacob A. Riis* (New York, 1974). One of America's finest photographers and critics, Ansel Adams, has also done the preface to an important book on Riis: Alexander Alland, *Jacob Riis: Photographer and Citizen* (Millerton, NY, reissued 1993).

Even for those readers whose photographic expertise is limited to a mastery of George Eastman's injunction ("You press the button . . ."), a number of books provide clear discussions of the photographic medium, its potentialities, and its limitations. Susan Sontag, in her *On Photography* (New York, 1977), provides many stimulating ideas, particularly in her first essay, "In Plato's Cave," and most recently, she reconsidered some of those ideas in *Regarding the Pain of Others* (New York, 2003). All followers of photographic art owe a debt to Beaumont Newhall, *The History of Photography from 1839 to the Present Day* (New York, 1964), and Robert Taft, *Photography and the American Scene* (New York, 1938; reissued 1964). For views that contrast with Riis's scenes of New York, see the Museum of the City of New York's *Once Upon a City: New York from 1890 to 1910* (New York, 1958).

One significant pleasure in a field as untapped as photographic evidence comes from doing original research yourself. Many photographs of historic value are on file and readily available to the public in the Library of Congress Prints and Photographs Division and the National Archives Still Picture Branch. Readers may download them from the Library of Congress's American Memory Web site (http://memory.loc.gov). Almost all readers will have access to family albums, yearbooks, newspaper files, Web sites, and other sources from which to do their own investigating.

## PAST AND PRESENT
# Why Can't I See Them Now?

People marveled in the 1880s at the miracle that George Eastman's Kodak system wrought. They pointed the lens, pushed the button, and sent the camera off to Eastman's factory to have their pictures developed. Soon, they had their cameras back, loaded with a new roll of film. No heavy gear, messy chemicals, or finicky darkrooms. So imagine how home photographers felt some sixty years later when Edwin Land invented his Polaroid "Land" camera. Point, shoot, open the back of the camera, and pull off the developed photograph. Near instant gratification. Land had solved the problem many parents faced when their children asked, "Why can't I see them now?"

Could Land top that achievement? In 1972 he did, as Polaroid introduced the SX-70, an instant color camera. Where the original Land camera used roll film, the SX-70 used a square cartridge, which emitted a color picture that developed automatically once the shot was taken. As one art critic commented, "Mystery clung to each impending image as it took shape, the camera conjuring up what was right before one's eyes, right before one's eyes." Some users complained because they could not make copies of the original. But for police photographers, that shortcoming became a virtue. When they took a mug shot or photographed a crime scene, no shady lawyer could suggest that the pictures had been doctored.

Thirty-five years after Land's miracle, Polaroid disappeared, driven out of business by digital cameras. These electronic wizards offer gratification that is even more instant and less complicated. If a picture disappoints, hit the delete button and shoot again without wasting film. Digital cameras have become so miniaturized they fit into cell phones that give almost anyone the ability to communicate images to distant places with unpredictable possibilities.

In late April 2004, for example, U.S. television news-magazine *60 Minutes II* broke a story involving abuse and humiliation of Iraqi inmates at Abu Ghraib prison. The story included photographs showing prisoners being tormented. Where did these incriminating images come from? Guards and soldiers at Abu Ghraib had routinely used their cell phone cameras to send photos of their activities back to friends and family at home. The resulting scandal shocked the nation and damaged the claim that the United States had a humanitarian mission in Iraq. The military learned its lesson, however. It banned soldiers from bringing cell phone cameras into Iraq. The "mirror with a memory" can also open windows into the dark corners of our lives.

# CHAPTER 10

# USDA *Government Inspected*

*They claimed to use every bit of the pig "except the squeal." Were meatpackers business visionaries or a threat to public health whose industry required public regulation?*

All our essays tell a story, and this one is no exception. But our present tale, by its very nature, partakes in large measure of the epic and the symbolic. It is a political tale, compiled largely from the accounts of politicians and the journalists who write about politicians; which is to say, it possesses much of the stuff of a good, robust fairy tale. As we shall shortly discover, there are logical reasons for such larger-than-life overtones, and they deserve serious scrutiny. But the story must come first: an exciting tale of a bold president, an earnest reformer, some evil political bosses, and a lot of pork and beef. It begins ("once upon a time") with the president, Teddy Roosevelt, who turns out to be the hero of the tale. There was nothing ordinary about Teddy, including the fact that he was ever president at all. People from the Roosevelts' social class disdained politics and would never encourage their sons to take it up as a profession. But then again, Teddy was not like other members of his social class, nor like his fellow students at Harvard. Anything he did, he did with gusto, and if being the best meant being president, then Teddy would not stop short of the White House.

His path to success was not an easy one. As a child Teddy was sickly, asthmatic, and nearsighted. He spent long hours pummeling punching bags, swinging on parallel bars, doing push-ups, and boxing in the ring to build a body as robust as his mind. When he went west in the 1880s to take up ranching, he had to overcome his image as an effete eastern "dude." He soon amazed many a grizzled cowboy by riding the Dakota badlands in spring mud, blasts of summer heat, and driving winter storms. He fought with his fists and once rounded up a band of desperados at gunpoint. Back East, when Teddy played tennis, he showed the same determination, his record being ninety-one games in a single day. When he led the Rough Riders through Cuba in 1898, he raised troop morale by walking the sentry line, whistling cheerfully while his men crouched low to avoid the bullets flying overhead. As president he advised others to speak softly and carry a big stick, though he himself more often observed only the latter half of his maxim.

**TR, displaying characteristic gritted teeth** and holding a moderately big stick. When he spoke, Roosevelt chopped every word into neat, staccato syllables, with a rhythm that bore no resemblance to the ordinary cadences of the English language. "I always think of a man biting tenpenny nails when I think of Roosevelt making a speech," remarked one acquaintance.

Teddy's favorite expressions, seldom spoken softly, were "Bully!" and "Dee lighted!"—uttered because he usually got his way.

By 1906 Teddy had the White House firmly in his grasp. Just two years earlier he had won a resounding victory. His many achievements included the Nobel Peace Prize for his role in bringing an end to the Russo-Japanese War. But Teddy could never rest on his laurels. In February a storm broke that challenged his skill as leader of both the nation and the Republican Party.

The thunderclap that shattered the calm was the publication of *The Jungle*. The book told a lurid tale about Chicago's meatpacking industry. Its author, Upton Sinclair, was not only a reformer but a socialist as well. Most Americans of the day believed that socialists were dangerous people who held extreme and impractical opinions. Despite that skepticism, readers could not ignore the grisly realities recounted in *The Jungle*. It related, in often revolting detail, the conditions under which the packers processed pork and beef, adulterated it, and shipped it to millions of American consumers. Breakfast sausage, Sinclair revealed, was more than

*The Jungle told a lurid tale about Chicago's meatpacking industry.*

**Hogs being scalded** preparatory to scraping at a Swift and Company plant, 1905. The packers boasted that they used every bit of the pig "except the squeal," and they were probably more than right, given some of the extraneous ingredients that went into the canned goods of the period. Although modern viewers may be taken aback at the unsanitary appearance of the plant, this photograph was a promotional shot illustrating some of the better conditions in packing facilities.

a tasty blend of ground meats and spices. "It was too dark in these storage spaces to see clearly," he reported,

> but a man could run his hands over the piles of meat and swap off handfulls of dry dung of rats. These rats were nuisances, and the packers would put out poisoned bread for them; they would die; and then rats, bread, and meat would go in the hoppers together. This is no fairy story and no joke; the meat would be shoveled into carts, and the man who did the shoveling did not trouble to lift out a rat even when he saw one.

Rats were but one tasty additive in the meat sent to dinner tables. Potted chicken contained no chicken at all, only beef suet, waste ends of veal, and tripe. Most shocking of all, Sinclair told of men in cooking rooms who fell into vats and, after being cooked for days, "all but the bones had gone out into the world as Durham's Pure Leaf Lard!"

In just one week a scandalized public had snapped up some 25,000 copies of *The Jungle*. Most readers missed the socialist message. Sinclair had hoped to draw their attention to "the conditions under which toilers get their bread." The public had responded instead to the disclosures about corrupt federal meat inspectors, unsanitary slaughterhouses, tubercular cattle, and the packers' unscrupulous business practices.

No reader was more outraged than President Theodore Roosevelt. Few politicians have ever been as well informed as TR, who devoured books at more than 1,500 words per minute, published works of history, and corresponded with the opinion makers of his day. Roosevelt recognized immediately that the public would expect government at some level—local, state, or federal—to clean up the meat industry. He invited Sinclair for a talk at the White House, and though he dismissed the writer's "pathetic belief" in socialism, he promised that "the specific evils you point out shall, if their existence be proved, and if I have the power, be eradicated."

Roosevelt kept his promise. With the help of allies in Congress, he quickly brought out a new bill, along with the proverbial big stick. Only four months later, on June 30, he signed into law the Meat Inspection Act that banned the packers from using any unhealthy dyes, chemical preservatives, or adulterants. The bill provided $3 million toward a new, tougher inspection system, one in which government inspectors could be on hand day or night to condemn animals unfit for human consumption. Senator Albert Beveridge of Indiana, Roosevelt's progressive ally in Congress, gave the president credit for the new bill. "It is chiefly to him that we owe the fact that we will get as excellent a bill as we will have," he told reporters. Once again, Americans could put canned meats and sausages on the dinner table and eat happily ever after. Or so it would seem.

# THE SYMBOLS OF POLITICS

The story you have just read is true—as far as it goes. It has taken on a legendary, even mythic quality in the telling. Politics is, after all, public business. And the public, especially in that era, treated their politicians a bit like celebrities, with the result that the tales of national politics almost inescapably took on epic proportions. In such situations, symbolic language serves to simplify highly complex realities. It makes those realities more comprehensible by substituting concrete and recognizable actors and objects in the place of complicated, though often ordinary, situations. In doing so, symbols and symbolic language serve as a means of communication between political leaders and their constituencies. Skillful politicians generally have

**Boss William Tweed of New York,** in life and in art. During the latter half of the nineteenth century, cartoons played an important part in defining the symbols of political discourse. Occasionally the representations were readily recognizable in more than a symbolic sense. When Tweed fled the United States to escape a jail term, he was arrested in an out-of-the-way Spanish village. The Spanish constables, it turned out, had recognized him from this Thomas Nast cartoon. The symbolic aspect of the drawing escaped them, however; they thought they had apprehended a notorious child kidnapper.

the ability to dramatize their actions so as to appear to address deeply felt public concerns.

Jacksonian Democrats pioneered many of the modern uses of campaign imagery. They touted their candidate, Old Hickory, as the symbolic embodiment of the American frontier tradition. In their hands Jackson became the uncommon "Common Man." As president, he waged war against the Second Bank of the United States, fittingly symbolized by its enemies as the Monster Bank. His Whig opposition had quickly grasped the use of such symbols; they nominated a popular general of their own, William Henry "Tippecanoe" Harrison. Their campaign rhetoric invoked a log-cabin motif and other appropriate frontier images, although in reality Harrison came from a distinguished Virginia family and lived in an elegant house. Thus, along with a two-party system of politics, Americans had developed a body of symbols to make complex political issues familiar and comprehensible to the voters.

Symbols as a mode of political discourse took on a new power in a form that matured in the late nineteenth century: the political cartoon. Earlier cartoonists had portrayed Old Hickory's epic struggle with the Monster Bank, but they lacked the sophistication and draftsmanship achieved by Gilded Age caricaturists such as Thomas Nast. Week after week, newspapers carried cartoons that established readily identifiable symbols. Nast conceived the elephant as a representation of the GOP (the Republicans, or Grand Old Party) and the donkey for the Democrats. To Nast and his fellow cartoonists we owe our image of the Political Boss, decked out in his gaudy suit that assumes a striking resemblance to a convict's striped outfit. So, too, we have the Monopolist, or greedy capitalist, his huge, bloated waistline taking on the aspect of a bag of silver dollars. A scraggly beard, overalls, and wild, crazed eyes denoted the Populist. In place of the Monster Bank stood the Trust, vividly pictured as a grasping octopus. Such cartoons by their very nature communicated political messages of their day.

The cartoonists seldom had a better subject than Teddy Roosevelt. His gleaming, oversized front teeth, bull neck, pince-nez glasses, and, of course, big stick begged to be caricatured. Cartoonists did not have to stretch the imagination to cast Teddy larger than life; he specialized in that department long before he reached the White House.

He offered himself up as the gun-toting cowboy, the New York police commissioner in his long, black cape, and the Rough Rider charging up Tea Kettle Hill. Thus it was easy during the political battles of the Progressive Era to conceive of the actors in symbolic terms. In one corner stood the reformers: Roosevelt, a policeman, clubbing the opposition with his big stick; or Sinclair, wild-eyed like all political radicals. In the other corner, during the meat-inspection fight, stood the Beef Trust: Armour, Swift, and the other packers, with their "public-be-damned" attitudes.

*Cartoonists did not have to stretch the imagination to cast Teddy larger than life.*

Yet as we have already noted, such symbolic representations inevitably oversimplify the political process to the point of distortion. As rendered by the cartoonist, shades of gray become black and white. Even more subtly, distortion arises because symbols come to personalize complex situations and processes. Inanimate institutions (trusts, political machines, Congress) appear as animate objects (a grasping octopus, predatory tigers, braying donkeys) with human motives and designs.

Consequently, we tend to visualize political events as the result of individuals' actions. The story of the meat-inspection law is reduced to the tale of Roosevelt, Sinclair, and their enemies. The tale, as we saw, is quite simple: (1) Sinclair's revelations scandalize the president; (2) Roosevelt determines to reform the meatpacking industry; (3) with his usual energy, Roosevelt overwhelms the opposition and saves the consumer.

Such an explanation masks the crucial truth that the actors—whether individuals, groups, or institutions—often have complicated motives and confused objectives. The outcome of a situation may bear slight resemblance

WILLIE AND HIS PAPA.

(COPYRIGHT, 1901, BY W. R. HEARST.)

"Trouble again, Willie?  Well, what now?"
"Teddy says this is the way he is going to arrange the Inaugural Parade."

**Caricaturists had a field day** with Roosevelt's energetic and good-natured self-aggrandizement. In this cartoon by Frederick Opper, Vice-President-Elect Roosevelt has rearranged the inaugural parade of 1901 so that President William McKinley is forced to bring up the rear. Teddy, of course, displays his teeth as well as a load of hunting trophies from western exploits, while the characteristic Trust figure looms in the background as "Willie's Papa."

to the original design of any of the participants. As a result, symbolic explanations do not adequately portray the process through which political actors turn their intentions, both good and bad, into law.

Political historians, then, must handle symbolic language and explanations with caution. They cannot simply dismiss or debunk the symbolism, for it can, by influencing opinion, affect the political process. At the same time, historians cannot allow symbols to obscure the information necessary to narrate and explain political events. Granted, Roosevelt played the reformer in seeking to curb the packers' worst abuses, but how successfully did he translate his intentions into an effective political instrument? Senator Beveridge, it is true, praised both the new law and the president's role in securing its passage, yet other supporters of inspection reform did not share Beveridge's enthusiasm. "The American consumer and the ordinary American farmer have been left out of the question," Senator Knute Nelson complained shortly after the act passed. "I must say I feel disappointed. . . . When I go home I will go home like a licked dog."

In fact, prominent Republicans in the Senate, led by Beveridge himself and Roosevelt's good friend Henry Cabot Lodge of Massachusetts, had fought to defeat the law only a few days before Roosevelt signed it. They believed, as Nelson had argued, that the bill was intended "to placate the packers; next to placate the men who raise cattle; and, third to get a good market for the packers abroad." In short, many senators viewed the Meat Inspection Act as a victory for the packers and a defeat for reform. In that light, Beveridge's praise has a symbolic meaning that our story thus far cannot explain.

So the historian must seek to set aside the mythic story and its symbols in order to reconstruct the way in which the real story unfolded. The outcome must be treated not as the inevitable triumph of good over evil but as just one of the many possible outcomes and not necessarily the best at that. The political historian's task is also to determine how the complex procedural tangle by which a bill becomes law limits the impact of individual actors no matter how lofty or base their motives.

## THE TANGLE BEHIND *THE JUNGLE*

The mythic tale of the Meat Inspection Act begins with the publication of *The Jungle* in February 1906. That, so the story goes, sparked the outrage against the packers and their unscrupulous methods. Yet although as many as one million people read *The Jungle*, we may legitimately wonder whether a single book could by itself generate such widespread controversy. For better or worse, we have no opinion polls from 1906 to measure public response to Sinclair's lurid exposé. But if we poke around in earlier stories about the meat industry, we find that *The Jungle* was merely a final chapter, albeit a telling one, in a long train of unfavorable stories about the packers.

As early as the 1870s, some European governments had begun to ban what they had found to be unhealthy American meat products. Over the years American exports declined as the Europeans tightened their restrictions. In 1891 the worried packers persuaded Congress to pass a federal meat-inspection act in order to win back their foreign customers. The federal stamp would show that all meats in interstate and foreign sales had been subjected to antemortem (preslaughter) inspection. That measure succeeded until 1897, when "embalmed meat" scandals renewed outrage at the

**Roosevelt with his Rough Riders.** TR's distrust of the packers reached as far back as the Spanish-American War, when packers had sold the American army quantities of rotten and chemically adulterated meats. Humorist Finley Peter Dunne took note of the situation—as well as the disorganized state of the regular army—when he had his fictional Irish bartender, Mr. Dooley, remark on the invincible American army of "injineers, miners, plumbers, an' lawn tinnis experts, numberin' in all four hundhred an' eighty thousand men," sent to do battle against the Spanish "ar-rmed with death-dealin' canned goods."

industry's unsavory practices. A few unscrupulous packers had supplied the army fighting in Cuba with rotten and chemically adulterated meats. As the commander of the Rough Riders, Colonel Teddy Roosevelt had seen troops die from poisonous meats, as well as from Spanish bullets.

Roosevelt had not forgotten what he interpreted as treachery. In 1905 he found an opportunity to punish the packers. He ordered his attorney general to bring suit against the packinghouses under the Sherman Antitrust Act. The president was particularly offended by what he viewed as the packers' brazen disregard for public safety. Armour, Swift, and others boasted openly that they used every bit of the pig "except the squeal." Roosevelt was therefore beside himself when he heard that the judge had dismissed the government's suit on narrow procedural grounds. Suspicious that the packers had resorted to bribery, he instructed his attorney general to release a confidential report revealing perjury in the Beef Trust case. Roosevelt scarcely needed to read *The Jungle* to believe that with their public-be-damned attitude the meat barons might be guilty of any manner of irresponsible behavior. Furthermore, the president recognized that the existing meat-inspection law left much to be desired. Under it, Congress allocated money for an inspection force, but never enough to do the job well. Given the limited funds, most inspectors worked only during the day, leaving the packers free to commit their worst abuses at night. Even if inspectors did find diseased cattle at antemortem inspection, they had no power to have the animals destroyed. In fact, the packers often sold those tainted animals to other plants not under federal supervision.

The federal government actually had almost no authority over the packers. Nothing under the system forced compliance with government standards. The inspectors could only threaten to leave the premises (and take their stamps with them) if the packers ignored their rulings. And though the law did prevent the industry from exporting meat without the federal stamp of approval, no similar provision protected American consumers. Once a carcass passed the inspector, the government had no further power to impose sanitary standards anywhere in the plants. Roosevelt was aware of these deficiencies and eager to see them corrected.

The public, too, had grounds for suspicion. Sinclair's accusations had already been published in a popular socialist journal. In doing his research, Sinclair had received information from *The Lancet*, a distinguished British medical journal that had investigated earlier meat-industry scandals. In 1905 *The Lancet* renewed its investigation of the packinghouses. Investigators discovered filth that jeopardized both workers and consumers. At the same time, Samuel Merwyn, a well-known muckraking journalist, had written articles charging the packers with deliberately selling diseased meats.

Muckrakers like Merwyn had much in common with the political cartoonists. Toward the turn of the century, journalists had discovered that the public possessed an almost insatiable appetite for sensational stories. Muckrakers' investigations uncovered villains who made convenient, easily recognizable symbols. Evil could be personified as the Monster Trust, the Self-Serving Politician, or the Avaricious Capitalist. These villains were much like the greedy landlords Jacob Riis had condemned. Like Riis, muckrakers told Americans what was wrong with their society, but with few suggestions about how to fix the problems. Somehow the exposure of the symptoms of evil was supposed to motivate reformers and an aroused public to cure the disease. In keeping with the popular style of muckraking, Sinclair had pointed an accusing finger at the packers without offering any specific suggestions for cleaning up the meat industry.

*Journalists discovered that the public possessed an almost insatiable appetite for sensational stories.*

But just as *The Jungle* can be understood only within the context of the muckraking era, so too the Meat Inspection Act stood within the context

"**An Alphabet of Joyous Trusts**" was Frederick Opper's subject in a 1902 series of cartoons. Predictably, "B" stood for the Beef Trusts. The same Trust figure is back (compare it with the one in Opper's Roosevelt cartoon on page 000), although here Opper plays on the monopolist's traditional control over market prices rather than on the unsanitary practices of the packing industry.

of Progressive reform. Despite Sinclair's lack of analysis, many Americans had identified the sources of such corporate arrogance and had prepared an agenda for politics. Theodore Roosevelt embodied much of the temperament of those Progressive reformers. He shared their hostility to excessive concentrations of power in private hands, their approval of executive regulatory agencies, their faith in democratic forms of government, their humanitarian sensibilities, and their confidence in the people's capacity to shape their future intelligently.

The Progressives were actually a diverse group seeking to turn government at all levels into a weapon for social justice. They included rural reformers, good-government and moral-uplift advocates, economic regulators, antitrusters, and political liberals and conservatives. Roosevelt's faith in traditional institutions might easily have led him to oppose the reformers, but he was never a diehard conservative who railed against change. "The only true conservative is the man who resolutely set his face to the future," he once told a Progressive supporter.

It was preoccupation with morality that brought the reform movement together and that attracted Roosevelt to Progressivism. "His life, he felt, was a quest for the moral," wrote one biographer. The reformers of the early twentieth century saw themselves rooting out evil, which more often than not they defined as "corporate arrogance." Seeking to maximize profits, a railroad might leave a road crossing unguarded; a water company might eliminate safeguards against typhoid fever. "Such

*A preoccupation with morality brought the reform movement together and attracted Roosevelt to Progressivism.*

**Chicago packers pioneered the moving (dis)assembly line.** Live pigs were lifted by their hind feet onto the overhead rail. Their throats were cut, and after they bled to death, the carcasses moved along as each worker cut off a particular part until virtually nothing was left. This process revolutionized work by reducing complex operations to simple steps.

incidents made the corporation look like a killer," wrote historian David Thelen. "These specific threats united all classes; anyone's child might be careless at a railroad crossing; and typhoid fever was no respecter of social origins."

Such problems were particularly acute because rapidly growing city populations depended on processed foods. Other food industries had no better sanitary standards than the meatpackers. Milk dealers, for example, regularly increased their profits by diluting their product, using chalk, plaster, and molasses to fortify the color and taste. A popular ditty of the day expressed the widespread skepticism with processed foods:

> Things are seldom what they seem;
> Skim milk masquerades as cream;
> Lard and soap we eat for cheese;
> Butter is but axle grease.

As a result, the public was prepared to think the worst of the meat industry. The campaign for improved meat inspection had all the ingredients that aroused Progressive ire. The packing industry fit Roosevelt's definition of a "bad" trust, since its apparent disregard for even minimum health standards threatened all classes of Americans.

Yet we must remember how politicians like to cast issues in black and white terms. Were the packers the villains that reformers painted them to be? To be fair, we should hear the packers' side of the case before we rush to judgment. Some packers stated publicly that improved federal inspection was the best way to restore public confidence in their products. J. Ogden Armour, head of the packinghouse that bore his name, confidently invited the public to visit local packing plants "to see for yourself how the hated packer takes care of your meat supply." But he frankly admitted that "no packer can do an interstate or export business without government inspection."

In their way, the packers were as revolutionary as the crazed socialists that Roosevelt condemned. Over a twenty-year period the industry had fundamentally altered the way Americans bought and ate meat. Whereas at one time customers would buy meat only from a local butcher, they now felt confident eating meats prepared in distant packinghouses. To get meat safely to consumers, the packers had invented the moving assembly line (disassembly might be a better term as the engraving indicates), refrigerated railroad cars, and a national marketing system. Urban consumers benefited because they had a greater variety of meat products at lower costs.

## Armour's Estimates of Dressed Beef By-Product Costs and Profits

| | |
|---|---|
| Steer, 1,260 lbs @ $3.25 per cwt* (becomes 710 lbs dressed beef) | $   40.95 |
| Cost of killing, processing, salt, icing, etc. | 1.75 |
| Freight on 710 lbs @ $0.45 per cwt | 3.20 |
| New York selling charges @ $0.35 per cwt | 2.48 |
| Costs of purchase, processing, and transport | $  −48.38 |
| Sale in NW of 710 lbs dressed beef @ 5⅜¢ per lb | $   38.17 |
| (Net loss on dressed beef in NW) | −$10.21 |
| Sale of hide, 70 lbs @ $.09 per lb | 6.30 |
| Sale of by-products | 4.50 |
| Yield from all by-product sales | 10.80 |
| Net profit from all transactions | 0.59 |

From *Nature's Metropolis: Chicago and the Great West* by William Cronon. Copyright © 1991 by William Cronon. Reprinted by permission of W. W. Norton & Company, Inc.

*hundred-weight

ckers had succeeded in large part because they used "everything but the squeal." Put another way, packers made a profit from what local butchers threw away. As one historian wrote, "[Armour] had built his empire on waste." To reformers, "this seemed akin to making something out of nothing." Look at the table on page 241, and you can see what these comments mean. Had Armour sold only the dressed beef, how much money would he have lost per head? Instead, the packers established chemical research labs that developed products out of the wastes once flushed down the sewers. Margarine, bouillon, brushes, combs, gut stringing, stearin (used in soap and candles), and pepsin (to aid digestion) were among their innovations. They even found uses for ground bones, dried blood, and hooves and feet (for glues). Today we might praise the packers for their aggressive approach to recycling. Reformers, however, mistook the careful attention to profit margins as corporate greed and a disregard for public health. Much of what the packers sold to make a profit the reformers thought they should throw away.

The innovative side of the packers' success was lost in the outcry over *The Jungle*. Under the shadow Sinclair had cast, millions of Americans altered their eating habits. Many foreign countries banned American meats. An industry representative confessed that the loss of public confidence was "hurting us very, very materially." The decline in both domestic and foreign meat sales persuaded Armour that only improved inspection would save the industry.

Thus the historical context surrounding meat-inspection reform reveals that the dramatic appearance of *The Jungle* was only the most conspicuous—and therefore the most obviously symbolic—event among a whole series of developments. All the necessary ingredients were on hand to produce legislation for a more stringent federal law. And on hand was Theodore Roosevelt, the master political chef who would whip all the ingredients into a dish that consumers could taste with confidence.

## THE LEGISLATIVE JUNGLE

In order for public outrage to find a constructive outlet, politicians must channel it into law. And historians, for their part, must trace a path through the congressional maze in order to see what compromises and deals shaped the final bill. The legislative process is so constituted that willful minorities can sometimes thwart the will of determined majorities. Skillful manipulation of legislative procedures may allow senators and representatives to delay the legislative process until support for a bill dissolves. It is during the legislative phase that the historian discovers that support for improved inspection was not so universal as it first seemed. Meat inspection, like many reforms of the Progressive Era, raised issues more controversial than the question of sanitary standards. Many of those larger issues affected the roles of the individual actors. President Roosevelt, for example, had expressed his determination "to assert the sovereignty of the National Government by affirmative action" against unchecked corporate wealth and power. When added to the Hepburn bill that allowed the government to set railroad shipping rates and that included the Pure Food and Drug Act, a new meat-inspection bill would mark a major extension of public regulatory authority over private corporations.

Many people who favored improved inspection had given no indication that they would accept Roosevelt's sweeping definition of executive authority. The popular doctrine of *caveat emptor* (let the buyer beware) placed the burden for policing the marketplace on the consumer, not the government.

*The popular doctrine of* caveat emptor *placed the burden for policing the marketplace on the consumer.*

As recently as 1895, in the case of *E. C. Knight,* the Supreme Court had severely restricted government regulation of commerce. The packers, for their part, had given no indication that in agreeing to inspection reform they would accept a bill that in any way limited their control of the meat industry. Misguided rules might ruin their business. So behind a mask of general agreement, many actors entered the legislative process with conflicting motives and objectives. Much of that conflict would be expressed not as disagreement on major legal or philosophical issues, but as seemingly petty bickering over the details of the proposed law.

To persuade conservatives to accept the tough bill he wanted, Roosevelt knew he needed more ammunition than Sinclair's exposé. His agriculture secretary, James Wilson, had ordered an internal investigation of the Bureau of Animal Industry (BAI), which ran the inspection system. But Wilson and Roosevelt both suspected that the investigation would not "get to the bottom of this matter." Therefore, they asked Commissioner of Labor Charles P. Neill and New York attorney James Reynolds to undertake an independent investigation. Both men had been active in "good government" causes, though neither had any familiarity with the meat industry. Once they reported back, Roosevelt would have the evidence he needed to determine whether Sinclair or the meatpackers were the "malefactors" in this case.

Agriculture Department investigators whitewashed the BAI, just as Roosevelt suspected they would. Sinclair had grossly exaggerated conditions in the plants and treated "the worst . . . which could be found in any establishment as typical of the general conditions," the investigators charged. Although the system could stand reforming, they argued that Sinclair's accusations were "willful and deliberate misrepresentations of fact."

Neill and Reynolds suggested, quite to the contrary, that if anything, conditions in the packinghouses were even worse than Sinclair had claimed. Their official report described slime and manure covering the walks leading into the plants. The buildings lacked adequate ventilation and lighting. All the equipment—the conveyors, meat racks, cutting tables, and tubs—rotted under a blanket of filth and blood. Meat scraps for canning or sausages sat in piles on the grimy floors. Large portions of ground rope and pigskin went into the potted ham. Just as Sinclair had charged, foul conditions in the plant proved harmful to the health of both the workers and the consumers of the products they prepared.

The Neill-Reynolds report gave Roosevelt the big stick he liked to carry into any political fight. Should the packers prove resistant, he could threaten to make the secret report public. "It is absolutely necessary that we shall have legislation which will prevent the recurrence of these wrongs," he warned. In Senator Albert Beveridge of Indiana he found a willing ally, already at work on a new inspection bill. Beveridge, like Roosevelt, had caught the rising tide of Progressive discontent over corporate misconduct. He sensed, too, that leadership on this issue would win him the popular acclaim he craved. Assisted by Agriculture Department experts, Beveridge had a bill drafted by the middle of May 1906. He urged Roosevelt to pave the way for Senate approval by releasing the damning Neill-Reynolds report.

For the moment, the politically adept Roosevelt heeded his own admonition to speak softly. For all his bluster, the president was generally a cautious man. An unnecessary confrontation with the powerful Beef Trust offended his sense of political practicality. Why waste his political ammunition if he could have his way without a fight? "The matter is of such far-reaching importance," he confided to Neill, "that it is out of the question to act hastily." Besides, having once been a rancher himself, he was reluctant to injure the livestock raisers, who bore no responsibility for the packers' scandalous behavior.

The packers had indicated that they would resist efforts to regulate their business, but had privately admitted that all was not well in their plants. One had begged Neill to withhold his report, promising in return that the packers would carry out any "reasonable, rational, and just recommendations" within thirty days. After that Neill and Reynolds would be free to reexamine the plants. When Neill refused, packer Louis Swift rushed off to confront the president. He found Roosevelt equally unsympathetic to any scheme involving voluntary compliance. The president assured Swift that he would settle for no less than legislation to "prevent the recurrence of these wrongs."

Beveridge by now had his bill ready. On May 2, 1906, he introduced it as a Senate amendment to the House Agriculture Appropriation Bill. Why, we might well ask, did such a major reform make its debut as an amendment tacked on to a House bill? Here, we begin to see how the legislative process affects political outcomes. Beveridge recognized that effective inspection required adequate funds. Previous congresses had undermined the system by refusing to vote the money needed. Many smaller plants had no inspection at all, and the largest ones had no inspectors at night. Beveridge, therefore, had proposed to shift the funding from the small amount allotted in the House Agriculture Appropriation Bill to a head fee charged for each animal inspected. As the industry processed more animals, the funds for the Bureau of Animal Industry would increase. But since the Constitution requires the House to initiate all money bills, Beveridge had to amend a House bill pending before the Senate rather than introduce a separate measure.

**Following the public outcry,** meatpackers tried to create a better image of conditions in their plants and of the thoroughness of government inspection. In fact, when this picture was taken in 1906, postmortem inspection, as shown here, had not been at all common.

Beveridge included two other important changes. The old law did nothing to force the packers to indicate on the label of canned meats either the date on which they were processed or the actual contents. (Neill and Reynolds, for example, discovered that the product called potted chicken contained no chicken at all.) The new law required dating and accurate labeling. It also invested the secretary of agriculture with broad authority to establish regulations for sanitary standards in the plants. Inspectors could then enforce those conditions as well as ensure the health of animals prior to and after slaughtering. If the owners challenged an inspector, the secretary had authority to make a "final and conclusive" ruling.

Yet this bill, which Beveridge confidently introduced in May, was hardly the same bill Roosevelt signed on June 30, 1906. By then an annual $3-million

riation replaced the small head fee. No longer did the secretary of agri-
have "final and conclusive" authority. That authority was shifted to the
federal courts, which could review his rulings. And the final measure said nothing about dating canned meats. In those discrepancies undoubtedly lies the
source of Senator Nelson's dismay with the outcome of the meat-inspection
battle. What the historian must now explain is why, if the reformers entered
the fray holding the high cards, they had given so much away.

In fact the battle had begun well for Roosevelt and Senate reformers.
When the packers first tried to stall Beveridge with promises to make voluntary improvements, the senator threatened them with more damaging
disclosures. To show he meant business, he had Neill brief representatives
for livestock raisers and western cattle-state senators on the contents of
his report. The packers had counted on those men as allies in their fight
against overly stringent federal regulation. But faced with the prospect of
more adverse publicity, the meat and cattle interests beat a hot retreat. The
Beveridge Amendment passed in the Senate without a single negative vote.
Never known for his modesty, Beveridge touted his measure as "the most
perfect inspection bill in the world."

Roosevelt hoped that the smashing Senate victory would lead to equally
swift action by the House. The packers, however, had no intention of giving up without a fight. In the House, they had far more substantial support,
particularly on the critical Agricul-
ture Committee. Its chairman, James       *The packers had no intention*
Wadsworth, a Republican from New         *of giving up without a fight.*
York, was himself a cattle breeder. He
regarded *The Jungle* as a "horrid, untruthful book" that, he claimed, had
temporarily unhinged the president. To orchestrate the opposition, Wadsworth could count on the unflagging support of "Blond Billy" Lorimer, a
senior committee member, a notorious grafter, and the Republican representative from Chicago's packinghouse district. The Beveridge bill roused
Lorimer like a red flag waved before a bull: "This bill will never be reported
by my committee—not if little Willie can help it."

The packers had another, even more powerful, ally—time. Summer
adjournment for Congress was only six weeks away. In the days before air
conditioning, most public officials left Washington to escape the oppressive
summer heat. While Congress vacationed, the public would most likely forget all about *The Jungle*, and as popular outrage waned, so would much of the
pressure for reform. Only new and more damaging disclosures could rekindle
the fervor that had swept Beveridge's amendment through the Senate. So
long as the Neill-Reynolds report remained secret, Roosevelt could save it as
a way to rekindle the public outcry. But by the time the Beveridge bill reached
the House, Sinclair had grown impatient. To goad the president, he published
new charges embellished with even more lurid details. Finally, unable to contain his frustration, he leaked the details of the Neill-Reynolds report to the
*New York Times*, and newspapers across the country picked up the story. Having lost its shock value, Roosevelt's big stick had become a twig.

The packinghouse forces sensed the worst was behind them. They could now afford to delay a vote on the Beveridge bill and in that way force reformers to make vital concessions. The requirement for stringent labeling, packers argued, would force the industry to abandon many well-known brand names. Dating would prejudice consumers against perfectly healthy canned meats. Nor could the packers abide investing such broad discretionary powers in the secretary of agriculture. Such a step, one spokesman claimed, would in effect "put our business in the hands of theorists, chemists, and sociologists, etc., and the management and control taken away from men who devoted their lives to the upbuilding and perfecting of this great American industry." In short, the packers argued that the secretary's arbitrary authority could deprive them of their property without the constitutional safeguard of due process in the courts.

Although they were likely to gain materially from more effective inspection, the packers most objected to the imposition of head fees. Condemned animals, they claimed, already cost them millions each year. Now the government proposed to saddle them with the additional burden of paying inspectors' salaries. Given the thin margins on which they operated, even a few pennies could make a difference. But that argument artfully concealed another reason the packers opposed a self-financing system. As many reformers pointed out, the small head fee (no more than 3 to 5 cents per animal) could easily be passed on to consumers. But a more effective inspection service might force the packers to abandon some of their most profitable, if unhealthy, practices. They could, for example, reroute cattle rejected at antemortem inspection to other parts of their plants. Furthermore, the old law allowed the packers to undermine the inspection system whenever it hurt profits, simply by arranging for their congressional allies, Lorimer and Wadsworth, to cut the BAI budget in the name of government economy. Forced to lay off inspectors, the BAI could not effectively supervise the plants. The Beveridge head-fee system eliminated that possibility. So what seemed like a minor issue had the potential to make or break the new inspection system.

When the packers lobbied Congress, they shrewdly pitched their arguments to other interests as well as their own. Control over annual appropriations gives the House and its members much of their political clout. By making his system self-financing, Beveridge would have weakened the House's jealously guarded grip on federal purse strings, depriving some congressional representatives of potential influence. Other representatives who were traditional champions of private enterprise agreed that restrictions on labels and dates, combined with the secretary of agriculture's discretionary authority, constituted unwarranted government interference in private enterprise. Beveridge had unwittingly reinforced his opponents' claims when he boasted that his bill was "THE MOST PRONOUNCED EXTENSION

*Beveridge boasted that his bill was "THE MOST PRONOUNCED EXTENSION OF FEDERAL POWER IN EVERY DIRECTION EVER ENACTED."*

OF FEDERAL POWER IN EVERY DIRECTION EVER ENACTED." Representative E. D. Crumpacker of Indiana warned House members that "the passage of the meat-inspection bill as it came from the Senate would mean the ultimate federalization of every industry in the United States."

With support growing in the House and the damning Neill-Reynolds report defanged, the packers went on the offensive. Wadsworth and Lorimer introduced a substitute bill in late May that eliminated each feature the packers opposed. Dates on the cans were not required. In place of the head fee, they had restored the annual appropriation. And in two other sweeping revisions, they removed the proposed ban on interstate transportation of uninspected meats and gave packing firms the right to appeal any Agriculture Department ruling to the federal courts. That last provision promised to be the most destructive of all. By appealing each unfavorable decision to the sympathetic courts, the packers could paralyze the inspection system.

The Wadsworth-Lorimer substitute outraged President Roosevelt. "It seems to me," he wrote Wadsworth, "that each change is for the worse and in the aggregate they are ruinous, taking every particle of good from the suggested Beveridge amendment." He then made good on his threat to expose the packers. On June 4 he sent the Neill-Reynolds report to Congress, along with a sharply worded message calling for a stringent inspection bill.

As might have been expected, Roosevelt's message in no way routed the packinghouse forces. Lorimer returned from a hasty trip to Chicago in time to denounce the Neill-Reynolds report as a "gross exaggeration of conditions." Armour accused the president of doing "everything in his power to discredit them and their business." All that rhetoric, of course, was a part of the symbolic language that so often monopolizes the public stage of politics. Each side adopts an uncompromising posture and accuses the opposition of all manner of villainy. The combatants strike heroic postures as champions of a larger public or national interest. They use such "disinterested" allies as Neill and Reynolds to legitimize their position. But at this point, when no accommodation seems possible, the negotiation and compromise begin. After all, both sides preferred some bill to no bill at all.

Faced with Roosevelt's demand for quick action, the House sent both the Beveridge bill and the Wadsworth-Lorimer substitute measures to the Agriculture Committee. In doing so, it followed a well-established procedure for reviewing legislation through its committee system. Congress first established committees to streamline its functioning. Rather than have the entire body deliberate every bill, these smaller groups consider measures relevant to their areas of special interest before making recommendations to the entire House or Senate. A trade bill may go to the Commerce or Foreign Relations Committees, a pork-barrel water project to the Rivers and Harbors Committee, and a farm bill to the Agriculture Committee. Those bills, encompassing a variety of features, have to go through several committees. All bills must eventually pass through the Rules Committee, which establishes parliamentary rules, such as the time allotted for floor debate or the conditions for amendment.

Yet if the committee system promotes efficiency, it also can provide an undemocratic means to defeat a popular bill. Committees can eliminate or amend central provisions or even refuse to return a bill to the floor for a vote. In sending the Beveridge bill to the Agriculture Committee, the House had routed it through an enemy stronghold. Wadsworth and Lorimer were both members of the committee; they had only to gain ten of eighteen votes from their colleagues in order to replace the Beveridge bill with their substitute. Other members of the House might never have a chance to vote on the original bill, even if a majority favored it.

Diligently, Wadsworth and Lorimer set out to undermine the Beveridge bill. They opened their attack by holding committee hearings to which they invited only witnesses sympathetic to the packers. As the hearings closed on June 9, Wadsworth eked out a narrow margin of victory, his substitute bill passing by only eleven to seven. Four Republicans had been so disgusted by the "bullyragging" aimed at Neill and Reynolds that they voted against the substitute. The president exploded when he saw Wadsworth's handiwork. The provisions in the new bill struck him as "so bad that . . . if they had been deliberately designed to prevent remedying of the evils complained of, they could not have been worse."

*The president exploded when he saw Wadsworth's handiwork.*

Two provisions particularly infuriated Roosevelt. The Agriculture Department had suggested as a compromise that Congress authorize an annual appropriation, but also grant the secretary standby power to levy a head fee if the appropriation proved inadequate. Lorimer and Wadsworth insisted on an annual sum of $1 million, scarcely enough to meet current costs. And once again, they had shifted final authority under the act from the secretary of agriculture to the federal courts.

The president did not deny that the packers, like anyone else, were entitled to "due process." But he also believed that court review should be restricted to a narrow procedural question: had the secretary been fair in reaching his decision? The committee granted the courts power to rule on substantive questions of fact. "You would have the functions of the Secretary of Agriculture narrowly limited so as to be purely ministerial," Roosevelt told Wadsworth, "and when he declared a given slaughter house unsanitary, or a given product unwholesome, acting upon the judgment of government experts, you would put on a judge, who had no knowledge of conditions, the burden of stating whether the Secretary was right."

Wadsworth refused to be cowed by the president's angry outburst. "You are wrong, very, very wrong in your estimate of the committee's bill," he responded. He even criticized the president for "impugning the sincerity and competency of a Committee of the House of Representatives" and called his substitute measure "as perfect a piece of legislation to carry into effect your own views on this question as was ever prepared by a committee of Congress." Lorimer, too, vowed to continue his defiance of the president.

All that sniping would not deserve a historian's attention except for one important detail—all the antagonists belonged to the same party. The meat-inspection battle had pitted a popular and powerful Republican president and his Senate friends against the Republican majority in the House. Senator Henry Cabot Lodge of Massachusetts, perhaps the president's closest political ally, had made the intraparty schism that much more public when he denounced the "greedy" packers for their attempt to derail the reform bill. Sensing the growing embarrassment among Republicans, House Democrats sought to deepen the rift. They insisted that the Beveridge bill be given a full vote on the House floor, even though it had not been voted out of the Agriculture Committee. "Czar" Joseph Cannon, the dictatorial Republican speaker, temporarily retrieved the situation for his party by ruling the motion out of order.

Cannon was now the man on the hot seat. The catfight among Republicans threatened to weaken party unity and with it the political empire he ruled so ruthlessly. His personal and political sympathies lay with the packers and conservatives who opposed government regulation of the free enterprise system. His power came, however, not from leading any particular faction, but from bringing together all the elements of his party. With his power base wobbling, Cannon sought some way to break the impasse between Republican reformers and conservatives. Since Roosevelt, too, had an interest in party unity, the speaker went to see him at the White House. The president proved amenable to a suitable compromise. They agreed that Wisconsin Representative Henry Adams, a moderate and a member of the Agriculture Committee, was the best person to work out the details. Adams had endorsed earlier compromises and, as a former food commissioner and champion of pure-foods legislation, he was free of the taint that clung to Wadsworth and Lorimer. Adams, Reynolds, and Agriculture Department lawyers had soon produced a new bill. From the Wadsworth-Lorimer measure they dropped the civil service waiver, added a provision for dating canned meats, gave the secretary standby fee authority, and eliminated the section on broad court review. Roosevelt declared their measure "as good as the Beveridge amendment."

While Cannon and Roosevelt negotiated, Wadsworth and Lorimer were away from Washington. When they returned, they vowed to reverse the president's apparent victory. Cannon, however, had no appetite for further infighting. He urged the Agriculture Committee to work out yet another compromise. Wadsworth and Lorimer immediately deleted the secretary's standby fee authority from the Adams bill, though they did raise the appropriation to $3 million, more than enough to meet current costs. Their axe next fell on the dating requirement, and, in return, they kept out the civil service waiver, while explicitly authorizing inspectors to visit plants "day or night."

One crucial issue remained. What would be the scope of court review? Wadsworth was willing to drop his demand for broad review if the president took out the Senate's phrase giving

*What would be the scope of court review?*

the secretary "final and conclusive" authority. Roosevelt agreed to that horse trade, which one historian aptly described as "purposeful obscurity." In other words, the bill obscured whether final authority would rest with the secretary or with the courts. To achieve improved inspection, Roosevelt was willing to have the courts decide the actual scope of judicial review. He regretted the absence of mandatory dating but did not consider the issue sufficiently important to upset the hard-won compromise. Roosevelt often criticized those diehards who would go down fighting for a "whole loaf" when "half a loaf" was the best they could expect. With the president behind the final committee bill, the entire House passed it on June 19.

The battle was not yet won, however, for Beveridge and the reformers in the Senate continued their fight, threatening to keep the two Houses deadlocked until recess. The Indiana senator had strong support from Redfield Proctor, chairman of the Senate Agriculture Committee. Although nearly crippled by rheumatism, Proctor had stayed on in Washington to ensure passage of an effective meat bill. Like Beveridge, he believed a consumer had the right to know whether canned meats were five days or five years old. And if the government stamp would be worth millions in free advertising for the packers, Proctor thought the industry, not the taxpayer, should bear the cost. The Senate, therefore, voted to reject the House bill in favor of its own.

Once again, process more than substance determined the outcome. When the two Houses pass different versions of the same bill, they create a conference committee to iron out the discrepancies. With time too short for long wrangling over each point, Roosevelt intervened. He first urged the House members to reconsider their position on dating and fees. They refused so vehemently that Roosevelt turned to the Senate conferees instead. Proctor and Beveridge recognized that further resistance meant total defeat. On June 29, the day before adjournment, they raised the white flag "to make sure of the greater good," and the Senate passed the House bill. The next day, after Roosevelt signed the bill, the Meat Inspection Act of 1906 became the law of the land.

## OUT OF THE JUNGLE

Was it time to uncork the champagne for a celebration? Despite their opposition to certain compromises, Roosevelt and Beveridge had endorsed the final measure as a triumph for reform. If historians let the case rest here, however, they would not know whether to accept Roosevelt and Beveridge's enthusiasm or Knute Nelson's despair. Who, after all, had won this legislative battle? Certainly, reformers were heartened to see that the old toothless law had been replaced by a system that required "day and night" inspection, banned uninspected meats from interstate commerce, gave the secretary authority to establish sanitary standards, and provided ample funding for the immediate future at least. Yet the final bill contained no provisions for head fees or dating and still left the courts as the final judge of the secretary of agriculture's rulings.

Roosevelt, Beveridge, and Nelson had reacted to the provisions in the bill as Congress passed it. The real impact of any new law, however, remains uncertain until it is applied by the executive branch and tested in the courts. In the case of the Meat Inspection Act, future presidents might appoint agriculture secretaries sympathetic to the packers. The standards established might be either too vague or too lax to enforce proper sanitation. More important, the courts might yet call Roosevelt's bluff and assume their prerogative for broad review. Historians must learn how the new system worked over time before they can decide whether the compromises vindicated Roosevelt or proved "half a loaf" worse than none at all.

As it happens, the subsequent history of meat inspection confirms the wisdom of the president's compromise strategy. The $3-million appropriation more than adequately funded the "beefed-up" inspection system. By the end of 1907 Secretary Wilson reported that new and more efficient procedures had substantially reduced operating costs. The BAI spent only $2 million the first year, and costs dropped even though the industry grew.

Roosevelt had been shrewdest in his resort to "purposeful obscurity." The packers made no attempt to dismantle the inspection system in the courts—the first important case did not arise for more than ten years. Then in 1917, in *United States v. Cudahy Packing Co., et al.*, a federal judge affirmed the secretary's authority. Congress, he ruled, could "delegate authority to the proper administrative officer to make effective rules." Two years later the Supreme Court adopted narrow rather than broad review. In an opinion for a unanimous Court in the case of *Houston v. St. Louis Independent Packing Company,* Justice John Clarke wrote that a decision over proper labeling of meat "is a question of fact, the determination of which is committed to the Secretary of Agriculture . . . , and the law is that the conclusion of the head of an executive department . . . will not be reviewed by the Courts, where it is fairly arrived at with substantial support." After thirteen years, the reformers could finally claim victory, though the outcome by then was scarcely in doubt. Not until 1968 did another generation of reformers, spurred by Ralph Nader, find it necessary to launch a new campaign to strengthen the inspection system. And in the twenty-first century, the health of the nation's meat remains a widespread concern.

*Roosevelt had been shrewdest in his resort to "purposeful obscurity."*

The controversy over meat inspection reminds the historian that when a legislative issue involves the disposition of economic and political power, all three branches of government influence the outcome. This input does not mean, however, that their roles are equal. In this case a politically shrewd and popular executive had shown greater capacity to affect the political process at critical moments. Roosevelt used the power of his office, his control over the Republican Party, and his ability to generate publicity to overcome opposition on both sides. Beveridge admitted that even in the face of widespread public outrage, Congress would not have acted "if the President had not picked up his big stick and smashed the packers and their agents in the

House and Senate over the head with it." Yet Roosevelt prevailed in the end only because he recognized compromise as an essential feature of the political process. He had yielded on points he considered less consequential in order to achieve his larger objective.

Just as historians must expand their field of vision to weigh the effects on a law of all three branches of government, so too they must establish the historical context of a bill over time. As we discovered, the meat scandal had a long history before the publication of *The Jungle*. We discovered, too, the existence of near-unanimous support for stricter inspection, though there was little understanding of what form a new law might take. Only when the bill made its way through the legislative process did we find that the widespread cry for reform masked a deep conflict over the roles of private and public agencies in determining satisfactory standards. The packers wanted the benefits of a new bill without having to relinquish control over their business. Reformers had both a moral goal and a political one. First, they wanted to punish the packers for their disregard for the public good. Second, and more consequentially, reformers sought to assert the authority of the federal government to police "corporate arrogance." The success of that effort remained in doubt until well after the bill's enactment, when the Supreme Court adopted narrow review.

It becomes clear, then, why the Meat Inspection Act could generate both Beveridge's enthusiasm and Nelson's dismay. The outcome had been a total victory for neither reformers nor packers. As is so often the case, the political system achieved results only after the visible symbols and myths of public discourse had been negotiated, debated, and compromised in the procedural tangle at the heart of the legislative process. Gone from our analysis are those wonderful symbols of corporate villainy and presidential heroism. But in their place we have a more complex story revealing the political processes that shape our history.

# *Additional Reading*

This chapter grew out of an Early Concentration History seminar at Yale University in which students had an opportunity to reconstruct history from primary sources. Many of the students in that seminar showed remarkable initiative in locating additional materials. In particular, they discovered the section in John Braeman's "The Square Deal in Action: A Case Study in the Growth of 'National Police Power'" that discusses the constitutional questions the new meat-inspection law raised. That essay appears in Braeman et al., *Change and Continuity in Twentieth Century America*, vol. 1 (Columbus, OH, 1964), pp. 34–80. Historians took much longer to discover certain urban and ecological factors involved in this episode. William Cronon, *Nature's Metropolis: Chicago and the Great West* (New York, 1991), places the industry in its urban context and establishes its links to a rural hinterland. Cronon, while no fan of big-business practices, recognizes the revolutionary nature of what the Chicago packers accomplished with such innovations as the moving (dis)assembly line and the refrigerated railcar. Like Cronon, Michael McGerr, *A Fierce Discontent: The Rise and Fall of the Progressive Movement in America, 1870–1920* (New York, 2003), and Elizabeth Sanders, *Roots of Reform: Farmers, Workers, and the American State, 1877–1917* (Chicago, 1999), offer a more modulated view of business and reform. The older muckrakers' bias is reflected in two books by Upton Sinclair, *The Jungle* (New York, 1906) and his often autobiographical *The Brass Check* (Pasadena, CA, 1919). On Theodore Roosevelt and traditional debate over Progressivism, see George Mowry, *The Era of Theodore Roosevelt* (New York, 1958); Gabriel Kolko, *The Triumph of Conservatism* (New York, 1964); and Lewis Gould, ed., *The Progressive Era* (1973). Another helpful secondary work is Joel Tarr, *Boss Politics* (Chicago, 1964), which examines the career of "Blond Billy" Lorimer. David Thelen's "Not Classes, But Issues," which first appeared in the *Journal of American History* 1 (September 1969): 323–334, offers a stimulating review of the many explanations of Progressivism, as well as a substantial interpretation of his own. That historiography was updated by Dan Rogers, "In Search of Progressivism," *Reviews in American History* 10 (1982). Robert Crunden, *Ministers of Reform: The Progressives' Achievements in Modern America, 1889–1920* (Urbana, IL, 1982), gives additional insight into the reform impulse that swept the nation. A reconsideration of Sinclair and other reformers comes in Walter Brasch, *Forerunners of Revolution: Muckrakers and the Social Conscience* (New York, 1990).

The documents in this case study are available in good research libraries and can be assembled. Such newspapers as the *New York Times*, *Chicago Tribune*, *Chicago Record-Herald*, and *Chicago Inter-Ocean* covered the entire controversy, though the Chicago papers did so in greater depth. Much of Roosevelt's thinking can be found in Elting Morison et al., *The Letters of Theodore Roosevelt*, vol. 5 (Cambridge, MA, 1953). Access to some contemporary magazines, including *Everybody's Magazine*, *The Lancet*, *Cosmopolitan*, and specifically J. Ogden Armour, "The Packers and the People," *Saturday Evening Post* 177, 37 (March 10, 1900)—a key document in Kolko's interpretation—will provide a picture of the debate over meatpacking and other muckraking issues.

This chapter drew most heavily on government documents. Readers should see *Congressional Record*, 59th Congress, 1st Session; House Committee on Agriculture, 59th Congress, 1st Session, *Hearings . . . on the So-called "Beveridge Amendment" to the Agriculture Appropriation Bill—H.R. 18537* (Washington, DC, 1906); Bureau of Animal Industry, *Twenty-Third Annual Report* (Washington, DC, 1906); *House Document 873*, 59th Congress, 1st Session (June 1906)—the Neill-Reynolds report and Theodore Roosevelt's cover letter; and the Agriculture Committee's minority and majority reports in *House Report 4935*, pts. 1 and 2, 59th Congress, 1st Session (June 14 and 15, 1906), and *House Report 3468*, pt. 2, 59th Congress, 1st Session (June 15, 1906). Additional materials can be found in the Roosevelt Papers (Harvard University, Widner Library) and Beveridge Papers (University of Indiana).

# CHAPTER 11
# *Sacco and Vanzetti*

*The Commonwealth of Massachusetts "demands no victims,"
insisted the court—or did it when it executed Sacco and Vanzetti?*

In the years after World War I, armed robberies occurred at an alarming rate. In such anxious times, anyone handling large sums of money had reason to be cautious. In December 1919 a gang of bandits had attempted an unusually brazen daylight payroll heist in Bridgewater, Massachusetts. After a brief gunfight the bandits had fled empty-handed, and no one was hurt. Still, Frederick Parmenter, paymaster for the Slater and Morrill Shoe Company of nearby South Braintree, normally used a car to deliver his payroll boxes to the lower factory building. On the afternoon of April 15, 1920, however, the car was not ready. His boss, Rexford Slater, encouraged him to walk the short distance from the office to the factory. So he and his assistant, Alessandro Berardelli, set off together with two steel boxes containing $15,776.51.

Halfway to their destination, a man approached Berardelli from the side of the road, spoke to him briefly, and then suddenly shot him. As Parmenter turned to flee, another bandit fired, mortally wounding him. Berardelli struggled to his knees. The gunman then fired several more shots, leaving him dead in the street. A blue Buick pulled from its parking place. The two assailants and their lookout jumped into the car and fled toward Bridgewater. The robbery had lasted little more than a minute. To discourage pursuers, the bandits threw tacks onto the streets. When the Buick reached a railroad crossing, the guard raised the gate. "Put them up or we'll put a hole through you," the bandits warned. The guard put up his hands, but they shot at him anyway. Narrowly missing, they sped on. Two miles from Braintree they abandoned the Buick and escaped in another car.

Bridgewater Police Chief Michael Stewart thought he recognized a pattern in the Braintree crime. The same foreigners who bungled the December heist, he guessed, had probably pulled off the Braintree job. Stewart's investigation put him on the trail of Mike Boda, an Italian anarchist. Unable to locate Boda, Stewart kept watch on a car Boda had left at Simon Johnson's garage for repairs. Whoever came to get the car would, according to Stewart's theory, become a prime suspect in both crimes.

**Nicola Sacco and Bartolomeo Vanzetti,** accused of committing a payroll robbery of the Slater and Morrill Shoe Company in South Braintree, Massachusetts. When police asked witnesses to identify the two men, instead of using a lineup, officers made Sacco and Vanzetti stand alone in the middle of a room and pose as bandits.

His expectations were soon rewarded. On May 5, 1920, Boda and three other Italians called for the car. Mrs. Johnson immediately slipped next door to alert the police, but the four men did not wait for her return. Boda and one friend, Riccardo Orciani, left on a motorcycle, while their companions walked to a nearby streetcar stop. Apparently nervous, they moved on to another stop a half mile away. There they boarded the trolley for Brockton. As the trolley car moved down Main Street, Police Officer Michael Connolly climbed on. Having spotted the two foreigners, he arrested them. When they asked why, he replied curtly, "suspicious characters."

Thus began the epic story of Nicola Sacco and Bartolomeo Vanzetti, two obscure Italian aliens who became the focal point of one of the most controversial episodes in American history. Within little more than a year after their arrest, a jury deliberated for just five hours before convicting both men of robbery and murder. Such a quick decision came as a surprise, particularly in a trial that had lasted seven weeks, heard more than 160 witnesses, and gained national attention.

Nor did the controversy end with the jury's decision. Six years of appeals turned a small-town incident of robbery and murder into a major

international uproar. The Italian government indicated that it was following the case with interest. Thousands of liberals, criminal lawyers, legal
scholars, civil libertarians, radicals, labor leaders, prominent socialites,
and spokespersons for immigrant groups rallied to Sacco and Vanzetti's
cause. Arrayed against them was an equally imposing collection of the
nation's legal, social, academic, and political elite.

The case climaxed on April 9, 1927. Having denied some eight appeals,
trial judge Webster Thayer sentenced Sacco and Vanzetti to die in the electric
chair. His action triggered months of protests and political activities. Around
Charleston Prison (where the two men were held) and the State House in
Boston, Sacco and Vanzetti's supporters marched, collected petitions, and
walked picket lines. Occasionally vio-
lence erupted between protesters and
authorities, as mounted police attacked
crowds in Boston and clubbed them off
the streets in New York. On August 22,
the morning before Sacco and Vanzetti
were scheduled to die, Charleston Prison
appeared like an embattled fortress. Ropes circled the prison grounds to
keep protesters at bay as 800 armed guards walked the walls. In New York's
Union Square, 15,000 people gathered to stand in silent vigil. Similar crowds
congregated in major European cities. All awaited the news of the fate of "a
good shoemaker and a poor fish peddler."

*In New York's Union Square,
15,000 people gathered to stand
in silent vigil. Similar crowds
appeared in European cities.*

The historian confronting that extraordinary event faces some perplexing
questions. How did a case of robbery and murder become an international
cause célèbre? How was it that two Italian immigrants living on the fringe of
American society had become the focus of a debate that brought the nation's
cherished legal institutions under attack? Or as one eminent law professor
rhetorically posed the question:

> Why all this fuss over a couple of "wops," who after years in this country had
> not even made application to become citizens; who had not learned to use
> our language even modestly well; who did not believe in our form of govern-
> ment; . . . who were confessed slackers and claimed to be pacifists but went
> armed with deadly weapons for the professed purpose of defending their
> individual personal property in violation of all the principles they preached?

## THE QUESTION OF LEGAL EVIDENCE

Lawyers reviewing events might answer those questions by arguing that the
Sacco and Vanzetti case raised serious doubts about the tradition of Anglo-
Saxon justice so venerated in the United States. More specifically, many
legal scholars then and since have asserted that the trial and appeals process
failed to meet minimum standards of fairness, particularly for a criminal case
in which the defendants' lives hung in the balance.

In the first flush of Sacco and Vanzetti's arrest, prosecutors seemed to have good reason to label the two men "suspicious characters." Both Sacco and Vanzetti were carrying loaded revolvers. Not only that, Sacco had twenty-three extra cartridges in his pockets, while Vanzetti carried several shotgun shells. When questioned, both men lied about their activities. They claimed not to know Mike Boda or to have been at the garage to pick up Boda's car. But suspicious behavior was one matter; proof that Sacco and Vanzetti had committed the Braintree murders was another. As the police and prosecutors went about making their case, they followed distinctly irregular procedures.

To be sure, in 1920 the police were allowed to conduct an investigation with far greater latitude than the law permits today. The Supreme Court decisions in *Miranda* (1966) and *Escobedo* (1964) established that criminal suspects have the right to remain silent, to be informed of their rights, and to stand in an impartial lineup for identification. None of those guarantees existed in 1920. Even so, District Attorney Frederick Katzmann and Chief Stewart showed unusual zeal in constructing a case against Sacco and Vanzetti. At no time during the first two days of questioning did they tell either suspect why they had been arrested. Chief Stewart repeatedly asked them not about the robbery, but about their political beliefs and associates. The district attorney did obliquely inquire about their activities on April 15, though he never mentioned the Braintree crimes. Furthermore, when the police asked witnesses to identify the suspects, they did not use a lineup. Instead, they forced Sacco and Vanzetti to stand alone in the middle of a room posing as bandits.

As the investigation continued, the case came close to collapsing for lack of evidence. Of the five suspected gang members, all but Vanzetti could prove they had not been in Bridgewater during the December holdup attempt. Despite an intensive search of the suspects' belongings, including a trunk sent to Italy, Katzmann was never able to trace the money, even among radical political groups with whom the suspects were associated. Fingerprint experts found no matches between prints lifted from the abandoned Buick and those taken from the suspects.

Faced with those gaps in the evidence, Katzmann still decided, first, to prosecute Vanzetti for the December Bridgewater holdup and, second, to charge both Sacco and Vanzetti with the Braintree murders in April. Historians cannot be sure just why he chose to do so, but from the patterns of his life they can make a convincing circumstantial argument. District attorneys and prosecutors tend to be politically ambitious people and Katzmann was no exception. He had made his way from working-class Boston to the elite atmosphere of Harvard College. After a brief career in business, he graduated from Boston University's night law school. Working for an upscale Boston firm gave him a taste for fine living and a desire to advance his career. By 1910 he inherited the job as district attorney for Norfolk County, south of Boston. Observers recognized him as "a man on the make" and many admired his tenacious style in the courtroom. A high-profile case such as the

Braintree robbery and murders offered an opportunity no ambitious district attorney could waste, nor afford to lose. Besides, he had an even more compelling motive. He knew in his heart that Sacco was guilty and was confident that Vanzetti was as well. These two anarchists threatened the society that had opened its doors to people like him.

Arguing the Bridgewater case in June 1920 before Judge Webster Thayer, Katzmann presented a weak case against Vanzetti on the charge of assault with intent to rob. Still, he did manage to make the jury aware of Vanzetti's anarchist views and persuade them to convict. Judge Thayer then meted out an unusually severe sentence (twelve *Katzmann saw anarchists as a threat to an America that offered opportunity to people like him.* to fifteen years) to a defendant with no criminal record for a crime in which no one was hurt and nothing was stolen.

That conviction allowed Katzmann to proceed with the second trial, to be held in the suburban town of Dedham. Since this trial would be a special session of the superior court, a judge had to be appointed to hear the case. Judge Thayer asked his old college friend, Chief Justice John Aiken, for the assignment, even though he had presided over Vanzetti's earlier trial and could scarcely consider himself impartial. Thus the second trial opened with a judge who already believed unequivocally in the defendants' guilt. Thayer's presence on the bench proved critical to the outcome of the case. Unlike Katzmann, Thayer came from the right side of the tracks. His middle-class parents sent him to private school and Dartmouth College. In 1917 a Dartmouth classmate appointed him to the bench, where he specialized in divorce cases. If Thayer had a defining characteristic, it was his sense of duty and loyalty to country. He once remarked of the anarchists who threatened his beloved country with violence, "Oh, how unfortunate that any such a doctrine, so destructive in its character and so revolutionary in all its tendencies[,] should ever have reached the sacred shores of these United States." Sacco and Vanzetti were not the first anarchists he faced in his court. When the bailiff opened the trial saying, "Oyez, oyez . . . God save the Commonwealth of Massachusetts," that is what Webster Thayer intended to do.

At Dedham, District Attorney Katzmann built his case around three major categories of evidence: (1) eyewitness identification of Sacco and Vanzetti at the scene, (2) expert ballistics testimony establishing Sacco's gun as the weapon that fired the fatal shot at Berardelli and Vanzetti's gun as the one taken from Berardelli during the robbery, and (3) the defendants' evasive behavior both before and after arrest as evidence of what is legally termed "consciousness of guilt."

The prosecution, however, had a difficult time making its case. Of the "eyewitnesses" claiming to place Sacco and Vanzetti at the scene, one, Mary Splaine, claimed to have observed the shooting from a window in the Slater and Morrill factory for no longer than three seconds at a distance of about 60 feet. In that time she watched an unknown man in a car traveling about 18 miles an hour. Immediately after the crime Splaine had difficulty describing any of the bandits, but one year later she picked out Sacco, vividly recalling such details as his "good-sized" left hand. She refused to recant her testimony even after the defense demonstrated that Sacco had relatively small hands.

Louis Pelzer testified for the prosecution that upon hearing shots, he had observed the crime from a window for at least a minute. He pointed to Sacco as the "dead image" of the man who shot Berardelli. Two defense witnesses, however, controverted Pelzer's story. Upon hearing the shots, they recalled, the intrepid Pelzer had immediately hidden under his workbench—hardly a vantage point from which to make a clear identification.

Lola Andrews, a third witness, claimed that on the morning of the crime she had stopped near the factory to ask directions from a dark-haired man working under a car. She later identified Sacco as that man. But a companion, Julia Campbell, denied that Andrews had ever spoken to the man under the car. Instead, Campbell testified, Andrews had approached a pale, sickly young man who was standing nearby. Other witnesses had recalled the same pale person. A second friend swore that he had heard Andrews say after she returned from police headquarters that "the government took me down and wanted me to recognize those men and I don't know a thing about them." Nor did Andrews's reputation as a streetwalker enhance her credibility. Yet in his summation, prosecutor Katzmann told the jury that in eleven years as district attorney he had not "ever before . . . laid eye or given ear to so convincing a witness as Lola Andrews."

Against Katzmann's dubious cast, the defense produced seventeen witnesses who provided the defendants with alibis for the day or who had seen the crime but had not seen Sacco or Vanzetti. One, an official of the Italian Consulate in Boston, confirmed Sacco's claim that he had been in Boston on April 15 acquiring a passport. The official remembered Sacco because he had tried to use a picture over 10 inches square for his passport photo. "Since such a large photograph had never been presented before," the official recalled, "I took it in and showed it to the Secretary of the Consulate. We laughed and talked over the incident. I remember observing the date . . . on a large pad calendar." Others said they had met Sacco at a luncheon banquet that day. Witnesses for Vanzetti claimed to have bought fish from him. Katzmann sought to persuade the jury that the witnesses had little reason to connect such a mundane event with a specific date.

In the face of contradictory eyewitness testimony, the ballistics evidence might have decided the case. To prove murder, Katzmann wished to show that the fatal shot striking Berardelli had come from Sacco's gun. Ballistics specialists can often identify the gun that fired a bullet by characteristic marks, as distinct as fingerprints, that the barrel and hammer make on the projectile and casing. Two experts, Captains William Proctor and Charles Van Amburgh, connected the fatal bullet to a Colt

*In the face of contradictory eyewitness testimony, the ballistics evidence might have decided the case.*

pistol similar to and possibly the same as Sacco's. But neither of Katzmann's witnesses made a definitive link. "It is consistent with being fired by that pistol," Proctor replied to Katzmann. Van Amburgh also indicated some ambiguity: "I am inclined to believe that it was fired . . . from this pistol."

For unknown reasons, defense attorneys never pursued the equivocation of those testimonies. Instead, they called their own ballistics specialists who stated with absolute certainty that the fatal bullet could not have come from Sacco's gun. In addition, they controverted the prosecutor's claim that Vanzetti had taken Berardelli's gun during the holdup. Shortly before his murder, Berardelli had left his pistol at a repair shop to have the hammer fixed. Shop records, though imprecise, indicated that the gun was .32 caliber, not a .38 such as Vanzetti was carrying. The records also supported Mrs. Berardellis's sworn testimony that her husband had never reclaimed his pistol. The defense then argued that the hammer on Vanzetti's gun had never been repaired.

Since the defense had weakened the ballistics evidence, Katzmann based his case primarily on "consciousness of guilt." To convict on those grounds, he had to convince the jury that Sacco and Vanzetti had behaved like men guilty of the crime, both before and after arrest. Here, Katzmann made his case with telling effect. Why had the defendants been carrying guns when they were arrested? They had gone hunting that morning, they claimed. But if that were the case, why were they still carrying hunting weapons and extra ammunition at night, when they set out to pick up Mike Boda's car? They were in such a hurry, Sacco and Vanzetti replied, that they forgot to leave their revolvers at home. But Katzmann continued his onslaught. Why did the two men lie at first about knowing Mike Boda or having visited the garage? Surely this evasion indicated a clear consciousness of guilt.

*Why had the defendants been carrying guns when they were arrested?*

To explain their clients' lies, defense lawyers were forced to introduce the inflammatory issue of Sacco and Vanzetti's political beliefs. For indeed, both men proudly proclaimed themselves to be anarchists, rejecting the authority of any government. Capitalism, they believed, was little more than an organized system of banditry under which the rich and powerful extorted the poor. Sacco and Vanzetti had both been active in the strikes and labor unrest of the era. As a result, they had been alarmed by the government crackdown on radicals that began in 1919. When Officer Connolly arrested them, the two men assumed that they, too, had been snared in the government's dragnet. They acted evasively, defense lawyers argued, not because they were criminals but because radicals were being persecuted and deported. Once arrested, Sacco and Vanzetti's fears were only confirmed by the police's constant questions about their political beliefs.

Similar worries accounted for their peculiar actions at Johnson's garage, the defense argued. Shortly before his arrest, Vanzetti had conferred with the Italian Defense Committee of New York, then inquiring into the fate of a fellow anarchist, Andrea Salsedo. The committee knew only that Salsedo was being held by Justice Department agents; members warned Vanzetti that he and his friends might be in danger of being jailed or deported. Only a week later, newspapers across the nation reported that Salsedo had fallen to his death from a twelfth-floor window. The police insisted the case had been a suicide, but many anarchists thought Salsedo had been pushed. Before he died, had he provided the government with the names of other anarchists? If so, Vanzetti and Sacco were at risk. Anyone found with anarchist literature could be arrested and deported. It was for that reason, Sacco and Vanzetti told the court, that they had gone to retrieve Mike Boda's car: they needed it to carry away the radical pamphlets stored in their homes, something they hardly wished to admit to police questioning them about radical activities.

The revelations of the defendants' radical politics could hardly have raised the jury's opinion of the two men. And their explanations did not stop Katzmann from focusing on consciousness of guilt in his final summation. Nor did Judge Thayer take into account their explanations in his charge to the jury. In theory, a judge's charge guides the jury as it interprets conflicting evidence: in separating the relevant from the irrelevant and in establishing the grounds for an objective verdict. But Thayer made his sympathies all too clear. In discussing the ballistics testimony, he wrongly assumed that Katzmann's expert witnesses had unequivocally identified Sacco's gun as having fired the fatal shot. And he spent no time weighing the defense's argument that prosecution eyewitnesses had been unreliable. Only when he discussed consciousness of guilt did the judge become expansive and specific. He lingered over the evidence offered by the police and the garage owner while ignoring Sacco and Vanzetti's explanations.

Lawyers and legal historians have raised other telling criticisms—excesses in the trial procedures, prejudice on the part of both judge and prosecutor, bungling by the defense lawyer. Inevitably, these criticisms have influenced the way historians have approached the controversy. Most of them have centered on the issue of proof of guilt. Contrary to popular opinion, the courts do not determine whether a person is guilty or innocent of a crime. They decide merely whether the prosecutor has assembled sufficient evidence to establish guilt. The judge may even suspect a defendant is guilty, but if the evidence does not meet minimum standards of legal proof, the court must set the accused free. As one court concluded, "the commonwealth demands no victims . . . and it is as much the duty of the district attorney to see that no innocent man suffers, as it is to see that no guilty man escapes."

Thus lawyers tend to focus on narrow, yet admittedly important, questions. They are all the more crucial when human lives are at stake, as was the case with Sacco and Vanzetti. Believing that the legal system maintains vital safeguards of individual rights, lawyers in general seek to ensure that proper legal procedures have been followed, that evidence is submitted according to established rules, and, in accordance with those procedures, that guilt has been adequately determined. A lawyer answering the question "Why all the fuss over the Sacco and Vanzetti case?" would most likely reply, "Because the trial, by failing to prove guilt beyond reasonable doubt, perpetrated a serious miscarriage of justice."

# BEYOND GUILT OR INNOCENCE

So far in these essays we have considered enough historical methods to understand that history affords far more latitude in weighing and collecting evidence than does the legal system. The law attempts to limit the flow of evidence in a trial to what can reasonably be construed as fact. A judge will generally exclude hearsay testimony, speculation about states of mind or motives, conjecture, and vague questions leading witnesses to conclusions. But those are sources of information upon which historians can and do draw in their research. Historians can afford to speculate more freely, because their conclusions will not send innocent people to jail or let the guilty go free. In one instance, for example, appeals judges refused to act on defense claims that Judge Thayer had allowed his prejudices against Sacco and Vanzetti to influence his conduct of the trial. They ruled that remarks made outside the courtroom, no matter how inappropriate, had no bearing on what occurred inside. By contrast, the historian can accept the fact of Judge Thayer's prejudice, regardless of where he revealed it.

Given their broader canons of evidence, historians might be tempted to do what the lawyers failed to do—establish whether Sacco and Vanzetti actually did commit the robbery and murders at Braintree. To succeed in such an investigation would at least lay the controversy to its final rest. Yet that approach does not take us beyond the lawyers' questions. We are still dealing with only two men—Sacco and Vanzetti—and one central question—guilty or innocent?

We must remember, however, that when historians confront such either-or questions, their overriding obligation is to construct an interpretation that gives full play to all aspects of the subject being investigated, not just the question of guilt or innocence. They must look beyond Sacco and Vanzetti to the actions of the people and society around them. What political currents led the prosecutor to bring those two men to trial? How much were Judge Thayer, District Attorney Katzmann, and the men in the jury box representative of Massachusetts or of American society in general? Of just what crime did the jury actually convict the defendants? In answering those questions,

*Historians' obligations go beyond the question of guilt or innocence.*

historians must lift their drama out of the Dedham courtroom and into a larger theater of action. In short, we cannot answer our original question "Why all the fuss?" merely by proving the defendants guilty or innocent. Historians want to know why this case provoked such sharp controversy for so many years.

Any historian who studies the climate of opinion in the early 1920s cannot help suspecting that those who prosecuted Sacco and Vanzetti were far

Going to Join the Indian and Buffalo?

The sturdy old American breed that wrested this country from the wilderness might now try a hard, quick shove toward the middle of the bench

**Many "old stock" Americans from northern Europe** feared that the new flood of immigrants from southeastern Europe would, by sheer force of numbers, displace them from their dominant place in society. Even a Progressive like George Creel, who had been sympathetic to immigrants during World War I, turned hostile and referred to the newcomers as "so much slag in the melting pot." Respected academics published research that purported to prove "the intellectual superiority of our Nordic groups over the Alpine, Mediterranean, and negro groups."

more concerned with who the defendants were and what they believed than with what they might have done. Throughout the nation's history, Americans have periodically expressed hostility toward immigrants and foreign political ideas that were perceived as a threat to the "American way of life." Nativism, as such defensive nationalism has been called, has been a problem at least since the initial waves of Irish immigrants came ashore in the first half of the nineteenth century. Until then, the United States had been a society dominated by white Protestants with a common English heritage. The influx of the Catholic Irish and then political refugees from the 1848 German revolution diversified the nation's population. Native-born Americans became alarmed that immigration threatened their cherished institutions. Later waves of newcomers from Asia, the Mediterranean, and eastern Europe deepened their fears.

The tides of nativism tend to rise and fall with the fortunes of the nation. During periods of prosperity, Americans often welcome immigrants as a vital source of new labor. In the 1860s, for example, many Californians

**The rabid patriotism of the war led** to widespread abuses of civil liberties. Here, angry servicemen on the Boston Commons destroy a Socialist Party flag seized during a 1918 peace march. The same spirit of intolerance was also reflected in the Red Scare, during which an Indiana jury deliberated only two minutes before acquitting a defendant who had shot and killed a radical for yelling, "To hell with the United States!"

cheered the arrival of Chinese coolies, without whom the transcontinental railroad could not have been so quickly completed. In the 1870s, as the nation struggled through a severe industrial depression, the same Californians who once welcomed the Chinese now clamored for laws to restrict the number of Asian immigrants.

The period following World War I, which one historian labeled the "Tribal Twenties," marked the high tide of nativism. Several factors accounted for its resurgence. World War I had temporarily interrupted the flow of immigrants who, since the 1880s, had increasingly included a preponderance of Catholics and Jews from countries with strong radical traditions. In 1914 alone, more than 138,000 of a total of 1.2 million immigrants to the United States were Jews. During the war, the number fell to just 3,672 newcomers in 1918 (out of a total of 110,000), but then rose to 119,000 (out of 805,000) in 1921, the last year of unrestricted immigration. A similar pattern occurred among Italians. In the entire decade of the 1870s, fewer than 50,000 Italians came to the United States. More than ever, nativists protested that these

**Seeking to screen out those immigrants who were "undesirable,"** many nativists urged Congress to adopt a literacy test. Although campaigns for such a law had been mounted since the 1890s, only in 1917 did a literacy requirement pass Congress. The cartoon shown here disparages such exclusionist policies, but in the 1920s the pressure for even tighter restrictions mounted, to be embodied (as one Minnesota representative put it) in a "genuine 100 per cent American immigration law."

THE AMERICANESE WALL, AS CONGRESSMAN
BURNETT WOULD BUILD IT.
Uncle Sam: You're welcome in—if you can climb it!

undesirable foreigners threatened to destroy cherished institutions, weaken the genetic pool, or in other ways undermine the American way of life.

The rocky transition to a peacetime economy further aggravated resentment toward immigrants. Returning veterans expected jobs from a grateful nation; instead, they found crowds of unemployed workers around factory gates. The army had discharged millions of soldiers almost overnight. The government dismissed hundreds of thousands of temporary wartime employees and canceled millions of dollars' worth of contracts with private businesses. As the economy plunged downward, native-born Americans once again looked on new immigrants as a threat to their livelihoods. Organized labor joined other traditional nativist groups in demanding new restriction laws.

Most business leaders were in no mood to compromise on union demands for higher wages, improved working conditions, and the recognition of collective bargaining. They resented the assistance the government had given organized labor during the war. Now, they not only rejected even the mildest union demands but also sought to cripple the labor movement. Conservatives launched a national campaign to brand all organized labor as Bolsheviks, Reds, and anarchists. They called strikes "crimes against society," "conspiracies against the government," and "plots to establish communism." As the market for manufactures declined, employers had little reason to avoid a showdown. Strikes saved them the problem of laying off unneeded workers.

Radicals played a minor role in the postwar labor unrest. Most union leaders were as archly conservative as the employers they confronted. Still, the constant barrage of anti-Red propaganda turned public opinion against the unions. And American radicals fed that hostility by adopting highly visible tactics. The success of a small band of Bolsheviks in capturing Russia's tottering government in October 1917 had rekindled waning hopes and at the same time startled most Americans. Two years later, the Bolsheviks boldly organized the Third Communist International to carry the revolution to other countries. Communist-led worker uprisings in Hungary and Germany increased conservative anxiety that a similar revolutionary fever might infect American workers, especially after a Comintern official bragged that the money spent in Germany "was as nothing compared to the funds transmitted to New York for the purpose of spreading Bolshevism in the United States."

*". . . spreading Bolshevism in the United States."*

Only a few shocks were needed to inflame the fears of Americans caught in the midst of economic distress, labor unrest, and renewed immigration from southern and eastern Europe. Those shocks were provided by a series of anarchist bombings inspired by Luigi Galleani, an Italian immigrant who had settled in New England. Although authorities at the time did not know it, members of Galleani's circle were the source of a series of thirty parcels mailed in April 1919 to eminent officials, including Attorney General A. Mitchell Palmer, Supreme Court Justice Oliver Wendell Holmes, members of Congress, and mayors, as well as the industrial magnates John D. Rockefeller and J. P. Morgan. Only one of the deadly packages detonated (blowing off the hands of the unsuspecting servant who opened it), but in June a series of even more lethal explosions rocked seven cities. The most spectacular explosion demolished the entire front wall of Attorney General Palmer's home. The device exploded prematurely, blowing to bits the man who was crouching by the front steps. Palmer's Washington neighbor, Franklin D. Roosevelt, called the police.

The American public had already learned to associate such deeds with anarchists: the Haymarket Square explosion of 1886 as well as the assassination of President William McKinley in 1901 by radical Leon Czolgosz. ("The anarchist is the enemy of humanity, the enemy of all mankind," proclaimed McKinley's successor, Teddy Roosevelt.) Following the bombings of 1919, Attorney General Palmer reacted swiftly, launching a roundup of as many radicals as he could find, branding each "a potential murderer or a potential thief." That the majority were only philosophical anarchists who had never undertaken any violent acts toward the government did not deter Palmer. That the majority were foreign-born served only to raise his patriotic bile: "Out of the sly and crafty eyes of many of them leap cupidity, cruelty, insanity, and crime; from their lopsided faces, sloping brows, and misshapen features may be recognized the unmistakable criminal types."

*ignored all laws*

For more than a year, Palmer and his young, Red-hunting assistant J. Edgar Hoover organized government raids on homes, offices, union halls, and alien organizations. Seldom did the raiders pay even passing attention to civil liberties or constitutional prohibitions against illegal search and seizure. One particularly spectacular outing netted more than 4,000 alleged subversives in some thirty-three cities. Most of those arrested, though innocent of any crime, were detained illegally by state authorities either for trial or Labor Department deportation hearings. Police jammed suspects in cramped rooms with inadequate food and sanitation. They refused to honor the suspects' rights to post bail or obtain a writ of habeas corpus.

The public quickly wearied of Palmer and the exaggerated stories of grand revolutionary conspiracies. Not one incident had produced any evidence of a serious plot. Palmer predicted that on May 1, 1920, radicals would launch a massive attempt to overthrow the government. Alerted by the Justice Department, local police and militia girded for the assault. But May Day passed without incident. The heightened surveillance did, however, have profound consequences for Nicola Sacco and Bartolomeo Vanzetti. Both men were on a list of suspects the Justice Department had sent to District Attorney Katzmann and Chief Stewart. Just four days after the May Day scare, Officer Connolly arrested the two aliens.

Sacco and Vanzetti fit the stereotypes that nativists held of foreigners. Sacco arrived in the United States in 1908 at the age of seventeen. Like so many other Italians, he had fled the oppressive poverty of his homeland with no intention of making a permanent home in America. Most of the young men planned to stay only until they had saved enough money to return home and improve their family fortunes. Although born into a modestly well-to-do family, Sacco was no stranger to hard labor. Shortly after his arrival, he found steady work in the shoe factories around Milford, Massachusetts.

*Sacco shoe worker*

Resourcefulness and industry marked Sacco as the kind of foreign worker whose competition American labor feared. Although he lacked formal schooling, Sacco understood that skilled labor commanded steadier work and higher wages, so he paid $50 out of his earnings to learn the specialized trade of edge trimming. His wages soon reached as high as $80 per week. By 1917 he had a wife and child, his own home, and $1,500 in savings. His employer at the "3 K" shoe factory described him as an excellent worker and recalled that Sacco often found time, despite his long workdays, to put in a few hours each morning and evening in his vegetable garden.

Vanzetti conformed more to the nativist stereotype of shiftless foreigners who drifted from one job to the next. Born in 1888 in the northern Italian village of Villafalletto, he had come in 1908 to America, where, like many other immigrants, he found a limited range of jobs open to him. He took a job as a dishwasher in hot, stinking kitchens. "We worked twelve hours one day and fourteen the next, with five hours off every other Sunday," he recalled. "Damp food hardly fit for a dog and five or six dollars a week was the pay." Fearing an attack of consumption, Vanzetti migrated to the countryside in search of open-air work. "I worked on farms, cut trees, made bricks, dug ditches, and quarried rocks. I worked in a fruit, candy and ice cream store and for a telephone company," he wrote his sister in Italy. By 1914 he had wandered to Plymouth, where he took a job in a cordage factory.

If that sketch captured the essence of Sacco and Vanzetti's lives, they would most likely never have come to the attention of Justice Department agents. But because they were aliens and anarchists, they embodied the kind of foreign menace American nativists most feared. Although not a student of politics like Vanzetti, Sacco was a rebel. He identified closely with the workers' struggle for better wages and the right to organize. In 1912 he and Vanzetti had independently participated in a violent textile strike at Lawrence, Massachusetts. Three years later, plant owners around Plymouth had blacklisted Vanzetti for his role in a local strike. Sacco had walked off his job to express sympathy for the cordage workers. Soon after a local labor leader organized a sympathy strike to support workers in Minnesota, authorities arrested Sacco and convicted him of disturbing the peace. All this time, he and his wife regularly joined street-theater productions performed to raise money for labor and radical groups.

*Sacco and Vanzetti embodied American nativists' dark fears.*

American entry into World War I created a crisis for both men. Their anarchist beliefs led them to oppose any war that did not work to overthrow capitalism. Sacco even refused the patriotic pressures to buy war bonds. He quit his job rather than compromise his principles. Both began to dread the law requiring them to register (though in fact, as aliens they were ineligible for military service). They decided to join a group of pacifists who in May 1917 fled to Mexico, where the two first became personal friends. The hard life and absence from his family finally drove Sacco to return home under an alias, though he did reclaim his name and former job after the war. Vanzetti returned to Plymouth and soon outfitted himself as a fish peddler.

So in the eyes of many Americans, Sacco and Vanzetti were guilty in at least one important sense. As self-proclaimed enemies of the capitalist system, they had opposed "the American way of life" that nativists cherished. Their suspicious behavior, which Katzmann successfully portrayed as consciousness of guilt, was all too real, for they knew that their radical beliefs might subject them to arrest and deportation, the fate hundreds of other friends and political associates had already faced.

Certainly, the trial record shows that nativism influenced the way judge and jury viewed the defendants. Almost all the eyewitnesses who identified Sacco and Vanzetti were native-born Americans. That they saw a resemblance between the Italian suspects and the foreign-looking criminals proved only, as Harvard law professor Felix Frankfurter remarked, that there was much truth in the popular racist song "All Coons Look Alike to Me." On the other hand, almost all the witnesses substantiating the defendants' alibis were Italians who answered through an interpreter. The jury, also all native-born Americans, would likely accept Katzmann's imputation that foreigners stuck together to protect each other from the authorities.

The choice of Fred Moore as chief defense counsel guaranteed that radicalism would become a central issue in the trial. In his earlier trial, Vanzetti had been defended by a conservative criminal lawyer, George Vahey. The guilty verdict persuaded Vanzetti that Vahey had not done all he could have, especially when Vahey entered into a law partnership with Katzmann shortly after the trial. For the Dedham trial, friends, local labor leaders, and anarchists created a defense fund to see that no similar betrayal by counsel occurred. From Elizabeth Gurley Flynn, an Industrial Workers of the World agitator and wife of anarchist publisher Carlo Tresca, the defense-fund committee learned of Moore, who had participated in the trials of numerous radicals, including two Italian anarchists charged with murder during the Lawrence strike. Only later did the committee learn that Moore had contributed little to the acquittal of the Lawrence defendants. Moore's participation must have reinforced the impression that Sacco and Vanzetti were dangerous radicals. He spent the bulk of defense funds to orchestrate a propaganda campaign dramatizing the plight of his clients and the persecution of radicals. He gave far less attention to planning defense strategy, left largely in the hands of two local cocounsels, Thomas and Jeremiah McAnarney.

Yet in the courtroom, Moore insisted on playing the major role. The McAnarneys soon despaired of making a favorable impression on the jury. An outsider from California, Moore wore his hair long and sometimes shocked the court by parading around in his shirtsleeves and socks. Rumors abounded about his unorthodox sex life. And at critical moments he sometimes disappeared for several days. Judge Thayer once became so outraged at Moore that he told a friend, "I'll show them that no long-haired anarchist from California can run this court." Not until 1924 did Moore finally withdraw in favor of William Thompson, a respected Massachusetts criminal lawyer.

Nativism, particularly antiradicalism, obviously prejudiced Judge Thayer and District Attorney Katzmann. We have already seen how Thayer used his charge to the jury to underscore Katzmann's construction of the evidence in the trial. Outside the courtroom, Thayer consistently violated the canons of judicial discretion by discussing his views of the case. George Crocker, who sometimes lunched with Thayer, testified that on many occasions the judge "conveyed to me by his words and manner that he was bound to convict these men because they were 'reds.'" Veteran court reporter Frank Silbey had been forced to stop lunching at the Dedham Inn to avoid Thayer and his indiscreet remarks. Silbey later recalled, "In my thirty-five years I never saw anything like it. . . . His whole attitude seemed to be that the jurors were there to convict these men."

From the moment the trial opened, Thayer and Katzmann missed few opportunities to strike a patriotic pose or to remind the jury that both defendants were draft dodgers. Thayer told the prospective jurors at the outset, "I call upon you to render this service . . . with the same patriotism as was exhibited by our soldier boys across the sea." Katzmann opened his cross-examination of Vanzetti with a cutting statement dressed up as a question: "So you left

Plymouth, Mr. Vanzetti, in May 1917 to dodge the draft did you?" Since Vanzetti was charged with murder, not draft evasion, the question served to arouse the jury's patriotic indignation.

Katzmann struck hardest in his questioning of Sacco, whose poor command of English often left him confused or under a misapprehension. Judge Thayer never intervened to restrain the overzealous prosecutor, even when it became clear that Sacco could neither follow a question nor express his thoughts clearly. Playing again upon the residual patriotic war fervor, Katzmann hammered away at the defendant's evident disloyalty:

> KATZMANN: And in order to show your love for this United States of America when she was about to call upon you to become a soldier you ran away to Mexico. Did you run away to Mexico to avoid being a soldier for the country that you loved?
>
> SACCO: Yes.
>
> KATZMANN: And would it be your idea of showing love for your wife that when she needed you, you ran away from her?
>
> SACCO: I did not run away from her.

When the defense objected, Thayer ruled that this line of questioning would help establish Sacco's character. But instead of showing Sacco's philosophical opposition to war, Katzmann made the defendant appear, as one critic expressed it, "an ingrate and a slacker" who invited the jury's contempt. With such skillful cross-examination, Katzmann twisted Sacco's professed love of "a free country" into a preference for high wages, pleasant work, and good food.

The prosecutor summed up his strategy in his final appeal to the jury: "Men of Norfolk do your duty. Do it like men. Stand together you men of Norfolk." There was the case in a nutshell—native American solidarity against alien people and their values. Whether he had proved Sacco and Vanzetti guilty of murder mattered little, for he had revealed their disloyalty. In case the point was lost, Judge Thayer reiterated it in his charge:

*"Men of Norfolk, do your duty. Do it like men . . ."*

> Although you knew such service would be arduous, painful, and tiresome, yet you, like the true soldier, responded to the call in the spirit of supreme American loyalty. There is no better word in the English language than "loyalty."

And just who were those "men of Norfolk" to whom the judge and prosecutor appealed? Could they put aside inflammatory rhetoric and render a just verdict? Not a single foreign name, much less an Italian one, appeared on the juror's list. Because Fred Moore had rejected any "capitalists" during jury selection, a few prospective jurors whom the McAnarneys knew to be fair-minded were kept off the jury. Those jurors selected were drawn from the tradespeople and other respectable Protestants of the town. None would share the defendants' antipathy to capitalism; few would have had any compassion for the plight of Italian immigrants or union members. Even worse, the jury foreman, Harry Ripley, was a former police chief who outdid himself in persuading his fellow jurors to convict. He violated basic rules of evidence in a capital case by bringing into the jury room cartridges similar to those placed in evidence. A short time before, he had told his friend William Daly that he would be on the jury in "the case of the two 'ginneys' charged with murder at South Braintree." When Daly suggested that they might be innocent, Ripley replied, "Damn them, they ought to hang anyway."

By using the concept of nativism to gain a broader perspective, the historian has come to understand the answer to a question lawyers need not even ask: what factors accounted for the conviction of Sacco and Vanzetti where convincing evidence was so clearly lacking? Nativism explains many prejudices exhibited in the trial record. It also explains why those attitudes were so widespread in 1920–1921. We must accept the truth of law professor Edmund M. Morgan's assertion that it was "almost impossible to secure a verdict which runs counter to the settled convictions of the community." Sacco and Vanzetti symbolized for a majority of Americans and the "men of Norfolk" alien forces that threatened their way of life. To be fair, we should admit that the jurors denied that the defendants' politics had influenced their verdict. They saw the judge as fair and the prosecutor's case as persuasive, especially on the point of consciousness of guilt. All the same, none of those "men of Norfolk" had even passing familiarity with the lives of Italian immigrants.

Yet, having answered one important question, the historian still faces another. Granted, a jury convicted two alien radicals of robbery and murder in 1921, but "why all the fuss?" as we asked earlier, in the years that followed? After all, Sacco and Vanzetti were not sentenced until 1927, long after the virulent nativist mood had passed. The Immigration Acts of 1921 and 1924 had severely curbed the flow of newcomers from Italy and eastern Europe. The damage from unsuccessful strikes, management opposition, and government hostility had sent organized labor into a decline from which it would not recover until the New Deal years. The historian must still explain how a local case extended its impact beyond Norfolk County to the nation and even the international community.

No single answer, even one so broad as nativism, can account for the notoriety. Certainly, from the beginning the case had sent ripples across the nation. Socially prominent individuals, intellectuals, the American Federation of Labor, immigrant groups, and radicals had all contributed to the defense fund for the Dedham trial. Those people represented a small minority without great political influence. But by tracing out the appeals process, the historian discovers a series of events that enlarged the significance of the case, heightened the public's awareness of the crucial issues involved, and raised the stakes many groups risked on the judicial outcome.

## A NATION STIRRED

In the American legal system, the right of appeal is designed to protect defendants against any miscarriage of justice rising out of the original trial. But in 1920 the appeals process in Massachusetts contained a provision that ultimately proved fatal to Sacco and Vanzetti. Any motion for a retrial based on new evidence had to be granted by the original trial judge. On each of eight motions made by the defense, including substantial evidence of prejudice on the part of the judge, the person who heard that appeal was none other than Webster Thayer! Thayer did not have to determine whether new information proved the men innocent, only whether another jury might reasonably reach a different verdict.

The next higher court, the Supreme Judicial Court, had only narrow grounds on which to reverse Thayer's decisions. It could review the law in each case but not the facts. Those grounds meant that the court could determine only if the procedure conformed to the criteria of a fair trial established under state and federal constitutions. Although it found some irregularities in procedure, the Supreme Judicial Court ruled that those irregularities did not prejudice the verdict against the defendants. At no time did that court review the weight of evidence presented at the trial or on appeal. It determined, instead, that a reasonable judge might have acted as Thayer did.

And what of the American Supreme Court, the ultimate safeguard of civil liberties? On three separate occasions the defense attempted to move the case into the federal courts. Defense attorneys argued that Sacco and Vanzetti had been the victims of a sham trial, particularly given Judge Thayer's overwhelming prejudice. Justice Oliver Wendell Holmes Jr., long a champion of civil liberties, wrote that the court could rule only on the grounds of constitutional defects in Massachusetts law. Since none existed, he refused in 1927 to grant a writ of certiorari allowing the Supreme Court to review the weight of evidence. Thus the appeals procedure created a formidable barrier to reversing the verdict rendered at Dedham.

In the face of such inequities, the defense spent six years fighting to overturn the conviction. Between July 1921 and October 1924 it presented five motions for a new trial. The first involved the behavior of jury foreman Harry Ripley. In response, Thayer completely ignored the affidavit from Ripley's friend William Daly and ruled that Ripley's tampering with evidence had not materially affected the verdict. Eighteen months later the defense uncovered an important new witness, Roy Gould, who had been nearly shot at point-blank range by the fleeing bandits. Gould had told his story to police immediately afterward, but Katzmann never called him to testify. Eventually defense lawyers uncovered Gould and realized why he had been kept off the stand. Gould had been so close to the escape car that one shot passed through his overcoat; yet he swore that Sacco was not one of the men. Judge Thayer rejected that appeal on the grounds that since Gould's testimony did no more than add to the cumulative weight of evidence, it did not justify a new trial.

Later appeals attempted to show that the prosecutor had tampered with the testimony of two key witnesses. Both witnesses had recanted their courtroom statements and then later recanted their recantations. Rather than find Katzmann guilty of impropriety, Thayer condemned Moore for his "bold and cruel attempt to sandbag" witnesses. Yet another motion came after the prosecution's ballistics expert, Captain Proctor, signed an affidavit in which he swore that on many occasions he had told Katzmann that there was no evidence proving Sacco's gun had fired the fatal shot. He warned that if the prosecutor asked a direct question on that point, Proctor would answer no. Katzmann had, therefore, carefully tailored his questions during the trial. By the time Thayer heard this motion, Proctor had died. The judge ruled that the jury had understood perfectly what Proctor meant and that Katzmann had not been unfairly evasive.

After that setback, Fred Moore finally withdrew from the case in favor of William Thompson, a distinguished trial lawyer who devoted the rest of his career to Sacco and Vanzetti's cause. Thompson made the first appeal to the Supreme Judicial Court. He argued that the accumulated weight of new evidence and the repeated rejection of appeals demonstrated that Thayer had abused his authority out of hostility to the defendants. Unlike historians, who would render judgment on the basis of the totality of evidence, the appeals judges turned down the defense arguments case by case, point by point. In each separate instance, they ruled that Judge Thayer had acted within his proper authority.

Throughout this drawn-out process, public interest in the case had steadily dwindled. But after November 18, 1925, controversy exploded once again. Sacco received a note from a fellow inmate that read, "I hear by [*sic*] confess to being in the South Braintree shoe company crime and Sacco and Vanzetti was not in said crime. Celestino F. Medeiros." Medeiros was a young prisoner facing execution for a murder conviction.

The defense soon connected Medeiros to the Morelli gang of Providence, Rhode Island. In the spring of 1921, the Morellis badly needed money to fight a pending indictment and so had ample reason to commit a payroll robbery. Joe Morelli carried a .32 Colt pistol and bore a striking resemblance to Sacco. Another gang member carried an automatic pistol, which could have accounted for spent cartridges found at the scene. Mike Morelli had been driving a new Buick, which disappeared after April 15. Another member fit the description of the pale, sickly driver. A number of defense and prosecution witnesses identified Joe Morelli when shown his picture. The New Bedford police had even suspected the Morellis of the Braintree crime.

Once again, the district attorney's office refused to reopen the case. The defense then appealed to Thayer to order a new trial. In reviewing the evidence, Thayer did not have to determine if it conclusively demonstrated Medeiro's guilt or Sacco and Vanzetti's innocence. He had only to decide that a new jury might now reach a different verdict. It took Thayer some 25,000 words to deny this motion.

That decision, more than any other, unleashed the torrent of outrage that surrounded the last months of the Sacco and Vanzetti case. Felix Frankfurter, an eminent Harvard Law School professor and later Supreme Court justice, published a lengthy article in the *Atlantic Monthly* in which he questioned the conduct of Thayer and Katzmann and the state appeals court's refusal to grant either clemency or a new trial. "I assert with deep regret, but without the slightest fear of disproof," he wrote, "that certainly in modern times Judge Thayer's opinion [on the Medeiros motion] stands unmatched for discrepancies between what the record discloses and what the opinion conveys." Frankfurter described the document as "a farrago of misquotations, misrepresentations, suppressions, and mutilations." The *Boston Herald* rebuked Thayer for adopting "the tone of the advocate rather than the arbiter." Once a staunch supporter of the prosecution, the *Herald* now called on the Supreme Judicial Court to overturn this ruling. Once again, the court refused to weigh the evidence. It ruled in rejecting the appeal that the defense motion involved questions of fact lying totally within the purview of the trial judge.

> "... *a farrago of misquotations, misrepresentations, suppressions, and mutilations.*"

That decision, in combination with Frankfurter's blistering attack, shifted public sympathy to Sacco and Vanzetti. A mounting body of evidence seemed to indicate that the two men were innocent. Yet, as the courts remained deaf to the defense appeals, more and more reasonable people came to suspect that, indeed, powerful men and institutions were conspiring to destroy two people perceived as a threat to the social order. Thayer's sentence of death by electrocution seemed but a final thread in a web of legal intrigue to commit an injustice.

Sacco and Vanzetti played an important part in winning broad popular support for their cause. Steadfastly, in the face of repeated disappointments, they maintained their innocence. Sacco, the more simple and direct of the two, suffered deeply as a result of separation from his family. During the first trying years, he went on a hunger strike and suffered a nervous breakdown. From that point on, he stoically awaited the end, more preoccupied with saving his wife further anguish than with saving himself. To assist the defense effort, however, he had begun in 1923 to study English, though with little success. A letter written to his teacher in 1926 conveys his energetic, simple idealism. Sacco had wanted to explain to his teacher why he had been unable to master the language:

> No, it isn't, because I have try with all my passion for the success of this beautiful language, not only for the sake of my family and the promise I have made to you—but for my own individual satisfaction, to know and to be able to read and write correct English. But woe is me! It wasn't so; no, because the sadness of these close and cold walls, the idea to be away from my dear family, for all the beauty and joy of liberty—had more than once exhaust my passion.

**Many artists, intellectuals, and literary figures** sympathized with Sacco and Vanzetti. Maxwell Anderson wrote a play, *Gods of the Lightning*; Upton Sinclair, the novel *Boston*; and Edna St. Vincent Millay, a series of sonnets. Artist Ben Shahn, himself an immigrant from Lithuania, received recognition during the 1930s for his series of twenty-three paintings on Sacco and Vanzetti. When the painting shown here is compared with the photograph of the two men on page 257, Shahn's source becomes evident. But the artist transformed the photograph in subtle ways. Given our earlier discussion of photographic evidence, how do the changes lend more force to his painting?

Vanzetti's articulate, often eloquent speeches and letters won him the respect of fellow prisoners, defenders, and literary figures drawn to the case, including Upton Sinclair, whose reformist instincts had not deserted him since writing *The Jungle* twenty years earlier. (Vanzetti was "one of the wisest and kindest persons I ever knew," Sinclair wrote, "and I thought him as incapable of murder as I was.") When at last Vanzetti stood before Judge Thayer on the day of his sentencing, he spoke passionately of the first principles that moved him:

> Now, I should say that I am not only innocent of all these things, not only have I never committed a real crime in my life—though some sins but not crimes—not only have I struggled all my life to eliminate crimes, the crimes official law and official moral condemns, but also the crime that the official moral and official law sanctions and sanctifies,—the exploitation and the oppression of man by man, and if there is reason why you in a few minutes can doom me,

it is this reason and nothing else . . . I would not wish to a dog or to a snake, to the most low and misfortunate creature of the earth—I would not wish to any of them what I have had to suffer for things that I am not guilty of. But my conviction is that I have suffered for things I am guilty of. I am suffering because I am a radical and indeed I am a radical; I have suffered because I was an Italian, and indeed I am an Italian; I have suffered more for my family and beloved than for myself; but I am so convinced to be right that if you could execute me two times, and if I could be reborn two other times, I would live again to do what I have done already.

The question of guilt or innocence, Vanzetti seemed to suggest, involved more than courtroom evidence. Despite the safeguards of the rule of law, society had used a broad constellation of attitudes, beliefs, and prejudices embedded in American culture to judge Vanzetti guilty. And, a historian might add, from out of Vanzetti's own constellation of beliefs, attitudes, and prejudices, he continued to condemn all governments as oppressive, all institutions as evil. This was the anarchist philosophy he lived by—the "Idea," as he and fellow believers termed it. Vanzetti reaffirmed his right to war against American society and against "the crime that the . . . official law sanctions and sanctifies."

As the debate and protests continued, public support for the execution began to erode. Yet an equally vocal element of the populace hailed Thayer's conduct as a message to "Reds" that they could not subvert the Commonwealth of Massachusetts. Thus Governor Alvan Fuller faced a difficult decision when he received a plea from Vanzetti for executive clemency.* To ease the political pressure on him, Fuller appointed a blue-ribbon panel to review the entire trial and appeals process. The three men he chose were symbols of the commonwealth's social and educational elite. Retired Judge Robert Grant was a New England patrician and novelist devoted to the Anglo-American traditions of Massachusetts. Samuel Stratton, president of Massachusetts Institute of Technology, was clearly overshadowed by the committee chair, A. Lawrence Lowell—a pillar of Boston society, a lawyer by training, and the president of Harvard. Lowell had already demonstrated his capacity for ethnocentrism, having introduced quotas to limit the number of Jewish students admitted to Harvard. As the liberal *New Republic* remarked of the committee, "the life of an Italian anarchist was as foreign to them as life on Mars."

For more than ten days the three men heard testimony on the evidence, much of it new. The defense also submitted a lengthy brief. But the committee's deliberations were short. On July 27 it filed its final report, upholding both the verdict and sentence against Sacco and Vanzetti. Sympathizers reacted with a mixture of despair and disgust. "What more can immigrants from Italy expect?" asked editorial writer Heywood Broun. "It's not every prisoner who has the President of Harvard throw the switch for him."

---

* Sacco refused to sign. Although he agreed with Vanzetti's arguments, he did not want to violate his anarchist principles by appealing to government authorities—or to give his wife further vain hopes.

By the time all appeals were exhausted, the Sacco and Vanzetti case had brought to public attention not only issues of guilt and innocence, but more fundamental tensions in American society. On one side were arrayed immigrants, workers, and the poor for whom Sacco and Vanzetti stood as powerful symbols. On the other stood Thayer, the "men of Norfolk," the Protestant establishment, and those who believed that America should tolerate only certain peoples and ideas.

On the night of August 22, 1927, John Dos Passos, a young writer, stood with the crowd outside Charleston Prison waiting for news of Sacco and Vanzetti's fate. Shortly after midnight word came—the "good shoemaker and poor fish peddler" were dead. Grief and anger raked the crowd. Some wept, others cried out in the name of justice, and many tore their clothes in anguish. The scene outside the prison was repeated in New York and other cities around the world. Years later, Dos Passos expressed the outrage he felt against those who had persecuted Sacco and Vanzetti:

> they have clubbed us off the streets they are stronger they are rich they hire and fire the politicians the newspapereditors the old judges the small men with reputations the collegepresidents the ward heelers (listen college presidents judges America will not forget her betrayers). . . .
>
> all right you have won you will kill the brave men our friends tonight there is nothing left to do we are beaten. . . .
>
> America our nation has been beaten by strangers who have turned our language inside out who have taken the clean words our Fathers spoke and made them slimy and foul. . . .
>
> they have built the electric chair and hired the executioner to throw the switch
>
> all right we are two nations

Two nations—that was the reason for "all the fuss."

Will the real truth of the case ever be known? Perhaps not—at least not "beyond a reasonable doubt," to borrow the language of the courts. Yet historians have unearthed enough additional information to provide, if not the certainties of fact, at least a few ironies of probability. After Sacco and Vanzetti's execution, Upton Sinclair began to collect material for a novel about the case. As a socialist who had staunchly defended the two men during their years in prison, he was able to interview scores of friends and associates. While Sinclair remained convinced that Sacco and Vanzetti were innocent of the Bridgewater and Braintree robberies, he became less sure whether the two men were merely philosophical anarchists. Both had "believed in and taught violence," he discovered. "I became convinced from many different sources that Vanzetti was not the pacifist he was reported to be under the necessity of defense propaganda. He was, like many fanatics, a dual personality, and when he was roused by the social conflict he was a very dangerous man."

Historian Paul Avrich, investigating the anarchist community of which the two men were a part, noted that Vanzetti was indeed a close friend of Luigi

Galleani, the firebrand whose associates had launched the letter bombs of 1919 and dynamited Attorney General Palmer's home. "We mean to speak for [the proletariat through] the voice of dynamite, through the mouth of guns," announced the anarchist leaflet found nearby. Carlo Valdinoci, the man who was blown up carrying out his mission, had been a good friend of both Sacco and Vanzetti. Indeed, after Valdinoci's death, his sister Assunta moved in with Sacco and his family. Then, too, rumors within the anarchist community suggested that Vanzetti himself had assembled the bomb that demolished a judge's home in Boston the night Valdinoci had done his work in Washington.

"But my conviction is that I have suffered for things I am guilty of," Vanzetti told Thayer at the end. Perhaps there was pride as well as indignation in this response. What, in the end, was the guilt of which Sacco and Vanzetti were so conscious during the trial? Was it the knowledge that their radical pamphlets, if found, would get them deported? But both men had been preparing to flee the country anyway, before being arrested. (Recall Sacco's outsized passport photo.) Could their evasive behavior have resulted from the fact that they had more to conceal at home than a few pamphlets?

Upton Sinclair came to believe so. After the execution, Fred Moore confided to him that Sacco and Vanzetti had admitted "they were hiding dynamite on the night of their arrest, and that that was the real reason why they told lies and stuck to them." If true, Sacco and Vanzetti, like Valdinoci, had been willing to commit acts of anarchism that, by the laws of American society, would have been punishable by death. Sacco made clear his own distinction between being tried for his beliefs and being arrested for mere bank robbery. "If I was arrested because of the Idea I am glad to suffer. If I must I will die for it. But they have arrested me for a gunman job."

*"If I was arrested because of the Idea I am glad to suffer."*

Is the final irony that Sacco and Vanzetti were willing to die—perhaps even to kill others—for their Idea? Just as the "men of Norfolk" and the officials of Massachusetts were willing to execute Sacco and Vanzetti on behalf of their idea of what America should be? ("Damn them, they ought to hang anyway," remarked juror Ripley.) The historian must suspect that on that August night in 1927, citizens were not merely fighting over a matter of guilt or innocence, but (as Dos Passos put it) over the meaning of those "clean words our Fathers spoke." Sacco and Vanzetti had forced the nation to ask who in their own times best embodied the principles of freedom and equality inherited from 1776. Perhaps neither historians nor lawyers can resolve that question to the satisfaction of a divided nation.

# *Additional Reading*

Periodically a new book comes along that reframes our understanding of the case and the controversy surrounding it. Most recently, Bruce Watson, *Sacco and Vanzetti: The Men, the Murders, and the Judgment of Mankind* (New York, 2007), offers what we consider the most lucid explanation so far. Among those works that have sought to establish the guilt of Sacco, Vanzetti, or both, the most forceful presentation is made by Francis Russell, *Tragedy in Dedham* (New York, 1971). To our minds, the following works have made a far stronger case. Readers might best start with Felix Frankfurter, *The Case of Sacco and Vanzetti* (New York, 1962), an expanded version of his famous *Atlantic Monthly* critique of the case. This book reveals why the establishment reacted so violently—to the extent that the Justice Department tapped Frankfurter's phone until after the execution. Any reader who wishes to encounter Sacco and Vanzetti through their own words can read Marion Frankfurter and Gardner Jackson, eds., *The Letters of Sacco and Vanzetti* (New York, 1960). Richard Newby, *Kill Now, Talk Forever: Debating Sacco and Vanzetti* (Bloomington, IN, 2001), provides another valuable source of documents.

One work that recognized that this case had a social as well as a legal side is Edmund M. Morgan and Louis Joughlin, *The Legacy of Sacco and Vanzetti* (New York, 1948). Morgan, like Frankfurter, a Harvard law professor, used his expertise on rules of evidence to analyze the legal issues, while Joughlin, an English professor, traced the strong effects of the case on intellectuals and writers. Another compelling treatment of the evidence, trial, and appeals procedure is Herbert Ehrmann, *The Case That Will Not Die* (Boston, 1969). Erhmann entered the case as an assistant to William Thompson. His first assignment was to research the Medeiros confession. From that experience he developed a lifelong commitment to establish Sacco and Vanzetti's innocence. Reinforcement of Ehrmann's case against the Medeiros gang is offered in Frank D'Allesandro, *The Verdict of History: Sacco and Vanzetti* (Providence, 1997).

After eighty years in which many people have spent nearly a lifetime of digging, it might seem that historians would be hard-pressed to produce any new evidence about this case. But William Young and David Kaiser, *Postmortem: New Evidence in the Case of Sacco and Vanzetti* (Amherst, MA, 1985), uncovered startling evidence of police improprieties, including extensive wiretaps of the defense and its friends and tampering with the ballistics evidence. Young and Kaiser make a powerful case that Sacco and Vanzetti were innocent of robbery and murder. Paul Avrich, *Sacco and Vanzetti: The Anarchist Background* (Princeton, 1991), focuses attention on the anarchist movement itself, including many previously untapped sources in Italian, that help clarify Sacco and Vanzetti's involvement with the Idea and with a philosophy of violence. Among the book's most startling revelations: Mike Boda, apparently outraged by the arrest of Sacco and Vanzetti, drove a wagon full of dynamite to Wall Street. The ensuing blast, notorious in American history, killed thirty-three people in September 1920.

# The Mending Wall?

The same year that officer Michael Connolly arrested Sacco and Vanzetti, Congress passed the National Origins Act of 1921. The act aimed to close America's borders to "the good-for-nothing mongrels of Central America and Southeastern Europe." Some eight decades later, American nativists were still anxiously trying to close the United States' porous borders.

The problem of how to control the southern border was a complicated one. On the one hand, by 2006 some 11 million illegal aliens already lived in the United States. They provided a vital source of labor for tens of thousands of farms and businesses. But each year millions more found their way across a 1,951-mile-long border. In response, Congress adopted a plan for fencing the most densely crossed areas. Two years later the Department of Homeland Security announced that more than 500 miles of fence had been constructed.

Many Americans objected in the 1920s that immigration restriction violated the spirit of the United States as a refuge for "huddled masses yearning to breathe free." The barrier across the U.S.-Mexican border proved even more controversial. The battle was not simply between Democrats and Republicans or liberals and conservatives. President George W. Bush and 2008 presidential nominee John McCain, both Republicans and conservatives, backed a "guest worker" program that would preserve the flow of workers, as well as a plan to legalize the status of illegals already in the country. Many equally conservative Republicans wanted the borders closed and the illegal aliens ousted. All the two sides could agree on was a wall.

Even that solution provoked controversy. Three Native American tribes objected because the barrier cut their lands in two. Human rights advocates pointed out that the barrier pushed those crossing the border into the Sonoran Desert, causing an increase in immigrants' deaths from dehydration and exposure. Environmentalists were especially unhappy when in April 2008 the Department of Homeland Security announced plans to waive more than thirty environmental laws to speed construction. Critics in Arizona and Texas asserted that the fence endangered migratory species and fragile ecosystems along the Rio Grande. Laredo Mayor Raul G. Salinas warned that the border wall would devastate his city. The people crossing the border "are sustaining our economy by forty percent, and I am gonna close the door on them and put [up] a wall? You don't do that. It's like a slap in the face."

Perhaps poet Robert Frost best understood the controversy a wall could bring. In his poem "Mending Wall," written on the eve of the 1921 restriction act, he described how each spring he and his neighbor set out to repair the wall that divided their properties. As they worked, his neighbor liked to say, "good fences make good neighbors." So the narrator asked him why this is so and added:

> Before I built a wall I'd ask to know
> What I was walling in or walling out,
> And to whom I was like to give offence.

His neighbor refused to speculate about the nature of walls and simply repeated, "Good fences make good neighbors." But do they?

## CHAPTER 12

# *Dust Bowl Odyssey*

*Who were the millions who flooded into California during the Depression? The census makes the invisible more visible.*

The story begins with dust—not the thin coating on the shelf or the little balls in the corner, but huge dark clouds of it. When the winds blew, they sucked the dust into the sky to create blizzards. The dust storms began in earnest on May 9, 1934. High winds captured dirt from Montana and Wyoming—some 350 million tons of it—and carried it eastward. By noon the dust began falling in Iowa and Wisconsin. That evening a brown grit fell like snow on Chicago—four pounds for each inhabitant. Then the storm moved on. It was dark in Buffalo at noon the next day, and the midday gloom covered five states. On May 11 the dust sifted down as far south as Atlanta and as far north as Boston. The following day, ships some 300 miles off the East Coast noticed a film of brown dust on their decks.

Every year more storms blew: twenty-two in 1934 to a peak of seventy-two by 1937, then a gradual decline until finally the rains returned in the 1940s. Residents of the high western plains remembered 1935 as the worst year. February brought temperatures in the seventies. With no snow cover and no vegetation to hold it, the dirt flew. Even on calm days, a pervasive grit fell everywhere on the southwestern plains. "In the morning," John Steinbeck wrote, "the dust hung like fog, and the sun was as red as ripe new blood. All day the dust sifted down from the sky, and the next day it sifted down. . . . It settled on the corn, piled on the tops of the fence posts, piled on the wires; it settled on roofs and blanketed weeds and trees." On May 15 Denver sent a warning that a dust storm was rolling eastward. Under a clear blue sky, folks in Kansas paid little attention until around noon, when the sky suddenly blackened. One movie patron leaving a theater expected to walk into the blinding glare of daylight. Instead, he thought a prankster had thrown a bag over his head. As he stepped outside, he bumped into a telephone pole, tripped on cans and boxes, and finally found his way by crawling along the curb. A young boy was less fortunate. He wandered out the door, became disoriented, and suffocated in a dust drift.

284

**The enormity of the dust storms** at first inspired amazement and awe. That sense of wonder soon gave way to despair as the constantly blowing dust turned day into night and left people asking if "this was the wrath of God."

No matter what they tried, people could not escape the dust. Open the door and the dust beat in your face. Shut the door tight and still "those tiny particles seemed to seep through the very walls. It got into cupboards and clothes closets; our faces were as dirty as if we had rolled in the dirt; our hair was gray and stiff and we ground dirt between our teeth."

Was this the wrath of God, as some plains dwellers thought? "This is the ultimate darkness," one woman wrote in her diary. "So must come the end of the world." Still, though the story of the Dust Bowl remains one of the saddest chapters in American history, its coming could be explained by causes more proximate than divine wrath. Drought had been a recurring feature of the high plains that stretched northward from the Texas panhandle, New Mexico, and western Oklahoma all the way through portions of Colorado, Kansas, Nebraska, Wyoming, and the Dakotas. To survive extremes of heat and cold, wind and drought, prairie grasses had developed deep roots. Those grasses fed the buffalo and held the soil in place.

In the late nineteenth century, farmers had seen the grass as a nuisance to be plowed under so they could exploit the rich soil beneath. Land that had been suitable enough for grazing was turned into fields of cotton, wheat, and corn. Little did farmers heed the warning of those who described the area as the "Great American Desert," subscribing instead to the popular notion that "rain follows the plow." Homestead

*"Rain follows the plow," but more often dust followed.*

farmers sought to create an agrarian kingdom in which they "busted" and "broke" the land into farms to feed their families, the nation, and the world.

**Photographer Dorothea Lange** liked to place displaced Oklahoma migrants against a background that suggested a central irony of the Depression era—want in the midst of plenty. This picture reminded viewers that there was more than one way to make the trip to California.

In 1934 the dust storms combined with the Great Depression to shatter dreams of the West as the land of opportunity. The rains failed the farmers, their crops withered, and the winds hurled the loose soil across the nation. As the soil eroded year after year, so did farmers' resources and hopes.

John Steinbeck told that story in his novel *The Grapes of Wrath*, and director John Ford turned it into one of the most critically acclaimed movies of all time. Most Americans now associate the Depression era with the Okies—dispossessed farm families out of Oklahoma and other Dust Bowl states—and their rickety cars packed high with all they owned and heading along Route 66 to California. Whether in Steinbeck's words, in Ford's images, in the ballads of folk singer Woody Guthrie, or in the pictures taken by Farm Security Administration (FSA) photographers such as Dorothea Lange, the Okies and their flight from the Dust Bowl put a face on the tragedy of America during the Great Depression.

Steinbeck's novel told of the Joad family in a near-biblical parable of suffering, endurance, and dignity in the face of adversity. The name Joad echoes the name Job, and the voice of God comes through the Reverend Jim Casy, whose initials link him to Jesus Christ. The Joads' trek across the desert to the promised land reminds us of Israel's lost tribes. It is a compelling story with three major sections: the opening in Oklahoma, in which the Joads are driven from their land; their odyssey across the desert on Route 66; and their wanderings through California in a desperate search for work.

The Joads are a simple family who for decades struggled to wrest a living cropping cotton on a forty-acre plot near Sallisaw, Oklahoma. At first there were five years of good crops "while the wild grass was still in her." Then it became an "ever' year" kind of place. "Ever' year," Tom Joad tells his friend Jim Casy, "we had a good crop comin' an' it never came." Bad crops forced the Joads to borrow from the bank. The crops kept failing, the debt kept growing, and soon the bank owned their farm. The Joads, along with hundreds of thousands of plains farmers, became sharecroppers who each year gave the better part of their crop to a landowner or the bank. When Tom

> "They was gonna stick her out when the bank come to tractorin' off the place."

Joad returns home after a stint in prison, he finds his family gone. His friend Muley Graves explains that they have been driven from their farm: "they was gonna stick her out when the bank come to tractorin' off the place." The tractor that leveled the farmhouse also severed the vital connection between the Joads and their land. They were almost literally uprooted and displaced.

Now the question became where to go. In the 1930s California beckoned more than any other destination. The agrarian dream of economic sufficiency and independence still glittered in the West. So the Joads pile all their worldly goods and a family of twelve onto a jalopy and head down Route 66. Steinbeck described the highway as

> the path of a people in flight, refugees from dust and shrinking land, from the numbers of tractors and shrinking ownership, from the desert's slow northward invasion, from the twisting winds that howl up out of Texas, from the floods that bring no richness to the land and steal what richness is there. From all of these the people are in flight.

The road proves a cruel taskmaster. Each repair of their weather-beaten auto eats into the Joads' shrinking cash reserve. The weaker members of the family die or wander off. In the roadside camps, however, the Joads often meet other refugees who give help and comfort, share what little they have, and join the Joads in reestablishing ties to the places they have left behind.

In California the dream turns into a nightmare. The Joads do indeed discover the land of milk and honey. Rich farms and fertile fields roll across a vast landscape. Yet that abundance is off-limits to the Okies. Californians treat them like vermin, vigilante mobs attack them, labor agents cheat them, strikebreakers threaten them, and worst of all, work at a living wage proves nearly impossible to find. Unable to provide, the men lose their place at the head of the family. In the end, Ma Joad's faith holds the remnants of the family together. But in a final irony, these Dust Bowl refugees face the peril of rising floodwaters.

## THE SPECIFIC VERSUS THE COLLECTIVE

Many Americans come away from the Joads' story convinced that Steinbeck recorded the central tragedy of America in the 1930s. Yet no single story, however powerful or popular, can capture the collective experience of hundreds of thousands, even millions, of people. A historian wants to know just how typical the Joads were—of Americans, of migrants to California, or even simply of Okies during the Great Depression. After all, Steinbeck was a novelist seeking to tell a story of people dispossessed from the land. Unlike a historian, he was not bound by strict rules of evidence and explanation, only by the desire to explore the human condition. Yet Steinbeck gained the respect of his readers in part because he based much of his novel on direct observation. Like many writers of the 1930s, he used a reporter's techniques to research his story, visiting Oklahoma, traveling Route 66, and touring California's migrant labor camps.

Social scientists and government officials of Steinbeck's day confirmed much of what he wrote. They, too, reported the drought conditions that drove farm families out of the plains, the hostility of Californians to refugees, and the destitution of many migrants. Yet we have already seen that the historian must rigorously question the testimony of social scientists and journalists as much as novelists. Even the apparently objective photographs taken by that "mirror with a memory" need to be scrutinized.

Take, for example, the case of photographer Dorothea Lange and her husband, Paul Taylor, an agricultural economist from the University of California at Berkeley. Like Steinbeck, Lange and Taylor followed the migrant trail from Oklahoma through Texas and across the desert to the migrant camps in California. Lange was one of many photographers hired by the FSA to document rural life in the 1930s. She and Taylor published a book, *An American Exodus: A Record of Human Erosion*, that described the destruction of the plains and the impoverishment of a proud people. Yet Taylor and Lange were hardly disinterested observers—much to their credit, one can argue. Like Steinbeck, they believed that the migrants needed help. And all three went looking for evidence to make that case.

The story of Lange's most famous photograph is instructive. One March morning in 1936 she was driving up California Highway 101 toward San Francisco. Eager to be home, she hurried past a hand-painted sign directing passersby to a pea-pickers' camp. Some impulse made her turn back. What she saw staggered her, even though she had spent months investigating the conditions of migrant farm laborers. The camp contained more than two thousand men, women, and children huddled against the cold and driving rain in ragged tents and flimsy wood shelters. They had come to pick peas,

**The collection of Dorothea Lange's work** in the Library of Congress shows that she was far more than a "one-picture" photographer. She traveled extensively and photographed a wide variety of Depression-era scenes. "Migrant Mother," her most famous photograph, was actually taken as the final in a series of six separate shots. What is it about "Migrant Mother #6" (*left*) that makes it more affecting than "Migrant Mother #1" (*right*)?

but the weather left them without work or wages. And with nowhere to go and no relief from local, state, or federal officials, they waited. First their money ran out, then their food. By the time Lange arrived, they were desperate. How was she to give voice to their need?

That day Lange took a photograph that must rank as one of the most widely viewed images of the decade. She entitled it "Migrant Mother." Her subject was Florence Thompson, age thirty-two, the recently widowed mother of six children. What Lange captured was the quiet dignity of a woman at the end of hope, cradling an infant in her arms with two young children clinging to her shoulders. She had just sold the tires off her car to buy food for her family. As Lange intended, the image put a personal face to a need so compelling that few people could turn away. Along with Steinbeck's tale of the Joads, "Migrant Mother" made Americans aware of the story of the Dust Bowl refugees.

Lange and other FSA photographers did not simply arrive at a camp and begin taking pictures. To get the image she wanted, Lange often posed her subjects. She sometimes even suggested to them where to look or what to do with their hands. In the case of Florence Thompson, Lange recalled, "she seemed to know that my pictures might help her, and so she helped me. There was a sort of equality about it." Lange took six different photographs, each time looking for a more compelling shot. In the first, one child was smiling at the camera, defusing the desperation of the situation. Lange then

**EXTENT OF AREA SUBJECT TO SEVERE WIND EROSION**
**1935–1940**

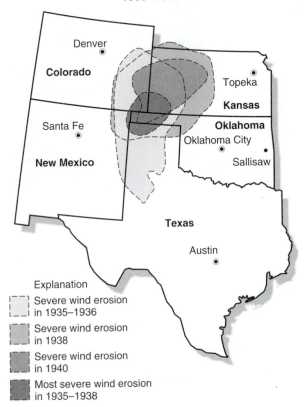

Explanation

- Severe wind erosion in 1935–1936
- Severe wind erosion in 1938
- Severe wind erosion in 1940
- Most severe wind erosion in 1935–1938

tried a longer view of the tent; then moved in to focus on the mother and her baby. In the final, telling shot, Thompson, of her own accord, raised her hand to her chin. "LOOK IN HER EYES," ran the headline in *Midweek Pictorial* when it first ran the photo. "This woman is watching something happen to America and to herself and her children who are part of America."

Both Lange and Steinbeck adopted the time-tested literary technique of allowing a part to stand for the whole. The two created images so vivid, stories so concrete, they would be remembered long after the bland generalizations of bureaucratic reports were forgotten. Yet here, in the matter of the concrete and the specific, is precisely where historians so often begin their skeptical cross-examinations. One way of identifying biases or limiting perspectives is to examine a broader sample. To what degree do Steinbeck's vivid stories and Lange's wrenching photographs reflect the collective reality they are taken to symbolize?

Even a casual glance at the Joads' story suggests that Steinbeck painted with a broad, sometimes imprecise brush. To begin with, the Joads did not live in what was physically the Dust Bowl. While drought affected a vast region from the Dakotas to Texas, geographers place the Dust Bowl in an area in the Texas-Oklahoma panhandle that spills over into western Kansas and eastern parts of Colorado and New Mexico. Sallisaw, from which the Joads hailed, lay in the eastern part of Oklahoma, several hundred miles outside the Dust Bowl. Rolling hills and oaks, not prairie and short grasses, formed the landscape. And corn, rather than cotton, was the primary crop. As one historian remarked, "Steinbeck's geography, like that of most Americans, was a bit hazy; any place in Oklahoma, even on the Ozark Plateau, must be Dust Bowl country, he assumed."

Still, this point seems a small one, given the wide reach of those rolling black clouds. Even if the Joads were not technically from the Dust Bowl, surely most of the Okies who migrated to California were farm refugees from the dust storms. Or were they? Here, too, the facts get in the way of the image Steinbeck made popular. Statistics show that California gained more than a million new residents in the 1930s. In fact, however, no more than about 15,000 to 16,000 of those people came from the Dust Bowl—well under 2 percent. In imagining the Joads, Steinbeck was implicitly portraying a much broader group of southwestern emigrants from four states: "agricultural laborers" and "farm workers" not only from Oklahoma but also Arkansas, Texas, and Missouri. Because this group amounted to about one-third of the newcomers to California, we might say that, strictly speaking, the Joads are more accurately representative of displaced agricultural labor than of Dust Bowl refugees.

The minute we begin talking about collective experiences, of course, we run headlong into numbers. To understand the great migration of the Depression decade, historians must place the Joads in a statistical context. What links them to the million people who reached California between 1930 and 1940? Unfortunately the mere mention of numbers—statistics or columns of figures—is enough to make the eyes of many readers glaze over. It is only natural to prefer Steinbeck's way of personifying the Dust Bowl refugees.

Yet the numbers cannot be avoided if we are to paint an accurate picture. The challenge for the historian lies in bringing statistics to life so they tell a story with some of the human qualities that Lange and Steinbeck invested in their subjects. In looking at the 1930s in particular, historians are lucky because social scientists and government officials tried hard to quantify the human circumstances of the era. In particular, historians of the Dust Bowl era have

*The challenge for the historian lies in bringing statistics to life so they tell a story.*

been able to benefit from the federal population count of 1940, which was the first modern census.

The federal census had been taken every decade since 1790, because its data were needed to apportion each state's seats in the House of Representatives, in accordance with the provisions of the Constitution. For the first fifty years, federal marshals did the actual counting, by locating households within their districts and recording the number of people living there. Over time the nature of the information collected became broader and more detailed; it included social statistics about taxes collected, real estate values, wages, education, and crime. In 1880 Congress shifted responsibility for the census from the marshals to specially appointed experts trained to collect not only population statistics but also data on manufacturing and other economic activities. By 1890 punch cards stored data, and an electric tabulating machine processed those cards. Mechanization, by vastly reducing calculation time, made it possible to accumulate more complex and varied information.

The census of 1940, because of advanced statistical techniques used by the enumerators, was even more comprehensive than its predecessors. Social scientists and opinion pollsters such as George Gallup had experimented during the 1930s with probability sampling. To measure unemployment rates in 1940, for example, they constructed a group of some 20,000 households to represent a cross section of the nation as a whole. The data from this small sample gave the social scientists statistics that accurately (though not exactly) reflected the national employment pattern. Other questions in the 1940 census were asked of just 5 percent of the households. That allowed the Census Bureau to publish detailed tables on many more subjects, not the least of which was internal migration. In so doing, they provided historians with a way of determining how representative the Joads actually were of the Dust Bowl refugees.

# History by the Numbers

Historian James Gregory went to the census records in his own attempt to analyze the Dust Bowl migration. In each of the censuses from 1910 to 1970, he was able to find statistics on Americans born in western regions of the South (Texas, Oklahoma, Missouri, and Arkansas) who had moved to California. By comparing these numbers decade to decade, he could also estimate how many new southwesterners arrived every ten years. Take a moment to look at the table below.

## Western South Natives Living outside the Region, 1910–1970

|  | Living outside region | Living in California | Net Calif. increase | Percentage of Calif. pop. |
|---|---|---|---|---|
| 1910 | 661,094 | 103,241 |  | 4.3% |
| 1920 | 1,419,046 | 187,471 | 84,230 | 5.5% |
| 1930 | 2,027,139 | 430,810 | 243,339 | 7.6% |
| 1940 | 2,580,940 | 745,934 | 315,124 | 10.8% |
| 1950 | 3,887,370 | 1,367,720 | 621,786 | 12.9% |
| 1960 | 4,966,781 | 1,734,271 | 366,551 | 11.0% |
| 1970 | 5,309,287 | 1,747,632 | 13,361 | 8.8% |

*Sources:* U.S. Bureau of the Census, Census of the United States, Population: 1910, Vol. 1, 732–733; 1920, Vol. 11, 628–629; 1930, Vol. H, 155–156; 1940, State of Birth, 17–18; 1950, State of Birth, 20–24; 1960, State of Birth, 22–23; 1970, State of Birth, 28–29.

The story of the Joads would lead us to hypothesize that between 1930 and 1940 a large number of migrants left the southwestern plains states for California. Drought and economic hardships drove them out. Because so many settled in California, we would further assume that conditions special to that state drew the refugees there.

At first glance, the statistics support the hypothesis. The number of southwesterners in California in 1940 was 745,934. Subtracting the residents that were already there in 1930 (430,810), we discover that some 315,124 southwesterners moved to California during the decade in which the severe dust storms took place (this number is shown for 1940 under the column heading "Net California Increase"). Of course, there is a certain false precision here. Common sense tells us that at least some southwesterners living in California who were counted in the 1930 census must have returned home, moved to an entirely new state, or died over the next ten years. In that case, the actual number of migrants arriving must have been greater, though we have no reliable way of knowing how much greater. But the bureau has estimated that the total number of southwestern migrants might have been as many as 400,000. In other words, the number in our table—315,124—may have been off by 85,000 people, enough to populate a medium-sized city.

A migrant total approaching half a million is surely high. But we must ask another question. Is there a causal connection between the drought and migration, or is the link merely coincidental? The anecdotal evidence of one journalist suggests an intriguing clue. He reported seeing Oklahoma farmers "in their second-hand flivvers [inexpensive Model-T Fords], piled high with furniture and family . . . pouring through the divides by the hundreds." It is the kind of literary detail that might have come straight out of Steinbeck. The problem is that the reporter was writing in 1926, eight years before the first dust storm. We begin to see the reason that James Gregory, in compiling his table, sought data over a sixty-year period. The broader time span provides a better yardstick of comparison. To make the point visually, we have taken the information from the "Net California Increase" column and displayed it as a bar graph on page 294.

As the bar graph reveals, during the 1920s nearly a quarter of a million southwesterners migrated to California—nearly as many as came during the "dirty thirties" of the Dust Bowl years. Small wonder that a reporter could speak, in 1926, of hundreds of flivvers crowding the mountain passes.

*Numbers suggest that factors besides drought, dust storms, and the Depression were driving people from the southwestern plains.*

And the 1920s, by contrast, were years of average rainfall. Equally notable, the number of arrivals virtually doubles during the 1940s, a time when rain and better economic times had returned to the Southwest, mostly because of massive industrial growth stimulated by World War II. Even in the postwar decade of 1950–1960, the migration of southwesterners remained heavy. Such numbers suggest that factors besides drought, dust storms, and the

## WESTERN SOUTH NATIVES ARRIVING IN CALIFORNIA, 1910–1970

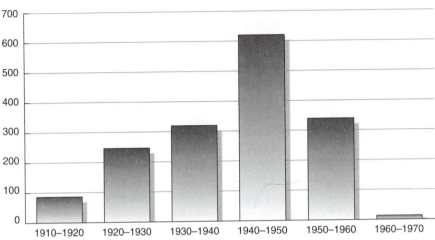

Depression were driving people from the southwestern plains or drawing them to California.

Steinbeck's powerful imagery provides one suggestion for explaining this broader trend: the tractor that knocked down the Joads' house. Why, we might ask, were tractors rumbling across the farmland, driving people from their homes? Steinbeck offered an explanation: "At last the owner men came to the point. The tenant system won't work any more. One man on a tractor can take the place of twelve or fourteen families. Pay him a wage and take all the crop." The owners took no responsibility for what they and their tractors did. It was "the bank" that gave the order, and the bank was "something more than men. . . . It's the monster. Men made it, but they can't control it." When the tenants protest that their families had "killed the weeds and snakes" to make way for their farms, the owners show cold indifference. "The bank, the fifty-thousand-acre owner, can't be responsible," they explain. "You're on land that isn't yours." When the tenants complain that they have no money and nowhere else to go, the owners responded, "Why don't you go to California? There's work there and it never gets cold."

The tractor symbolized a complex process of agricultural reorganization through absentee landownership, mechanization, and corporatization. During the late nineteenth century, farmers had flooded into the southwestern plains—the nation's final agricultural frontier. Through World War I they realized generally high prices for their crops. All the same, many farmers had arrived with few resources other than the labor they and their families could perform. One bad crop, one dry year, and they were facing debt. Once in debt, they had to buy on credit and borrow on future crops. As a result, sharecropping and tenantry had become widespread even in flush times.

During the 1920s, though industry boomed, the agricultural economy went into decline. Prices for agricultural staples including cotton, wheat, and corn fell. Overfarming depleted the soil. Such factors created conditions under which too many people were trying to farm land that could no longer support them. Between 1910 and 1930, well before the great dust storms, the number of farmers and agricultural workers in the region fell by about 341,000 and some 1.3 million people left, of which about 430,800 settled in California. A majority of the farmers who remained in the region rented land or cropped on shares. By the 1930s landowners had come to realize that they could increase profits by driving off their tenants, by consolidating their acreage into larger, more efficient farms, and by using tractors and other machines rather than human labor.

So the explanation for the exodus from the plains would need to include a discussion of agricultural reorganization and the mechanization of farming. Steinbeck's vivid portrait of the bankers' tractors acknowledged this reality, but the novel's pervasive images of dust overwhelm it somewhat. These findings do not mean we should dismiss *The Grapes of Wrath*, merely that we should study the numbers on migration a little more closely. Were those migrants who left between 1910 and 1930 the same kinds of people who left in the 1930s? Did they leave for the same reasons?

Because the 1940 census was so much more comprehensive than those that preceded it, we actually know more about the Dust Bowl–era migrants than about those who traveled in previous decades. The 1930 census tells us, for example, that the population of rural counties in Oklahoma, Missouri, and Arkansas dropped in the 1920s, but not whether people left the region. Many may have gone into the cities or to work in the booming oil fields. All the same, it seems most likely that the migrants of the 1920s were a more prosperous group than those of the next decade. Despite the popular image of the West as a "safety valve" for the poor from the East, over the course of American history the majority of pioneer farmers were neither rich nor poor. The West attracted largely middle-class folk drawn to the promise of economic opportunity rather than driven out by harsh circumstances.

Elbert Garretson seems representative of the middling sort of people making up migrants before the Great Depression. Garretson saw that lower crop prices and declining soil fertility had weakened his chances to succeed at farming. So he packed up his family and took a job in a California steel mill. His plan was to get on his feet financially so he could continue to farm in Oklahoma. Several times the Garretsons returned to Oklahoma, but each time the lure of California proved stronger. Finally, Garretson sold the farm as a bad bet.

During the 1920s the lure for migrants was even stronger because California farmers faced a shortage of agricultural labor. To attract workers, they often paid the railroad fares of southwesterners who would emigrate. "The farmers would meet you at the trains," one woman recalled. Another family went "because we could see the promise of the cotton future here, and we were cotton ranchers." Poorer people like the Joads surely felt the draw, too, but they were more likely tied by debt to their "ever' year" farms.

What differed in the 1930s was not so much the numbers of those who went but their identities. Of all the regions of the United States, none suffered more economic devastation during the Great Depression than the southwest plains. The once-robust oil industry collapsed in a glut of overproduction. Unemployment in the region hit one-third of all workers. Infestations of locusts and boll weevils added to the woes of farmers long afflicted by drought and low crop prices. In the two years before Franklin Roosevelt became president, creditors foreclosed the mortgages of some 10 percent of Oklahoma's farms. As a result, the migrants of the 1930s included many more desperately poor and displaced families like the Joads.

When Franklin Roosevelt launched the New Deal in 1933, he placed the agricultural crisis at the top of his agenda. Still, it was far from clear what government could do to ease the farmers' plight. One of the New Deal's most ambitious measures during the president's Hundred Day program for relief, recovery, and reform was the Agricultural Adjustment Act. New Dealers sought to ease farm distress by providing credit, reducing overproduction, and raising prices. One strategy was to offer farmers a cash subsidy to take land out of production. Over the next eight years, desperate southwestern farmers so eagerly sought the subsidy that they reduced their cotton acreage by 12.5 million acres, or more than 50 percent.

This strategy contains one of the central ironies of the Dust Bowl crisis. Along with the drought and the "monster" bank, the good intentions of the federal government helped to account for the wave of tractors driving people like the Joads from their land. To receive a crop subsidy, landowners had to reduce the acreage they planted. The easiest way to do that was to evict tenants. Landowners could consolidate their best lands and farm them with tractors, while letting tenant lands return to grass. One landlord boasted that "I bought tractors on the money the government give me and got shet o' my renters." So common was that practice that by 1940, tenantry had decreased by 24 percent. "They got their choice," the same landlord remarked curtly. "California or WPA [Works Progress Administration, a federal relief agency]."

If only the choice had been so simple. Unlike the 1920s, when California and the urban centers of the Southwest attracted rural folk with new opportunities, displaced tenants in the 1930s had few practical options. By this time California had a glut of agricultural workers, and the southwestern cities had higher unemployment than the rural counties did. The New Deal did offer help. During the early duster years of 1934 and 1935, the Federal Emergency Relief Administration provided funds to some 2.5 million southwestern families, about 20 percent of the population. But the aid proved woefully inadequate. In most areas of the country, the states supplemented federal relief payments, but not in the Southwest. Throughout the 1930s, some 20 percent to 35 percent of all families in the region suffered from extreme poverty and unemployment. This situation is one area in which the story of the Joads brings the plight of 1930s migrants into clear focus.

# THE ROAD

As the Great Depression worsened, Roy Turner and his family migrated to a shantytown outside the Oklahoma City stockyards. These encampments (often nicknamed Hoovervilles, after President Herbert Hoover) appeared in many urban areas. In Oklahoma City, the Turners joined some 2,000 others living off a mixture of relief, part-time jobs, and declining hopes. The Turners described their home as "old automobiles, old lard cases, buckets, paste board." For food they had little more than the milk from the stock-pen cows. When conditions became unbearably grim, the family pulled together what few belongings they had and headed down Route 66—"walking, me and my wife and two babies," hoping to hitch rides on the 1,200-mile trip to California.

Here indeed is a family much like the Joads, though their path to California involved a stop for several years in an urban center. But the Turners and Joads—desperately poor, without jobs, and without prospects—were only one element of the southwestern surge to California. When James Gregory examined the Census Bureau statistics as well as other surveys, he discovered some surprising percentages. For example, in 1939 the Bureau of Agricultural Economics surveyed the occupations of about 116,000 families who had come to California in the 1930s. The results of that data are displayed in the graph on page 298.

As the chart indicates, only 43 percent of southwesterners were doing farmwork immediately before they migrated. Farmers were a definite minority. In fact, nearly one-third of all migrants were professional or white-collar workers. The 1940 census showed similar results. Southwesterners who moved to California between 1935 and 1940 were asked to list their residence as of April 1, 1935. Only 36 percent reported that they were living on a farm.

With these numbers, as with all statistics, it is important to look critically at the method of collection. The census enumerators of 1940 reported that rural residents, to simplify answering the question of residence, would sometimes merely list the nearest town or city, which gave the mistaken impression that those people lived in an urban area. Even taking these biases into account, however, it seems that Steinbeck (and many historians as well) have exaggerated the numbers of farmers in the migrant stream. Other factors distinguish the actual migrants from the Joads. Of the twelve travelers in the Joads' old Hudson, five were well over forty years old. By contrast, most of the actual migrants were younger—60 percent of the adult travelers were under age thirty-five. Unlike the Joads, the actual migrants were slightly better educated than those who remained behind. The Joads were typical in gender balance, since the majority of migrants traveled as families. (In the broader history of American migration, this family movement is rather unusual, because single males more commonly predominate among migrating populations.) All the same, large extended families like the Joads were rare. The average southwestern migrant family had 4.4 members.

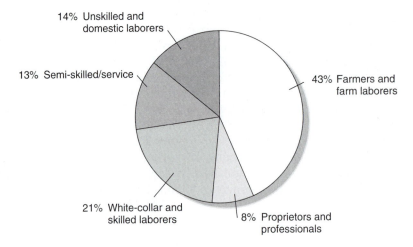

14% Unskilled and domestic laborers

13% Semi-skilled/service

43% Farmers and farm laborers

21% White-collar and skilled laborers

8% Proprietors and professionals

**Premigration occupations of California migrants from west south-central states.** (Data from *American Exodus: The Dust Bowl Migration and Okie Culture in California* by James N. Gregory. Copyright © 1991 by James N. Gregory. Used by permission of Oxford University Press, Inc.)

Finally, there is the matter of race. Like 95 percent of all southwestern migrants to California, the Joads were white. This was not because few African Americans lived in Missouri, Arkansas, Texas, or Oklahoma. In 1930 the black population in those four states was approximately 1.7 million. Many of these African Americans were farmers or agricultural laborers, and thousands left the region between 1910 and 1930. However, most migrated to urban centers in the North and upper Midwest, such as Chicago and Pittsburgh, where they already had relatives or friends. Among those black southwesterners who headed to California, the great majority settled in Los Angeles. Even so, by 1940 the black population there was only about 64,000 out of 1.5 million residents. (And a mere 5,000 African Americans resided in San Francisco.)

Steinbeck's account of the Joads' trip west leads us to another question—about the quality of the trip itself. *The Grapes of Wrath* devotes a third of its tale to the Joads' struggle to reach California. The book gives no exact dates, but the Joads were on the road long enough to have many hardships and adventures. They reached California weeks after their journey began. Reading of such tribulations, a reader might well wonder why so many people risked the trip if it was such an ordeal.

But the collective portrait that historians have assembled about migration journeys suggests that, for most people, the odyssey was not so wrenching. Here, the evidence is mostly anecdotal. The census collected no systematic *For most people, the odyssey was not so wrenching.* information on the length of the journey or conditions along the way. But social scientists and reporters interviewed Okies and recorded oral histories of their experience. Although the individual misfortunes that Steinbeck ascribed to the Joads no doubt happened to some migrants, most found the trip less harrowing.

Take, for example, the hopes that drew people to the road. To the Joads, California was little more than a blurry set of ideas based on rumors, legends, gossip, and handbills sent to Oklahoma by labor agents. Certainly, many people headed for California with unreasonable expectations. Two young researchers who were hired by the Library of Congress to collect folklore recorded this verse:

> They said in California
> that money grew on trees,
> that everyone was going there,
> just like a swarm of bees.

State tourist agencies encouraged such illusions. California was the place to come for a grand vacation of sun and fun. The Hollywood film industry portrayed the state as a glamorous alternative to the dark urban settings it used for films about social problems and crime.

But precisely because California officials feared that destitute job seekers would overrun their state, they repeatedly sought to dispel such fantasies, sending word that conditions in California were desperate. More than one migrant family must have thought twice about the journey after seeing a billboard along Route 66 near Tulsa announced in bold letters:

> NO JOBS in California.
> If you are looking for work—KEEP OUT
> 6 men for every job
> No State Relief available for Non-residents

Neither the dire warnings nor the glamorous tourist brochures were accurate. Although California's economy suffered and unemployment remained serious, the state in the 1930s was much better off than most of the nation. Its farms grew some one hundred different crops, and such diversification made California agriculture less vulnerable to overproduction and falling prices. Other industries also weathered the depression better than most. Industrial workers in California generally received higher hourly wages than did the same workers in other regions. The state economy actually grew during the 1930s. For those unable to find work or who lost jobs, the state had the nation's best relief benefits—$40 per month as opposed to $10 to $12 in the Southwest. All these facts suggest that folks who left the southern plains had reason to pick California as their destination. As one Texan remarked, "Well, if they have lots of work out there and if relief is good, then if I don't find work I'll still be all right."

Furthermore, unlike the Joads, many of the migrants traveling along Route 66 had relatives and friends already living in California. By 1930 more than

400,000 former southwesterners resided in the state, creating a solid base for what demographers call "migration chains." Much like worldwide immigrants to America did, southwesterners wrote home to relatives. Such letters "gits the folks back home to talkin' that work is pretty good in California," explained one Oklahoman, "so they decide to pull up stakes and come." One message made a particularly powerful impression: "Everyone writes back that he's heeled. He's got him a job." Equally important, relatives offered newly arrived migrants a place to stay and help in getting started. During the 1920s and 1930s, entire communities of Okies and Arkies (migrants from Arkansas) sprang up in California's agricultural valleys. Unlike the Joads, more than half of the Dust Bowl migrants left for California with a destination in mind.

Novelists and reporters dramatized the hardships of the road because it made a good story; indeed, much of *The Grapes of Wrath* fits the popular literary genre of a "road novel." Just as Huck Finn's character deepened as he and the runaway slave Jim floated down the broad Mississippi, so the Joads were transformed by their trials along Route 66. But as one historian observed, Steinbeck wrote in tones "more justly reserved for the era of covered wagons." By the 1930s good highways, bus routes, and railroads linked the southwestern plains to California. A family with a decent car could make the trip in about three or four days.

## CALIFORNIA

About 150 miles after crossing the state line, Route 66 entered the town of Barstow, California. There, travelers faced a significant choice. Should they follow the highway as it veered south into the sprawling city of Los Angeles? Or should they take the smaller road out of Barstow, not entirely paved, that wound through the Tehachapi Mountains and into the San Joaquin Valley? The decision was a fateful one.

The Joads chose the route to the valley. But as you may have suspected (based on the census data we have already reviewed), most southwestern migrants did not. The majority hailed from urban areas, and during the years 1935 to 1940 at least, nearly 70 percent chose to make their residence in urban California. That figure is somewhat misleading because, as we shall see, many agricultural laborers settled in cities and migrated to various farm jobs from season to season. Still, Los Angeles remained the most popular destination for southwesterners, attracting more than one-third of all migrants.

Only 28 percent of the Dust Bowl's refugees found their way, like the Joads, to the San Joaquin Valley. Most of those who did harbored the same dreams that had inspired so many Americans throughout the nineteenth century: to take possession of their own family farms. California, after all, boasted plenty of cotton fields, just like back home. Migrants assumed they could work in the fields at a living wage until they could save enough to purchase some land. It was the same pattern of hope that had sent many of their forebears to the Southwest. But California surprised them.

The sights greeting newcomers to the San Joaquin Valley were both tantalizing and troubling. As the Joads roll down the highway, Pa stares at the countryside transfixed: "I never knowed they was anything like her." Before him lie the "peach trees and the walnut groves, and the dark green patches of oranges." Just the look of the place struck *"Where are the farmhouses?"* migrants as somehow vaster and stranger than the plains they left behind. And something else seemed odd. Amidst the broad fields and orchards spreading for miles and miles, migrants saw few signs of the agrarian kingdom of small farms they were expecting. "Where are the farmers?" one newcomer asks. And even more puzzling: "Where are the farmhouses?"

To be sure, farms had hardly vanished from the landscape. In 1929 some 90 percent of California's 135,000 farms produced crops valued at less than $30,000 a year. Thirty percent had crops worth less than $1,000. But those smaller farmers lacked political or economic clout. Of all American farms producing crops worth more than $30,000 a year, more than one-third lay in California. Thus large corporations and landowners dominated the state's agriculture. Some crops, including citrus fruits and raisins, were organized into centrally controlled marketing cooperatives. (Sunkist was one such example.) Cotton, the crop Okies knew best, was a bit less organized. Even so, just four companies ginned two-thirds of the cotton, and a web of corporate farms, banks, and the San Joaquin Valley Agricultural Bureau kept a tight rein on production levels and labor costs. In fact, California only permitted farmers to grow one kind of high-quality cotton.

Most migrants coming into the valley had little time to think of buying land; they faced the more pressing task of simply surviving. Like the Joads, most timed their arrival in California for September, the beginning of the cotton harvest. Growers estimated that a good worker might earn $3 to $4 a day, about twice the wage in the Southwest. But agricultural employment in cotton virtually ceased between December and March. That was the rainy season, when temperatures, though milder than back home, often dipped into the thirties. Some lucky families found shelter in labor camps. A few landowners allowed migrants to stay on in one-room shacks. More often, home was a squatter village of tents, old cars, and shanties made from wood scraps. Under conditions of poverty and malnutrition, disease spread quickly, especially among the old and young. This was the scene that Dorothea Lange discovered when she photographed her "Migrant Mother."

So *The Grapes of Wrath* remains closest to history when Steinbeck describes the plight of the Joads during 1937–1938, the worst and wettest California winter of the era. In 1937, when the Roosevelt administration cut back on spending in the belief that the nation was on its way to recovery, the economy collapsed. Unemployment returned to levels much like those before the New Deal. Not surprisingly, migration reached a peak that year. And then the rains came. Floods, as Steinbeck depicted, wiped out entire squatter camps, often leaving the residents homeless. The situation became so desperate that private charities and government agencies finally swung into action—just as Lange and Steinbeck had hoped. The FSA offered medical care and relief to families who could not meet California's one-year residency requirement for public assistance.

After that winter, the worst was over. Within two years the rains returned to the plains, while World War II brought back prosperity and a virtual end to unemployment. No longer did migrants face the same struggle for survival that the Joads experienced in California.

# THE OTHER MIGRANTS

The collective portrait of the Okies, drawn by Gregory and other historians, demonstrates the strengths of Steinbeck's searing novel as well as its limitations. In effect, the census and other numerical data serve as a framework, within which we can set not only Steinbeck's specific tale but also the newspaper reports, photographs, contemporary sociological studies, and oral recollections that have been left behind in the historical record. The structure of the numbers allows us to give Steinbeck and the other evidence its proper due without mistaking a part for the whole.

In the same way, the discipline of the numbers is also invaluable for placing the newly arrived Okies within their larger California context. Because Steinbeck's tale focuses on the Okies alone, historians have come to appreciate that the tale is inevitably partial in the picture it gives of California's agricultural labor force. Another set of numbers makes the point. In 1930 that labor force was 43 percent white, 21 percent Mexican, 17 percent European, 8 percent Filipino, and 7 percent Japanese.

That multicultural influence is mirrored by another data set, this one illustrating the wide diversity of crops grown in the San Joaquin Valley. The map on page 303 shows not only cotton but also grapes, potatoes, peaches, plums, olives, figs, oranges, rice, beans, cherries, tomatoes, and so on. Small wonder Pa Joad was taken aback. And the diversity of both the agriculture and its labor force are related. Americans today take for granted the variety of California produce. But these crops are hardly "natural." Most were not raised by the original Spanish settlers, nor were they the choice of Anglo newcomers from the East during the mid-nineteenth century, whose preference was to plant familiar crops like wheat. The diversity of California agriculture arose only in the late nineteenth century—at the same time that its labor force was becoming increasingly diverse.

To begin with, the Chinese who arrived in the wake of the 1848 gold rush played a vital part in introducing fruit orchards. Many Chinese immigrants who had once farmed along the Pearl and Yellow Rivers turned their energies in America to constructing irrigation channels, dikes, and levies in the delta regions of the San Joaquin and Sacramento Rivers. Swampy land that sold for only $28 an acre in 1875 was soon being snapped up at $100 an acre. The Chinese also brought valuable horticultural experience in growing orchard and garden crops. One immigrant to the United States, Ah Bing,

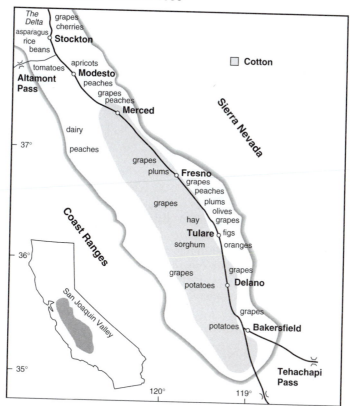

**SAN JOAQUIN VALLEY 1930**

**A rich array of fruits and vegetables** grow in California's San Joaquin Valley. Such variety reduced the impact of the Depression on the state's agricultural economy and helps explain why the valley became a destination for families like the Joads. (From *American Exodus: The Dust Bowl Migration and Okie Culture in California* by James N. Gregory. Copyright © 1991 by James N. Gregory. Used by permission of Oxford University Press, Inc.)

bred the renowned Bing cherry; in Florida, Lue Gim Gong developed a frost-resistant orange.

Anti-Asian nativism, especially strong in California, led Congress to pass the Chinese Exclusion Act, banning the entry of Chinese laborers after 1882. Nevertheless, increasing numbers of Japanese immigrants continued the transformation of California agriculture, especially after 1900. By 1910 Japanese farmers were producing 70 percent of California's strawberries. By 1940 they grew 95 percent of its snap beans as well as spring and summer celery, and they actively cultivated a host of other crops. As Colonel John Irish, president of the California Delta Association, commented in 1921, Californians

**Mexican farmworkers** organized a number of major labor actions against California's growers. Such action is one reason the growers were so willing to replace them with southwestern migrants. The Dust Bowl migrants had no similar tradition of labor activism and community organization. The Mexican women on this truck were making an appeal to strikebreakers to join their strike.

had seen the Japanese convert the barren land like that at Florin and Livingston into productive and profitable fields, orchards and vineyards, by the persistence and intelligence of their industry. They had seen the hardpan and goose lands in the Sacramento Valley, gray and black with our two destructive alkalis, cursed with barrenness like the fig tree of Bethany, and not worth paying taxes on, until Ikuta [a Japanese immigrant] decided that those lands would raise rice. After years of persistent toil, and enduring heartbreaking losses and disappointments, he conquered that rebellious soil and raised the first commercial crop of rice in California.

The restrictive immigration acts of the 1920s, however, once again reshaped California's labor pool, drastically limiting the inflow of workers from most nations and banning Asian immigration entirely. No longer could Californians find European or Japanese immigrants to tend their fields. Facing a labor shortage, they turned to Mexicans and, to a lesser extent, to Filipinos, who were still allowed entry because the Philippines was a U.S. territory.

A look at the numbers and background of Mexican laborers dispels a stereotype similar to the one we have already rejected about southwestern migrants. Most Mexicans who labored in California in 1930 were hardly simple peasants straight from the Mexican countryside. More often they were laborers possessing a variety of skills, whose migration resulted from the industrialization spreading through Mexico after the 1890s. For example, Braulio López, a worker who picked cotton in the San Joaquin Valley, had worked on the Mexican railroad before coming north. In the United States López had also

**The faded Spanish** on the older sign to the left offers mute testimony to the shift from Mexican to southwestern migrants in California agriculture. Notice that the Hotchkiss Ranch has been able to expand production of cotton despite the Depression (from 10,000 to 15,000 acres in cultivation and from 3,000 to 10,000 acres in cotton). The glowing description on the signs is a far cry from the actual conditions under which most migrants lived and worked.

worked as a miner, laid tracks for the streetcar in Los Angeles, and worked on road construction between Los Angeles and San Diego.

This pattern of varied labor was common among both Mexicans and Filipinos. Although many workers called Los Angeles or some other city their home, they moved seasonally to jobs they knew they could count on. "You start out the year, January," one Filipino laborer recalled, "you'd find a place and it was usually an asparagus camp. . . . From asparagus season, we would migrate to Fairfield, to Suisin and there the men worked out in the orchards picking fruits while the women and even children, as long as they could stand on their boxes, worked cutting fruits." Historian Devra Weber has argued that these more regular patterns of migration became a source of stability in a chaotic labor regime by providing a combination of jobs that allowed families to make ends meet.

Now that we are aware of these patterns of agricultural labor, we can place the Okies' arrival in context. In doing so, it becomes evident that not one but two large migrations were going on during the 1930s. Over the decade, as we have seen, as many as 400,000 southwesterners came to the state. During that same period, however, anywhere from half a million to a million Mexicans returned to Mexico from the United States. (Exact figures for migration in and out of Mexico are difficult to obtain.) With the coming of the Depression and scarce employment, many local governments either encouraged or coerced Mexican laborers into leaving the country. Many laborers who were forced out had been born in the United States and thus were legal citizens. "My father left his best years of his life in this country because he worked hard in the mines and in the fields," recalled one San Joaquin Valley resident, "and when hard times came around, we were expendable, to be thrown like cattle out of this country."

These odysseys were as wrenching as those of the Okies, and very similar. Life was "muy dura," recalled Lillie Gasca-Cuéllar—very hard.

> Sufrió uno mucho. Mucho trabajo. No teníamos estufa. No teníamos camas. Dormíamos no más con cartónes, no teníamos casa—y a veces en las calles durmiéndonos.
>
> [We suffered a lot. Lots of work. We didn't have a stove. We didn't have beds. We had only cartons to sleep on, we didn't have a house—and at times we slept in the streets.]

By 1940, whites constituted 76 percent of the workforce in the San Joaquin Valley, an area that formerly had been a stronghold of Mexican labor. Of those white workers, half were southwestern migrants.

As we have seen, the Okie migration was unusual in that it consisted more often of families than of single individuals. Even so, the newcomers in the 1930s lacked the extensive network of family and community connections built up by Mexican families during the previous two decades. Those southwesterners who already had family in California adapted best. But other newcomers could not anticipate the harvest schedules of crops they had never grown, so that they sometimes arrived at picking fields early, losing precious time, or came too late, when there was no work to be had. Furthermore, the picking style for California cotton proved different from that of the plains. Jessie de la Cruz, an experienced Mexican picker, noticed that some Texans in her field "weren't used to this kind of picking. . . . It had to be clean, no leaves, you had to leave nothing but the stalk." The newcomers picked forty-five pounds to her hundred. Such difficulties compounded the problems faced by newcomers like the Joads.

In theory, southwestern migrants might have made common cause with Mexican and Filipino laborers to strike for better wages and working

**California had both ladder crops**—tree fruit that workers climbed to pick—and stoop crops—those that required long hours of painful bending and squatting to pick. Growers of stoop crops generally preferred Filipino and other Asian American workers because those workers had conditioned themselves to the painful positions involved. Such conditioning did not mean they did not suffer greatly from the physical demands of the work.

conditions. As migrants poured into the San Joaquin Valley, established local residents treated them with increasingly open hostility. *The Grapes of Wrath* portrays the comments of a service station attendant at Needles, California: "Them Okies got no sense and no feelings. They ain't human. A human being wouldn't live like they do. A human being couldn't stand it to be so dirty and so miserable. They ain't a hell of a lot better than gorillas." Other journalists and investigators reported similar prejudices. "You take some of these guys," complained a California grower, "and give them the best land in the Garden of Eden and they'd starve to death."

But cultural prejudices made cooperation between ethnic groups difficult. Okies often found California's ethnic and racial diversity threatening. Compared to the southwest plains, California simply had too many "foreigners." As one Okie put it, "the farmers ain't got no business hirin' them fer low wages when we native white American citizens are starvin'." At an FSA labor camp in Arvin, California, migrants from Texas objected when a Mexican family moved in. "Remember the Alamo! Either us or them," they told the camp manager. "Can't have both of us here."

The competition for jobs intensified resentments. Some Okies found it degrading to pick for Italian and Japanese growers or to find work through Hispanic labor contractors—*contratistas.* There were certain kinds of farmwork the Okies could not or would not do. Vegetables like asparagus required them "to squat and walk, like a Mexican," which most could not. Mexicans and Asians did the more backbreaking work associated with ground crops like vegetables and potatoes. "White men can't do the work as well as these short men who can get down on their hands and knees, or work all day long stooping over," commented a California newspaper editor in 1930, and his sentiments were echoed by a Japanese farmer, who applied the same prejudice to the Filipino workers he hired. "The Fils do all the stoop labor. They are small and work fast." As might be expected, such judgments were not shared by the workers themselves. "Many people think that we don't suffer from stoop labor, but we do," remarked one Filipino.

In the end, the oversupply of labor drove wages down, making life worse for Okie, Mexican, Filipino, and Japanese laborers alike. The census shows that with the influx of southwestern migrants, the income for all workers fell. Even so, the Okies earned more than the minorities they displaced. Once again the census provides key evidence. In 1940 southwesterner families who arrived in the valley before 1935 had average annual incomes of $1,070. Those who arrived between 1935 and 1940 averaged $650, while other white Californians received $1,510. Those Mexican families who had not returned to their homeland earned just $555 a year and usually found even New Deal relief programs beyond their reach. California law barred alien Mexicans from public work projects, and local rules also kept many Mexicans, even those who were American citizens, from WPA jobs.

In short, the structure and dynamics of agricultural labor in California were far more complex than *The Grapes of Wrath* could suggest within the tale of a single family's tribulations. Why did Steinbeck ignore the darker sides of that complexity? The answer is perhaps not so difficult to understand. Instinctively, he viewed the Okies as victims, not victimizers. From his perspective, the real tragedy of the farm crisis of the 1930s was the destruction of Jeffersonian agrarian ideals. Steinbeck wanted the government to give the Joads more than a handout; he advocated a second revolution that would recreate an America of small farmers rooted in the land. He failed to acknowledge that the ideals he cherished too often applied only to white Americans and, in any case, had become increasingly irrelevant to the kind of industrial agriculture that was transforming America.

In the seven decades since the dust storms swept across the southwestern plains, the United States has been transformed by a civil rights revolution. It has been reminded, too, of its diversity, by the renewed tide of immigration springing up in the wake of the Immigration Reform Act of 1964. Historians have worked to give voice to that diversity. In doing so, they have drawn not only on statistics but folk songs, photographs, anecdotes, and observations from ordinary people like the Turners, the Garretsons, and Lillie Gasca-Cuéllar. Among this abundance of evidence, the impersonal numbers of the census may have seemed, at first blush, the most lifeless of voices. But in the aggregate, the mass of their ones and zeros provides the structure that gives a collective portrait weight and balance. And with proper study, the tales those numbers tell can prove to be nearly as gripping as those of a novel.

# *Additional Reading*

Because the narrative in this chapter begins with "dust," interested readers might well begin with Donald Worster, *The Dust Bowl: The Southern Plains in the 1930s* (New York, 1979). For an idiosyncratic view, Worster would direct readers to James Malin, *The Grasslands of North America* (New York, 1956). John Steinbeck actually began *The Grapes of Wrath* (New York, 1939) as a series of articles for the *San Francisco News* and published them as *Their Blood Is Strong* (New York, 1938). A similar study that historians find valuable is Carey McWilliams, *Factories in the Fields* (Boston, 1939). On "Migrant Mother" we recommend Dorothea Lange and Paul Schuster Taylor, *An American Exodus: A Record of Human Erosion* (New York, 1939). That book may be hard to find, but Lange and her work are the subject of Milton Meltzer, *Dorothea Lange: A Photographer's Life* (New York, 1978). Dorothea Lange, *Photographs of a Lifetime* (New York, 1996), is a recent reprint with much of her work. The story of "Migrant Mother," *The Grapes of Wrath* as both novel and movie, and other aspects of the Dust Bowl in American cultural memory are wonderfully told and illustrated in Charles J. Shindo, *Dust Bowl Migrants in the American Imagination* (Lawrence, KS, 1997). Many of Lange's photographs, including "Migrant Mother 6," are available online through the Library of Congress at its American Memory site: http://memory.loc.gov.

The work of two historians has contributed heavily to this essay. James Gregory, *American Exodus: The Dust Bowl Migration and Okie Culture in California* (New York, 1989), not only conceptualizes the problem of collective history, he also models the way in which quantitative analysis and anecdotal narrative interact to produce history that is both informative and easy to read. In that same spirit, Devra Weber, *Dark Sweat, White Gold: California Farm Workers, Cotton, and the New Deal* (Berkeley, 1994), has captured the migrant farmworkers' experience with special attention to Mexicans. The footnotes from these many sources inevitably lead back to the U.S. Bureau of the Census, *Historical Statistics of the United States, Colonial Times to 1970*, 2 vols. (Washington, DC, 1975), which is supplemented annually. Internet users can access the Census Bureau at http://www.census.gov.

# CHAPTER 13

# The Decision to Drop the Bomb

*President Harry Truman claimed he gave the order to drop the atom bomb in order to end the war with Japan quickly. Many historians wonder if that is the whole story.*

Just before dawn on July 16, 1945, a few clouds hung over the still New Mexico desert. To the anxious observers in the blockhouse, several large towers on the horizon appeared as little more than spikes stuck in the sand.

Suddenly, from one of the towers a brilliant fireball erupted, searing the air and instantly replacing the dawn's pastels with a blazing radiance. With the radiance came heat—an incredible, scorching heat that rolled outward in waves. Where seconds before the sand had stretched cool and level in every direction, now it fused into glass pellets. The concussion from the fireball completely vaporized the tower at its center, created a crater a quarter of a mile wide, and obliterated another forty-ton steel tower one-half mile away. Above the fireball an ominous cloud formed, shooting upward, outward, then back upon itself to form the shape of a mushroom, expanding until it had reached 8 miles in the air. The effects of the fireball continued outward from its center: the light, followed by the waves of heat, and then the deadening roar of the concussion, sharp enough to break a window more than 125 miles away. Light, heat, concussion—but first and foremost, the brilliance of the light. At the edge of the desert a blind woman was facing the explosion. She saw the light.

In the blockhouse at Alamogordo, where scientists watched, feelings of joy and relief were mixed with foreboding. The bomb had worked. Theory had been turned into practice. And devastating as the explosion appeared, the resulting fireball had not ignited the earth's atmosphere, as some scientists had predicted. But the foreboding was impossible to shake. Humankind now had in its hands unprecedented power to destroy.

General Leslie R. Groves, director of the atom bomb project, shared none of the scientists' fears. Groves could barely contain his joy when he wired the news to President Harry Truman, who was meeting allied leaders at Potsdam outside the conquered city of Berlin. "The test was successful beyond the most optimistic expectations of anyone," reported Groves. Buoyed by the message, Truman returned to the conference a changed man. British Prime Minister Winston

**At 0815 hours August 6, 1945,** the bomber Enola Gay and its flight crew received weather clearance and proceeded toward Hiroshima. An hour later, flying at 328 miles per hour, it dropped its bomb directly over the city, from 31,000 feet. It then turned and dove sharply in order to gain speed. The bomb detonated at about 2,000 feet above Hiroshima in order to increase the effective radius of its blast; the resulting cloud, photographed by a nearby observation plane, reached 50,000 feet into the air and was visible for 390 miles. The final statistic: approximately 100,000 people killed and thousands dying from radiation poisoning.

Churchill noticed the president's sudden self-confidence. "He stood up to the Russians in a most decisive and emphatic manner," Churchill remarked. "He told the Russians just where they got on and got off and generally bossed the whole meeting." Since the British were partners on the bomb project, Churchill understood why Truman suddenly seemed so confident.

Less than three weeks later, on August 6, 1945, a second mushroom cloud rose, this time above Hiroshima, Japan. That explosion destroyed an entire city; it left almost 100,000 people dead and thousands more dying from radiation poisoning. Three days later another bomb leveled the city of Nagasaki. Only then did World War II come to an end, the bloodiest and costliest war in history. Ever since, the world has lived with the stark prospect that in anger or in error, some person, group, or government might again unleash the horror of atomic war.

The New Mexico test of the first atom bomb marked the successful conclusion of the Manhattan Project, the code name for one of the largest scientific and industrial efforts ever undertaken. Between 1941 and 1945 the United States spent more than $2 billion to build three atom bombs. Twenty years earlier that amount would have equaled the entire federal budget. The project required some thirty-seven factories and laboratories in nineteen states and Canada, employed more than 120,000 people, and monopolized many of the nation's top scientists and engineers during a period when their skills were considered essential to national survival. Leading universities, as well as some of the nation's largest corporations—DuPont, Eastman Kodak, and General Electric—devoted substantial resources to the undertaking.

The Manhattan Project marked the trend in modern industrial society for physicists and other scientists to conduct their work within large organizations. For much of the nineteenth century, scientists, like artists, worked alone or in small groups, using relatively simple equipment. Thomas Edison, however, led the way toward rationalized, business-oriented research and development, establishing his own "scientific" factory at Menlo Park, New Jersey, in 1876. Like a manufacturer, Edison subdivided research tasks among inventors, engineers, and toolmakers. By the first decades of the twentieth century, Westinghouse, DuPont, U.S. Rubber, and other major corporations had set up their own industrial labs.

Then, too, World War I demonstrated that organized, well-funded science could be vital to national security. During the war, scientists joined in large research projects to develop new explosives, poison gases, optical glass for lenses, airplane instruments, and submarine-detection devices. In less than two years, physicists and electrical engineers had doubled the advances of radio technology over the previous ten years. The government, for the first time, funded research on a large scale.

*World War I demonstrated that organized, well-funded science could be vital to national security.*

But scientists were as much committed to the notion of laissez-faire as any conservative robber baron. They were suspicious of any "scheme in which any small group of men, appointed as a branch of the government, attempt to dominate and control the research of the country," as one scientist put it.

The end of the war halted government direction and financial support. Still, like most Americans, scientists shared in the prosperity of the 1920s. Economic boom meant increases in research budgets. Success in the laboratory attracted contributions from private foundations and wealthy individuals. American science began to produce both theoretical and applied results that rivaled the quality of science in Europe.

The Depression of the 1930s forced researchers to tighten their belts and lower their expectations. The government, though seldom an important source of funding, drastically cut the budgets for its scientific bureaus. Even when the New Deal created jobs for scientists, it did so primarily to stimulate employment, not research. But by the late 1930s private foundations had resumed earlier levels of support. One of their most prominent beneficiaries was Ernest Lawrence, a physicist with a flair for showmanship who had established himself as the most famous, most funded, and most bureaucratically organized scientist in the United States. During the 1930s Lawrence built what he called a cyclotron, a machine designed to accelerate atomic particles in a focused beam in order to penetrate the nucleus's shell and unravel its structure and dynamics. By 1939 his Radiation Lab at the University of California at Berkeley was raising the unprecedented sum of $1.5 million to build an enormous, 100-million-volt cyclotron.

The movement of science toward organization and bureaucracy reflected similar forces at work elsewhere in American society. As Lawrence expanded his laboratory at Berkeley, the New Deal was establishing new regulatory agencies, social welfare programs, and other government organizations that reached into many areas of daily life. Furthermore, much that the New Deal instituted through government and politics in the 1930s, large corporations had accomplished in the preceding era. Centralized slaughterhouses, with their elaborate distribution system involving railroads, refrigerated warehouses, and trucks, replaced the local butcher as the source of meat for many American tables. What Armour and Swift did for meatpacking, Heinz did for the pickle, Henry Ford for the automobile, and other corporations for the multitude of food, clothing, and goods used in American homes and industry. To understand the nature of the modern era, to grasp an undertaking as vast as the making of an atomic bomb or a decision as complex as how to use it, historians must understand how large organizations work.

## MODELS OF DECISION MAKING

"Truman dropped the atom bomb in order to win the war as quickly as possible." Historians routinely use such convenient shorthand in their historical narratives. Yet physically, of course, Truman was nowhere near Japan or the bomb when it was dropped. He was halfway around the world, returning from the Potsdam Conference with Stalin and Churchill. The actual sequence of events was rather more complicated. President Truman did give an order. It passed through the Pentagon to an airbase on the island of Tinian in the western Pacific. The base commander ordered a specially trained crew to arm an American airplane with a single atom bomb, designed and built by scientists and technicians under the authority of the War Department. The pilot of the plane then followed an order, conveyed through the military chain of command, to proceed to a target in Japan, selected by the secretary of war in consultation with his military advisers, in order to destroy a Japanese city and thereby hasten the end of the war.

The difference in meaning between "Truman dropped the atom bomb" and what actually happened encapsulates the dilemma of a historian trying to portray the workings of a systematized, bureaucratic modern society. The first explanation is coherent, clear, and human. It accords with Harry Truman's own well-known maxim "The buck stops here"—implying that the important, truly difficult decisions were his and his alone. The second explanation is cumbersome and confusing, but more comprehensive and descriptive. It reflects the fact that the president stood at the tip of a pyramid of advisers, agencies, bureaus, offices, and committees, all going about their own business. And such organizations create their own characteristic ways of gathering information, planning, working, and acting. To a large extent, what Truman decided or did not decide depended on what he learned from those organizations. To that extent also, the shorthand "Truman dropped the atom bomb" conceals as much as it reveals.

*Harry Truman's own well-known maxim "The buck stops here"—implied that the important, truly difficult decisions were his and his alone.*

To better analyze the workings of organizations, historians have borrowed a technique from the social sciences. They work with interpretive models. For many people, the term *model* might bring to mind an object like a small plastic airplane or an electric train. For social scientists, a model, not unlike the small plane, reduces the scale of reality and increases the researchers' capacity to describe the characteristics of what they observe. Models can be applied to systems as basic as individual behavior or as grand as the world's climate. If the average daily temperature goes up, will we have more or less rain? If the amount of carbon dioxide in the atmosphere increases, will temperatures rise? A computer model of weather patterns allows meteorologists to test the relationship between such variables in the climate. Even so, the number of variables is so great that meteorologists are forced to speak of probabilities, not certainties. While their model provides insights into several components of a weather system, it inevitably simplifies as well. In that sense models, too, have limits.

The phrase "Truman dropped the atom bomb" typifies the application of what some social scientists have called a "rational actor" model. This interpretive framework may be what historians most often adopt without even thinking about models. Rational actor theory treats the actions of governments and large organizations as the acts of individuals. Further, it assumes that the individual actor, like Adam Smith's capitalist, behaves rationally in that he or she uses the most efficient means to pursue ends that are in his or her self-interest. When forced to choose among a range of possible actions, government leaders will select the option that achieves the best result at the lowest cost. One does not use a bat to swat a fly, nor would a government go to war to collect a small debt, unless war served some larger purpose.

The appeal of this model lies in its predictive powers. Often enough, governments do not make clear why they act. On other occasions, they announce their goals but keep their strategies for achieving them secret. By applying standards of rational behavior, an analyst can make inductive leaps about a government's unclear goals or hidden actions. If we know that a government has suddenly ordered highly mobile assault troops to the borders of its nation but we lack evidence about its goals, we might still conclude that a rational actor would not use mobile assault troops merely to defend borders: an invasion is planned. The process works in reverse as well. If analysts know what goals a nation has at hand, they can guess with some confidence what its leaders might do in a situation, given their resources.

Franklin Roosevelt's decision to launch the Manhattan Project presents historians with an example of how rational actor analysis can help reveal motivations and goals. Roosevelt was not an easy person to read—either for his advisers or for historians. Often enough, his orders to different people seemed contradictory. Or he would encourage competing bureaucracies to implement the same policy. In setting in motion the bomb project, Roosevelt left little evidence about why he made his decision. But the rational actor model suggests that Roosevelt recognized the military potential of nuclear fission; calculated that the United States had the financial, industrial, and scientific resources needed; and concluded that the nation's security demanded full-scale research and development.

The available evidence does support that conclusion. The Manhattan Project owed its beginnings to several physicists, primarily refugees from fascist Germany and Italy who feared that recent atomic research would allow the Nazis to develop a weapon of unparalleled destructive force. In March 1939 Enrico Fermi, a Nobel Prize–winning physicist who had fled from Mussolini's Italy, paid his own way to Washington to warn the military. Fermi himself had been on the verge of discovering fission reactions in 1934 but had not then recognized the meaning of his results. If he had, the fascist powers might have applied his results to military use. Although Fermi had become an American citizen and a faculty member at Columbia University, navy technical experts ignored his warning. Other refugee physicists, led by Leo Szilard, joined the campaign. Szilard persuaded Albert Einstein, the world's most admired scientist, to lend his name to a letter explaining their concern to President Roosevelt. Alexander Sachs, an economic adviser to the president, acted as their emissary. After Roosevelt read the letter and heard Sachs out, he remarked, "Alex, what you are after is to see they don't blow us up."

The president took immediate action, but he did not yet set in motion a massive research project. That step would have been irrational, for as Sachs had made clear, the scientists had not yet found a way to harness the power of fission for war. Instead, Roosevelt merely created a Uranium Committee to promote American nuclear research. The project got under way slowly, for the committee requested only $6,000 for its first year of operations. Other, more promising experimental efforts competed for funds that were particularly scarce since the United States was not yet at war.

In England, however, two German emigrés developed an understanding of how a "superbomb" might work. Scientists Otto Frisch and Rudolph Peierls determined that the fast neutrons needed to set off an explosive chain reaction could be produced with either plutonium or uranium 235, a fissionable isotope that could be separated from uranium 238. They also suggested ways to separate uranium 235 from uranium 238. The amount of fissionable material needed would be small enough to fit into a bomb that existing aircraft could carry. Such a bomb, Frisch and Peierls calculated, could probably be built within two years. What was more frightening, German physicists were known to have made similar discoveries. Allied scientists feared the Germans might be as much as two years ahead in the race to build a bomb.

When the British passed this information along to the American administrators supervising war research, the head of the National Defense Research Committee (NDRC), Vannevar Bush, immediately brought the news to Roosevelt in June 1941. "If such an explosive were made," Bush told the president, "it would be thousands of times more powerful than existing explosives, and its use might be determining." The British research had given the rational actor—in this case President Roosevelt—cause to commit the United States to a larger project. To accelerate the research effort, Roosevelt replaced the ineffective Uranium Committee with a group called S-1. The membership of the committee reflected the new priority of the bomb project. It included Bush, now head of the Office of Scientific Research and Development; his successor at NDRC, James Conant (the president of Harvard University); Vice President Henry Wallace; Secretary of War Henry Stimson; and Chief of Staff General George Marshall. Bush and Conant assumed primary responsibility for overseeing the project and keeping the president informed. In September 1942 General Leslie Groves, who supervised construction of the Pentagon, assumed command over the construction and operation of the rapidly expanding facilities that were named the Manhattan Project.

For three years, American, British, and emigré scientists raced against time and what they feared was an insurmountable German lead. At first, research focused on the work of scientists at the Chicago Metallurgical Laboratory (another code name). There, on a squash court under the old University of Chicago football stadium, Fermi and his associates achieved the first self-sustaining chain reaction. The next goal was the separation of enough pure uranium 235 or sufficient plutonium to build a bomb. That goal required the construction of huge plants—an expense that now seemed rational, in light of the work at Chicago. Conant authorized Groves to begin building facilities at Oak Ridge, Tennessee, and Hanford, Washington.

Actual design of the bomb took place at a remote mountain site near Los Alamos, New Mexico. Los Alamos was the choice of physicist Robert Oppenheimer. As director of the design laboratory, Oppenheimer sought a

**J. Robert Oppenheimer** directed the construction, completion, and testing of the first atomic bomb at a remote desert site near Los Alamos, New Mexico. He was an intense, introspective man and a chain-smoker early in his career; he confessed he found it nearly impossible to think without a cigarette in his hand. The burden of the Manhattan Project took its toll on him: the chain-smoking commenced again, and his weight, normally only 130 pounds, dropped to 116.

place to isolate the most outstanding collection of experimental and theoretical physicists, mathematicians, chemists, and engineers ever assembled. Free from the intrusions of the press and inquisitive colleagues, world-renowned scientists rubbed elbows with brilliant, eager young graduate students, all applying the abstract theories of physics to the question of how to produce an atomic weapon.

By the summer of 1944 the race with the Nazis had ended. Spies discovered that German physicists had long since given up hope of building a bomb. As Allied forces marched into Berlin in April 1945, scientists knew that peace would come to Europe before the bomb was ready. The war against Japan, however, had grown more ferocious. Fearing heavy American casualties during an invasion of Japan's home islands, President Roosevelt had asked Stalin to enter the Pacific war. Yet as the tide of battle began to favor the Allies, the president became more reluctant to draw the Soviets into Japan. If the bomb could win the war for the United States, all the sacrifices of time, personnel, and materials would not have been in vain. Oppenheimer, Groves, and the Manhattan Project scientists redoubled their efforts to produce a working bomb.

Thus the rational actor model explains adequately the progression of events that brought about the bomb's development: (1) physicists saw the potential of nuclear fission and warned the president; (2) Roosevelt ordered a speedup in research; (3) scientific breakthroughs led to greater certainty of eventual success, causing the president to give bomb research top priority; (4) the race with Germany, and then Japanese resistance in the Far East, encouraged scientists to push toward success.

Although this outline of key decisions proceeds logically enough, there are troubling features to it, suggesting limits to the rational actor model. Certainly Roosevelt could be viewed as the rational actor. But we have already seen that a host of committees and subgroups were involved in the process. And the model becomes murkier when we seek answers to a number of controversial questions surrounding the decision actually to use the bomb. Did the military situation in the summer of 1945 justify launch-

*Who did the United States really want to shock with its atomic bomb? Japan or the Soviet Union?*

ing the attacks without warning Japan? Could a nonmilitary demonstration of the bomb's power have persuaded the Japanese to surrender without immense loss of life? Why drop a second bomb on Japan so soon after the first? And finally, who did the United States really want to shock with its atomic might—Japan or the Soviet Union?

To be sure, rational actor analysis provides answers to these questions. The problem is, it provides too many. Historians have offered contradictory answers to the way a rational actor might have been expected to behave under the circumstances. To begin with, what was the most crucial problem to be solved by a rational actor in that summer of 1945? On the one hand, convincing Japan to surrender was the primary goal of the war—something the use of atomic bombs would be expected to hasten. On the other hand, military and diplomatic planners had already begun to focus on the transition from war to peace. Increasingly, they worried about the postwar conduct of the Soviet Union. Following the surrenders of Italy and Germany, the Russians had begun consolidating control over Eastern Europe. Many British and American officials feared that Stalin saw victory as a way to extend the global reach of communism. The larger the role assumed by the Soviets in the Pacific, the greater their opportunity for expansion there too.

But what if the bomb were used to end the war before Stalin's troops could make any headway in the Far East? Wasn't it likely Stalin would become more cooperative once he saw the awesome power of such a weapon? That "rational" line of reasoning raises an unsettling possibility. Did the United

States drop the bomb primarily to send a warning to the Soviet Union? So concluded historian Gar Alperovitz, who argued that after Franklin Roosevelt's untimely death in April 1945, President Truman was more concerned with containing the Soviet Union than with defeating Japan.

Alperovitz came to that conclusion by examining the information available to Truman and his advisers in the summer of 1945. That data, he argued, should have convinced Truman (or any rational actor) that the United States had no compelling military reason to drop atomic bombs on Japan. The American navy had already established a tight blockade around Japan, cutting off delivery of raw materials and threatening the Japanese economy with widespread starvation. Allied land-based bombers had leveled whole sections of Tokyo without opposition from Japanese fighters. By July 1945 Japan was ready to consider capitulation, except that in 1943 Roosevelt had laid down uncompromising terms of "unconditional surrender." The Japanese feared that the United States would insist that their emperor leave his throne, a humiliation they wished at all costs to avoid. Their only hope was to negotiate terms of surrender, using the Russians as intermediaries, to obtain a guarantee that the institution of the emperor would be preserved.

Truman knew that the Japanese had made overtures to the Soviet Union. "Unconditional surrender is the only obstacle to peace," the Japanese foreign minister had cabled his emissary in Moscow, in a coded message intercepted by American intelligence. Still, Truman refused to deviate from Roosevelt's policy of unconditional surrender. At the Potsdam Conference, Allied leaders issued a vaguely worded proclamation warning the Japanese that they faced "prompt and utter destruction" if they fought on. Nowhere did the proclamation mention the existence of a new superbomb. Nor did it offer hope that the Allies might permit the Japanese to keep their emperor. When the Japanese ignored the warning, the Americans concluded that Japan had resolved to continue fanatic resistance.

In fact, the emperor himself had taken unprecedented, though cautious, steps to undermine the war party. He had decided that the military extremists must accept surrender on Allied terms. But the bombing of Hiroshima, on August 6, followed two days later by a Russian declaration of war, threw the Japanese government into confusion. Before it could digest this double shock, Nagasaki was leveled on August 9. Even then, the Japanese surrendered only when the United States made an implicit commitment to retain the emperor. Despite Truman's insistence on an "unconditional" surrender, in the end it had been conditional.

Alperovitz's conclusion is sobering. If ending the war had been Truman's only goal, the rational response would have been to give Japan the extra few days or weeks to negotiate a surrender. There would have been no need to drop the bomb. But of course it was dropped. Therefore (so the logic goes) the president's primary goal must have been to intimidate the Soviets. This possibility was one that Alperovitz understandably condemned, for it would have meant that Truman had wantonly incinerated hundreds of thousands of Japanese for reasons that had little to do with the war itself. Furthermore, if Truman had hoped to intimidate the Russians into cooperating, he seriously erred—for the Soviet Union became, if anything, more intractable after Japan's surrender. Failure to achieve a nuclear arms control agreement with Stalin while the United States and Britain had a monopoly on atomic weapons led to a postwar arms race. Possession of the atom bomb resulted finally in a decrease in American security and a loss of moral stature. Those consequences are not the desired results of rational decision making.

Alperovitz's reconstruction of Truman's choices placed most emphasis on the diplomatic effects of dropping the bomb. But were these the factors that weighed most heavily on the minds of Truman and his advisers? Other historians have placed more emphasis on the military circumstances behind the development of the bomb—not only in 1945 but in the years preceding it. In doing so, they have constructed an alternate set of motivations that might have influenced a rational actor.

Franklin Roosevelt was the first president who had to consider whether the bomb would actually be used. And merely by approving the massive effort to build a weapon, there was an implicit assumption on the president's part that it would be used. "At no time," recalled former Secretary of War Stimson, "did I ever hear it suggested by the President, or by any other responsible member of the government, that atomic energy should not be used in the war." Robert Oppenheimer, whose leadership at Los Alamos played a critical role in the success of the project, confirmed Stimson's point about the bombs: "we always assumed if they were needed, they would be used."

In fact, Roosevelt was proceeding a bit more cautiously. He discussed the delicate subject with British Prime Minister Winston Churchill when the two men met at Roosevelt's home in Hyde Park in September 1944. At the end of their private interview, with only the two of them present, they signed a memorandum summarizing their attitudes. Both men agreed that the bomb would be kept a secret from the Russians, an action that made it clear (as Alperovitz contended) that the leaders recognized how valuable a lever the weapon might be in postwar negotiations. As for the war itself, Roosevelt and Churchill agreed that the bomb might be used against Japan after "mature consideration," while warning the Japanese "that this bombardment will be repeated until they surrender."

If Roosevelt had lived, conceivably he might have proved more flexible than Truman. But if he had any serious doubts about using the bomb, they died with him. None of his military and diplomatic advisers were aware of the Hyde Park memorandum. After Roosevelt's death, responsibility for atomic policy shifted largely to Secretary of War Stimson, the cabinet officer in charge of the Manhattan Project. The new president, Truman, knew nothing about the bomb or, for that matter, most other critical diplomatic and military matters. Roosevelt had seldom consulted the vice president or even met with him. Once, while acting as chair of a Senate committee, Truman had stumbled onto information about the vast sums being spent on some unknown project, only to be persuaded by Stimson that secrecy should prevail. As the war approached its end and the new president faced a host of critical decisions, Stimson cautiously introduced him to the bomb. "I mentioned it to you shortly after you took office," the secretary prompted him on April 23, 1945, "but have not urged it since on account of the pressure you have been under. It, however, has such bearing on our present foreign relations . . . I think you ought to know about it without further delay."

To present his case, Stimson prepared a memorandum setting out his two most pressing concerns. He wanted Truman to recognize the monumental importance of the bomb for postwar relations, particularly with the Soviet Union. And he wanted to emphasize the bomb's capacity to shorten the war. Stimson displayed no qualms about using it against Japan and considered no steps to avert a postwar nuclear arms race. But the two men did agree that Stimson should form a committee to formulate further policy options. It would seem that the rational actor was at work: if Truman wanted to weigh all his options, the committee would provide him with a full range from which to choose.

The Interim Committee, as the group was known, met three times. It also created a scientific panel that included Oppenheimer, Fermi, Lawrence, and Arthur Compton (head of the Chicago lab) to advise the committee. During its meetings, it scarcely touched the question of whether to drop the bomb on Japan. "It seemed to be a foregone conclusion that the bomb would be used," Arthur Compton recalled. "It was regarding only the details of strategy and tactics that differing views were expressed." When those issues were debated, some members briefly considered a nonmilitary demonstration in place of a surprise military attack. They asked Oppenheimer how such a demonstration might be prepared. Since the bomb had yet to be tested, Oppenheimer could only estimate its power. He replied that he could not conceive of any demonstration that would have the impact of an attack on a real target of factories and buildings. Furthermore, the committee had to consider what might happen if Japanese representatives were taken to a test site and the mighty atomic "demonstration" fizzled. And if the Japanese were given advance warning about a superbomb, wouldn't that allow them to prepare their defenses or move American prisoners of war to likely bombing targets?

For all those reasons the Interim Committee decided against giving any advance warning. In addition, it made several assumptions about Japan that predetermined its recommendations to the president. First, committee members considered the military leadership of Japan so fanatic that only a profound shock such as an atomic attack would persuade them to surrender. Kamikaze attacks by Japanese pilots, as well as other resistance, continued to claim a heavy toll in American lives. General Douglas MacArthur, who had led the Western Pacific campaign against Japan, discounted the effectiveness of either a naval blockade of the home islands or continued air raids with conventional bombs. Only a full-scale invasion, MacArthur argued, would compel surrender. The army continued to organize an invasion for November 1, anticipating as many as a half million American casualties.*

---

* This casualty figure has become quite controversial. Historian Martin Sherwin has discovered that a number of prominent military figures offered a much lower estimate, which would have made an invasion a more reasonable option.

In any case, by 1945 committee members had become somewhat hardened to the idea of killing enemy soldiers or civilians. Conventional fire-bombing had already proved as horrifying as the atom bomb promised to be. In one incendiary raid, American bombers leveled one-quarter of Tokyo, left 83,000 people dead, and wounded another 40,000. Having lived with the fear that the Germans might use an atom bomb against the United States, committee members had ample reason to see it as a potential weapon against the Japanese. Since it promised to save American lives, the committee sensed that the public would want, even demand, combat use. And finally, though the members were far from agreement, the committee decided that a combat demonstration would facilitate negotiations with the Russians. From those assumptions they reached three conclusions: (1) the bomb should be used as quickly as possible against Japan; (2) to maximize the shock value, the target should be a war plant surrounded by workers' homes; (3) no warning should be given. When Stimson communicated those views to Truman, he included a recommendation that both bombs scheduled for completion by August should be dropped in separate raids, in order to maximize the shock and convince Japanese leaders that further resistance meant certain destruction.

> *By 1945 committee members had become somewhat hardened to the idea of killing enemy soldiers or civilians.*

In only one small but vital way did Truman deviate from the committee's determination of how and why to use the bomb. A group of scientists at the Chicago laboratory, led by Leo Szilard, had become persuaded that combat use of the bomb without warning would lead to a postwar arms race between the Soviets and the Americans. They urged Truman and his advisers to tell the Russians about the bomb and to plan a demonstration before using it in combat. In a concession to Szilard and his colleagues, the Interim Committee recommended that Truman disclose the bomb to Stalin in order to help gain his cooperation after the war. At Potsdam, Truman chose not to discuss the bomb or atomic energy. But he did make an oblique reference to Stalin "that we had a weapon of unusual destructive force." Stalin was equally cryptic in his reply. "He was glad to hear it and hoped we would make 'good use of it' against the Japanese," the president recalled. And so Truman acted.

By retracing the series of decisions made over the entire year preceding the attack on Hiroshima, it becomes clearer that, for Truman, military considerations about how to end the war with a minimum number of casualties remained paramount. Resolution of Soviet-American differences was a secondary goal, though rapidly becoming the administration's chief concern. Using the bomb would also forestall any criticism in Congress for having spent $2 billion on the secret Manhattan Project. Thus the bombing of Hiroshima and Nagasaki appeared to be the optimum way to reach the administration's primary objective, with the additional virtue of promoting secondary goals as well. When applied at the level of presidential decision making, rational actor analysis suggests that the decision to drop the bomb was consistent with perceived American goals.

# A MODEL OF ORGANIZATIONAL PROCESS

Despite those results, the rational actor model exhibits definite limitations. It leads us to focus attention on the policy-making debates of key actors like Roosevelt and Truman, or even on scientists like Szilard and Oppenheimer. But in truth, our narrative of events has involved numerous committees far from the top of the organizational pyramid: the Uranium Committee, S-1, the National Defense Research Council, and the Interim Committee. Roosevelt and Truman relied on the recommendations of those groups in making decisions. Should their participation make any difference to our explanations?

Imagine, for a moment, the government as a kind of giant clock. Rational actor analysis would define the telling of time as the visible movements of the hands controlled by a closed box. Inside are the gears, springs, and levers that move the clock's hands: the bureaucracy supporting decision makers at the top. In the rational actor model, these gears are seen as neutral cogs in the machine, passing along the energy (or in government, the information) that allows the hands to do their highly visible work. But suppose we look at the decision-making process using a model that focuses on the organizational processes themselves. Is there something about their structure or behavior that influences the outcome of decisions made by supposedly rational actors?

Of course, the actions of bureaucracies and agencies are usually less regimented than the movements of a clock. Often enough, the subgroups that make up a government end up working at cross-purposes or pursuing conflicting objectives. While the Surgeon General's office has warned that cigarette smoking is "hazardous to your health," the Department of Agriculture has produced films on the virtues of American tobacco. Perhaps, then, it would be better to envision not a clock but a football team. If we observe a game from the stands, the players can be seen moving in coordinated patterns, in an effort to control the movement of the ball. Rational actor analysis suggests that the coach, or another centralized decision maker like the quarterback, has selected the strategies best suited to winning the game. That larger strategy, in turn, determines the plays that the offense and defense use.

After closer observation, we begin to sense that the play is not as centrally coordinated as we anticipated. Different groups of players move in patterns determined by their positions as well as by the team strategy. We come to understand that the team is made up of subgroups that execute regularly assigned tasks. Linemen block; ends run pass patterns. On each down, the players do not try to think anew of the best imaginable play. Rather, they repeat actions they have been trained to perform. A halfback will generally advance the ball by running and leave the passing to the quarterback. On some plays, we observe that a few players' actions seem inappropriate. A halfback runs when he should be blocking. Whereas the rational actor model might interpret such a move as a purposeful attempt to deceive the opposing team, a model focusing on organizational processes might recognize it as a breakdown of coordination among subgroups. What one model treats as planned, the other treats as a mistake.

Thus the organizational process model leads the historian to treat government behavior not as centralized acts and choices, but as the actions of bureaucracies functioning in relatively predictable patterns. Organizations begin by breaking problems into parts, which are assigned to the appropriate subgroups to solve. The subgroups do not have to understand the larger problem, only the piece assigned to each

*SOPs allow organizations to coordinate the independent activities of many groups and individuals.*

of them. They follow what the military refers to as SOP—standard operating procedure. If the quarterback decides on a sweep to the right, the lineman's SOP is to block left; on a sweep to the left, he blocks right; for a pass, straight ahead. SOPs allow organizations to coordinate the independent activities of many groups and individuals.

While SOPs make coordination possible, they also limit the actions of organizations. The more specialized a subgroup, the fewer tasks it is able to perform. Its training is more narrowly focused, its equipment is more specialized, and the information available to it is more limited. All those factors make it difficult for the group to deviate from regular routines. The weather bureau, for example, would find it impossible to apply its computer programs and specialized knowledge to predicting changes in the economy rather than the weather. Furthermore, the rational actor is presumed to weigh all available choices to select the best one, but in the real lives of organizations, SOPs determine the range and pattern of choices that are considered. Specialized groups are generally content to choose standardized and previously determined policies rather than searching for new or improved ones.

Since organizations are generally as much concerned with avoiding failure as with gambling on success, they also tend to be more conservative. Although the rational actor might weigh the potential benefits against possible consequences and then make a bold new departure, organizations tend to change in small, incremental steps. Corporations, for example, like to test-market a product before investing in expensive new plants, distribution networks, and advertising. And we have already seen that the American government moved relatively slowly in producing an atomic bomb. In authorizing the quest for a bomb, Roosevelt was ordering the government to do something it had never done before: conduct nuclear research. He soon discovered that the military and scientific bureaus could not readily execute such an unprecedented decision. They lacked the scientific personnel, equipment, and research routines that made the Manhattan Project possible. In the end, Roosevelt and project managers such as Groves, Conant, Bush, and Oppenheimer had to create new organizations and routines.

By treating the decision to drop the bomb not as a single act but as the outcome of many organizational routines, historians can see more clearly why progress on the bomb came slowly. In fact, the project could not have gotten under way in the first place if emigré scientists had not broken through the bureaucratic chain of command. When Fermi first approached navy officials, none of them could even comprehend the concept of nuclear power. Only by writing the president directly did scientists attract the support they needed. To get the project under way, Roosevelt was forced to create an ad hoc committee to investigate the military potential of nuclear fission. His decision to appoint Lyman Briggs, a government physicist, as head of the Uranium Committee may have delayed the project by at least a year. As the director of the Bureau of Standards, Briggs knew little about nuclear physics. He was by temperament "slow, conservative, methodical"—ideal bureaucratic qualities totally unsuited to the bold departure Roosevelt sought. Not until the president created the National Defense Research Committee did nuclear physics gain adequate support.

In other areas, organizational behavior resulted in delays. President Roosevelt had established two incompatible priorities for NDRC head Vannevar Bush: speed and security. The scientists felt speed should come before security; military administrators opted for security over speed. Military SOP had well-established ways to safeguard classified material. Officers were required to operate strictly within the chain of command and were provided information only on a "need-to-know" basis. Thus each soldier performed only a portion of a task without knowledge of the larger mission and without talking with anyone beyond his or her immediate circle. In that way, information was "compartmentalized"—securely protected so that only a few people at the top of the chain of command saw the entire picture.

To maximize security, Groves proposed placing the laboratory at Los Alamos under military control. All scientists would don uniforms and receive ranks based on their importance. As a group, however, scientists were among the least likely candidates for military regimentation. Their dress was more informal than most working professionals (sloppy might have been the adjective that jumped to the military mind). In their laboratories, they operated with a great deal of autonomy to pursue research as they saw fit. Oppenheimer could not recruit many scientists to come to Los Alamos until he assured them the project would not be militarized.

Compartmentalization, also promoted by Groves, seriously inhibited research. Physicists insisted that their work required access to all relevant information. They thought best when they understood the wider implications of their work. Groves disdained their habit of engaging in creative, freewheeling discussions that regularly drifted far afield of the topic at hand. Scientists should stick to their jobs and receive information only on a need-to-know basis. "Just as outfielders should not think about the manager's job of changing pitchers," Groves said to justify his system, "each scientist had to be made to do his own work." While compartmentalization promoted security, it denied researchers vital information from other areas of the project. Some scientists, like Szilard, simply violated security procedures whenever they chose to. Oppenheimer eased the problem at Los Alamos by conducting seminars during which his staff could exchange ideas and

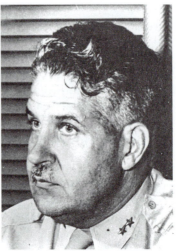

**In 1942 General Leslie Groves** was placed in charge of the construction and operation of the Manhattan Project. He got the job in part because he was a good organizer, having supervised the construction of the Pentagon, still unfinished in this 1942 photo. The building became the largest office facility in the world, containing 16 miles of corridors, 600,000 square feet of office space, and a capacity to house 32,000 workers. As historian Warren Susman recognized, it also became a symbol of its era: "For the age it climaxed indeed the triumph of order, science, reason. . . . And yet, for the age being born it was the home of the atom bomb and a frightening bureaucratic structure, the beginning of a brave new world of anxiety."

information. But information never flowed freely among the many research and production sites.

Security procedures indicate, too, that long before the war ended, many policy makers saw the Soviet Union as their chief enemy. Few precautions were designed against Japanese or even German agents. Military intelligence concentrated its counterespionage against Soviet and communist spies. Known communists or scientists with communist associations were kept under constant surveillance. Had intelligence officers prevailed, they would have barred Oppenheimer from the project because of his previous involvement with communist-front organizations. To his credit, Groves overruled the nearsighted sleuths in army intelligence and saved the project's most valuable member. In the meantime, security precautions against a wartime ally continued to work to the advantage of the Nazis by delaying the project.

The military was not solely responsible for project bottlenecks. The procedures of organized science caused delays as well. Scientists recruited from private industry did not share their academic colleagues' preoccupation with speed. Work in industry had conditioned them to move cautiously, with an eye toward efficiency, permanence, and low risk. Academic scientists felt such industrial values "led to a considerable retardation of the program." But the traditions of academic science also created problems. The bulk of research money had most often been directed to the celebrities in each field. Ernest Lawrence's reputation made him a magnet for grants and contributions. Manhattan Project administrators automatically turned to him as they sought methods to refine the pure uranium 235 needed for the bomb. Much of the money spent at Oak Ridge, Tennessee, went into Lawrence's electromagnetic process based on the Berkeley cyclotron.

In the end, Lawrence's program proved to be a conspicuous failure. By 1944 Oppenheimer had the design for a uranium bomb but scarcely any uranium 235. In desperation he looked toward a process of gas diffusion developed four years earlier by Harold Urey and a young, relatively unknown physicist named John Dunning. Lawrence had been so persuaded of the superiority of his own method that Groves gave it priority over the process developed by Urey and Dunning. And compartmentalization prevented other physicists from learning more about gas diffusion. As Dunning recalled, "compartmentalization and security kept news of our program from filtering in to Ernest and his Laboratory [the Radiation Lab at Berkeley]." Physicists soon acknowledged that electromagnetic separation was obsolete, but in the meantime, the completion of the uranium bomb, "Little Boy," was delayed until July 1945.

## A MODEL OF BUREAUCRATIC POLITICS

Clearly, bureaucratic structures and SOPs played major roles in determining how the bomb was developed. Yet the example of an energetic and forceful Vannevar Bush makes clear that within that organizational framework, not all bureaucrats were created equal. Powerful individuals or groups can often override the standard procedures of organizations as well as the carefully thought-out choices of rational actors. It makes sense, then, for historians to be alert to decisions shaped by the politics within government institutions.

If we return to our vantage point in the football stadium, we see linebackers blocking and receivers going short or long—all SOPs being executed as parts of a complex organization. The team's coach—the rational actor—remains prominent, pacing the sidelines, deploying forces. But we notice now that often an assistant sends in a play, or the quarterback makes a decision at the line of scrimmage. The field has not just one decision maker, but many. And the play finally chosen may not reflect rational choice, but bargaining and compromise among the players and the coach. Although final authority may rest with the coach or the quarterback, other players, such as a star halfback, gain influence and prestige from the skill with which they play their positions.

*The play finally chosen may not reflect rational choice, but bargaining and compromise among the players and the coach.*

A historian applying those insights, in what might be called a model of bureaucratic politics, recognizes that a person's official position as defined by the organization does not alone determine his or her bargaining power. According to an organizational flowchart, the most influential members of the executive branch, after the president, would be the secretaries of state, defense (war and navy), and treasury. Yet American history abounds with examples in which power has moved outside normal bureaucratic channels. Sometimes a political actor, through astute jockeying, may convert a relatively less influential office into an important command post, as Henry Kissinger did when he was Richard Nixon's national security adviser. Kissinger, through forceful advocacy, shaped foreign policy far more than Secretary of State William Rogers. Colonel Edward M. House, the most influential adviser to Woodrow Wilson, held no formal position at all. House achieved his power by maintaining a low profile and offering the president seemingly objective counsel. For Attorney General Robert Kennedy, family ties and political savvy, not his office, made him a powerful figure in his brother's administration.

In the case of the atom bomb, the lines of political influence were shifted by President Roosevelt's untimely death. When Harry Truman assumed the presidency, all the old institutional and informal arrangements of decision making had to be readjusted. Truman had had little access to the Roosevelt administration's information and decision-making channels. Ignorance of Roosevelt's policies forced Truman to rely far more heavily on a wider circle of advisers. Stimson, for one, suddenly found that for several months the need to initiate the president into the secrets of S-1 or the Manhattan Project greatly enhanced his influence.

Thus during the same months that Truman was trying to set up his own routines for decision making, individuals within various bureaucracies were jockeying for influence within the new order. And amid all this organizational turmoil, key decisions about the bomb had to be made—decisions that were neither clear-cut nor easy. Would a Soviet entry into the war force Japan to surrender? Would conventional bombing raids and a blockade prove sufficient to end the war? Did Japan's peace initiatives indicate victory was at hand? Would a compromise on unconditional surrender, specifically a guarantee for the emperor, end the war? Would a demonstration of the bomb shock the Japanese into suing for peace?

As critics of Truman's decision have pointed out, each of those options had significant advocates within government circles. And each presented policy makers with reasons to avoid dropping the bomb—something that, as historian Barton Bernstein pointed out, was "precisely what they were not trying to do." But why not? Why did the decision makers who counseled use of the bomb outweigh those who championed these various alternatives? By applying the bureaucratic politics model, historians can better explain why the alternatives were never seriously considered.

The chief advocates for continued conventional warfare came from the navy. From the beginning, navy leaders had been skeptical of nuclear fission's military potential. Admiral William Leahy, the senior navy representative on the Joint Chiefs of Staff and also an expert on explosives, always doubted the bomb would have anywhere near the force scientists predicted. The Alamogordo test laid his argument to rest. Chief of Naval Operations Admiral Ernest King believed a naval blockade would successfully end the war. King had no qualms about developing the bomb, but as a loyal navy officer, he hated to see the air force end a war that his service had dominated for four years. He feared, too, that the bomb might undermine the navy's importance after the war. Among military brass, Admirals Leahy and King had somewhat less influence than General George Marshall, army chief of staff. Marshall, along with General Douglas MacArthur, felt that further delay would necessitate an invasion and an unacceptable loss of American lives. Since they favored using the bomb instead, the navy lost that round.

Some members of the State Department, led by Acting Secretary of State Joseph Grew, believed that diplomacy should end the war. As early as April 1945 Grew had urged administration officials to extend some guarantee that the imperial throne would not be abolished. Without that assurance, he felt, the peace party could never overcome the military's determination to fight on. As former ambassador to Japan, Grew knew more about Japanese politics and culture than any major figure in the Truman administration. On the other hand, he had spent much of his career as a foreign service officer far from Washington. Thus he could exert little personal influence over Truman or key advisers. Even within the State Department, Assistant Secretaries Dean Acheson and Archibald MacLeish, both more influential than

> *Grew knew more about Japanese politics and culture, but had spent much of his time far from Washington, so he had little influence over Truman.*

Grew, opposed his position. They considered the emperor as the symbol of the feudal military tradition they hoped to see destroyed. By the time of the Potsdam Conference, Grew had made just one convert for negotiations—Secretary Stimson—and a partial convert—Harry Truman. "There was [*sic*] pretty strong feelings," Stimson recalled, "that it would be deplorable if we have to go through the military program with all its stubborn fighting to the finish." Truman showed sufficient interest to arrange talks between Grew and the military chiefs, but he did not feel he could bring congressional and public opinion in line with Grew's position on the emperor.

The ghost of Franklin Roosevelt proved to be Grew's major opponent. Lacking Roosevelt's prestige, popularity, and mastery of government, Truman felt bound to pursue many of FDR's policies. Any move away from "unconditional surrender" posed political risks at home and military risks abroad that Truman did not feel strong enough to take. Acheson and MacLeish reminded their colleagues that Americans despised Emperor Hirohito as much as they did Hitler. The Joint Chiefs of Staff argued that premature compromise might reduce the emperor's incentive to subdue military extremists after the armistice.

James Byrnes emerged as the leading defender of unconditional surrender. In contrast to Grew, Byrnes had little training in foreign affairs. His importance in the government reflected his consummate skill at domestic politics. During the war, many people considered him second in power only to Roosevelt.

In fact, Truman himself had risen to prominence as Byrnes's protégé and had repaid his debt by making Byrnes secretary of state. Deep down, Byrnes could not help feeling that he, not Truman, was the man best qualified to be president. He never got over thinking of himself as Truman's mentor.

Byrnes was exceptionally sensitive to the political risks of modifying unconditional surrender. More important, among Truman's advisers he was the most preoccupied with the growing Soviet threat. Using the bomb quickly would minimize Russian demands for territorial and political concessions in Asia, he believed, as well as strengthen the United States in any postwar negotiations. Since Byrnes's chief opponents, Grew and Stimson, were old and near retirement, and since he had strong support in both the military and State Department, his position carried the day. If the Japanese "peace feelers" to Moscow had been followed by more substantive proposals, to either the Russians or the Americans directly, perhaps some compromise might have been reached. But no other proposals were forthcoming. Thus at Potsdam, Byrnes and Truman remained convinced that the peace party in Japan would never marshal enough support against the military unless American attacks made further resistance seem futile. And it was again Byrnes who persuaded Truman to delete a provision in the Allied declaration that would have guaranteed the institution of the emperor.

By now it must be obvious why none of Truman's advisers wanted to rely on Soviet entry into the war as an alternative to dropping the bomb. By the time of the Potsdam Conference, Japan's military position had become hopeless. Why encourage Stalin's ambitions, especially when the bomb was available for use?

Some Americans proposed that the bomb be demonstrated before a group of international observers instead of being dropped on Japan without warning. But advocates of this alternative were found largely among scientists working at the Chicago Metallurgical Laboratory. This group had been the first to finish its work on the bomb. While the Los Alamos lab rushed to complete the designs for Little Boy and Fat Man, the Chicago lab began discussing the postwar implications of nuclear weapons and the threat of an international arms race. The eminent scientist Niels Bohr had already raised those issues with Roosevelt and Churchill. Yet as we have seen, Churchill and Roosevelt agreed at their 1944 Hyde Park meeting to keep the bomb secret from Stalin, hoping to use it to advantage in any postwar rivalry with the Russians.

Unaware of the Hyde Park agreement, scientists continued to press their case against a surprise nuclear attack. "It may be very difficult," Nobel Prize–winner James Franck observed, "to persuade the world that a nation that was capable of secretly preparing and suddenly releasing a weapon as indiscriminate as the [German] rocket bomb and a million times more destructive, is to be trusted in its proclaimed desire of having such weapons abolished by international agreement." As powerful as that argument was, it was a moral, not a military, one. Equally important, scientists lacked the political influence to change policy. Only leaders such as Truman, Byrnes, and Stimson had the power to do so. The decisions key officials debated, then, were not

**Fat Man,** also familiarly known to scientists working on the project as Fat Boy. The graffiti on the tail included the notation "Chicago is represented in here more than once."

whether to drop the bombs, but where and when to use them. Here, too, our models reveal both organizational processes and bureaucratic politics at work. To select the targets, Groves appointed a target committee composed of scientists and ordnance specialists. Their priorities reflected both the military's desire to end the war quickly and the scientists' hope to transmit a dramatic warning to the world. They sought cities that included military installations, but they also wanted a site with a large concentration of structures subject to the blast, in case the bomb missed its primary target. Kyoto, the ancient cultural and political center of Japan, topped their list.

Secretary of War Stimson vetoed that choice. As a former secretary of state and a person of broad cultural and political experience, he believed that the destruction of Kyoto would engender in the Japanese an undying bitterness toward the United States. Any hopes of integrating a revitalized and reformed Japan into a healthy postwar Asia might die with Kyoto. Stimson's position near the top of the organizational hierarchy gave him a different perspective from lower-level planners who weighed other issues. On the final target list Hiroshima ranked first, Nagasaki ranked fourth, and Kyoto not at all.

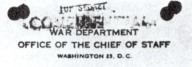

WAR DEPARTMENT
OFFICE OF THE CHIEF OF STAFF
WASHINGTON 25, D.C.

25 July 1945

TO:    General Carl Spaatz
       Commanding General
       United States Army Strategic Air Forces

1. The 509 Composite Group, 20th Air Force will deliver its first special bomb as soon as weather will permit visual bombing after about 3 August 1945 on one of the targets: Hiroshima, Kokura, Niigata and Nagasaki. To carry military and civilian scientific personnel from the War Department to observe and record the effects of the explosion of the bomb, additional aircraft will accompany the airplane carrying the bomb. The observing planes will stay several miles distant from the point of impact of the bomb.

2. Additional bombs will be delivered on the above targets as soon as made ready by the project staff. Further instructions will be issued concerning targets other than those listed above.

3. Dissemination of any and all information concerning the use of the weapon against Japan is reserved to the Secretary of War and the President of the United States. No communiques on the subject or releases of information will be issued by Commanders in the field without specific prior authority. Any news stories will be sent to the War Department for special clearance.

4. The foregoing directive is issued to you by direction and with the approval of the Secretary of War and of the Chief of Staff, USA. It is desired that you personally deliver one copy of this directive to General MacArthur and one copy to Admiral Nimitz for their information.

THOS. T. HANDY
General, G.S.C.
Acting Chief of Staff

**The letter outlining SOP** for dropping the bomb. It authorized the "509 Composite Group, 20th Air Force" to "deliver its first special bomb as soon as weather will permit visual bombing after about 3 August 1945 on one of the targets: Hiroshima, Kokura, Niigata and Nagasaki." In a reflection of protocol, as well as a hint of the rivalry between the army and navy, the letter instructs General Spaatz, in paragraph four, to inform General MacArthur and Admiral Nimitz of the decision personally.

It was the weather and the routines of organization, not diplomatic or military strategy, that sealed Nagasaki's fate. After the bombing of Hiroshima and the Russian declaration of war, Japanese leaders decided to sue for peace. Advocates of surrender needed only enough time to work out acceptable terms and to reconcile military officers to the inevitable. As the Japanese discussed policy, the Americans followed standard military procedure. Control shifted from the commander in Washington, President Truman, to the commander of the bomber squadron on the island of Tinian in the Pacific. Plans called for Fat Man, a plutonium bomb, to be ready by August 11. Since work went faster than expected, the bomb crew advanced the date to August 9. The forecast called for clear skies on the ninth, followed by five days of bad weather. Urged on by the squadron commander, the crew had Fat Man armed and loaded on the morning of the ninth. And again following military SOP, the pilot shifted his attack to Nagasaki when clouds obscured his primary target.

Had the original plan been followed, Japan might well have surrendered before the weather cleared. Nagasaki would have been spared. But the officer who ordered the attack had little appreciation of the larger military picture that made Nagasaki a target or that made the Soviet Union a diplomatic problem connected with the atom bomb. He weighed factors important to a bomb squadron commander, not to diplomats or political leaders. The bombing of Nagasaki slipped from the hands of policy makers not because of some rogue computer or any power-mad, maniacal general, but simply because of military SOPs.

And so two bombs were dropped and the world entered the atomic age.

If historians based their interpretations on a single model, they would never satisfy their desire to understand the sequence of events leading to Nagasaki. Each model provides its own particular perspective, both clarifying and at the same time limiting. The use of several models allows the historian the same advantage enjoyed by writers of fiction who employ more than one narrator. Each narrator, like each model, affords the writer a new vantage point from which to tell the story. The facts may not change, but the reader sees them in another light. As organizations grow more complex, models afford historians multiple perspectives from which to interpret the same reality.

And yet we must remind ourselves that models do not work miracles, for their potential to reveal new insights depends on the skills of the people who build and apply them. If poorly applied, their seeming precision, like reams of computer printout, conveys a false sense of empirical legitimacy. Data specialists have coined the acronym GIGO to suggest the limits of such mechanical devices—"garbage in, garbage out." In the end, historians must remember that organizations are open systems existing within a broader historical and cultural context. Even when our models have accounted for goals, strategies, SOPs, and political influence, there remain those pieces of the picture that are still irreducible: from scientists' dismay at the devil

**The reaction of scientists** watching the detonation of the first atomic bomb in New Mexico was recalled by Robert Oppenheimer: "A few people laughed, a few people cried, more people were silent. There floated through my mind a line from the Bhagavad Gita in which Krishna is trying to persuade the Prince that he should do his duty: 'I am become death, the shatterer of worlds.' I think we all had this feeling, more or less." The photograph is of an atomic blast detonated at Bikini Island in July 1946.

of their creation to the inanimate, complex meteorological forces that combined to dissipate the clouds over Nagasaki in August 1945.

Some elements of history will always remain stubbornly intractable, beyond the reach of the model builders. The mushroom clouds over Japan did not merely serve as a dramatic close to World War II. The afterglow of their blasts destroyed a sense of security that Americans had enjoyed for almost 150 years. After the war, the nuclear arms race turned the United States into an armed camp. Given the limits of human understanding, who in 1945 could have appreciated all the consequences that would result from the decision to drop the atom bomb?

# Additional Reading

The creation and use of the atomic bomb ranks with slavery, democratic reform, civil rights and liberties, economic justice, and possibly even the Civil War as issues critical to the understanding of American history. During the early cold war, most Americans willingly accepted the rationale for dropping the bombs offered in official accounts such as Harry S. Truman, *Memoirs, 1945: Year of Decisions* (New York, 1955); Henry Stimson (with McGeorge Bundy), *On Active Service in Peace and War* (New York, 1947); Leslie Groves, *Now It Can Be Told* (New York, 1962); and Richard Hewlett and Oscar Anderson, *The New World: 1939–1946*, vol. 1 of *A History of the United States Atomic Energy Commission* (University Park, PA, 1962). A useful and full-length study of the controversy over casualty estimates is John Ray Skates, *Invasion of Japan: Alternative to the Bomb* (Columbia, SC, 1994). Another student of the bomb controversy, J. Samuel Walker, has summarized much of the evidence in *Prompt and Utter Destruction: Truman and the Use of the Atomic Bombs Against Japan* (Chapel Hill, NC, 1997).

Then in 1965 came Gar Alperovitz's bombshell, *Atomic Diplomacy* (New York, 1965; rev. ed., 1985). Suddenly the rationale for building and using the bomb seemed much less obvious. Alperovitz raised difficult questions about official justifications of the decision to bomb Hiroshima and Nagasaki. Herbert Feis defended the official view in *The Atomic Bomb and the End of World War II* (Princeton, NJ, 1966). The debate was continued with critical studies by Martin Sherwin, *A World Destroyed*, rev. ed. (New York, 1985), and Barton Bernstein, "Roosevelt, Truman, and the Atomic Bomb: A Reinterpretation," *Political Science Quarterly* 90 (spring 1975): 23–69. McGeorge Bundy reviewed the moral and political debates about the bomb in *Danger and Survival* (New York, 1988). George Kennan, the father of the cold war policy of containment, became more cautionary of nuclear diplomacy in later years, as reflected in his *Nuclear Delusion* (New York, 1982). Alperovitz and a team of research assistants responded to critics of his *Atomic Diplomacy* in a thoroughly researched new book, *The Decision to Use the Atomic Bomb* (New York, 1996).

An excellent collection of primary documents on the bomb's development can be found in Michael Stoff, Jonathan Fanton, and R. Hal Williams, eds., *The Manhattan Project: A Documentary Introduction to the Atomic Age* (New York, 1990). Many of the diaries, letters, and top-secret memoranda are reproduced in facsimile form. The decision-making models we discuss are more fully developed in another context in Graham Allison and Philip Zelikow, *The Essence of Decision: Explaining the Cuban Missile Crisis*, 2d ed. (Boston, MA, 1999 ). Richard Rhodes, *The Making of the Atomic Bomb* (New York, 1986), has written the most comprehensive and readable account of the bomb project. Kai Bird and Martin Sherwin, *American Prometheus: The Triumph and Tragedy of J. Robert Oppenheimer* (New York, 2006), draw an intriguing portrait of the scientist most responsible for the Manhattan

Project's success. They make clear that Oppenheimer was in no way disloyal, as some of his enemies claimed. Daniel Kevles, *The Physicists* (New York, 1977), and Nuel Pharr Davis, *Lawrence and Oppenheimer*, reprint (New York, 1986), provide background on members of the science community who helped create the bomb. Many went on to raise profound questions about what they had done and how their work was put to use. Gregg Herken, *Brotherhood of the Bomb: The Tangled Lives and Loyalties of Robert Oppenheimer, Ernest Lawrence and Edward Teller* (New York, 2003), traces the relationship of the three key physicists and the issues over which they divided.

# *Truckstop Atomic Science*

The scientists and engineers who designed the first atomic weapon were among the most brilliant in the world. Few, however, ever spoke publicly about the bombs' inner workings. And for more than a half century, the U.S. government has kept information about the design a secret, fearing that enemies or terrorists might exploit it.

Recently, however, a detailed reconstruction of the bomb's inner workings has emerged—written not by a physicist, engineer, or historian, nor even by a college graduate. John Coster-Mullen was a truck driver from Waukesha, Wisconsin, who earlier in his career had worked as a photographer. His book, published at the local Kinko's copy shop, appeared under the title *Atom Bombs: The Top Secret Inside Story of Little Boy and Fat Man*. Its accuracy astonished scientists.

Coster-Mullen began his fanatical quest to discover the bomb's design when he and his son Jason constructed a model of Little Boy in his garage. He wanted to get the details right and began gathering clues from the public record, visiting museums from London to West Point to Los Alamos. He pored over old photographs, even measured the bomb casings on display. But what fit inside? And how?

At the Smithsonian's National Air and Space Museum, the bomb casing had cryptic numbers scribbled on it: 36 and 52 on the side, 12 on the nose. What did they mean? 52 struck a chord. A book on the Enola Gay described Little Boy as possessing a 52-inch wooden gun barrel—used, supposedly, to create a critical mass needed to detonate the bomb. Coster-Mullen knew that a gun barrel made of wood was preposterous and that 52 inches was far too long for the barrel itself. But another book had described a 24-inch channel bored within the back of the bomb. Adding the 12-inch notation on the bomb's nose yielded 36 inches. Other sources indicated that the projectile used in the gun mechanism was 16 inches: 16 plus 36 totaled 52. Suddenly, Coster-Mullen had a clearer sense of how the parts fit together.

His background in photography paid dividends, too. Coster-Mullen examined a photo of two Los Alamos scientists carrying a box housing a plutonium assembly. One bomb machinist had told him that the mechanism inside was 11 or 12 inches long. Directly behind the box was a car he identified as a 1942 Plymouth. One day he spied just that model parked at an antique auto dealership. By measuring the height of its door, estimating the distance of the photographer from the car in the photo, and determining the ratios, he calculated the size of the box at 10½ inches. Clearly, an object in the box had to be shorter than 11 or 12 inches.

And so it went, step by excruciating step. What fueled Coster-Mullen's obsession to get the details right? Partly, it was a mental challenge, not unlike solving a complex crossword puzzle. But he also objected to what he saw as a foolish attempt to keep secrets. Any terrorist could find an atomic bomb design on the Internet. As historian Richard Rhodes commented, a group bent on creating havoc "hardly needs the help of us poor souls, who aren't even scientists" to build a bomb. For Rhodes and Coster-Mullen, officials seemed guided largely by the principle "I can have the truth and you can't."

So a truck driver defeated government efforts to keep an antique secret that nuclear technology had long ago passed by. In the future, a scientist suggested, security officials might want to work more closely with Coster-Mullen, so "if there really *is* something they want to keep close, they might have a clearer idea how to do it."

# CHAPTER 14
# *From Rosie to Lucy*

*If the media of the 1950s brainwashed women to be contented housewives and mothers, how did so many women of the 1960s develop a feminist consciousness?*

It was 1957. Betty Friedan was not just complaining; she was angry for herself and uncounted other women like her. For some time, she had sensed that the discontent she felt as a suburban housewife and mother was not peculiar to her alone. Now she was certain, as she read the results of a questionnaire she had circulated to about 200 postwar graduates of Smith College. The women who answered were not frustrated simply because their educations had not properly prepared them for the lives they were leading; rather, these women resented the wide disparity between the idealized image society held of them as housewives and mothers and the realities of their daily routines.

True, most were materially well off. The majority had families, a house in the suburbs, and the amenities of an affluent society. But amid that good fortune they felt fragmented, almost as if they had no identity of their own. And it was not only college graduates. "I've tried everything women are supposed to do," one woman confessed to Friedan.

> Hobbies, gardening, pickling, canning, being very social with my neighbors, joining committees, running PTA teas. I can do it all, and I like it, but it doesn't leave you anything to think about—any feeling of who you are. . . . I love the kids and Bob and my home. There's no problem you can even put a name to. But I'm desperate. I begin to feel I have no personality. I'm a server of food and putter-on of pants and a bedmaker, somebody who can be called on when you want something. But who am I?

A similar sense of incompleteness haunted Friedan. "I, like other women, thought there was something wrong with me because I didn't have an orgasm waxing the kitchen floor," she recalled with some bitterness.

This growing unease led her to raise some disturbing questions. Why, she wondered, had she chosen fifteen years earlier to give up a promising career in psychology for marriage and motherhood? What was it that kept women from using the rights and prerogatives that were theirs? What made them feel guilty for anything they did in their own right rather than as their husbands' wives or children's mothers? Women in the 1950s, it seemed to Friedan, were not behaving quite the way they had a decade earlier. During World War II the popular press extolled the virtues of women like "Rosie the Riveter"—those who left homes and families to join the workforce. Now, Rosie was no longer a heroine. The media lavished their praise on women who devoted themselves to family and home. In the closing scene of one 1957 *Redbook* article, the heroine, "Junior" (a "little freckle-faced brunette" who had chosen to give up her job), nurses her baby at two in the morning, sighing, "I'm so glad, glad, glad I'm just a housewife." What had happened? "When did women decide to give up the world and go back home?" Friedan asked herself.

Questions like those have engaged historians since the 1970s, but they were not ones housewives of the 1950s were encouraged to ask. For a red-blooded American to doubt something as sacred as the role of housewife and mother was to show symptoms of mental disorder rather than a skeptical or inquiring mind. Whatever the label attached to such feelings—neurosis, anxiety, or depression—most people assumed that unhappy women needed only to become better adjusted to who and what they were.

Friedan, however, was no ordinary housewife. At Smith College she fought against anti-Semitism and, as a graduate student at Berkeley, associated with Bay Area radicals. Before starting her family, she had written for labor union publications and as a newspaper reporter; even after her children were born, she wrote regularly for the major women's magazines. Opposition to inequality and exploitation shaped her worldview. By 1957 she was fed up with the endless stories about breast-feeding, the preparation of gourmet chip dips, and similar domestic fare that was the staple of *Redbook*, *McCall's*, and *Ladies' Home Journal*. She had noticed many women like herself who worked outside the home and felt guilty because their jobs threatened their husbands' roles as providers or took time away from their children. Thus Friedan began to wonder not only about herself as a woman, a wife, and a mother, but also about the role society had shaped women to play.

The results of the Smith questionnaire suggested to Friedan that she was onto a story bigger than anything she had ever written. But when she circulated an article describing the plight so many women were experiencing, the male editors at the women's magazines turned it down flat. It couldn't be true, they insisted; women could not possibly feel as guilty or discontented as Friedan claimed. The problem must be hers. "Betty has gone off her rocker," an editor at *Redbook* told her agent. "She has always done a good job for us, but this time only the most neurotic housewife could identify." Friedan was not deterred. If the magazines would not print her story, she would do it as a book. For five years, she researched and wrote, exploring what she called the "feminine mystique," a phenomenon she saw embedded in American culture:

> The new mystique makes the housewife-mother, who never had a chance to be anything else, the model for all women . . . it simply makes certain

**A happy housewife with a week's work.** By 1947 many women laborers were back in the home full-time and the baby boom was under way. *Life* magazine celebrated the labors of a typical housewife by laying out a week's worth of bed making, ironing, washing, grocery shopping, and dish washing for a family of four. An incomplete tally shows more than 250 plates being washed and thirty-five quarts of milk consumed a week. Did the wife drink the majority of the six cups of coffee that seem to have been consumed per day?

concrete, finite, domestic aspects of feminine existence—as it was lived by women whose lives were confined by necessity to cooking, cleaning, washing, bearing children—into a religion, a pattern by which all women must now live or deny their femininity.

By the time Friedan was finished, the book had become a crusade. "I have never experienced anything as powerful, truly mystical, as the forces that seemed to overtake me as I wrote *The Feminine Mystique*," she later admitted. Published in 1963, the book soon joined the ranks of truly consequential books in American history. What Harriet Beecher Stowe did for slaves in

*Uncle Tom's Cabin,* Jacob Riis for the urban poor in *How the Other Half Lives,* Upton Sinclair for public health in *The Jungle,* or Rachel Carson for the environment in *Silent Spring,* Friedan did for women. No longer would they bear their dissatisfaction in silence as they confronted the gap between their personal aspirations and the limited avenues society had left open to them. Friedan helped inspire a generation of women to demand the equal rights and opportunities that men routinely claimed.

# RETREAT FROM REVOLUTION: A DEMOGRAPHIC PROFILE

The feminist movement that blossomed in the wake of the civil rights movement of the 1960s had a profound impact on the study of history as well. After all, many of the questions Friedan raised were the sort that historians are trained to explore. Was it true that women hadn't followed up on the gains in employment they experienced during World War II? What caused society in postwar America to place so much emphasis on home and family? What was the image of women that the mass media, scholars, and other opinion makers presented? Friedan, however, was a journalist, not a historian. True, historians and journalists share many methods in common. Both write more confidently when they can confirm their story from multiple sources. Like many historians, Friedan turned to the social sciences for theory and methods. She canvassed articles in popular women's magazines, studied the recent scholarship, and talked to psychologists, sociologists, and marriage counselors who regularly treated women. She conducted in-depth interviews with women of varying ages, backgrounds, and social classes.

It was not her methods, however, that influenced the study of history. Rather, it was the subject she chose to probe. Prior to the 1970s, history as a discipline gave slight attention to the experience of women, even though they constituted more than half the world's population. The vast majority of studies (most of which were written by men anyway) concentrated on topics in the public arena. Politics, business, intellectual life, diplomacy, war—all were areas in which males defined the terms of action. The few women who

> *Prior to the 1970s, history as a discipline gave slight attention to the experience of women.*

did enter the history books were there most often because, like Eleanor Roosevelt, they had lived a public life; like Jane Addams, they initiated social reform; like Margaret Mead, they contributed in major ways to the social sciences; or like Willa Cather, they stood among the nation's leading writers and artists. Those women were exceptional, and it was the exceptional, not the commonplace, that historians generally preferred to study.

Still, history has by no means been confined to the rich, powerful, famous, and male—as we have seen in earlier chapters. And particularly for the twentieth century, documentary materials like the census made it possible to study ordinary people in a macrocosmic sense, looking at the actions of millions of people in the aggregate. Along with the new statistical census procedures adopted in 1940 came sophisticated opinion polling. Advertisers in the 1930s sought to discover more about consumer preferences so they could pitch their products more effectively. George Gallup developed survey techniques that allowed pollsters to determine mass opinions on a multitude of issues. Polling had been done before Gallup began his work, but he and his rivals undertook it much more systematically, devising better ways of recording opinions, more sophisticated techniques for minimizing margins of error, and more scientific means of asking questions.

In the academic world, the expansion of social science theory enlarged the kinds of information people thought worth having as well as the means for interpreting such data. As we saw in Chapter 12, social scientists were able to learn much about the causes for mass migrations in the 1930s. Thus when historians began investigating women's status in the mid-twentieth century, they could draw on a good deal of statistical information. The data they found in some ways challenged Friedan's picture of women being pushed out of the workforce, but in other ways her view was strikingly confirmed. Census data and other governmental records indeed show that many women entered higher-paying and more-skilled jobs as early as World War I. But those gains were short-lived. With the return of peace, women faced layoffs, renewed wage discrimination, and segregation into female-only jobs such as teaching and nursing. Women made little headway over the next decade, despite the hoopla about the emancipated "new woman" of the twenties. Behind the stereotype of the smart-talking flapper with her cigarette, bobbed hair, and boyish clothes, traditional ideas about women and their proper roles prevailed in the labor marketplace. In 1920, 23 percent of women worked; by 1930, the figure rose to only 24 percent. Access to the professions increased but remained heavily restricted. For example, women earned more than 30 percent of all graduate degrees but accounted for only 4 percent of full professors on college faculties. Most women workers were young, single, and without children, and they toiled at unskilled jobs. Between 1920 and 1930, the percentage of women in manufacturing fell from 22.6 (the same as in 1910) to 17.5, while the percentages of women in both domestic service and clerical work—the lowest-paying jobs—rose.

Real gains for women came during World War II. A rapidly expanding war economy absorbed most of the reserve labor force of underemployed or unemployed male workers. The military alone siphoned off some 15 million men and women. That left married women as the single largest untapped labor reserve. Suddenly, the propaganda machinery that had once discouraged women from competing with men for jobs urged them to enlist in the workforce. The patriotic appeal had the desired effect. What faithful wife could sit at home when the media warned that her husband in the service might die from the lack of ammunition? Commando Mary and Rosie the Riveter became symbols of women who heeded their country's call to join the production line.

Patriotism by itself did not explain the willingness of married women to take jobs. Many found higher war wages an attractive inducement. Indeed, with so many husbands earning low military pay, families needed additional income to survive. Absent husbands also meant that domestic life was less central. Women had more time and opportunity for work outside the home. And wartime restrictions on leisure activities made jobs a more attractive outlet for women's energies. Whether stated as raw numbers or percentages, the statistical gains for women were impressive. From 1940 to 1945 some 6.5 million women entered the workforce, more than half of them for the first time. Women accounted for just 25 percent of workers in 1940 but 36 percent in 1945. Perhaps more significant were the kinds of women who now found employment outside the home. Young, single women no longer dominated. By 1950 married women were a majority of the female workforce, compared with only a third in 1940. Similarly, older women between ages fifty-five and sixty-four became a major working group, rising from 17 percent in 1940 to 35 percent by 1960.

It was not only the numbers of working women that soared but also the quality of their jobs. Women had an opportunity to work in skilled areas of manufacturing and to earn much higher wages. Black women in particular, who had been stuck in low-paying farm and domestic jobs, rushed to the factories that offered higher pay and better hours. Women on the assembly lines shaped sheet metal, built airplanes, and performed a host of skilled tasks. Suddenly, stereotypes about traditional male and female roles had shattered.

Yet for all these undeniable gains, the situation brought about by a world at war was a special case, and most Americans perceived it that way. The men returning home intended to pick up their jobs, and most men assumed that women would return to their traditional household duties. As a result, the war led to few structural changes affecting women's economic roles. For example, working mothers needed some form of day care for their young children. The government was slow to provide it, and even where it existed, many mothers were reluctant to use it. For them, the responsibilities of the job were secondary to those of the home.

Most professions continued to maintain barriers against women. Among the female workers who flooded government bureaucracies and factories, few received managerial status. And many employers found ways to avoid government regulations requiring equal pay for men and women. General Motors, for example, simply changed its job classifications. Jobs once designated

*Most professions continued to maintain barriers against women.*

as male or female became "heavy" or "light." Women generally were assigned to the light, lower-paying categories. Fearful that rapidly rising wages would spur inflation, the government was slow to enforce its own rules protecting women from discrimination.

Certain social trends seemed to underscore the traditional resistance to working mothers. Some public officials worried about statistics indicating that wartime stresses threatened to undermine the family. Americans have always seen the family as the foundation of the social order, and wartime did nothing to change that view. The increase in alcohol abuse, divorce, and juvenile delinquency all suggested a weakening family structure. Apparently, so did emotional problems among children such as bed wetting, thumb sucking, and truancy.

Observers were quick to blame those problems on one cause—maternal neglect. In fact, there was no clear evidence that the families of working women had any disadvantage over those whose mothers stayed home. Extraordinary wartime mobility, not the fact that the mothers worked, seems to have accounted for many of those problems. The sudden rush of workers, both male and female, to industrial centers overtaxed all manner of public services, including housing and schools, which were of particular importance to families with young children. The war disrupted families whether mothers worked or not.

What is striking is that by 1945, despite all the gains women had made, most attitudes about women and work had not changed substantially. Surveys showed that Americans, whether male or female, continued to believe that child rearing was a woman's primary job. Thus the marked demographic shift of women into the workforce was revolutionary in import, but it brought no revolution in cultural attitudes toward gender roles. As historian William Chafe commented, "The events of the war years suggested that most Americans would accept a significant shift in women's economic activities as long as the shift was viewed as 'temporary' and did not entail a conscious commitment to approve the goals of a sexual revolution."

Despite the general expectation that women would return to the home after the war, female laborers did not simply drop their wrenches and pick up frying pans. Many continued to work outside the home, although mostly to support their families, not to find career alternatives. As peace came in 1945, polls indicated that more than 75 percent of all working women wanted to continue at their jobs. About 88 percent of high school girls surveyed said they hoped for a career as well as the role of homemaker. Although employment for women did shrink slightly, a significantly higher percentage of women were working in 1950 than in 1940 (28 percent versus 24 percent). Even more striking, that figure continued to rise, reaching 36 percent by 1960. Those numbers included older women, married women with children, and women of all social classes.

Such statistics would seem at first to undercut Friedan's notion that the vast majority of American women accepted the ideal of total fulfillment through housework and child rearing. Some 2.25 million women did voluntarily return home after the war, and another million were laid off by 1946. At the same time, 2.75 million women entered the job market by 1947, leaving a net loss of only half a million.

But even if Friedan was mistaken in seeing a mass female exodus from the workforce, a significant shift did take place in the types of work performed. When women who had been laid off managed to return to work, they often lost their seniority and had to accept reduced pay in lower job categories. Employment in almost all the professions had decreased by 1960. Despite gains in some areas, women were concentrated in jobs that were primarily extensions of their traditional responsibility for managing the family's physical and emotional well-being: they were nurses, not doctors; teachers, not principals; tellers, not bankers. Far more worked in service jobs (as maids or waitresses, for example) than in manufacturing. Overwhelmingly, job opportunities were segregated by gender. About 75 percent of all women workers held female-only jobs. In fact, gender segregation in the workplace was worse in 1960 than in 1900—and even worse than segregation by race. Thus, even though women's participation in the workforce remained comparatively high, it did not inspire a corresponding revolution in attitudes about women's roles in society.

## Retreat from Revolution: The Role of Mass Media

Attitudes, of course, were at the center of Friedan's concerns in *The Feminine Mystique*, and the demographic profile we have sketched underlines the reason for her focus. If the percentage of women holding jobs continued to increase during the 1950s and if young women, when polled, said they hoped to combine work in some way with motherhood, how did the cult of the "feminine mystique" become so firmly enshrined? If wartime laboring conditions produced a kind of revolution in fact but not in spirit, what elements of American culture reined in that revolution and kept it from running its course?

As Friedan was well aware, economic and demographic factors played a crucial role in renewing the concern with home and family living. The hard times of the Depression had discouraged couples from starting large families. But as war production renewed prosperity and soldiers headed off to war, the birthrate began to climb. With the return of peace in 1945, GIs were eager to do more than kiss their wives hello. For the next fifteen years the United States had one of the highest birthrates in the world, rising from an average of 1.9 to 2.3 children for each woman of childbearing age. Large families became the norm. The number of parents with three children tripled, while those with four quadrupled. Women also married younger. The average age of marriage dropped from 22 in 1900 to 20.3 in 1962. The United States had the highest rate of marriage of any nation in the world, and American men and women chose to organize their lives around family.*

Clearly, material conditions not only pushed women out of the workplace as GIs rejoined the peacetime economy but also pulled women back into the home as the birthrate rose. Friedan acknowledged these changes but noted

---

* At the same time, the United States had the world's highest divorce rate. Enthusiasm for marriage was apparently no guarantee of success.

**Women of the *Saturday Evening Post*, Part One.** In the midst of the war, the *Post*'s "cover girl" was this confident Rosie, patriotic buttons across her chest, goggles over her eyes, macho watchband around her wrist, and biceps calculated to make Charles Atlas envious. As one real-life Rosie commented about welding, "We were happy to be doing it. We felt terrific. Lunch hour would find us spread out on the sidewalk. Women welders with our outfits on, and usually a quart of milk in one hand and a salami sandwich in another. It was an experience that none of us had ever had before."

that the birthrates of other economically developed nations—such as France, Norway, and Sweden—had begun to decline by 1955. Even more striking, the sharpest rise in the United States came among women ages fifteen to nineteen. In Great Britain, Canada, and Germany, on the other hand, the rise was more equally distributed among age groups. What was it that made so many American teen brides give up the chance of college and a career for early marriage and homemaking?

Friedan's answer was to look more closely at the mass media. Magazines, radio, movies, and television had all come to play a predominant role in the modern era. They exposed Americans to powerfully presented messages conveying the standards and ideals of the culture. The media, observed sociologist Harold Lasswell in 1948, had come to perform many of the tasks that the Catholic Church assumed in medieval Europe. Like the church, the media possessed the capacity to send the same message to all classes at the same time, with confidence in their authority to speak and to be heard universally. Friedan, for her part, believed that in the postwar era the media's message about women—what they could dream of, set their sights on, and accomplish—underwent a marked shift. From her perspective, the purveyors of popular culture suddenly seemed determined to persuade women that they should not just accept but actually embrace the idealized image of women as wives and mothers.

Having written for the mass-circulation women's magazines, Friedan already knew they played a role in promoting the feminine mystique. What surprised her was how much the image of women had become domesticated in the postwar era. In the 1930s, the woman most likely to appear in a magazine story had a career and was as much concerned with a goal of her own as with getting her man. The heroine of a typical *Ladies' Home Journal* story in 1939 is a nurse who has "strength in her hands, pride in her carriage and nobility in the lift of her chin . . . she left training, nine years ago. She had been on her own ever since. She had earned her way, she need consider nothing but her heart." And unlike the heroines of the 1950s, these women did not have to choose invariably between marriage and career. If they held strongly to their dreams, they could have both. Beginning in 1950s fictional magazine stories, however, new heroines appeared. These, Friedan noted, were most often "young and frivolous, almost childlike; fluffy and feminine; passive; gaily content in a world of bedroom and kitchen, sex, babies, and home." The new women did not work "except housework and work to keep their bodies beautiful and to get and keep a man." "Where," Friedan asked rhetorically, "is the world of thought and ideas, the life of the mind and the spirit?"

*The new women did not work "except housework and work to keep their bodies beautiful and to get and keep a man."*

Talking with some of the few remaining editors from the 1930s, Friedan discovered one reason for the change. "Most of the material used to come from women writers," one explained. "As the young men returned from the war, a great many women writers stopped writing. The new writers were all men, back from the war, who had been dreaming about home, and a cozy domestic life." Male editors, when queried, defended themselves by contending that their readers no longer identified with career women, no longer read serious fiction, and had lost almost all interest in public issues except perhaps those that affected the price of groceries. "You just can't write about ideas or broad issues of the day for women," one remarked.

In the 1930s, magazines, newspapers, radio, and movies had set the fashion. By the 1950s, those media had begun to lose their audience to television. Women who had once gone to the matinee stayed home to watch the latest episode of *As the World Turns*. In 1951, cities with television networks

**Women of the *Saturday Evening Post*, Part Two.** Biceps and riveting guns had deserted *Post* covers by 1956. Instead, these two women—like Margaret in *Father Knows Best*—can barely get their cars out the driveway, let alone down the street. No doubt, however, they could stir up a mean Jell-O salad.

reported a 20 percent to 40 percent decline in movie attendance. Almost overnight, television became the preeminent mass medium, carrying images—feminine or otherwise—of American culture into the home. By 1949, there were about a million sets and 108 licensed stations, most in large urban markets. By 1952, 15 million Americans had bought sets; by 1955, the figure had jumped to 30 million; by 1960, television had entered 46 million homes. In fact, more American homes had television sets than had bathrooms! Obviously, if we are to understand how the mass media of the 1950s shaped the image of women, our inquiry must focus on television.*

And indeed, television portrayed women of the fifties in predictable ways. Most often they were seen in domestic dramas or comedies in which Mom

---

* The technology of broadcasting had been available in the 1920s, but only after World War II did commercial application begin in earnest. As secretary of commerce, Herbert Hoover had his image transmitted in 1927, making him the first president to appear on television, although this appearance occurred before his election in 1928. Franklin Roosevelt was, in 1939, the first sitting president in office to appear on television.

and Dad were found living happily with their two or three cute children and possibly a live-in maid or relative to provide additional comic situations. The homes in which they lived, even that of blue-collar airplane riveter Chester Riley (*The Life of Riley*, 1949–1950, 1953–1958), were cheerfully middle class, with the antiseptic look of a furniture showroom. As for Mom herself, she never worked outside the home and seldom seemed to do much more than wave a dust cloth or whip up a three-course meal at a moment's notice. Sometimes, as in *The Adventures of Ozzie and Harriet* (1955–1966), she is competent, cool, and collected. Ozzie, in fact, often seems rather a lost soul when turned loose in his own castle and has to be guided gently through the current week's predicament by Harriet. In other series, such as *The George Burns and Gracie Allen Show* (1950–1958), women like Gracie Allen and her friend Blanche play the role of "dizzy dames," unable to balance checkbooks and sublimely oblivious to the realities of the business world. When Harry Morton announces to his wife, Blanche, "I've got great news for you!" (he's been offered a new job), Blanche replies, "When can I wear it?"

Perhaps the domestic comedy that best portrayed the archetypal family woman was *Father Knows Best* (1954–1962). The title says it all: Robert Young, playing Jim Anderson, never lacks a sane head, while his wife, Margaret, is stuck in the thrall of domestic life. She lacks Gracie Allen's originality yet still can be counted on as a source of genial humor who could on occasion correct the men in her family. Margaret is the fifties housewife personified.

In one sense, then, Friedan does have a case. The mass media of the 1950s, television prime among them, saturated the American public with the image of the new feminine mystique. But to establish that finding merely raises a much thornier issue: what sort of relationship is there between the media and reality? Friedan is arguing not merely that the institutions of mass communication promoted the feminine mystique; she is suggesting that, through their influence and pervasiveness, the media seduced women into the cult of domesticity. If Friedan was correct, we can understand why women's gains during the war did not translate into a revolution of the spirit.

# REFLECTION VERSUS MANIPULATION

What effect do the mass media have on real life? Obviously, that question is a complex one. Most Americans resist the idea that the images they see on television, in advertising, or in films have any purpose beyond plain and simple entertainment. But surely the reality is more complicated. Every day, Americans are bombarded by images that in ways both subtle and overt exert a powerful, though far from clearly understood, influence.

In sorting out possible answers, we can see two sharply contrasting hypotheses for gauging the media's impact. On the one hand is the argument that, in fact, the media have very little effect on the real world, since they merely reflect tastes and opinions that mass audiences already hold.

Confronted with a need to attract the largest number of consumers, media executives select programs that have the broadest appeal. Advertisers seek less to alter values than to channel existing ones toward a specific choice. Americans already value romantic love; once Ralph Lauren has his way, they wear his clothes to achieve it. In the most extreme form, this reflection hypothesis would see the media as essentially passive—a simple mirror to society. And with that argument, a good deal of Friedan's examination of female imagery might be instructive but beside the point. Women of the fifties were portrayed the way they were because, for whatever reasons, they had been transformed by the conditions of postwar culture.

But that extreme form of the reflection hypothesis breaks down for several reasons. First, if we argue that the mass media are merely reflections, then what are they reflecting? Surely not "real life" pure and simple. Only in commercials do women who use Fructis shampoo and men who wear Axe deodorant make their mates swoon. The parents on *Father Knows Best* are happily married with three children, hardly the statistical norm in America even then. Divorced, single-parent mothers were unknown in sitcom land. African American, Latino, or Asian families were virtually nonexistent. Obviously, while the media reflect certain aspects of real life, the reflection hypothesis must be modified to admit that a good deal of what is reflected comprises idealized values—what people would like to be rather than what they really are.

But if mass communications reflect ideals as much as reality, whose ideals are these? African American scholar bell hooks (she purposely lowercases her name) argued that "many audiences in the United States resist the idea that images have an ideological intent. ... Image making is political—that politics of domination informs the way the vast majority of images are constructed and marketed." That domination was precisely the problem Friedan addressed.

> *If mass communications reflect ideals as much as reality, whose ideals are these?*

As she pointed out, most of the editors, producers, directors, and writers of the 1950s were men. If male rather than female ideals and aspirations were being communicated (or, for that matter, white rather than Latino, middle-class rather than lower-class, or the ideals of any limited group), then it again becomes legitimate to ask how much the ideals of one segment of America are shaping those of a far wider audience.

Of course, many of the people involved in producing mass culture would argue that in the matter of dreams and ideals, they are not selling their own, they are merely giving the audience what it wants. But do audiences know what they really want? Surely they do sometimes. But they may also be influenced, cajoled, and swayed. Persuasion, after all, is at the heart of modern advertising. A fifties marketing executive made the point quite freely, noting that

> in a free enterprise economy, we have to develop the need for new products. And to do that we have to liberate women to desire these new products. We

help them rediscover that homemaking is more creative than to compete with men. This can be manipulated. We sell them what they ought to want, speed up the unconscious, move it along.

A better case for domination or manipulation would be hard to make. Perhaps the most obvious case of an audience susceptible to persuasion is children. Psychological research has indicated that among children, a process called modeling occurs,

> simply by watching others, without any direct reinforcement for learning and without any overt practice. The child imitates the model without being induced or compelled to do so. That learning can occur in the absence of direct reinforcement is a radical departure from earlier theories that regarded reward or punishment as indispensable to learning. There is now considerable evidence that children do learn by watching and listening to others even in the absence of reinforcement and overt practice.

Obviously, if young girls learn week in and week out that father does indeed know best and that a woman's place is in the home, the potential for asserting an ideology of male dominance is strong.

The hypothesis that the media may be manipulative contrasts sharply with the theory that they are only reflective. More realistically, though, the two alternatives are best seen as the poles of a continuum. In its extreme form, the reflection hypothesis sees the media as entirely neutral, with no influence whatever. The manipulative hypothesis, in its extreme form, treats the media as highly controlling, brainwashing viewers (to use a term popular in the anticommunist fifties) into believing and acting in ways they never would have on their own. But a young girl, no matter how long she watches television, is also shaped by what she learns from her parents, schoolteachers, religious instructors, and a host of other influences. Given those contending factors, how decisive a role can the media play?

Ironically, the more extreme forms of the manipulative hypothesis have been supported by both the left and right wings of the political spectrum. During the 1950s, for example, with worries of foreign subversion running high, conservative ideologues warned that communists had come to rely "more on radio and TV than on the press and motion pictures as 'belts' to transmit pro-Sovietism to the American public." On the other hand, liberal intellectuals charged that mass culture, at its worst, threatened "not merely to cretinize our taste, but to brutalize our senses by paving the way to totalitarianism."

Historians have stepped only gingerly into the debate over media influence. In part their hesitation may be because, like most scholars, they tend not to be heavy consumers of mass culture themselves. Preferring a symphony by Brahms to rap, Federico Fellini's *8 1/2* to *The Dark Knight*, or *Masterpiece Theatre* to *American Idol*, their instinctive reaction is to deem popular fare "worthy of attention only if it is created by unpaid folk and 'serious' artists who do not appear to think about making a living," as sociologist Herbert Gans has tartly remarked.

By temperament and training, most historians are also more comfortable with the traditional print media. When they seek to explicate a document, book, or diary, they can readily find the text and use common critical strategies to identify thematic, symbolic, or cultural content. Insofar as the author of the document is sensitive to issues that concern some significant sector of society, the text can be said to reflect on social reality.

But what if the "text" is a series of commercials plugging the virtues of Crest toothpaste or a year's worth of the soap opera *General Hospital*? In that case, historians confront two difficulties. A vast amount of broadcast material from the 1950s was ephemeral—not permanently recorded at the time it was broadcast and no longer recoverable. The actual content of many broadcasts can be reconstructed, if at all, only from file scripts or memories of viewers or participants. Even in situations in which television material has been saved and can be analyzed for its cultural content, a knowledge of how the audience received a program or commercial is crucial. As Gans has insisted, "cultural values cannot be determined from cultural content, until we know why people chose it." Do viewers watch a program intensely, or does it serve simply as background noise? Historians seldom have the means to answer that question satisfactorily.

Sociologists and cultural anthropologists are the scholars most likely to help historians determine the influence of the media—particularly television—in modern life. But while sociologists have run a number of interesting studies involving the effect of television violence and racial stereotypes on viewers, much less systematic evidence has been gathered on television's effect on women. The most promising work has centered on what is known as content analysis. A content-analysis researcher examines a body of evidence, scanning it systematically in order to answer a few objective questions. How often are sex and violence linked in network crime shows? The researcher picks a sample group of shows, views them on a regular basis, and counts the number of incidents involving sex and violence. The results, of course, are descriptive within fairly limited bounds. They can tell us, for example, how often women appear in certain roles, but not how the audience perceives or values those roles. Nor can we know, except indirectly, what the shows' producers actually intended. If women are always portrayed in inferior positions, we can infer that the producers saw women as inferior; but the inference remains unproved.

Content analysis of early programming has led sociologist Gaye Tuchman to conclude that television practiced the "symbolic annihilation of women." By that she meant that women were "demeaned, trivialized, or simply ignored." Surveys of television programs revealed that women, who constituted more than half the population, accounted for just 32 percent of the characters in prime-time dramas. Most of the women who did appear in prime time were concentrated in comedy series. Children's cartoons had even fewer female characters. In the shows in which women appeared most often—daytime soap operas—they still held inferior positions. A 1963 survey showed, in fact, that men held 80 percent of all jobs in prime-time shows.

Women were demeaned in other ways. They were most often the victims of violence, not the perpetrators. Single women were attacked more frequently than married women. The women most favorably portrayed were those who were court-ing or had a family role. In the 1950s two-thirds of all the women characters on television shows were married, had been married, or were engaged. Even in soap operas, usually set in homes in which women might presumably be allowed to act as leaders, women's roles were trivialized, for it was usually men who found the solutions to family problems.

*Even in soap operas, usually set in homes in which women might presumably be allowed to act as leaders, it was usually men who found the solutions to family problems.*

Much early content-analysis research was not designed to focus specifi-cally on women. But studies analyzing the settings of shows and the psycho-logical characteristics of heroes, villains, and supporting characters indirectly support Tuchman's conclusion, because they show that the world of televi-sion drama was overwhelmingly white, middle class, suburban, family cen-tered, and male dominated. In eighty-six prime-time dramas aired during 1953, men outnumbered women 2 to 1. The very young (under twenty) and the old (over sixty) were underrepresented. The characters were largely of childbearing age and were employed or employable. High white-collar or professional positions were overrepresented at the expense of routine white-collar or blue-collar jobs. Most characters were sane, law abiding, healthy, and white (more than 80 percent). Blacks, who accounted for 12 percent of the population, appeared in only 2 percent of the roles. Heroes outnum-bered heroines 2 to 1; and since heroic foreigners were more likely to be women, that left three American heroes for each American heroine.

In these same eighty-six shows, male villains outnumbered female vil-lains. Feminists might take this fact to heart as a more positive presenta-tion of women. Villains, however, had many traits that Americans admired. Although viewers saw them as unattractive, dishonest, disloyal, dirty, stingy, and unkind, villains also appeared brave, strong, sharper, or harder than most heroes, and had inner strength. Thus they were imposing, if undesirable, characters. In minimizing women as villains, television preserved a male-comforting stereotype while depriving women of yet another set of roles in which they could be effective. Similarly, television dramas presented the most favorable stereotypes of professions in which men dominated. Jour-nalists, doctors, and entertainers all had positive images, while teachers—a large majority of whom were women—were treated as the slowest, weakest, and softest professionals (though clean and fair).

So far as content analysis is able to go, then, it confirms that television did systematically reinforce the feminine mystique that Betty Friedan found so prevalent elsewhere. But along with the advantages of content analysis come limits. To be rigorous, the method of measuring must be standardized, and the questions asked must be fairly limited and objective. For example, one content analyst described her approach in this way:

> Between March 18 and March 31, 1975, I watched and coded the shows, according to pretested categories. Using a specially prepared timer, I examined the first verbal or nonverbal interaction clearly between two people in thirty seconds of one-minute segments of the programs. I recorded who was dominant, dominated, or equal in each interaction and noted the relevant occupation status, sex, race, and family role of each participant.

This approach is admirably systematic, but it leaves little room for more qualitative judgments—for evaluating the nuances of an image as well as its overt content. Sociologists, of course, would say that such subjective analysis is precisely what they are trying to avoid, because any nuances are likely to incorporate the prejudices of the researcher. As we know by now, historians have traditionally felt that this possible bias is a risk worth taking. They are inclined to examine documents for what they hint at or even do not say as much as for what they do. Because we are not in a position to undertake field research on how audiences of the fifties were affected by programs involving women, let us instead resort to a subjective analysis of television's product itself and see what its leading characters and dramatic themes reveal.

## MALE FRAMES AND FEMALE ENERGIES

The most promising programs for exploring gender issues are the sitcoms of the 1950s. As we have seen, other genres popular in the 1950s—crime shows, westerns, and quiz programs—tended to ignore women or place them in secondary roles. A majority of the sitcoms, however, take place in a domestic setting in which women are central figures. The plots regularly turn on misunderstandings between men and women over their relationships or the proper definition of gender roles. As a consequence, of all television programs, sitcoms had the most formative influence on the image of women.

As a genre, sitcoms had their roots in radio shows like *The Jack Benny Program*, *The Burns and Allen Show*, and *Amos 'n' Andy*.* That origin helps explain why comedy in television shows came to be more verbal than comedy in film, which blended physical and verbal humor. Sitcoms derived most of their laughs from puns, repartee, or irony. What the camera added were close-ups and reaction shots, since the small television screen limited the detail that could be shown. Tight focus revealed the visual delivery comedians often achieved through subtle gestures: a raised eyebrow, a curled lip, or a frown. "You know what your mother said the day we were married, Alice?" grumps the obese Ralph Kramden on *The Honeymooners*. [A close-up, here,

---

* *Amos 'n' Andy*, a show about a taxicab company operated by blacks, presented a special crossover problem. The white actors who starred in the show on radio were hardly appropriate for a visual medium.

for emphasis; the double-chin juts in disdain.] "You know what she said? I'm not losing a daughter; I'm gaining a ton." Or another time, when Ralph's vanity gets the better of him, he brags, "Alice, when I was younger, the girls crowded around me at the beach." "Of course, Ralph," replies Alice. "That's because they wanted to sit in the shade." [Cut to Ralph's bulging eyes.]

From the historian's point of view, the more intriguing sitcoms are not the predictable ones, such as *The Adventures of Ozzie and Harriet* or *Father Knows Best*, but those that do not seem to fit the standard mold. It is here—where the familiar conventions come closest to being broken—that the tensions and contradictions of the genre appear most clearly. In different ways, *Our Miss Brooks, I Love Lucy,* and *The Honeymooners* all feature unconventional characters and unusual plot situations. *Our Miss Brooks* stars Eve Arden as an aging, unmarried schoolteacher whose biting humor makes her a threat to the bumbling men around her. *I Love Lucy*, with Lucille Ball, follows the zany attempts of Lucy Ricardo to break out of her narrow domesticity into the larger world of show business or into some moneymaking venture. Although the Ricardos had a child midway through the series, he was not often featured in the show. *The Honeymooners* was perhaps the most offbeat sitcom of the fifties. It featured the blue-collar world of the Kramdens, a childless couple who lived in a dreary Brooklyn flat with their neighbors Ed and Trixie Norton, also childless. Ralph, a bus driver, and Ed, a sewer worker, seem unlikely subjects to reinforce the middle-class values of Friedan's feminine mystique. Despite their unusual formats, all three sitcoms were among the most popular shows of the fifties, and Lucy stayed at the top of the ratings for almost the entire decade. By looking at these sitcoms, we can better understand on what basis a show could deviate from traditional formats and still remain successful.

As it happens, none of these shows is as exceptional as it might first seem. All incorporate elements of the traditional family-show structure, with male authority remaining dominant, middle-class values applauded, and the proper order of society prevailing by the end of each episode. Still, there is more to them than the simple triumph of the feminine mystique. The three leading female characters—Connie Brooks, Lucy Ricardo, and Alice Kramden—reveal through the force of their comic personas certain tensions that conventional plot resolutions cannot hide. Each series offers glimpses of women's discontent as well as women able to cope with adversity.

The comic tensions in *Our Miss Brooks* arise from two primary sources: Miss Brooks constantly clashes with her authoritarian principal, Osgood Conklin, and at the same time has her amorous eye on the biology teacher, Mr. Boynton. Boynton seems oblivious to her sexual overtures yet is the best prospect to save her from spinsterhood. In one show she walks in with her arms full of packages. "Can I hold something?" he asks. "Sure, as soon as I put these packages down," she cracks, though he chooses not to notice.

Miss Brooks is oppressed on several levels. She recognizes that society places little value on her role as a teacher. There is no future in her job, where she is bullied, exploited, and underpaid. Marriage offers the only way out, but since she is superior in intellect and personality to the men and no longer young and fresh, her prospects are dim. Thus she faces a future in which she cannot fulfill her femininity. Her only hope is to use her wiles to trick Mr. Boynton into marriage. She must be passive-aggressive, because convention prevents her from taking overt initiatives. At the same time, she must accept a career situation that is beneath her talents. Rather than challenge the system that demeans her, she survives by treating it as comical and transcending it through the force of her superior character.

In the first episode of the series, Miss Brooks determines to arouse Mr. Boynton's romantic interest by starting a fight. That leads to a number of laughs as Mr. Boynton ducks each provocation. Before she makes headway, she is called on the carpet by Mr. Conklin, the principal. From behind his desk, Conklin radiates authority, glowering at her and treating her with disdain. But Miss Brooks hardly folds before the onslaught. She tricks him into reminiscing about his youth, and as he becomes more mellow (and human), she assumes greater familiarity, until she is sitting casually on the corner of his desk. By the end of the meeting, Connie has sent Mr. Conklin

*Male hierarchy is reestablished in the end, but before order returns, we have had a glimpse of a world in which women have power.*

on a wild-goose chase that leads to his arrest by the police. In his absence, she becomes acting principal, clearly relishing the sense of authority she gains from holding the seat of power, having subverted the duly constituted authority. Of course, male hierarchy is reestablished in the end, but before order returns, we have had a glimpse of a world in which women have power.

The liberties taken in the show, however, amount to scarcely more than shore leave. A traditional sense of domestic order underlies the surface mayhem. Even though the central characters are unmarried, the show does have a surrogate family structure. Despite her relatively advanced age, Miss Brooks's real role is that of a smart-talking teenage daughter. She lives in an apartment with a remarkably maternal housekeeper. One of the students at school, Walter (an essential nerd), serves as a surrogate son, while Mr. Conklin, of course, is the father figure. That leaves Mr. Boynton to be paired off as Miss Brooks's reticent steady. Her challenges to Mr. Conklin's male authority are allowed only because the principal is pompous, arbitrary, and occasionally abusive of his position. And Mr. Boynton is scarcely as dumb as he acts; indeed, at the end of the first episode, as Miss Brooks waits eagerly for a kiss that will demonstrate his interest, he holds back and winks at the audience—indicating that he can dish it out too. With Mr. Conklin back in charge and Mr. Boynton clearly in control, the male frame is reestablished. Miss Brooks has been chastened for her presumption, and the normal, male-dominated order has been restored.

Similar tensions operate in the *I Love Lucy* show. Lucy's efforts to escape the confines of domesticity threaten her husband, Ricky, and the well-being of the family. The plot generally thickens as Lucy cons her neighbor Ethel

**Ethel Mertz (Vivian Vance) and Lucy (Lucille Ball) look on** as Ricky Ricardo (Desi Arnaz) and Fred Mertz (William Frawley) react with shock to yet another of their schemes, this time to spend more time with their husbands by playing golf together. The women chose old-fashioned golf clothing, because they knew next to nothing about the game. Costuming was one of many recurring devices the show employed to develop storylines. Notice how Ricky and Fred use their eyes to express shock. Such small facial gestures were a common way in which early television achieved comic effects.

Mertz into joining her escapades. Ethel and Lucy then become rivals of their husbands. In an episode that could have generated biting commentary, Lucy and Ethel challenge Fred Mertz and Ricky to exchange their jobs for domesticity. The women will be the breadwinners, the men the housekeepers. Both, of course, prove equally inept in the others' domain. Ethel and Lucy, once they discover they have no significant job skills, end up working in a chocolate factory. Their boss is a woman who is far more domineering and arbitrary than Mr. Conklin ever was. In a parody of Charlie Chaplin's *Modern Times*, Lucy and Ethel fall hopelessly behind as they pack candies that run relentlessly along a conveyor belt. They stuff their pockets and their mouths until they are sick and the floor is heaped with fallen candies. By the end of the day they return home emotionally drained, humbled, and thwarted.

  In the meantime, Ricky and Fred have virtually destroyed the apartment. How much rice do they need for dinner? They decide on several pounds, so that the kitchen is soon awash. Just as Ethel and Lucy are relieved to return home, Fred and Ricky are overjoyed to escape the toils of domestic life. Each side learns to respect the difficulties facing the other.

Despite the schmaltzy ending, there is a real tension in the structure of this episode and the series as a whole. Within the orthodox framework (Lucy and Ricky are firmly middle class, worrying about money, friends, schools, and a house in the suburbs), the energy and spark of the show comes precisely because Lucy, like Miss Brooks, consistently refuses to recognize the male limits prescribed for her. Although Ricky manages to rein her in by the end of each episode, the audience realizes full well that she is too restless, too much restricted by four walls and a broom, and far too vivacious to accept the cult of domesticity. She will be off and running again the following week in another attempt to break loose.*

More than any other sitcom of the fifties, *The Honeymooners* seems to deviate from middle-American stereotypes. As lower-class, childless couples living in stark apartments, the Nortons and Kramdens would scarcely seem ideal reflections of an affluent, family-centered society. Ralph and Alice struggle to get by on his $67.50-a-week salary as a bus driver. Sewer worker Ed Norton and his wife, Trixie, live off credit. Whenever their appliances or furniture are repossessed, Ed replaces them with merchandise from another store. The show's main set is the Kramden's living room-cum-kitchen, with no television set, telephone, vacuum cleaner, or other modern appliances. They have only a bureau, a table and chairs, a standing sink, an icebox (literally), and a stove.

The show turns on Ralph's obsession with money and status. He is forever trying to get rich quick, earn respect, and move up in the world. All that saves him from himself and disaster is Alice's stoic forbearance. She has had to live through all his efforts to assert his authority—"I'm the boss, Alice, and don't you ever forget it!"—and to resist his harebrained schemes (diet pizza parlors, wallpaper that glows in the dark to save electricity). And it is Alice who cushions his fall when each new dream turns to

> *In no other show do the characters so regularly lay marriage, ego, or livelihood on the line.*

ashes. Like most middle-class American couples, Ralph and Alice bicker over money. Ralph is a cheapskate, not by nature but to mask his failure as a breadwinner. Alice must use her feminine wiles to persuade him to buy anything,

---

* The show's most successful moment might also serve as a model of 1950s family life. In its early years, television honored all the middle-class sexual mores. Even married couples slept in separate beds, and the word *pregnant* was taboo (since it implied that a couple had been sexually active—at least once). The producers of *Lucy* thus faced a terrible dilemma when they learned that their star was indeed with child. What to do? They made the bold decision to incorporate Lucille Ball's pregnancy into the show. For months, television audiences watched Lucy become bigger and more uncomfortable. On January 19, 1953, the big day arrived. The episode "Lucy Goes to the Hospital" (filmed earlier in anticipation of the blessed event) scored the highest rating (68.8 percent) of any show of the decade. In newspaper headlines, news of the birth of Desi Arnaz Jr. rivaled the inauguration of Dwight D. Eisenhower, which occurred the following morning.

**In a typical scene** from *The Honeymooners*, Ralph Kramden (Jackie Gleason) adopts a pompous pose before his skeptical wife, Alice (Audrey Meadows), and her anxious friend Trixie Norton (Joyce Randolph), while his friend Ed Norton (Art Carney) looks on with bug-eyed disbelief. Inevitably, Ralph's confidence shattered in the face of his bungling attempts to get rich quick, leaving Alice to pick up the pieces and put him back together again.

even a television or a telephone. To protect his pride, Ralph accuses her of being a spendthrift. Their battles have far more bite than those seen in any other sitcom of that era. In no other show do the characters so regularly lay marriage, ego, or livelihood on the line.

Why, then, did the audience like this show? For one thing, it is very funny. Ed Norton's deadpan is a perfect foil to Ralph's manic intensity. It is a delight to watch Norton take forever to shuffle a deck of cards while Ralph does a slow burn. And Alice's alternately tolerant and spirited rejoinders complete the chemistry. In addition, there is a quality to the Kramdens' apartment that separates it in time and space from the world in which middle-class viewers live. The mass audience is more willing to confront serious questions if such issues are raised in distant times or places. Death on a western does not have the same implications as a death on *Lassie*. Divorce for Henry VIII is one thing; even a hint of it for Ozzie and Harriet would be too shocking to contemplate. Thus the depression look of the Kramdens' apartment gives the audience the spatial and temporal distance it needs to separate itself from the sources of conflict that regularly trouble Ralph and

Alice. The audience can look on with a sense of its material and social superiority as Alice and Ralph go at it:

> RALPH: You want this place to be Disneyland.
> ALICE: This place is a regular Disneyland. You see out there, Ralph? The
> back of the Chinese restaurant, old man Grogan's long underwear on
> the line, the alley? That's my Fantasyland. You see that sink over there?
> That's my Adventureland. The stove and the icebox, Ralph, that's
> Frontierland. The only thing that's missing is the World of Tomorrow.
> RALPH (doing his slow burn): You want Tomorrowland, Alice? You want
> Tomorrowland? Well, pack your bags, because you're going to the moon!
> [Menaces her with his raised fist.]*

Underneath its blue-collar veneer, *The Honeymooners* is still a middle-class
family sitcom. Alice and Trixie don't have children; they have Ralph and
Ed. In one episode Trixie says to Alice, "You know those men we're married to? You have to treat them like children." Reversal of social class roles
makes this arrangement work without threatening the ideal of male authority. Because the middle classes have always
equated the behavior of the poor with that of     *"Baby, you're the greatest."*
children—and Ralph and Ed are poor—no
one is surprised by their childish antics. Trixie and Alice, both having married beneath their social status, maintain middle-class standards. At the end
of almost every episode, Alice brings Ralph back into the fold after one of his
schemes fails. Surrounding her in an embrace, he rewards her with his puppy
dog devotion: "Baby, you're the greatest."

One episode in particular reveals the price Alice paid to preserve her man/
child, marriage, and selfhood. A telegram arrives announcing, "I'm coming to
visit. Love, Mom." Ralph explodes at the idea of sharing his apartment with
his dreaded mother-in-law. Whenever she visits, she showers him with criticisms that wound his brittle pride. After numerous jokes at Ralph's expense,
along with some cutting commentary on mothers-in-law, Ralph moves in
upstairs with the Nortons. There he provokes a similar fight between Ed
and Trixie. But just as this upheaval threatens the domestic order, marriage
and family prevail over wounded pride. Kicked out by the Nortons, Ralph
returns home, only to discover that "Mom" is Mother Kramden. Alice, of
course, has welcomed her with the very warmth Ralph denies Alice's mother.
Alice's generosity of spirit once again reduces him to a shamefaced puppy.

This victory is so complete that it threatens to destroy Alice's relationship
with Ralph. Any pretense of masculine authority has been laid to ruin. As
if to soften the blow to Ralph's pride, Alice sits down to deliver her victory
speech. She lowers her eyes, drops her shoulders, and speaks in tones of
resignation rather than triumph. The episode ends as she reads a letter that

---

* Similarly, a show like *M\*A\*S\*H* could more easily explore topical issues such as racism because it
was set in Korea, not the United States, and in the 1950s, not the present, even though the issues
were contemporary.

describes mothers-in-law as having the "hardest job in the world." Ironically, the letter is one Ralph wrote fifteen years earlier to Alice's mother.
The sentiments expressed are so sappy that they virtually undercut the comedy. Like Ralph, the producers must have thought it better to eat crow than
leave a residue of social criticism. Their material had been so extreme, the
humor so sharp, and the mother-in-law jokes so cruel that they threatened
middle-American values.

Even after its apology, the show ends with a disturbing image. Mother
Kramden has gone off to "freshen up." A penitent Ralph admits his defeat,
then announces he is going out for some air—in essence, to pull himself
back together. But what of Alice? She is left alone in her kitchen, holding
nothing more than she had before—dominion over her dreary world. While
Ralph can escape, if only briefly, Alice's domestic role requires her to stay
with Ralph's mother. For Alice, there is no escape. When the show ends, she
is no better off than before the battle began. Her slumped posture suggests
that she understands all too well the hollowness of her triumph. We must
believe that many women in videoland identified with Alice.

*The Honeymooners, I Love Lucy,* and *Our Miss Brooks* all suggest that while
the male characters in the series maintain their ultimate authority, the
"symbolic annihilation" of women that Gaye Tuchman spoke of is, in these
comedies at least, not total. A battle between the sexes would not be funny
unless the two sides were evenly matched; and setting sitcoms in the domestic sphere placed women in a better position to spar. Further, although men
had an advantage through social position, rank, and authority, women like
Miss Brooks, Lucy, and Alice vied on equal terms. The authority that men
assumed through male hierarchy, these women radiated through the sheer
strength of their comedic personalities. The producers, of course, were
not closet feminists in permitting this female assertiveness to occur; they
simply recognized that the female characters accounted for much of their
shows' popularity. And the shows' ratings were high, we would argue, partly
because they hinted at the discontent many women felt, whether or not they
recognized the strength of their feelings.

If that conclusion is correct, it suggests that neither the reflective hypothesis nor the manipulative hypothesis explains how the mass media shape
popular culture. At bottom, the extreme forms of each explanation slight one
of the constants in historical explanation: change over time. If the mass communications industries simply reflected public taste and never influenced it,
they would become nonentities—multibillion-dollar ciphers with no causal
agency. All change would be the consequence of other historical factors. On
the other hand, if we assign a role to the media that's too manipulative, we
find it difficult to explain any change at all. As agencies of cultural hege-
mony, the media could stifle any attempt to change the status quo. How
was it, then, that millions of girls who watched themselves being symboli-
cally annihilated during the fifties supplied so many converts to the women's
movement of the sixties?

Perhaps the mass media, although influential in modern society, are not as monolithic in outlook as they sometimes seem. A comparison to the medieval church is apt, so long as we remember that the church, too, was hardly able to impose its will universally. Even where orthodoxy reigned, schismatic movements were always springing up. Today's heretics may be feminists rather than Anabaptists, but they are nonetheless responding to growing pressures within society. From a feminist point of view, we have not automatically achieved utopia merely because television since the 1980s has regularly presented sitcoms and dramas with women as their central characters. We should remember that the same mass culture industry that threatened women with symbolic annihilation also published *The Feminine Mystique*.

# *Additional Reading*

This chapter draws on material from three different fields—women's history, social history and popular culture, and the history of television. For overviews of the image of women in our culture, see Lois Banner, *American Beauty* (New York, 1983); Ann Douglas, *The Feminization of American Culture* (New York, 1977); and Molly Haskell, *From Reverence to Rape* (New York, 1974). Haskell's study of the image of women in movies confirms what we learn from examining other areas of popular culture. A most intriguing strategy for decoding gender signs in the mass media is Erving Goffman, *Gender Advertisements* (New York, 1976).

For readers more concerned with the feminist movement and women's history, Betty Friedan, *The Feminine Mystique* (New York, 1963), is one place to start. Her book retains the vitality that spurred its wide popularity and remains an interesting social history of the 1950s. Friedan, however, has argued for what one feminist critic described as a declensionist view of women's situation. She believed that between the 1930s and the 1950s, women had lost status and opportunity. Joanne Myerowitz, ed., *Not June Cleaver: Women and Gender in Postwar America, 1945–1960* (Philadelphia, 1994), finds more continuity than decline. A series of scholars offer evidence of successful, engaged women who defy the stereotype Friedan established. Friedan's political activism is the subject of Susan Oliver, *Betty Friedan: The Personal Is Political* (New York, 2007). Daniel Horowitz, *Betty Friedan and the Making of "The Feminine Mystique": The American Left, the Cold War, and Modern Feminism* (Amherst, 2000), connects her to the progressive politics of her youth and links to American Communists. Ruth Rosen, *The World Split Open: How the Modern Women's Movement Changed America* (New York: 2000), covers the roots of feminism in the 1950s. The explosion of thinking and writing in women's history makes it impossible to mention more than a few valuable studies. The historian who looks at both television and feminism is Susan Douglas, *Where the Girls Are: Growing Up Female with the Mass Media* (New York, 1995). Carroll Smith-Rosenberg has been a leader among women historians; her article "The New Woman and New History," *Feminist Studies* 3 (1975–1976): 185–198, offers useful perspectives.

As we mentioned, historians have not written extensively about television. A good starting point is Gary Edgerton, *The Columbia History of American Television* (New York, 2009), a comprehensive guide to all facets from programming to technology. James Roman, *From Daytime to Prime Time: A History of American Television Programing* (Santa Barbara, CA, 2007), gives a picture of evolving content. Eric Barnouw's *Tube of Plenty* (New York, 1990) is a pioneering work in broadcast history. Karal Ann Marling, *As Seen on TV: The Visual Culture of Everyday Life in the 1950s* (Cambridge, MA, 1994), has taken up the topic of this chapter. A couple of collections of essays are quite interesting: John O'Connor, ed., *American History, American Television*

(New York, 1983), and Raymond Williams, *Television: Technology and Cultural Form* (New York, 1975), have some of the most interesting insights into the evolution of television and its impact on society.

# CHAPTER 15
# *Sitting-In*

*Civil rights protests erupted all over the South in 1960 after four black students sat-in at a lunch counter in Greensboro, North Carolina. Was this a spontaneous act born of frustration, or were larger forces at work?*

Joseph McNeil felt hunger pangs as he stepped off the bus at Union Station in Greensboro, North Carolina. He received little comfort from the food counter, however: he was black, this was 1960, and across the South rigid "Jim Crow" lines segregated African Americans in almost all public places—schools, movie theaters, parks, churches, trains, buses, planes, and, of course, restaurants. So when McNeil asked for service, he was refused and returned hungry to his dormitory at North Carolina A&T, an agricultural and technical college where he was a first-year student. He poured out his frustration to his roommate, David Richmond. Two other A&T students from down the hall joined them: Franklin McCain and Ezell Blair Jr., who, like Richmond, hailed from Greensboro.

The four frequently held bull sessions about college life—the poor food, quirky professors, and elusive coeds. Often the conversations turned to indignities large and small that segregation imposed on black people. To McNeil and his friends, a white person walking down the street had to be addressed as "Mister," "Miss," or "Mrs." Whites, on the other hand, called blacks by their first names or simply as "boy." Facing a bathroom emergency, they could not enter a lavatory unless it was designated "colored." On city buses, they still sat in the back, despite the landmark 1954 Supreme Court ruling in *Brown v. Board of Education of Topeka*, which rejected the notion of "separate but equal" segregated facilities—and even after the Court explicitly addressed busing in December 1956, affirming Martin Luther King Jr.'s bus boycott in Montgomery, Alabama.

No doubt McNeil's most recent humiliation fired up the four friends, because on this evening their conversation took an unexpected turn. They had frequently criticized older blacks for passivity in the face of repeated racial insults. "We constantly heard about all the evils that are occurring and how blacks are mistreated and nobody is doing anything about it," Richmond recalled. "We used to question, 'Why is it that you have to sit in the balcony? Why do you have to ride in the back of the bus?'" Then McCain pointed out that they, too, were all talk and no action. The real question, they agreed, was what should be done to bring an end to Jim Crow, the system of racial segregation that stigmatized all black Americans as second-class citizens? More immediately and personally, what were *they* going to do about it?

A plan emerged. They decided to ask for service at the lunch counter at Woolworth's department store. Blacks were encouraged to shop anywhere in the store yet were allowed to eat only at a stand-up snack bar and bakery counter. The long L-shaped, stainless-steel lunch counter with cushioned stools was strictly off-limits. Woolworth's even posted Colored Only and Whites Only signs until 1958, when Dr. George Simkins, a local African American dentist and civil rights activist, asked the manager to remove the signs. The manager agreed, but only because other merchants were removing them as well. But even when the signs were gone, the lunch counters remained strictly segregated, so much so that only whites waited on customers, while blacks stayed in the background, cooking the food and cleaning up.

Simkins understood well the racial politics of Greensboro. The city had a reputation for its progressive approach to race relations, but Simkins recognized that city leaders made concessions to the black community only to avoid a confrontation that might tarnish the city's image. They remained determined to keep Jim Crow in place. Simkins, chapter president of the local National Association for the Advancement of Colored People (NAACP), was equally determined to end apartheid. In 1955 he had led three black friends to the first tee of the segregated Gillespie Park Golf course, a public facility. Local police arrested him, and a judge jailed him for criminal trespass.

On the afternoon of February 1, 1960, Simkins was seeing patients when he received word that something big was happening at Woolworth's. It turned out to be McCain, Blair, McNeil, and Richmond, who had set out on their mission. McCain, having been to an air force ROTC (Reserve Officers' Training Corps) class, still wore his uniform. Some people later thought he was making a patriotic statement, but in truth, the class had run late, leaving him no time to change. On their way to Woolworth's, the four passed a shop run by Ralph Johns, a local white business owner who had long urged blacks to stand up for their rights. They let him know that they finally had decided to act, and he called the local newspaper. Whatever outward bravado they displayed, on the inside they were scared. "I can tell you this," McCain said. "I was fully prepared mentally not to ever come back to the campus. . . . I thought the worst thing that could happen to us is we could have had our heads split open with a night stick and hauled into prison."

Pushing aside those dark thoughts, they pressed on. In the store they divided into pairs to make purchases—toothpaste, school supplies—that would establish them as legitimate customers. Then they made their way to the lunch counter. McCain and McNeil were the first to sit down.

What happened next took them by surprise. Nothing! The waitress at first ignored them. Geneva Tisdale, a black woman bussing dishes behind the counter, assumed they were from out of town. "I just thought there was somebody here from someplace else that didn't know they didn't serve blacks," she said, "so I kept on doing what I was doing." But when they tried to order sodas, doughnuts, and coffee, the waitress refused to serve them. Tisdale called them troublemakers whose actions would damage race relations.

Manager Charley Harris spoke to them next. His store was one of Woolworth's most profitable, and the lunch counter was his biggest moneymaker. An incident there might drive customers away. Despite his request, the four politely refused to leave. So off he went to see the local police chief, who declined to intervene since the four had done nothing disorderly. The chief did, however, send an officer to keep an eye on the situation. Just as the students were beginning to doubt their decision to sit-in, an elderly white woman approached. "Boys, I am just so proud of you," she said. "My only regret is that you didn't do this 10 or 15 years ago." McCain later recalled, "That pat on the shoulder meant more to me that day than anything else. . . . I got so much pride and such a good positive feeling from that little old lady. I mean, she'll never know it, but that really made the day for us." Harris then ended the standoff by closing the counter. The "Greensboro Four," as they would soon be known, told him they would be back. Outside, they ran into news photographer Jack Moebes, who took their picture walking four abreast.

The young men returned to the campus without their coffee and doughnuts. McCain remembered, "I've never felt so good in my life. I truly felt as though I had my going-to-the-mountaintop experience." Students on campus at first refused to believe what they had done. All the same, many pledged to join the protest. From 11:00 to 3:00 the next day, they sat at the counter, where a number of hostile whites came by to heckle them. Newspaper and television reporters also arrived, and when the news hit the campus, the response was beyond their wildest

> *"I've never felt so good in my life. I truly felt as though I had my going-to-the-mountaintop experience."*

imagining. A&T students greeted them as heroes. The college president, despite his previous deference to white community leaders, refused demands that he expel or suspend the demonstrators. All he wanted to know, he asked wryly, was why the four of them had decided to eat at Woolworth's, since the food there was no better than the campus cafeteria.

By February 3, a fever gripped the community. Students from other local colleges soon joined in, and on the fourth day the first white students as well as high school students sat in with them. Rather than face more demonstrations, Woolworth's closed the lunch counter, but the genie had escaped the lamp. The Greensboro spirit spilled over to other states and other communities. Cleveland Sellers, who would become a leading student activist,

**The Greensboro Four** (*from left to right:* David Richmond, Franklin McCain, Ezell Blair Jr., and Joseph McNeil), as photographed by Jack Moebes as they left Woolworth's on February 1, 1960.

felt "a shot of adrenaline" that ignited "a burning desire to get involved" when the news reached him in South Carolina. Up in New York City, a young high school math teacher, Robert Moses, saw news photos of the four Greensboro students exhibiting a defiance rare among southern blacks. Within months, Moses had headed south to join the student movement, and Sellers was leading a protest in Denmark, South Carolina. In Nashville, Tennessee, another group of students, who had already staged sit-ins the previous fall, sensed their time had come. So did students such as Lonnie King and Julian Bond in Atlanta, Georgia. When King saw the headlines from Greensboro, he shoved the paper in front of Bond and said, "Don't you think it ought to happen here?" Soon enough it did.

In February alone, students held sit-ins at lunch counters in eleven cities in North Carolina, seven in Virginia, four in South Carolina, three in Florida, two in Tennessee, one in Kentucky, and one in Maryland. Over time the circle of protest widened to Georgia, Texas, Louisiana, Arkansas,

West Virginia, and even Ohio. Established civil rights organizations such as the NAACP and the Southern Christian Leadership Conference (SCLC) seemed as much surprised by this eruption of protests as the local authorities who opposed them. The Congress of Racial Equality (CORE) rushed an organizer to the area, and some local chapters of the NAACP provided legal counsel and bail bond money, but the national NAACP often urged protesters to show more restraint. Its Legal Defense Fund at first refused to provide funds for jailed student protesters.

And jailed many were. In Raleigh, North Carolina, police arrested forty-one students at the Cameron Village Woolworth's. Nashville police arrested eighty-one student protesters, even though they behaved with courtesy and were committed to nonviolence. Whites who harassed them were not arrested. Most authorities assumed that the stigma of being jailed would stifle further protest and were thus surprised when many demonstrators chose jail rather than paying a fine. "Jail-ins" added another weapon to the protesters' arsenal. Even more surprising to authorities, the often-cautious leaders of the local black communities, whatever their initial reservations, threw their support behind the students.

In Nashville, where the Reverend James Lawson had been training students in the practices of nonviolent protest, the Greensboro sit-ins took civil rights organizers by surprise. That Friday, February 5, they held a mass meeting to plan local actions. Lawson urged students to move slowly. Few had received adequate training, he warned, and the local affiliate of the SCLC had less than $90 available for bail, once the police started to make arrests. The students insisted that, ready or not, it was time to act. As nineteen-year-old theology student James Bevel put it, "I'm sick and tired of waiting." Whatever their reservations, local black community leaders threw their wholehearted support behind the students. The Reverend Kelly Miller Smith opened the doors of the First Baptist Church to public meetings. Lawson provided a crash course in the tactics of nonviolent protest. Within several days, the local SCLC chapter raised $40,000 for bail. Many people put up homes and businesses as security for the bail fund. All fourteen local black lawyers offered free legal services. As Reverend Smith explained, "We had just launched out on something that looked perfectly crazy and scores of people were being arrested, and paddy wagons were full and people downtown couldn't understand what was going on, people just welcoming being arrested, that ran against everything they had ever seen."

First Greensboro, then Raleigh and Durham, then Nashville, and then all over the South. McCain, Richmond, McNeil, and Blair had let loose an avalanche. By the end of May, businesses in Nashville had accepted an integration plan. Greensboro took a bit longer, but there, too, stores opened their lunch counters to black customers. And the momentum did not stop with Greensboro. Student protesters gave the civil rights movement new energy and an urgency that culminated first in major civil rights legislation and eventually in the demand for "black power."

Looking back almost fifty years later, what should historians make of this extraordinary string of events? How did the decision of four young men, made in a late-night dormitory bull session, explode into a national crusade that transformed the civil rights movement? In an article he wrote for *Harper's* magazine in 1960, Louis Lomax, an African American journalist and early historian of the civil rights movement, offered an explanation for the impact of Greensboro. "Negroes all over America," he observed, "knew . . . that the spontaneous and uncorrelated student demonstrations were more than an attack on segregation: they were proof that the Negro leadership class, epitomized by the National Association for the Advancement of Colored People, was no longer the prime mover of the Negro's social revolt."

In that statement, Lomax made two major points about the Greensboro sit-ins: first that they were spontaneous—determined by the unprompted decision McNeil, Richmond, Blair, and McCain made to take action; and second, that they shifted the leadership and strategy in the civil rights movement away from traditional organizations to students. Civil rights veteran James Farmer reached a similar conclusion: "At long last after decades of acceptance, four freshman students at North Carolina A&T went into Woolworth and at the lunch counter they 'sat-in.'" Many historians agreed with Lomax. Howard Zinn, for example, wrote that "spontaneity and self-sufficiency were the hallmarks of the sit-ins; without adult advice or consent, the students planned and carried them through." As one college history text asserted, "The courage of the students transformed the civil rights movement. Their activism emboldened black adults to voice their dissatisfaction, and it brought young African Americans a new sense of self-respect."

## CONTINUITY VERSUS DISCONTINUITY

At heart, history as a discipline studies change over time. Historians routinely seek to explain why change occurs where and when it does and why it occurs in the particular way it does. So an event that appears to move history in new directions attracts close attention. Readers of this book have already encountered numerous events that transformed society, whether a trial of two relatively unknown anarchists for bank robbery, the dropping of two bombs on Japan at the end of World War II, or the writing of *The Feminine Mystique*. Such an event or moment constitutes what is popularly called a "tipping point" or a "watershed." Once John Brown attacked Harper's Ferry, the rush to civil war became irresistible. The decision to drop the atom bomb led to a nuclear arms race. Why is it, historians want to know, that in the steady flow of time some events are so much more consequential than others?

In their study of the past, historians generally gravitate toward one of two camps: those who see the past as a continuous flow with occasional pools and eddies and those who see the past as punctuated by periodic torrents, during which the ties between past and present are largely severed. As a shorthand we could label them the "continuity" and "discontinuity" schools, except at this level of abstraction the division amounts to less of a school than an instinctive disposition brought to the way one analyzes trends and events. Those in the continuity school tend to emphasize the links between major watershed moments and the events that precede them. They explain the volume of water at a falls by following the river upstream to locate the tributaries that turn what was once a brook into a river.

Many chapters in this book make the case for continuity. In analyzing the role of *The Jungle* in the controversy over tainted meat, we suggested that no matter how much Upton Sinclair shocked the nation, previous scandals had prepared the public to believe the worst of the meatpackers. And Theodore Roosevelt, in his ambition to increase the regulatory authority of the government, used the furor over *The Jungle* toward ends previously championed by a large and varied group of Progressive reformers.

The explanation of Greensboro offered by Louis Lomax and echoed by Howard Zinn emphasizes discontinuity, and historians who gravitate in this direction find much to work with in breakout events characterized as revolutions, whether they be political in nature (e.g., the French and Russian revolutions) or more intellectual or social (the scientific and industrial revolutions). With revolutions, old structures collapse, new authorities arise, and discredited ideas and values make way for new ones. Thus, when Lomax, Zinn, and others called the sit-ins spontaneous, they were suggesting that the four young men acted independently of and largely without consultation with any organized movement.

Certainly the chain of events following the Greensboro protest redirected the civil rights movement into a more confrontational phase, in which the young and especially students took the lead. In the wake of the Woolworth's sit-ins came the creation of the more radical Student Nonviolent Coordinating Committee (SNCC—pronounced *snick*), the Freedom Rides of 1961, James Meredith's integration of the University of Mississippi in 1962, student voter-registration drives during the Mississippi Freedom Summer of 1964, and ultimately the rise of the Black

*Without Greensboro, the civil rights movement would not have happened when it did and in the way that it did.*

Power movement. The increasing level of confrontation increased pressure on the system of racial segregation. It pushed President John Kennedy to introduce a civil rights bill in 1963; it prodded Martin Luther King to organize the March on Washington in August of that year, and Lyndon Johnson to pass the Civil Rights Act (1964) and Voting Rights Act (1965). Hence, the Greensboro sit-ins, historian William Chafe argued, would qualify as a watershed moment in the history of American racial politics. The movement might well have changed direction without Greensboro, but it certainly would not have happened when it did and in the way that it did without it.

Considerable evidence supports the Lomax-Zinn notion that the Greensboro sit-in was a "spontaneous" event. To begin with, none of the four central participants had been civil rights activists before they decided to act. In their late-night bull sessions, they were just as likely to question whether moral man should act against injustice as to debate over race and social activism. In that sense, they were armchair philosophers, like so many first-year college students. But the insult at the Greensboro bus terminal got under McNeil's skin. On the Sunday night that he returned to the dorm hungry, he said to his friends, "It's time we take some action now." What would they do? McCain remembered that they had no name for their tactic—they did not consider it a "sit-in" or "sit-down"—they just planned to go ask to be served. No one expected they would be; they just planned to order and stay put. As Ezell Blair commented, "Well, you know that might be weeks, that might be months, that might be never."

And why Woolworth's? None of the four had a special grievance against the chain store; it was simply a prominent local business and, they felt, a proper target. "They advertise in the public media, newspapers, radio, television, that sort of thing," McCain later explained. "They tell you to come in. 'Yes, buy the toothpaste; yes, come in and buy the notebook paper.' " Once blacks made their purchases, their money mingled in the cash register with white money. But sit down with white people at the lunch counter? "Never." "The whole system, of course, was unjust," McCain noted, "but that just seemed like insult added to injury." So when the waitress told them, "I'm sorry, we don't serve you here," they replied, "We just beg to disagree with you. We've in fact already been served," referring to their recent purchases. "We wonder why you'd invite us in to serve us at one counter and deny service at another."

Further evidence suggests that McCain and his friends had no notion they were starting a movement. Although all four participated in civil rights events on campus after the sit-in, they did not become activists after college. Ezell Blair spent a year in law school before moving to Boston, where he worked with the developmentally disabled, became a member of the New England Islamic Center, and took the name Jibreel Khazan. Franklin McCain became a chemist and then an executive for the Celanese Corporation. Joseph McNeil served as an officer in the air force before working for IBM and later the financial-services industry on Wall Street. David Richmond stayed around Greensboro as a community counselor and died from lung cancer at the age of 49. No matter how much they resented the injustices of Jim Crow in 1960, the Greensboro Four did not make the movement they inspired the focus of their adult lives.

## THE CASE FOR CONTINUITY

So a case can be made for "spontaneity" and discontinuity. Still, the context sketched thus far has centered mostly on the conversations these four men held in their first-year dorm. But what happens if we dig a little deeper into the influences on their lives before freshman year? First, three of the four students (McNeil was the exception) grew up in Greensboro and attended segregated Dudley High School. The teaching staff contained a number of civil rights activists, including Nell Coley, an English teacher who preached racial pride to her students. The curriculum included the literature and history of black protest. Ezell Blair remembered particularly the impact of Langston Hughes's poem, "The Negro Speaks of Rivers," which proudly evoked his African heritage:

> I bathed in the Euphrates when dawns were young.
> I built my hut near the Congo and it lulled me to sleep.
> I looked upon the Nile and raised the pyramids above it.
> I heard the singing of the Mississippi when Abe Lincoln went down to
> New Orleans, and I've seen its muddy bosom turn all golden in the sunset.
>
> I've known rivers:
> Ancient, dusky rivers.
>
> My soul has grown deep like the rivers.

Joseph McNeil grew up in Wilmington, North Carolina, but he, too, had teachers who were "dynamic and straightforward [and] who would tell you what your rights were as citizens, what you should have, what you don't have, how you're going to get them."

School was not the only place where these four heard the message of civil rights. Blair and Richmond attended Shiloh Baptist Church, where Pastor Otis Hairston recruited members for the NAACP. They also belonged to the local NAACP youth group that met in churches and on college campuses in the area. At meetings, they discussed protest activities both in Greensboro and across the South. The 1955 Montgomery bus boycott had inspired intense discussions that, as one participant recalled, "started a whole lot of things rolling." Martin Luther King also left his mark when he came to Greensboro in 1958. The president of North Carolina A&T, fearing that King was too controversial, refused to make the school's auditorium available. Willa Player, president of nearby Bennett College, had no such reservation. As head of a private women's college, Bennett was less vulnerable to reprisal from state officials. But Player also made her

*"This is a liberal arts college where freedom rings—so Martin Luther King can speak here."*

decision as an educator, saying "this is a liberal arts college where freedom rings—so Martin Luther King can speak here." Blair heard King's sermon. He recalled it as "so strong that I could feel my heart palpitating. It brought tears to my eyes."

Those at A&T who knew the four young men found Blair an unlikely person to launch a social movement. Where Franklin McCain was a large, imposing figure and McNeil, a physics major, was brainy, Blair was physically small and struck his friends as the "little brother" type. But Blair came from a home that resonated with civil rights consciousness. His father, Ezell Blair Sr., taught shop at Dudley High School and was a central figure among local civil rights activists. In 1957, when Greensboro adopted a strategy of token integration, it earned a reputation as a symbol of the "New South, astir with new liberalism," as *Newsweek* put it. Blair senior sized up the Greensboro integration plan for the charade that it was. "The white power structure was trying to appease . . . ," he noted, "so they could call Greensboro 'the Gateway City,' an all-American city—and they got it."

Two years later, as an NAACP member, Blair senior sparked an initiative to pressure merchants in a new shopping center to make "nontraditional" jobs (clerks rather than janitors) available to blacks. Then in 1959 he did something quite extraordinary—he briefly integrated the lunch counter at Woolworth's—the very one where his son would sit-in two months later. He had spent the day at Greensboro's Christmas parade. His daughter (who was with him) was hungry, he was tired, and they were in front of Woolworth's. So they went in and sat down at the counter. One of his students, who happened to be working that day, thought of Mr. Blair as "the type of teacher that when he asked you to do something you did it." So when he asked for sandwiches, she delivered them, even though she knew full well the store didn't serve blacks. After all, she was black herself. An assistant store manager immediately came over and directed the Blairs to the stand-up counter. Blair assured him they were "doing just fine" where they were, and they finished their sandwiches before leaving.

What Blair did was certainly confrontational, but it was an isolated incident observed by few people. Nor did he repeat the gesture in a more political context, as his son would soon do. However, the experience may explain why on the night of January 31, as the Greensboro Four planned their sit-in, they went to the Blairs' to discuss the idea with Ezell's father. He had not encouraged them, since he doubted their request for service would accomplish much. He only said, "If that's the way you feel, go ahead."

Blair Senior was not the only adult with whom the four shared their plan. Recall that on their way to Woolworth's they stopped to speak to Ralph Johns, a white shop owner. Why Johns? "Ruffles" Johns, as he was sometimes known, was no ordinary southern shopkeeper. As the son of Syrian immigrants, he knew firsthand from growing up in Pennsylvania steel towns what discrimination felt like. He arrived in Greensboro as a soldier during World War II and stayed on when he married a local woman. His father-in-law ran a small clothing store that had a largely black clientele. Johns soon gained a reputation as "a nigger lover" after he joined the NAACP and began to encourage local college students to challenge Jim Crow. An ever-changing sign in front of his store advertised his views: "God hates segregation," it might say one day; "Colored and white fountains are not the way of God or of Christians," it announced another. In 1949 Johns encouraged an A&T football player to challenge the segregated lunch counter at Woolworth's. The student was dumbfounded. "Man, what do you want to do? Get me arrested? All I want to do is get my diploma and get out of the South."

**Ralph "Ruffles" Johns,** the son of Syrian immigrants, understood prejudice. As a Greensboro businessman, he urged black students to fight against segregation.

Johns never gave up the dream of living in an integrated community. He continued to urge area college students to confront the hypocrisy at Woolworth's. Among those he encouraged was Joseph McNeil, whom he thought was unusually bright and promising. Johns admitted that anyone who carried out his plan might be arrested, but he was sure that with enough pressure, Greensboro's stores and restaurants would integrate. He even promised McNeil money for bail and legal fees. In December 1959 McNeil said he would do it. Johns, however, was skeptical. He remarked to his clerk, Dorothy Graves, "Just like the rest?" and then answered his own question, "Yeah, he ain't coming back." But of course, six weeks later McNeil did come back and brought three friends. Johns coached them in how to act and what to say and even gave them money to make their purchases. After they left, he tipped off the reporter at the *Greensboro News and Record.*

To call the Greensboro sit-ins spontaneous is to ignore Johns's ten-year effort to integrate Woolworth's and to discount the courageous example set by George Simkins, Otis Hairston, Willa Player, and numerous local leaders like Ezell Blair Sr. The Greensboro Four did not stumble onto the idea of testing the segregated lunch counter at Woolworth's. Parents, churches, local civil rights organizations, and civil rights leaders had prepared them to challenge Jim Crow.

## THE BIRTH OF A SOCIAL MOVEMENT

Of course, the real significance of the Greensboro sit-ins was not local, but regional and national. Historians of the civil rights movement generally agree that the militant phase of nonviolent protest began in earnest only after Greensboro. It was as if dry tinder had been gathering for years and Richmond, Blair, McNeil, and McCain struck a match and dropped it into the pile. The flame that erupted burned across the nation's racial landscape. Again, the historian wants to know why this match set the movement aflame rather than the sparks struck earlier. Why February 1960 and not 1957 in Little Rock, Arkansas, where nine students integrated Central High School? And why lunch counter sit-ins rather than school or bus desegregation? In short, why that place, at that time, and in that way?

To explain what differentiated the Greensboro sit-ins from other campaigns that preceded them, we need to consider the nature of social movements: how they begin, why some succeed, why others fail. Why did the movement choose nonviolent sit-ins rather than petitioning their elected representatives to change the law? Why do some people join a social movement rather than a political campaign to redress their grievances? To answer those questions, historians, political scientists, and sociologists alike have traditionally been drawn to models to explain the rise of social movements. We have previously discussed models as we explored the decision to drop the atom bomb at the end of World War II.

According to sociologist Doug McAdam, there are a number of long-standing theories of movement behavior that might be called the "classical explanatory models." They vary, but all agree on several central points. First, they treat American politics as pluralistic. Rejecting the Marxist idea of power controlled by a relatively small but coherent class of capitalists, pluralists see power spread among competing groups that occasionally come together to pursue common interests. "There does not exist a single set of all-powerful leaders," wrote sociologist Robert Dahl, "who wholly agree on their major goals and who have enough power to achieve their major goals." That lack of concentrated power creates a fluid political system in which even the relatively powerless have an opportunity to promote their ends. Or as Dahl explained, "whenever a group of people believes that they are adversely affected by national policies or are about to be, they generally have extensive opportunities for presenting their case and for negotiations that may produce a more acceptable alternative." Because groups can resolve their grievances through normal political channels, they are less likely to resort to violence. In that way, pluralists explain the relatively peaceful transfer of power within the American system. Electoral politics provide an effective alternative to revolution, terrorism, vigilantism, and other forms of violence.

Still, social movements acting outside of the normal political arena are common in American history. To explain their recurrence, theorists have added a second dimension to the classical model. A basic causal sequence describes how such movements arise:

Structural strain $\longrightarrow$ disruptive psychological state $\longrightarrow$ social movement

"Structural strain" is one way of saying that the basic framework of the social order is out of joint, and thus a group or groups within society feel threatened or discontented. The resulting tension leads them into a "disruptive psychological state" of mind; they sense the need to act but may feel powerless to do so through normal politics. To make society respond to their sense of grievance, these discontented individuals form a "social movement." The ability to do so, according to many sociologists, depends on the movement being organized by people who "feel both *aggrieved* about some aspect of their lives and *optimistic* that, acting collectively, they can redress the problem."

Does the classical model help understand how Greensboro affected the civil rights movement? Certainly, McCain, Richmond, Blair, and McNeil were aware of widespread discontent with segregation and the racial status quo in 1960. Indeed, they shared that discontent. So strong was that sense of injustice (their disruptive state) that they challenged each other to take action; they initiated a social movement "to redress the problem." Normal political channels were not open to them. Across the South, few blacks could vote, almost none held public office, and white leaders made no more than token concessions. Without resources to redress their grievances, blacks began to organize a social movement.

But this formulation, altogether too neat, does not really answer our questions about the why, where, and how of Greensboro. We may know why these four students acted when they did and why they sat-in at Woolworth's. But why didn't thousands of other black adults and students act before February of 1960? Blacks across the South had faced Jim Crow with a mounting sense of grievance for over seventy years. Neither sit-ins as a tactic, nonviolence as a strategy, nor restaurants as a target were new in 1960. CORE, a biracial organization founded in 1942, adopted the sit-in during World War

> *Why didn't thousands of other black adults and students act before February of 1960?*

II. After integrating a theatrical performance of Richard Wright's *Native Son* in Baltimore, the organization moved on to Stoner's Restaurant in Chicago in 1943. When a small group of blacks asked for service, waiters brought food covered with egg shells and other garbage, but eventually Stoner's decided to desegregate. Similar efforts succeeded in Denver and Detroit. CORE also integrated the federal prison in Danbury, Connecticut. But these were all places outside the South.

At that time Washington, DC, was largely southern in its orientation, officially segregated since the administration of Woodrow Wilson. Inspired by CORE's success, students at Howard University formed the Civil Rights Committee to picket and sit-in at segregated restaurants. They opposed discrimination as "contrary to the principles for which the present World War is being fought" and declared "the effort to end discrimination against a person because of race or color as a patriotic duty." Their means would be nonviolent. They would "use dignity and restraint at all times . . . no matter what the provocation." Outside Thompson's, a moderately priced restaurant favored by government workers, black and white demonstrators carried signs declaring, "We die together; let's eat together" and "Are you for Hitler's way or the American way?" Moved to act, six uniformed black soldiers and several students entered Thompson's and asked for service. The military police arrived and requested the soldiers to leave in order to avoid embarrassment to the army. The soldiers left, but the students stayed. Four hours later, Thompson's agreed to serve them.

CORE struggled to keep alive the momentum it created during the war. In April 1947, the organization sent eight white and eight black men on what it called a Journey of Reconciliation through Virginia, North Carolina, Tennessee, and Kentucky. Bringing attention to segregation in interstate travel, the sixteen men were arrested and jailed. They received wide publicity, but segregation remained firmly in place. CORE faded into the background, as the socialists, pacifists, and other leftists who dominated its membership fell under the dark cloud of McCarthyism. Leadership on civil rights passed to the NAACP and its legal strategy to end segregation. The 1954 decision in *Brown v. Board of Education* marked its greatest triumph, as the Supreme Court overturned the "separate, but equal" policy enshrined since 1895 in the case of *Plessy v. Ferguson.* Following through on that decision, NAACP activists like Rosa Parks ignited the 1955 bus boycott in Montgomery, Alabama.

In the midst of that success, a new organization, the Southern Christian Leadership Conference and its charismatic leader Martin Luther King Jr., gained new prominence. After 1955, preachers more than lawyers and church congregations rather than NAACP chapters took the initiative in the civil rights crusade, at least in the South. Yet despite the efforts of CORE, the NAACP, and SCLC activists, nothing so broad as a national social movement had emerged by the end of the 1950s. Instead, an array of grassroots movements revealed a pattern of localized discontent. Two deserve attention because they help understand why Greensboro transformed civil rights politics.

Most people think of hardcore segregation in the 1950s in terms of the Deep South—Mississippi, Alabama, and Georgia. Seldom does Oklahoma come to mind. However, as we saw in Chapter 12, many Okies arriving in California pressed local school districts there to segregate the schools. Clara Luper, sometimes referred to as "the mother of the civil rights movement," grew up in the segregated Oklahoma the Okies left behind. As a high school history teacher, Luper understood that most Americans did not know much about her state, "because we are a young state and people have not paid attention to us like they have in other states. We've had lynchings in this state. We've had burnings. In fact, my building was bombed." She pointed out that "during the debate on the Civil Rights Bill in 1964, one Senator stated that Oklahoma had the worst segregation laws in the United States, which is true."

To make the case for integration, Luper wrote a play honoring Martin Luther King, entitled *Brother President.* In 1957 she and a group of students traveled to New York City to see her play performed. While there, they experienced a sense of freedom they had never known before. They entered restaurants and ate at integrated lunch counters. Returning home through the Jim Crow South, Luper vowed to take on segregation. "I was always taught that segregation was wrong," she explained. "My dad was a veteran of World War I and he believed what Woodrow Wilson said: they were fighting to make the world safe for democracy. My mother was from Texas and

**Clara Luper,** known to many people as the mother of the civil rights movement, led sit-in protests in Oklahoma City in August 1958.

she saw a black person burned in Paris, Texas and she was afraid that would happen to anyone who spoke out against segregation."

Luper spoke out anyway. She embraced a plan put forward by the local NAACP youth council to integrate public accommodations. At first, she and her followers were a bit naïve, "We thought all we had to do was make our wishes known." Along with a friend, "who happened to be white," and "shared her excitement about the project," Luper went to a restaurant. "When we did that, all hell broke out because they would say to the white lady, come in, but Clara Luper, you can't come in." Despite the hostile reactions, Luper kept up her campaign, until even her students became involved. "And after seventeen months, the kids made reports and my daughter Marilyn said, let's go downtown and wait." They "selected the stores where most blacks traded. So we decided that night to go to Katz Drug Store. Katz Drug Store not only had drugs, it had a basement with tennis shoes and shirts and what have you. So we went in, 13 of us, and took seats." The students Luper escorted to the lunch counter ranged in age from six to seventeen. "People that had known us for years began to curse us. They called the police. Policemen came from all directions, but we were just sitting at the counter. We were not arrested," Luper told an interviewer.

**Sit-ins in Nashville** followed soon after those in Greensboro. They lasted from February through May and were notable for their disciplined nonviolence. Nashville merchants agreed to integrate before those in Greensboro.

That was 1958. Luper helped integrate many public facilities in Oklahoma City over a year before the sit-ins in Greensboro. Similar efforts succeeded in Tulsa and in Wichita, Kansas. Luper was truly a civil rights pioneer who acted as boldly as any heroes of the movement. Yet while most civil rights histories mention McNeil, Richmond, Blair, and McCain, few tell her story. Luper's success may have transformed the racial climate in Oklahoma, but it did not immediately inspire others to follow her example.

Civil rights activists in Nashville, such as John Lewis, Diane Nash, James Lawson, and Marion Barry, are better known today than Clara Luper and even the Greensboro Four. But that is less because of what they did to integrate Nashville and more because of the roles they later played on the national stage. All the same, anyone familiar with the civil rights movement in 1959 would have predicted that Nashville, not Greensboro, would become the cradle of the sit-in crusade. During the Civil War, Tennessee never joined the Confederacy, and Nashville

*Most observers in 1959 would have predicted that Nashville, not Greensboro, would become the cradle of the sit-in crusade.*

was known as "the Athens of the South" (it even allowed a few blacks on the school board, city council, and police force). But in all other matters racial, the state and city were as thoroughly segregated as any place in the South. By 1958 local black leaders were determined to integrate the city.

They formed the Nashville Christian Leadership Conference (NCLC) as an affiliate of Martin Luther King's Southern Christian Leadership Conference. Unlike the Greensboro Four, who mostly thought and talked about ways to push integration, students in Nashville actually trained for a sit-in campaign. Beginning in March 1958, they attended NCLC workshops on nonviolent tactics led by Reverend James Lawson, who had steeped himself in the teachings of Gandhi and King.

During November and December 1959, Nashville protesters actually held sit-ins at several downtown department stores. Anticipating the tactics used in Greensboro, students John Lewis, Diane Nash, James Bevel, Marion Barry, and several clergy bought goods and then attempted to desegregate the lunch counters. They stayed only long enough to have their requests for service denied and then left. Lawson continued to train other college students to participate in the protests. But these Nashville sit-ins, like Luper's in Oklahoma City, attracted no significant national attention. Only after Greensboro did Nashville's black college students launch their first full-scale efforts. For the next three months, they targeted the downtown stores as well as the Greyhound and Trailways bus terminals. Their principles of direct nonviolent protest and civil deportment became models for other protests. And as we have seen, when the police began to arrest protesters, the community rallied to provide financial and legal support. By May 10, 1960, Nashville began to desegregate its public facilities.

# WHY HERE? WHY NOW?

So we are still left to puzzle out why Greensboro and not Oklahoma City or Nashville? And why February 1960 and not 1957, 1958, or 1959? Fortunately, sociologists have other models that help historians focus on the circumstances peculiar to Greensboro in 1960 that may help us answer those questions. Doug McAdam applied a model of "political process" to explain the emergence of the activist phase of civil rights protest after Greensboro. His model brings our attention to three factors involved in the formation of social movements: first, "the level of organization within an aggrieved population"; second, "the collective assessment of the prospects for successful insurgency within that same population"; and third, "the political alignment of groups within the larger political environment."

Let's develop these concepts a little more so we see how they apply to our questions. Consider first what creates a level of organization that is strong and effective. McAdam identified four essential elements—members, solidarity incentives, communications channels, and leaders. Members are recruited into social movements along existing lines of interaction. So, for example, we have already seen that the Greensboro Four all had participated in NAACP youth groups and had other ties through church and high school. Further, social movements often gain members when preexisting groups merge into a new coalition. As one sociologist commented, "mobilization does not occur through the recruitment of large numbers of isolated and solitary individuals. It occurs as a result of recruiting blocs of people who are already highly organized and participants." This proved true at North Carolina A&T, where students who knew each other from campus organizations quickly mobilized to join the sit-ins.

The task of recruiting members, however, is complicated by what sociologists refer to as the "free rider" problem: individuals perceive that they can realize the benefits of collective action whether or not they join. Some potential recruits sit on the sidelines rather than accept the risks of protesting. Organizations counter this passivity by providing incentives to join—McAdam's second point—by offering a sense of belonging, praising members' contributions, and nurturing a sense of mutual achievement. Solidarity can be achieved more readily when movements communicate effectively—the third point. SCLC chapters in local churches had well-established lines of communication within the community and with other church congregations that were under the SCLC umbrella. Phone trees, letter chains, meeting halls, and common space allowed insurgents to reach significant numbers of like-minded people quickly. Finally, movements need leaders who consolidate and direct members. These leaders have often developed their skills in other organizations and can use their prestige to draw members into the social insurgency.

*The "free rider" problem complicates the recruiting of new members to a social movement.*

Even with strong organization, most movement groups face numerous disadvantages in the political arena. The same lack of power and political access that sparks minorities to mobilize also limits their chances for success. The likelihood that they will succeed, however, is not static over time. Key events or historical trends may arise that challenge the foundation on which the established power structure rests. Economic downturns, rising unemployment, shifts in population demographics, wars—all these and more can play a role in shifting the balance of power. After World War II, for example, the South became increasingly urban. Greensboro's population grew from about 75,000 to 120,000 between 1950 and 1960. The mechanization of cotton harvesting forced large numbers of African Americans to relocate to cities. In 1960 they accounted for over a third of Greensboro's population.

Because Jim Crow laws denied them the vote, urban blacks could not directly pressure city political establishments to address their grievances. As African Americans increasingly moved to the city, however, the NAACP and SCLC could more easily recruit new members and initiate indirect political action. That was the case during the 1955 bus boycott in Montgomery, Alabama, where many city businesses relied increasingly on African American customers. In this increasing dependence, civil rights organizations discovered "a structure of political opportunity." Faced with a threat to their businesses, white store owners often pressured politicians to help end the protests. Increased economic power gave the movements an effective means to overcome their relative political powerlessness. And the emerging dynamic was amplified over time. As the insurgents became more organized and more insistent, segregationists were forced to take ever more extreme measures to maintain Jim Crow. Growing pressure from the Supreme Court and other federal agencies further improved "the structure of political opportunities" facing prospective insurgents.

Turn now to the idea of "insurgent consciousness," which McAdam argued was also key to a movement's success. Enough people must come to recognize that the system they seek to overthrow is vulnerable and that new circumstances make success more likely. In the Declaration of Independence, Thomas Jefferson noted that "in the Course of human events," it had become "necessary for one people to dissolve the political bands, which have connected them with another." Here he was expressing an "insurgent consciousness" that the colonists had become "one people," united in the belief that circumstances impelled them to sever their ties with England.

Three "cognitions," or collective understandings, were embedded in Jefferson's assertion. First, the colonists had come to believe that the "system"—in this case England's North American empire—had lost its legitimacy. They were no longer willing to accept the authority of the king, Parliament, or the royal officials sent to govern them. Second, the colonists no longer viewed imperial rule as permanent or immutable. Finally, the colonists had become persuaded that they could successfully "dissolve the political bands" that had tied them to England. These perceptions were not based on any hard evidence; indeed, many people doubted that a group of ragtag revolutionaries could successfully revolt against the world's premier military power. Rather, rebel leaders persuaded each other that together they could and should push the cause of separation. They succeeded in large part because they had an organizational network in place (think the Continental Congress) and well-developed lines of communications (recall the Committees of Correspondence)—in short, indigenous organizational strength.

Organizational readiness, insurgent consciousness, and political opportunities: Were the same key factors in play at Greensboro? And were they more fully evolved there than in either Oklahoma City in 1958 or Nashville in December 1959? After all, the NAACP and SCLC were active in all three communities. All had civil rights leaders who were convinced that segregation was illegitimate and that the dependence of local merchants on black customers made the system vulnerable to boycotts and protests. What none of them could determine, as they planned their protests, was the level of repression that segregationists would use to keep Jim Crow in force.

Clara Luper found an effective way to restrain the authorities. Many of her student protesters came from the local elementary schools. Arrest or violence against young children would have exposed Oklahoma City to outside criticism or even federal intervention. Facing these youthful protesters, the authorities quietly gave in to demands for desegregation. Luper's success might have persuaded civil rights activists that similar success was possible elsewhere, but the low-key nature of her efforts inspired few demonstrations outside Oklahoma. Furthermore, Luper's use of young children had a downside. It posed a level of risk that many parents were not inclined to accept. Hence Luper's strategy was not readily exportable as a model for protest elsewhere.

The Nashville students were older than those in Oklahoma City, but they were guided by leaders from the NAACP and SCLC who were inclined to a "go slow" approach to insurgency. Having witnessed arbitrary arrests, beatings, and lynchings, the students' older mentors understood all too well the forces arrayed against them and the potential for violence. Thus when the Nashville students sat down at the lunch counters and placed their orders, they left as soon as they were refused service. On the positive side, the quick exit gave authorities little time to intervene or arrest anyone, nor the chance for violent mobs to assemble. Unfortunately, the same tactic also deprived the protest of much impact. The students had demonstrated courage and their sense of grievance, but they had established no "insurgent consciousness"—no conviction that peaceful sit-ins would actually undermine segregation.

Student leadership distinguished Greensboro from Nashville and Oklahoma City. Where Luper shepherded her elementary-school students into lunchrooms and James Lawson and other adult leaders coached the Nashville students on the strategies of nonviolent protest, the Greensboro Four acted on their own—not sure how long they might have to wait to be served but determined to hang in there as long as it took. In the days that followed, as the news media picked up the story, students from A&T and other area colleges joined in. And when the sit-ins spread to other communities, including Nashville, college students took the lead, even as many civil rights leaders counseled restraint. Though surprised by the Greensboro results, Nashville students eagerly came to the conclusion that sit-ins in public facilities could succeed in attacking segregation. The students shifted the focus and style of protest. Where the NAACP concentrated on school desegregation and the SCLC sought to integrate public transportation, the students adopted the sit-in as their primary tactic and public accommodations as their principle targets.

Not that student leaders pushed their elders aside. The student-led phase of the civil rights movement succeeded because it added a new layer of organizational resources to those that already existed. Local SCLC and NAACP chapters called on their members to support the spreading sit-ins with bail money, lawyers, and meeting places. SCLC leader Wyatt Tee Walker asked—and not just rhetorically—"If a Negro's going to have a meeting, where's he going to have it?" Publicly funded colleges and universities were normally out of the question. "The church is the primary means of communication," Walker insisted, "far ahead of the second best, which is

*"The church is the primary means of communication, far ahead of the second best, which is the Negro barbershop and beauty parlor."*

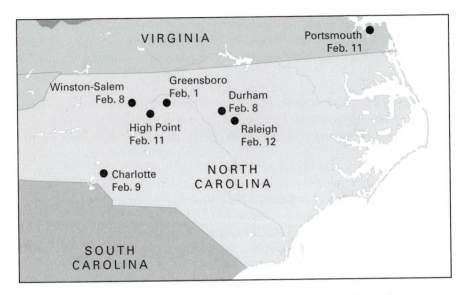

**The dates on this map** refer to protests that occurred after the Greensboro sit-in. They confirm Doug McAdam's conclusion that informal and formal communications encouraged nearby campus groups to follow the lead of the Greensboro protesters. Protests on campuses without those links took longer to organize. (*Source:* Doug McAdam, *Political Process and the Development of Black Insurgency, 1930–1970*, 2nd ed. Chicago, University of Chicago Press, 1999)

the Negro barbershop and beauty parlor." All the same, students possessed communication networks on and between campuses that were separate from those their elders had developed. Fraternities and sororities, service organizations, and even athletic teams provided essential links.

Doug McAdam, applying what sociologists call "diffusion theory," discovered that "student-initiated protest activity . . . occurred earlier at campuses closer to the original protest site—Greensboro, North Carolina—and only later at schools some distance removed." He made that assumption by noticing that the protests after Greensboro adopted both the same strategy (sit-ins) and similar targets (public accommodations). The information he compiled (represented in the map above) suggests that formal and informal communications links did influence the timing and location of the protests that spread from one city to the next. One sociologist even tied the pattern of protests to intercollegiate sports. Nearby colleges refused to be shown up. If a rival school sat-in, so would they. Eleven of the first fifteen protests took place in the Piedmont region within 100 miles of Greensboro. Five of those were at schools whose basketball teams played A&T within two weeks after the initial sit-in. McAdam thus concluded that as "in the case of both the NAACP and the black churches, the campuses afforded the burgeoning movement an effective communications network through which local protest units could be linked together to provide a broader geographic base."

Besides introducing new civil rights communications networks, the student movement greatly enhanced the organizational base. Sociologist E. Franklin Frazier had earlier dismissed black college students as too conservative and bourgeois to become involved in social protest. Greensboro demonstrated that he had been far too pessimistic. Campuses, in fact, provided social movements with a fertile source of new recruits. As sociologist Alton Morris observed, their communications networks made them ideal places "for rapid mobilization to occur." Students were also free of social and political pressures that inhibited their parents, teachers, and school administrators. They did not have "families to support, employers' rules and dictates to follow, or crystallized notions of what was 'impossible' and 'unrealistic.'" Equally important, students had the time and energy needed to protest effectively. Finally, as Morris concluded, "students were available to protest because, like ministers, they were an organized group within the black community who were relatively independent of white economic control." Unlike most adults, they could not be fired.

In that way Greensboro took advantage of new "political opportunities" that helped establish a new "insurgent consciousness." After McNeil, Richmond, Blair, and McCain sat-in, they were not arrested, beaten, nor expelled. Instead, they became heroes, and hundreds of would-be student protesters discovered a new sense of possibility. Sit-ins could *work*, the authorities were not invincible, and the risks involved were not as daunting as protesters previously assumed.

Social movement theory does help explain the genesis of Greensboro's protest and its relationship to the civil rights movement it helped spawn. The Greensboro Four's decision to integrate Woolworth's may have arisen spontaneously, but it had firm roots in the local and national civil rights movement. Greensboro spread so quickly and so far because the civil rights movement had reached a tipping point. As Rhone Frazer, a historian of the sit-ins wrote "The American civil rights narrative has too often been reduced to a tale of spontaneous invention, rather than the product of intense debate, meticulous planning and, often, tactical and strategic genius on the part of the organizers."

## SNCC AND THE DISORGANIZATION OF THE MOVEMENT

The student energy and initiative that inspired the sit-in movement added a vital element to the civil rights movement. Yet nothing that happened at Greensboro guaranteed that it was on a sure path to success. Indeed, over the next few years, student activism proved as much a disruptive as a unifying force. Again, social movement theory helps explain why the addition of college and university students to the insurgency contributed to the passage of the Civil Rights Act in 1964 and the Voting Rights Act of 1965 as well as to the splintering of the civil rights coalition and its crusade for integration and equal rights.

We can understand this apparent contradiction by asking a simple question: How did the insurgent consciousness of student protesters compare to that of traditional civil rights groups such as CORE, the NAACP, and the SCLC? The question's answer can be found in the organization that came to represent student protest—the Student Nonviolent Coordinating Committee. Credit for the creation of SNCC must go to Ella Baker, one of the original founders of the SCLC. In 1960, as the sit-ins erupted, Baker had grown so outspoken about the cautiousness of King and the ministers who ran the SCLC that they terminated her role as executive director. Looking to take the movement further and faster, Baker saw students as the basis for a new

> *Credit for the creation of SNCC must go to Ella Baker, one of the original founders of the SCLC.*

and more dynamic approach. As a graduate of a southern college, she worried about how little prepared these young civil rights activists were for the uncertain future ahead. Their initial successes gave them an unrealistic faith in the potential of direct-action protests to overturn segregation. In reality, student protesters had no organizing principles or leadership beyond their campuses. Baker believed that more coordinated action was needed to maximize their potential. To that end, in April 1960 she organized the Southwide Student Leadership Conference on Nonviolent Resistance to Segregation at Shaw University in Raleigh, North Carolina.

What would be the new group's link to established civil rights groups? Baker sensed that the major organizations wanted to capture the activists' energy and channel it into their own programs. The NAACP, SCLC, and CORE all sent observers to the Raleigh convention, as did sympathetic northern groups such as the Young People's Socialist League, the National Student Association, and Students for a Democratic Society (SDS). Julian Bond, a student activist from Atlanta, recalled, "NAACP wanted us to be NAACP youth chapters, CORE wanted us to become CORE chapters, SCLC wanted us to become the youth wing of SCLC." Baker urged students to cooperate with the traditional organizations on terms of equality but not to tolerate "anything that smacked of manipulation or domination." With her encouragement, the delegates "finally decided we'd be our own thing." The thing they chose was the Temporary Student Nonviolent Coordinating Committee, eventually dropping the temporary *T*.

While SNCC added a third level to the civil rights movement, it also introduced new tensions. Reverend James Lawson from Nashville pressed students to accept a religious commitment to nonviolence. "Love is the central motif of nonviolence," Lawson explained. "Such love goes to the extreme; it remains loving and forgiving even in the midst of hostility." Inspired by Lawson and Martin Luther King, the delegates agreed that their organization would be nonviolent, but, in line with Baker, most delegates wanted SNCC to be more action-oriented than its allies. SNCC would not simply coordinate the activities of local protesters. It aimed at becoming the vanguard of an ever-widening civil rights movement.

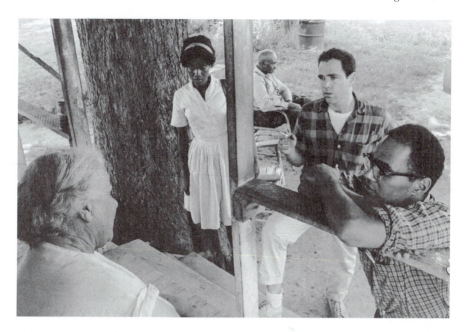

**Robert Moses** made a promise to Anzie Moore to bring students to Mississippi to promote voter registration. Here, during Mississippi Freedom Summer, he leads a mixed racial group of SNCC volunteers who canvased rural voters. The attention given to the integrated voter registration drive bothered some black SNCC veterans who had previously suffered beatings, arbitrary arrest, and even murder without much attention from the national media.

Despite its high ambitions, SNCC was always short of money and staff to carry out its mission. Baker arranged office space at SCLC's Atlanta headquarters, while the National Student Association provided additional resources. She also recruited Robert Moses, the math teacher from New York who went south after being inspired by news of the sit-ins. Moses was an unlikely person to determine SNCC's future. Slight of build, light in complexion, somber in manner, he led by quiet example rather than charisma. Though, as one reporter noted, Moses was "an outstandingly poor speaker," people found him accessible, a listener more than a talker. He urged SNCC to practice what was known as "participatory democracy"—allowing those most directly affected a central role in decision making. That approach was a departure from the lawyer-led NAACP and the preacher-led SCLC.

When Moses went to Mississippi to recruit local leaders to attend a SNCC conference in October, he met Anzie Moore, from Cleveland, Mississippi. Moore agreed to go to Atlanta in October but made clear that voter registration, not desegregation, was his agenda. Moore impressed Moses when he suggested that he send SNCC students down to help him register blacks in Cleveland. As a result, Moses promised to return in the near future. That promise would put voter registration on the SNCC agenda.

At the October conference, 140 people and about 80 observers from northern colleges met in Atlanta to consider SNCC's future. The mood had a new militancy. The invitation stressed that SNCC would be "action-oriented," because we are "convinced that only mass action is strong enough to force all Americans to assume responsibility" for the nation's racial injustice. Once again, the delegates affirmed their commitment to nonviolence. James Lawson, though no longer an active SNCC member, insisted that a "jail, no bail" strategy would have the most powerful impact. Lawson called it the start of a "nonviolent revolution" to destroy "segregation, slavery, serfdom paternalism."

The October conference was a turning point for SNCC. The organization turned away from the religiosity of King and Lawson to focus on political action. That shift brought SNCC and voter registration to Mississippi, just as Anzie Moore had urged. "Only when SNCC workers were prepared to initiate protests outside their own communities," noted historian Clayborne Carson, "could they begin to revive and extend the social struggle that had already become the central focus of their lives."

By 1963 SNCC, CORE, and the SCLC had conducted freedom rides, boycotts, sit-ins, and voter-registration drives. Those actions forced the Kennedy administration to give civil rights a higher priority. To push their agenda even further, the civil rights organizations needed to find new ways to spread their message. Some leaders suggested that they unite to pass the civil rights bill President Kennedy introduced in June of 1963. This was not the usual token measure designed to placate the civil rights movement without offending moderate southerners; Kennedy's bill attacked the very heart of Jim Crow. It would outlaw segregation in all public interstate facilities, authorize the attorney general to initiate school desegregation cases, and deny funds to federal programs that involved discrimination. As a blow against literacy tests as a barrier to voting, a key provision declared literate a person who had a sixth-grade education.

The introduction of the civil rights bill coincided with plans for a major march on Washington. The idea came from movement veteran A. Philip Randolph, who had planned a similar march for African American jobs and economic opportunities during World War II. Franklin Roosevelt had dissuaded him by issuing an executive order on discrimination in employment and adopting a Fair Employment Practices Commission. In 1963 Randolph resurrected his idea, since jobs for blacks were still hard to find. The White House convened a gathering of civil rights leaders, at which Kennedy firmly opposed the march. It would risk violence, harden segregationist opposition, and undermine his own political fortunes, he warned. Vice President Lyndon Johnson argued forcefully that the way to move Congress was not through demonstrations but through traditional political channels. Martin Luther King and the other march supporters would not back down. Their restive organizations demanded the kind of gesture the march would provide. In a compromise, civil rights leaders agreed that the theme of the march would be broadened to include support for the Kennedy bill.

The one significant holdout was John Lewis of SNCC. Too many times Lewis had seen fieldworkers in Mississippi harassed, beaten, and murdered

**The "Big Six" civil rights leaders met to plan the March on Washington.**
(*left to right*) John Lewis (SNCC), Whitney Young (Urban League), A. Philip
Randolph, Dr. Martin Luther King Jr. (SCLC), James Farmer (CORE), Roy
Wilkins (NAACP). Lewis's determination to deliver "a forceful speech" about the
"revolution" at hand upset the other leaders. Finally, Randolph made a personal
appeal for a softer speech. "I have waited all my life for this opportunity," he said,
"please don't ruin it."

while their demands for federal protection went largely unheeded. In January 1963 Robert Moses and his staff filed suit against Attorney General Robert Kennedy and FBI Director J. Edgar Hoover. They charged that these
officials had failed to protect SNCC workers from white supremacists in
Mississippi, who repeatedly violated their constitutional rights. Though the
suit failed, as Moses knew it would, it reflected the profound impatience
SNCC had with federal civil rights policies and the Kennedys' efforts to
work with southern moderates.

Out of growing frustration, SNCC grew more cynical and militant. In
Cambridge, Maryland, in June 1963 a SNCC demonstration turned into a
violent clash with local police. The governor sent some 400 national guards-
men to restore order. Such eruptions had become increasingly common. In
an estimated 930 protests in eleven southern states, some 20,000 demonstrators were arrested. Such direct-action strategies contrasted sharply in intent,
if not so clearly in consequence, from King's nonviolent approach. Most
white liberals continued to urge nonviolence as an alternative to SNCC's
growing militancy. King, too, experienced his share of disillusionment, but
he was more inclined to work through, rather than against, the system.

SNCC leaders saw the March on Washington, scheduled for August 1963,
not as an opportunity to support the Kennedy bill, but as a chance to criti-
cize the Justice Department. On the eve of the march, southern authorities

## MARCH ON WASHINGTON FOR JOBS AND FREEDOM
### AUGUST 28, 1963

### LINCOLN MEMORIAL PROGRAM

| | | |
|---|---|---|
| 1. | The National Anthem | *Led by* Marian Anderson. |
| 2. | Invocation | The Very Rev. Patrick O'Boyle, *Archbishop of Washington.* |
| 3. | Opening Remarks | A. Philip Randolph, *Director March on Washington for Jobs and Freedom.* |
| 4. | Remarks | Dr. Eugene Carson Blake, *Stated Clerk, United Presbyterian Church of the U.S.A.; Vice Chairman, Commission on Race Relations of the National Council of Churches of Christ in America.* |
| 5. | Tribute to Negro Women Fighters for Freedom<br>Daisy Bates<br>Diane Nash Bevel<br>Mrs. Medgar Evers<br>Mrs. Herbert Lee<br>Rosa Parks<br>Gloria Richardson | Mrs. Medgar Evers |
| 6. | Remarks | John Lewis, *National Chairman, Student Nonviolent Coordinating Committee.* |
| 7. | Remarks | Walter Reuther, *President, United Automobile, Aerospace and Agricultural Implement Wokers of America, AFL-CIO; Chairman, Industrial Union Department, AFL-CIO.* |
| 8. | Remarks | James Farmer, *National Director, Congress of Racial Equality.* |
| 9. | Selection | Eva Jessye Choir |
| 10. | Prayer | Rabbi Uri Miller, *President Synagogue Council of America.* |
| 11. | Remarks | Whitney M. Young, Jr., *Executive Director, National Urban League.* |
| 12. | Remarks | Mathew Ahmann, *Executive Director, National Catholic Conference for Interracial Justice.* |
| 13. | Remarks | Roy Wilkins, *Executive Secretary, National Association for the Advancement of Colored People.* |
| 14. | Selection | Miss Mahalia Jackson |
| 15. | Remarks | Rabbi Joachim Prinz, *President American Jewish Congress.* |
| 16. | Remarks | The Rev. Dr. Martin Luther King, Jr., *President, Southern Christian Leadership Conference.* |
| 17. | The Pledge | A Philip Randolph |
| 18. | Benediction | Dr. Benjamin E. Mays, *President, Morehouse College.* |

### "WE SHALL OVERCOME"

**Labor leaders, clergy** representing the major faiths, and civil rights leaders young and old all addressed, the crowd, but the day belonged to Martin Luther King Jr. His speech evoked the spirit of both the black church and the Founding Fathers.

began a number of legal actions designed to stifle desegregation and voting-rights efforts. The Justice Department actually joined one of the suits against SNCC demonstrators. Lewis planned to address these injustices at the Washington march. In the draft of a speech, he asked rhetorically, "Which side is the federal government on?" Reflecting SNCC's frustration, he warned that "we will not wait for the President, the Justice Department, nor Congress, but will take matters into our own hands and create a source of power outside of any national structure that could and would assure us victory." Civil rights leaders were most troubled that Lewis wanted to call for a "revolution." Even the militant Randolph found the idea excessive. "John, for the sake of unity, we've come this far," he argued. "For the sake of unity, change it." And change it Lewis did, if ever so reluctantly. The urgency and impatience with which students had energized the movement now threatened to be its undoing. Lewis and his SNCC comrades remained deeply ambivalent about the March on Washington.

All this behind-the-scenes maneuvering was invisible to most of the nation. The massive crowd in Washington on August 28, 1963, offered living proof that a social movement had been born. Organizers had worried that only a few thousand might show up; they hoped for as many as 100,000. That day some 250,000 marchers, perhaps 60,000 of them white, joined in peaceful witness to the cause of civil rights. Until that moment, few Americans appreciated the movement's force, and the voice that captured their attention belonged not to Lewis, but to Martin Luther King Jr. King's fervor stirred the crowd as he spoke of his people "crippled by the manacles of segregation," of their poverty, and of "the horrors of police brutality."

His real message, however, was not about past wrongs, but about his dream of a new beginning when "the sons of former slaves and the sons of former slave owners will be able to sit down together at the table of brotherhood," when even the state of Mississippi "will be transformed into an oasis of freedom and justice." Rather than complain of past divisions, he called for a new unity, evoking a majestic vision of the future:

> And when this happens and we allow freedom to ring, when we let it ring from every village and hamlet, from every state and city, we will be able to speed up that day when all God's children, black men and white men, Jews and gentiles, Protestants and Catholics, will be able to join hands and sing together in the words of the old Negro spiritual: "Free at last, Free at last. Thank God Almighty, we are free at last."

In that moment, King offered the nation a vision in which the spirit of brotherly love healed the wounds of race and slavery.

## DISUNION

In many ways August 28 marked an end, not a beginning. Most SNCC workers had by then lost faith in the gospel of nonviolent reform that King preached. Yes, the Civil Rights Act made its way through Congress, but under the guidance of Lyndon Johnson, not John Kennedy. By 1965 voting rights would become a reality. But for militants on either side of the race issue, the real battle had just begun. In New York City, an obscure Black Muslim named Malcolm X called on fellow African Americans to arm in self-defense. He dismissed King's event as the "Farce on Washington." "Whoever heard of angry revolutionists swinging their bare feet together with their oppressor in lily-pad park pools, with gospels and guitars and 'I Have A Dream' speeches?" Malcolm asked with naked sarcasm.

Despite all the models of the political scientists and sociologists, movements and individuals sometimes possess a logic of their own. Malcolm X would make an abrupt about-face, connecting with the international religion of Islam rather than the separatist movement of Elijah Muhammad, embracing brotherhood and cooperation before being gunned down, most likely by some of the violent followers he now scorned. "Black Power" would displace the inclusiveness SNCC had adopted just three years earlier, and SNCC itself would eventually expel its white members and collapse. Black Panthers would call for armed resistance rather than nonviolence. The same youthful idealism that gave the civil rights movement a new beginning in Greensboro, North Carolina, would also anticipate its collapse three and a half years later, even as a quarter of a million people sang, "We Shall Overcome Some Day."

Historians are often wary of models that try, usually after the fact, to explain the peculiarities and contingencies of history. Their skepticism is often merited, though such models do help clarify the structural aspects of any movement or revolution. There will always be a tension between contingency—the choices of individuals that often remain unpredictable by general models—and the need to step back and see larger structural patterns in society that move individuals in groups, in aggregates, in movements in a direction whose general course can no more be changed than can a river's course down a deep valley. If the vendor at the Union Station snack bar in Greensboro had offered to sell Joseph McNeil something on the side, would the Greensboro Four have ever achieved their place in the history of a movement? Contingency. Would the tinder then have been ignited—in June, perhaps, rather than January— if the Nashville students had decided not just to order and leave but rather insisted on service? We can see by tracing the backgrounds of the Greensboro Four that there were enough people out there pushing for change—from Ezell Blair Sr. to white store owners to NAACP youth groups—that the tinder would spark a larger movement. The structural preparation was there. Both perspectives supply necessary lenses in the quest to define and track a social movement that was larger than life.

# *Additional Reading*

To understand more about Greensboro as the cradle of the student sit-in movement, try William Chafe, *Civilities and Civil Rights: Greensboro, North Carolina, and the Black Struggle for Freedom* (New York, 1980). Miles Wolff's *Lunch at the 5 & 10* (New York, 1990) is rich in details of events. A broader view comes from Howell Raines, *My Soul Is Rested: The Story of the Civil Rights Movement in the Deep South* (New York, 1983). Clayborne Carson, *In Struggle: SNCC and the Black Awakening of the 1960s* (Cambridge, MA, 1995), describes the formation of the organization. Juan Williams's *Eyes on the Prize: America's Civil Rights Years, 1954–1965* (New York, 1987), is the companion volume to the powerful PBS series.

Doug McAdam, *Political Process and the Development of Black Insurgency, 1930–1970*, 2d ed. (Chicago, 1999), and Aldon Morris, *The Origins of the Civil Rights Movement: Black Communities Organizing for Change* (New York, 1984), place events in a coherent theoretical frame. Sidney Tarrow, *Power in the Movement: Social Movements and Contentious Politics*, 2d ed. (New York, 1998), combines sociological theory and history.

Happily, the Internet makes this a topic any student can explore. Many materials from and about the civil rights movement are readily available. The Web site *Greensboro Sit-ins: Launch of a Civil Rights Movement*, http://www.sitins.com/mccain.shtml, offers a rich variety of information and images. We also found helpful Amanda Strunk, "Oklahoma City and the Origins of the Modern Civil Rights Movement" (undated, East Central University, Oklahoma Gamma Chapter of Alpha Chi), http://www.harding.edu/alphachi/pdf/onlinepublishes/2002Under/OKCityandCivilRights.pdf. Lynda T. Wynn, "Nashville Sit-ins (1959–1961)," http://www.tnstate.edu/library/digital/nash.htm, is another place to look. You can easily find more on your own.

## CHAPTER 16
# *Breaking into Watergate*

*How did presidential tape recordings turn a "third-rate burglary attempt" into an impeachable offense? Historians move from print into the electronic age.*

Ron Ziegler, press secretary to President Richard Nixon, called the break-in at the Watergate luxury apartment complex "a third-rate burglary attempt" and warned, "certain elements may try to stretch this beyond what it is."

Ziegler was referring to the arrest of an unusual group of burglars who on June 7, 1972, had forced their way into Democratic Party headquarters in Washington, D.C. Despite Ziegler's disclaimer, the story would not go away. In the months that followed, reporters for the *Washington Post* linked the five intruders to officials on President Nixon's White House staff. In March 1973 a jury convicted not only the five burglars but also two former presidential aides. When the aides refused to say who had ordered the burglary, trial judge John Sirica angrily threatened prison terms of twenty to forty years. The threat seemed to have its effect, for one of the officials confessed that they had been under "political pressure to plead guilty and remain silent." Suddenly, high White House officials rushed to "lawyer up." By the summer of 1973 the "third-rate" Watergate burglary had blossomed into a full-fledged scandal that threatened to force Richard Nixon from office.

Americans got a close-up look at the events when a special Senate committee, convened by Senator Sam Ervin of North Carolina, televised hearings on what the entire country called "Watergate." Viewers saw a parade of witnesses testify that former Attorney General John Mitchell, the highest law-enforcement officer in the land, had been present at meetings in which one of the convicted officials outlined proposals for the Watergate burglary and other espionage attempts. Testimony confirmed that burglar G. Gordon Liddy had reported directly to John Ehrlichman, the president's chief domestic advisor, as part of a White House security group called "the Plumbers." Hired to investigate leaks to the press, the Plumbers, it was revealed, were no strangers to burglary. In 1971 they had broken into the office of a psychiatrist in search of damaging information about a former Defense Department official named Daniel Ellsberg.

**Former White House Counsel John Dean** consults a portion of his testimony as Senator Sam Ervin (*left*) speaks with Dean's lawyers. Dean's low-key manner, meticulous testimony, and remarkable memory impressed many listeners, but until the existence of the tapes became known, it was Dean's word against the president's.

The Ervin committee's most astonishing witness was John Dean. Dean, until recently White House legal counsel, looked like a cross between a boy scout and a choirboy. Testifying in a soft, precise monotone, he charged that the president had been actively involved in efforts to cover up White House connections to Watergate. When one of the convicted burglars had threatened to tell prosecutors what he knew, Dean met with the president and his aides on March 21, 1973, and approved hush money of up to a million dollars to buy the Watergate burglars' silence.

Of all the witnesses, only Dean directly implicated Richard Nixon in the cover-up. It was his word against the president's. Bearing down on Dean, Senator Howard Baker, the Republican Senate minority leader, subjected him to a vigorous cross-examination. Baker asked Dean to begin with the "central question" of the investigation: "What did the President know and when did he know it?" Dean remained unshaken in his testimony, but the president's allies challenged his account. Then came the most stunning revelation of all.

For months, investigators had noticed that certain White House figures, especially Nixon and White House Chief of Staff H. R. (Bob) Haldeman, showed a remarkable grasp of details when recalling past meetings at the

White House. On occasion the two had even provided direct quotes. Still, no one had thought to ask any witness whether the White House had a recording system of some kind. Ironically, it was an investigator for the Republican minority who popped the question.

Donald Sanders was a ten-year veteran of the FBI (Federal Bureau of Investigation) before he became a congressional staffer. Listening to the responses of several former presidential advisers, Sanders "felt a growing certainty that the summaries had to have been made from verbatim recordings." He further assumed that the president "would never have said anything incriminating on the record." Since Nixon's conversations would be "self-serving," Sanders concluded that the tapes "would prove the President's innocence." He had but one reservation. If there were recordings that cleared Nixon, "why hadn't the President revealed the system and used it to advantage?"

Hence Sanders approached his questioning of Haldeman aid Alexander Butterfield with some trepidation. Why, he asked the witness, might the president have taken Dean to one corner of the room and spoken to him in a whisper, as Dean testified? "I was hoping you fellows wouldn't ask me that," Butterfield replied. Reminded that the proceedings were official and that he was under oath, Butterfield then admitted that, "Well, yes, there's a recording system in the White House." When he gave televised testimony to that effect, his revelation stunned virtually everyone, from millions of television viewers to members of Congress and even the president himself, who had assumed that the secret of the tapes was safe. John Dean declared he was "ecstatic" at the promise of vindication. If the committee could listen to those tapes, it would no longer be Dean's word against the president's. The tapes could tell all.

*Reminded that he was under oath, Alexander Butterfield then admitted that, "Well, yes, there's a recording system in the White House."*

But obtaining the evidence did not prove easy. Archibald Cox, who in May had been appointed as special prosecutor to investigate the new Watergate disclosures, subpoenaed relevant tapes. The White House refused to provide them. When the courts backed Cox, the president fired him on Saturday, October 20, 1973. Reaction was swift and vehement. Nixon's own attorney general and his immediate subordinate resigned in protest. Reporters dubbed the firing and resignations the "Saturday Night Massacre." Members of the House introduced twenty-two separate bills calling for possible impeachment of the president, and the House Judiciary Committee began deliberations on the matter.

Under immense pressure, President Nixon named a new special prosecutor, Leon Jaworski of Texas, and released the subpoenaed tapes to Judge Sirica. Then came yet another jolt. The new White House counsel told the court that some sections of the requested tapes were missing. One contained a crucial eighteen-and-a-half-minute "gap." When asked if the erasure might have been caused by human error, one expert replied "it would have to be an accident that was repeated at least five times." Alexander Haig, the president's new chief of staff, could only suggest lamely that "some sinister force" was at work. By April 1974, Special Prosecutor Jaworski and the House Judiciary Committee had requested additional tapes. At first the president refused, then grudgingly agreed to supply edited transcripts. White House secretaries typed up more than 1,200 pages, which the president with a show of virtue made public.

The transcripts were damaging. They revealed a president who was often vindictive, vulgar, and small-minded. The pivotal meeting with John Dean on March 21, 1973, showed Nixon discussing in detail how his aides might, as he put it, "take care of the jackasses who are in jail." "How much money do you need?" Nixon asked Dean. "I would say these people are going to cost a million dollars," Dean estimated. "We could get that," replied the president. "You could get a million dollars. And you could get it in cash. I know where it could be gotten. I mean it's not easy, but it could be done."

In the following months, events moved swiftly. Since neither the Judiciary Committee nor Jaworski was satisfied with edited transcripts, Jaworski appealed directly to the Supreme Court to obtain the originals. In July, the court unanimously ordered the president to produce the tapes. The same month, the Judiciary Committee passed three articles of impeachment, accusing the president of obstructing justice, misusing his presidential powers, and refusing to comply with the committee's requests for evidence. In August, even the president's own lawyers insisted that he release transcripts of three conversations with Chief of Staff Haldeman recorded on June 23, 1972, only a few days after the Watergate burglary.

This tape soon became known as the smoking gun, for it demonstrated beyond all doubt that the president had been involved in the cover-up from the beginning. Haldeman had warned Nixon that the "FBI is not under control" and that agents had "been able to trace the money" found on the burglars. The two planned to frustrate the investigation by playing the CIA (Central Intelligence Agency) off against the FBI. "The FBI agents who are working the case, at this point, feel that's what it is. This is CIA," explained Haldeman. Nixon hoped that because four of the burglars were Cubans, the FBI would assume the break-in was a "Cuban thing" carried out as a part of a covert CIA operation. He suggested that the FBI be told, "'[D]on't go any further into this case,' period." With the release of these transcripts, all but the president's staunchest congressional supporters deserted him. Facing certain impeachment, Richard Nixon announced his resignation on August 9, 1974.

## PRESIDENTIAL TAPES

In the end, the president had been done in by reel upon reel of audiotape recordings he himself had authorized. For more than two decades, however, the National Archives allowed access to only sixty hours that had been available to the special prosecutor. In 1974, Congress legislated that all the Nixon presidential recordings be released "at the earliest possible date," but Nixon was equally determined the tapes would remain unheard. Eager to rehabilitate his reputation, he worked energetically until his death in 1994 to block the release of the tapes.

Historians wanted access to the tapes. They promised to provide details of the Nixon presidency that no recollection or memoir could match. In effect, they were the audio equivalent of the camera's "mirror with a memory": a snapshot of the words, inflections, laughs, stutters, and even coughs, exactly as they had been uttered.

*The presidential tapes were the audio equivalent of the camera's "mirror with a memory": a snapshot of the words exactly as they had been uttered.*

Although such documentation was unparalleled, it was not without precedent. A week after his election in 1968, Nixon toured the White House with President Lyndon Johnson, who proudly showed his successor an elaborate secret taping system he had in place. Such a system, he advised Nixon, would be vital for writing memoirs and keeping on top of events. "You've got to know what's happening, and the only way you can do that is to have a record of it," he explained. Nixon was less than impressed. Upon entering the White House, he ordered Johnson's system torn out. Two years into his presidency, however, for reasons that remain unclear, he ordered his own secret system installed.

No doubt Nixon said little about the tapes, because he understood that bugging the conversations of his staff, diplomats, and other visitors was difficult to justify. Indeed, once Alexander Butterfield acknowledged the existence of the tapes, many in the press and Congress condemned the practice. Nixon and his defenders responded that he was hardly the first president to make secret recordings. In fact, presidents had been doing so on and off for thirty years. In 1940 Franklin Roosevelt had a microphone hidden in a desk lamp so that he could secretly record his press conferences. The machine also caught Roosevelt promoting a whispering campaign to discredit his presidential opponent, Wendell Willkie. Willkie, it seems, had a mistress, and Roosevelt wanted the nation to know about her without being identified as the source of the rumor. That episode ended FDR's flirtation with bugging. Harry Truman was so offended at the idea of secret recordings that he had the equipment dismantled. President Dwight Eisenhower shared Truman's misgivings, but he mistrusted Washington politicians enough that he had a crude Dictaphone device installed. Eisenhower explained, "I want to have myself protected so they can't later report that I had said something else." All the same, he used the system little.

John F. Kennedy was the first president to make extensive audio recordings, though not until eighteen months after he assumed office. Like Nixon, Kennedy never revealed his motives for doing so. He had certainly showed no compunction about authorizing secret FBI bugging and wiretaps, which he agreed to more than once during his term. All the same, the system Kennedy installed was primitive. Secret Service agents placed microphones in light fixtures in the Cabinet Room and in the president's Oval Office desk. When Kennedy wanted the system turned on, he flipped several switches. He could also signal his secretary to start a separate machine for recording phone calls. Thus he had to make a conscious decision that he wanted a conversation recorded.

After Kennedy's assassination, several people made an effort to transcribe the tapes he had made, and Robert Kennedy consulted them in writing his memoir of the Cuban missile crisis of 1962. Otherwise, until the Watergate investigation, they remained a well-kept secret. When Nixon suggested that other presidents had similarly recorded conversations, Senator Ted Kennedy confirmed the existence of some 248 hours of taped meetings and 12 hours of telephone conversations from the Kennedy White House. The tapes primarily recorded meetings of ExCom, the high-level group of officials Kennedy convened during the missile crisis.

Efforts to decipher the tapes were frustrated not by Kennedy family obstruction, but by poor sound quality. Two historians, Ernest May and Philip Zelikow, later attempted to transcribe them. They reported that "the large majority of the tapes crackle, rumble, and hiss. Conversation is as hard to make out as on a factory floor or in a football stadium." But once May and Zelikow cleared away the static and verbal debris, the tapes told a riveting story. They showed the president and his advisers striving to respond, under intense pressure, to the secret placement of Soviet offensive nuclear missiles at launching sites in Cuba only ninety miles from American shores. With the world as close to all-out nuclear war as it has ever come, the tapes recorded what May and Zelikow suggested "may be the most harrowing episode in all of human experience."

Lyndon Johnson's tapes possessed their own distinct flavor. Unlike earlier presidents, Johnson began recording as soon as he moved into the Oval Office. In fact, as Senate majority leader, he had secretaries and aides eavesdrop on telephone conversations and take shorthand notes. As president, Johnson replaced Kennedy's system with better microphones installed in the Cabinet Room and Oval Office, in the kneeholes of his secretaries' desks, in the Situation Room, at the LBJ Ranch in Johnson City, Texas, and even in his White House bedroom. Johnson talked incessantly on the phone, whether in his office, his bedroom, or his bathroom. If he wanted a conversation recorded in his office, he twirled his finger in the air to let his secretary know that she should turn on the system. Shortly before he died in 1973, Johnson told his secretary, Mildred Steagall, that he wanted his tapes to remain private until fifty years after he died. She later transferred the sealed boxes to the Johnson Library under the conditions Johnson had set: the library director and chief archivist of the United States could not listen to them until 2023.

Given these precedents, Nixon could legitimately claim that in bugging his offices he was merely following a well-established practice. Yet, as in

**Lyndon Johnson** talked incessantly on the phone. When sculptor Jimilu Mason went to have Johnson pose, he tired of the constant phone interruptions. In that spirit, Mason finally decided to cast Johnson dashing around with a phone to his ear. That anecdote may help explain why the large majority of Johnson tapes preserve telephone conversations, while most of the tapes from John Kennedy and Richard Nixon are of face-to-face meetings.

many of his actions, Nixon did not simply mirror his predecessors. Once he decided to record private conversations, he went at it with a vengeance. Unlike earlier systems, his was voice-activated, starting up whenever someone spoke. Why he went to such lengths is not clear, though Alexander Butterfield commented to investigators that "the President is very history-oriented and history-conscious about the role he is going to play, and is not at all subtle about it, or about admitting it." Nixon reinforced this notion in an offhand remark recorded on the tapes themselves, when Chief of Staff Bob Haldeman commented that the Secret Service had told him the recording system was "extremely good. I haven't listened to the tapes." "They're for future purposes," the president assured him. In his memoirs Nixon offered a hint at what "future purposes" might be served by the tapes. They "were my best insurance against the unforeseeable future. I was prepared to believe that others, even people close to me, would turn against me just as Dean had done, and in that case the tapes would give me some protection."

While Nixon argued that the tapes were his private property, historian Stanley Kutler believed with equal fervor that the public had a right to know what they contained. In 1991 Kutler and the group Public Citizen sued

Nixon (and later the Nixon estate) and the National Archives to release the tapes. About the same time, a public uproar erupted following the release of Oliver Stone's film *JFK*. The film suggested that the CIA and other government officials had been involved in Kennedy's assassination. To satisfy public interest, Congress passed the John F. Kennedy Assassination Records Act. All government archives were required to release any documents bearing on the assassination.

The Johnson Library faced a quandary. On the one hand, Johnson had ordered his tapes kept under lock and key. On the other hand, the library director and LBJ's widow, Lady Bird Johnson, had together already determined that they could overrule Johnson's order sealing the tapes. Further, they worried that the tapes might deteriorate if left unattended. Finally, they wanted to avoid the kind of controversy that arose when Kutler sued the Nixon estate. Showing great regard for history and for the public's right to know about its government, they ordered the opening not only of the assassination records, but of the entire collection. And finally, in 1996, some two years after Nixon had died, Kutler reached an agreement in which the National Archives promised to release all 3,700 hours of Nixon's tapes within four years. The first batch included 201 hours of conversations that related specifically to Watergate, including some dealing with other illegal operations of Nixon's secret security unit, the Plumbers. Kutler published transcripts of excerpts from these tapes. At almost the same time, Ernest May and Philip Zelikow published transcripts of the Kennedy tapes, and Michael Beschloss, those of the early Johnson presidency.

> *Lyndon Johnson had ordered his tapes kept under lock and key.*

What, then, would the public learn from this sudden exposure of presidential secrets? The historians who had worked with the tapes believed they were like no evidence available before. "The material in this book offers the most complete set of data available on how a modern government actually made a set of important decisions," concluded May and Zelikow about the Kennedy tapes. Michael Beschloss observed that "LBJ was famous for concealing himself"; hence, the Johnson tapes were important because they "allow us to listen in on an American presidency from beginning to end." Compared with other records of the same events, the tapes have a "towering advantage," Beschloss observed. "Meaning is conveyed through not just language but tone, intensity, pronunciation, pauses, and other aspects of sound." And as Stanley Kutler commented, "The tapes of Richard Nixon's conversations with political intimates compel our attention as do few other presidential documents."

Opening of the presidential tapes inspired wide coverage in newspaper stories, magazine articles, and television news programs. As historian Bruce Shulman wryly noted, "Seldom do historical documents receive such lavish attention from the national media." Most commentators were thrilled that the tapes allowed Americans the rare opportunity to become "flies on the wall" inside the Oval Office. On the face of it, the tapes seemed less prone to the kinds of selective bias operative in the creation of photographic images or written accounts. Set the tape reels going, and they would record any sound within reach of the microphone. Observers in the media seemed persuaded that the public could now have history pure and simple, without the interfering hand of the historian. The tapes would tell all.

## The Tapes as Evidence

Readers who have followed us this far will hardly be surprised to discover that historians have been more skeptical—even those who transcribed the tapes. Michael Beschloss, for example, warned his readers that "a President who knows he is taping a conversation can manipulate or entrap an interlocutor who does not. He can also try to present the best face for history."

Then there is the problem of setting down on paper what the tapes actually contain. Only with repeated listening and extensive research can the conversations be transcribed with any degree of accuracy. Kutler, for example, traveled to the National Archives in Washington to listen to the original Nixon recordings. (They could not be removed from the archives.) Because no transcriptions were available for most tapes, he had professional court reporters and transcribers prepare a first draft. Then he and his research assistant listened to the tapes, trying to check for accuracy and fill in the many "unintelligibles" marked in the transcripts. "The process of deciphering the tapes is endless," Kutler admitted. "Different ears pick up a once unintelligible comment, or correct a previous understanding." Kutler also eliminated "what I believe insignificant, trivial, or repetitious"—comments like "right," "yeah," and "okay." Government archivists removed other materials that they considered sensitive for reasons of either personal privacy or national security. So from the beginning we must recognize that the transcripts as presented include omissions, deletions, and "unintelligibles."

Beschloss offered one striking example of how audiotapes can be misunderstood. Background noise, heavy accents, and scratchy voices all distorted the content of the more primitive Dictaphone recordings. On one occasion a White House secretary transcribed Lyndon Johnson as complaining in his Texas twang that he had a "pack them bastards" waiting to meet him. Only after Beschloss listened repeatedly and checked Johnson's daily diary did he realize that Johnson actually said he had the "Pakistan ambassador" waiting.

Such pitfalls aside, let us assume that the Nixon tapes are transcribed accurately enough that we can use them with reasonable confidence. What story do the tapes have to tell? Here is the transcription of the very first excerpt in Stanley Kutler's book *Abuse of Power* (1997). The conversation takes place almost a year before the Watergate break-in.

### JUNE 17, 1971: THE PRESIDENT, HALDEMAN, EHRLICHMAN, AND KISSINGER, 5:17–6:13 P.M., OVAL OFFICE

HALDEMAN: You maybe can blackmail Johnson on this stuff.

PRESIDENT NIXON: What?

HALDEMAN: You can blackmail Johnson on this stuff and it might be worth doing. . . . The bombing halt stuff is all in that same file or in some of the same hands. . . .

PRESIDENT NIXON: Do we have it? I've asked for it. You said you didn't have it.

HALDEMAN: We can't find it.

KISSINGER: We have nothing here, Mr. President.

PRESIDENT NIXON: Well, damn it, I asked for that because I need it.

KISSINGER: But Bob and I have been trying to put the damn thing together.

HALDEMAN: We have a basic history in constructing our own, but there is a file on it.

PRESIDENT NIXON: Where?

HALDEMAN: Huston swears to God there's a file on it and it's at Brookings.

PRESIDENT NIXON: Bob? Bob? Now do you remember Huston's plan? Implement it.

KISSINGER: Now Brookings has no right to have classified documents.

PRESIDENT NIXON: I want it implemented. . . . Goddamn it, get in and get those files. Blow the safe and get it.

HALDEMAN: They may very well have cleaned them by now, but this thing, you need to—

KISSINGER: I wouldn't be surprised if Brookings had the files.

HALDEMAN: My point is Johnson knows that those files are around. He doesn't know for sure that we don't have them around.

Taken by itself, this conversation is rather mysterious and more than a little unnerving. What is going on here? Perhaps we should begin with what we know for sure. The four participants are easy to identify, for they are the major figures in the administration: in addition to Richard Nixon, there are Chief of Staff Bob Haldeman, General Counsel John Ehrlichman, and National Security Adviser Henry Kissinger. As for the subjects of the conversation, "Johnson" was no doubt former President Lyndon Johnson. The reference to a "bombing halt" gives us a clue that "the stuff" they have on Johnson has something to do with the war in Vietnam. Johnson used the halts in American bombing raids to encourage the North Vietnamese to negotiate. But why does Nixon need "the stuff," and why is he trying to blackmail Johnson? Isn't blackmail illegal? There is no mention of the Watergate complex or Democratic headquarters, but there seems clearly to be some sort of burglary involved. "Blow the safe," suggests the president.

Whose safe? "Brookings" is easy enough to identify as the Brookings Institution, a Washington policy center not especially

*Had the president really just given an order for an illegal break-in and safe-robbery?*

**Richard Nixon sits on his desk** while conferring with his key aides (*from left to right*): National Security Adviser Henry Kissinger, General Counsel John Ehrlichman, and White House Chief of Staff Bob Haldeman. Few people ever saw the President in the Oval Office without prior approval from Haldeman.

sympathetic to Nixon or his administration. But who is Huston? What was his plan? Has the president really just given an order for an illegal break-in and safe-robbery? Was the order carried out? Even though we have the raw evidence of history before us, we are left with more questions than answers. In fact, however, Stanley Kutler did not reprint the transcript in quite the form we have presented above. As we have come to appreciate, historians are not simply messengers bringing us materials from the past. Even when selecting and printing documentary evidence, they usually have a case to make, based on their research. Kutler's research into Watergate persuaded him that he knew the answer to Senator Howard Baker's question: "What did the President know and when did he know it?" "The President knew everything about Watergate and the imposition of a cover-up, from the beginning," Kutler informed his readers. As a consequence, his annotations help to make the evidence clearer:

### JUNE 17, 1971: THE PRESIDENT, HALDEMAN, EHRLICHMAN, AND KISSINGER, 5:17–6:13 P.M., OVAL OFFICE

A few days after the publication of the Pentagon Papers, Nixon discusses how to exploit the situation for his advantage. He is interested in embarrassing the Johnson Administration on the bombing halt, for example. Here, he wants a break-in at the Brookings Institution, a centrist Washington think tank, to find classified documents that might be in the Brookings safe.

HALDEMAN: You maybe can blackmail [Lyndon B.] Johnson on this stuff [Pentagon Papers].

PRESIDENT NIXON: What?

HALDEMAN: You can blackmail Johnson on this stuff and it might be worth doing. The bombing halt stuff is all in that same file or in some of the same hands. . . .

PRESIDENT NIXON: Do we have it? I've asked for it. You said you didn't have it.

HALDEMAN: We can't find it.

KISSINGER: We have nothing here, Mr. President.

PRESIDENT NIXON: Well, damn it, I asked for that because I need it.

KISSINGER: But Bob and I have been trying to put the damn thing together.

HALDEMAN: We have a basic history in constructing our own, but there is a file on it.

PRESIDENT NIXON: Where?

HALDEMAN: [Presidential aide Tom Charles] Huston swears to God there's a file on it and it's at Brookings.

PRESIDENT NIXON: Bob? Bob? Now do you remember Huston's plan [for White House–sponsored break-ins as part of domestic counterintelligence operations]? Implement it.

HALDEMAN: Now Brookings has no right to have classified documents.

PRESIDENT NIXON: I want it implemented Goddamn it, get in and get those files. Blow the safe and get it.

HALDEMAN: They may very well have cleaned them by now, but this thing, you need to—

KISSINGER: I wouldn't be surprised if Brookings had the files.

HALDEMAN: My point is Johnson knows that those files are around. He doesn't know for sure that we don't have them around.

**Richard Nixon spent long hours alone** in his office pondering problems or planning political strategy. This photo of the Oval Office in 1971 shows Nixon in a characteristic contemplative pose.

The situation now is a little clearer. Nixon was angered by the publication of the Pentagon Papers, a classified 7,000-page report that analyzed the conduct of the Vietnam War under Presidents Kennedy and Johnson. The Pentagon Papers proved especially embarrassing for Johnson, because they provided evidence that LBJ had deceived the American public when he obtained permission from Congress to escalate the war. Nixon did not mind seeing Johnson embarrassed, but he worried that if the Pentagon Papers were published, other disgruntled officials might come forward exposing other government secrets. Hence the administration went to court to block the *New York Times* from publishing. That effort failed. At the same time, Nixon and his advisers saw a possibility that they could use similar classified files at the Brookings Institution to damage Johnson and, through Huston's domestic counterintelligence operations, other enemies as well.

Why does Kutler begin his book with this transcript about Brookings? This conversation suggests that Richard Nixon clearly had little compunction about breaking the law to advance his own political agenda. Even if he did not specifically order the Watergate break-in in June 1972, he had previously approved and encouraged illegal operations like this break-in at Brookings— and those who worked for him knew it. But there is an irony here. Even though we can come to these conclusions by reading the tape transcripts, historians have been able to piece together not only the story of Watergate but also the Brookings episode by using other sources. Here is the way

Stanley Kutler reconstructed Brookings in 1990, before he had access to the tapes:

> One of the more bizarre by-products of the Pentagon Papers affair was a plan either to raid or to firebomb the Brookings Institution and to pilfer papers there belonging to Leslie Gelb and Morton Halperin, former National Security Council aides. These papers allegedly represented a Pentagon Papers analogue for the Nixon years. The Brookings plan has been described by three people: Ehrlichman, Dean, and Caulfield. All agreed that Charles Colson pushed the idea, but all asserted that Nixon inspired it. . . . Dean claimed that Nixon had demanded he obtain the Gelb-Halperin papers, and he also learned from Egil Krogh that White House people thought Dean had "some little old lady" in him because of his reluctance to go along with the plan. Dean claimed credit for thwarting the plan, but his rival John Ehrlichman insisted that he had blocked it. Only later, Ehrlichman wrote, did he learn that Nixon knew about the plan. . . . Meanwhile, John Dean was not so passive. He gave Krogh copies of the Brookings tax returns and proposed to "turn the spigot off" by revoking some of the institution's government contracts.

This account is more informed and informative than the versions from the tapes. We learn, for example, that the mysterious files belong to Leslie Gelb and Morton Halperin, a former Kissinger assistant. New players appear—Charles Colson, Egil Krogh, and John Dean—all central Watergate figures. And two new crimes have been added. While Nixon had ordered his aides "to blow the safe," someone else apparently introduced a plan to destroy the documents by firebombing the Brookings Institution. So to plotting blackmail we can add a charge of plotting arson. As if that were not enough, John Dean, the president's White House counsel and a supposed "little old lady," illegally passed along tax information to Egil Krogh with the idea of undermining the Brookings Institution. Finally, we have reasonable evidence that, beyond Dean's abuse of the tax records, the plot against Brookings was never carried out. John Ehrlichman claims to have blocked it.

The historian's version does something the tapes alone could not do—it places the conversation in context. As Kutler's footnotes reveal, he consulted a host of other sources—in this instance, John Ehrlichman's memoirs, records of the Select Senate Committee staff that investigated Watergate, and the papers of John Dean. From this perspective, the tapes seem hardly the crucial source that will tell all but rather a sometimes vivid, sometimes cryptic record that cannot be fully understood without a great deal of additional digging. Far from being the key to the story, the tapes seem to be the proverbial icing on a cake that journalists and historians baked years earlier.

# THE TAPES AS A WINDOW INTO RICHARD NIXON

The reality that the tapes are not so central to the story would seem to dampen our enthusiasm about them. If the recordings tell us only part of the truth and much that they contain merely confirms what we already know, why get so excited? What is left for the tapes to tell? Kutler seemed to sense that problem when he published the transcripts. On the one hand, he had to admit that tapes "are far from the whole of the record of the Nixon presidency." The National Archives, the private and public papers of Nixon and his aides, the records of the news media—all have materials essential to understanding the subject. On the other hand, Kutler argued that the tapes still had great significance; they "are the bedrock in laying bare the mind and thoughts of Richard Nixon. They constitute a record of unassailable historical documentation he cannot escape." In other words, even if the outlines of Watergate are clear enough without the tapes, the transcripts remain invaluable in helping us understand Richard Nixon the man. The possibility is tantalizing, for Nixon has long been an enigma to historians.

In part this is because he was essentially a loner. Uncomfortable around most people, Richard Nixon had few close friends. In times of crisis he turned inward, often spending long, solitary hours brooding and planning his own course of action. Yet this loner chose to go into politics, the most public of careers and one that requires a facility for dealing with people.

> *The Nixon who distrusted the media devoted much of his career to convincing them that he should be portrayed as a tough, competent, resilient, and honest politician.*

The Nixon who distrusted the media devoted much of his career to convincing them that he should be portrayed as a tough, competent, resilient, and honest politician. In a private memorandum at the end of 1970, the president sat one night in the Lincoln Room of the White House, compiling a list of traits he wished to project in terms of "visible presidential leadership":

> compassionate, humane, fatherly, warmth, confidence in future, optimistic, upbeat, candor, honesty, openness, trustworthy, boldness, fights for what he believes, vitality, youth, enjoyment, zest, vision, dignity, respect, a man people can be proud of, hard work, dedication, openmindedness, listens to opposing views, unifier, fairness to opponents, end bombast, hatred, division, moral leader, nation's conscience, intelligent, reasonable, serenity, calm, brevity, avoid familiarity, excitement, novelty, glamour, strength, spiritual, concern for the problems of the poor, youth, minorities, and average persons.

This public persona—and the earnest, often awkward way Richard Nixon went about establishing it—was projected most strikingly early in Nixon's career, when his position as Eisenhower's vice presidential candidate in the election of 1952 was threatened by a scandal over a secret campaign slush fund that came to light. Facing calls to step down from the ticket, Nixon gave what became known as the "Checkers speech," in which he used his wife, the family's modest finances, their two little girls, and even their cocker spaniel, Checkers (a gift from supporters), to win public sympathy. "And you know the kids, like all kids, love the dog," Nixon told the 55 million people

**In 1952 a young Richard Nixon appeared on a television studio set** to give
what would become known as his "Checkers speech." His wife, Patricia Ryan
Nixon, looked on with a supportive smile. In private, Pat Nixon had doubts about
Nixon's exposure of his family's financial circumstances to arouse public sympathy.
The speech, however, won widespread public support for the beleaguered
Nixon and secured his position on the 1952 Republican presidential ticket.
(Corbis/Bettmann/UPI)

watching and listening, "and I just want to say this right now, that regardless of what they say about it, we're going to keep it." Critics thought the
presentation both saccharine and hypocritical (one condemned the speech,
hyperbolically, as "the most demeaning experience my country has ever had
to bear"). Even Nixon's wife, Pat, asked plaintively why her husband had "to
tell people how little we have and how much we owe?" The general public,
however, swamped national Republican headquarters with messages supporting Nixon. He remained on the ticket.

In 1962, two years after his loss to John Kennedy in the 1960 presidential
election, Nixon lost a race to become governor of California. At his concession speech he showed a different face: bitter, sarcastic, and self-pitying.
"You won't have Nixon to kick around anymore," the dejected candidate
told reporters. "Just think how much you're going to be missing." The press
quickly wrote his political obituary. Six years later a "new Nixon" arose from

the ashes of political defeat to become president. The respected liberal commentator Walter Lippmann applauded this version of Nixon as "a maturer, mellower man who is no longer clawing his way to the top . . . who has outlived and outgrown the ruthless politics of his early days." By 1972 Nixon had become a much-admired statesman who traveled triumphantly to Beijing and Moscow in a dramatic effort to ease cold war tensions with Communist China and the Soviet Union. Despite his successes, Nixon remained angry with anti–Vietnam War protesters, student radicals, and a list of personal political "enemies" both real and imagined. After winning a landslide reelection in 1972, a bitter Nixon plotted to settle old grudges by using, as he put it, "the available federal machinery to screw our political enemies."

Which of these images, then, was the real Richard Nixon? The humble man of modest means? The whiner who quit politics in 1962? The "new," more mature candidate of 1968? The world leader who redirected the cold war? The vindictive winner of the 1972 election? Precisely because there seems to be such a gap between the public and private Nixon, the tapes offer a window into the "real" Nixon—"uninhibited," in Kutler's words, "by the restraints of public appearance, [capturing] him in moments alone with trusted confidants."

This view of the real Nixon, of course, was one reason the earliest tape transcripts, released in April 1974, had such shock value; the private Nixon often departed radically from his public persona. Kutler's new transcripts reinforce that disjunction between the public and private image. Here, for example, is a meeting between Nixon and Haldeman:

*SEPTEMBER 13, 1971: THE PRESIDENT AND HALDEMAN, 4:36–5:05 P.M., OVAL OFFICE*

PRESIDENT NIXON: . . . But [the Reverend] Billy Graham tells an astonishing thing. The IRS is battering the shit out of him. Some sonofabitch came to him and gave him a three-hour grilling about how much he, you know, how much his contribution is worth and he told it to [John] Connally [the former governor of Texas and a Nixon supporter]. Well, Connally took the name of the guy. I just got to get that nailed down to Connally when you get back. He didn't know it. Now here's the point. Bob, please get me the names of the Jews, you know, the big Jewish contributors of the Democrats. . . . All right. Could we please investigate some of the cocksuckers? That's all. Now look at here. Here IRS is going after Billy Graham tooth and nail. Are they going after Eugene Carson Blake [President of the National Council of Churches, a liberal group]? I asked—you know, what I mean is, God damn. I don't believe—I just know whether we are being as rough about it. That's all. . . .

HALDEMAN: Yeah.

PRESIDENT NIXON: You call [Attorney General John] Mitchell. Mitchell could get—stick his nose in the thing. . . . Say, now, God damn it, are we going after some of these Democrats or not? They've gone after

Abplanalp. They've gone after Rebozo. They've gone after John Wayne. They're going after, you know, every one of our people. God damn it, they were after me. . . .

The comparison between the Richard Nixon in this conversation and the man who gave the Checkers speech is astonishing. Where the younger, public Nixon appeared modest and upright, this private Nixon is angry, vulgar, and vindictive. He is clearly persuaded that enemies in the Internal Revenue Service are out to attack supporters such as Robert Abplanalp and Bebe Rebozo, businessmen and social companions with whom Nixon liked to relax, and John Wayne, the actor, also noted for his conservative politics. Like Nixon himself, all three had faced IRS audits. The focus of this tape, however, is the Reverend Billy Graham, one of the most widely admired religious figures in America. Having developed a huge following as an evangelical preacher, Graham became a spiritual adviser to many presidents. He had been part of Nixon's political circle since the 1950s.

Given the volume of donations to Graham's ministry and the range of his related business dealings, the IRS may well have had some cause to examine his tax returns. Nixon, however, saw the audit not as a reasonable inquiry, but as an indirect effort to discredit the White House and its allies. Rather than make inquiries about the audit through proper channels, Nixon preferred to bring the wrath of the White House down on the unlucky agent and to suggest that, in return, the IRS be used illegally to harass political enemies. Billy Graham, for his part, later deplored "the moral tone implied in these papers" and regretted that Nixon had "used" him to promote his own image.

The tactic of using the tapes as a window onto a hidden—and therefore somehow more real—Nixon does carry risks. In replaying private conversations, we experience an almost unavoidable illicit pleasure of being privy to information not meant for our ears—and then magnifying that information precisely because it is hidden and forbidden and therefore more fascinating. Yet it would be misleading simply to replace the "public" with the "private" Nixon or to assume that the value of these audiotapes lies solely in the candor with which they catch their subjects. Candor is a tricky concept, and historians need to be just as cautious in assessing the tapes as they are in assessing any evidence.

*The tactic of using the tapes as a window onto a hidden—and therefore somehow more real—Nixon does carry risks.*

One way to impose a measure of prudence is to search for patterns in the tapes rather than picking out isolated events. Nixon's reference in the previous transcript to "big Jewish contributors" as "cocksuckers" is truly shocking, but it might be put down as an aberration—except that Kutler's transcripts include more than fifteen similar slighting or stereotypical allusions. None are quite so extreme, but the president makes offhand comments about "Jews with the Mafia," worries that a loyal aide investigating

Nixon's political enemies might "be soft on the Jews" because he is Jewish himself, and expresses disbelief that someone Jewish might be considered to run the FBI ("Christ, put a Jew in there?"). Equally striking, it is Nixon himself who always injects the reference into the conversation. He is not reacting to the comments of others. The pattern here reinforces the impression that Nixon's anti-Semitism was a part of his personality.

Similarly, transcripts covering the weeks after Nixon's suggestion of undertaking a Brookings burglary reveal a highly significant pattern. Nixon's tirade about blowing the safe is no momentary rage. Two weeks later, on June 30, the president again is telling Haldeman, "I want Brookings, I want them just to break in and take it out. Do you understand?" The following day, July 1, the demands continue: "Did they get the Brookings Institute raided last night? No. Get it done. I want it done. I want the Brookings Institute's safe *cleaned out* in a way that makes somebody else [responsible?]." Later in the day, at yet another meeting, the president complains to Ehrlichman that Henry Kissinger isn't pushing hard enough on the Brookings documents: "Henry welshed on these, you know. He's a little afraid. . . . John, you mop up. You're in charge of that. And I want it done today and I'd like a report." And in case his aides have somehow missed the point, again on July 2: "Also, I really meant it when—I want to go in and crack that safe. Walk in and get it. I want Brookings cut. They've got to do it."

More than Kutler's succinct summary, the tapes' repetitive, insistent, unremitting demands make clear how much Watergate was Nixon's own undoing. Indeed, the transcripts are full of laments by the president that he can find no one as ruthless as he. Kissinger, we have seen, is "a little afraid." Attorney General John Mitchell, known to the public as a stern-faced man, is not tough enough. "John is just too damn good a lawyer, you know," comments Nixon. "It just repels him to do these horrible things, but they've got to be done." Should John Ehrlichman and John Dean be anointed as hatchet men? Alas, they're good lawyers too, "always saying, well, we've got to win the court case [over the Pentagon Papers] through the court. . . . I don't want that fellow Ellsberg [who leaked the Pentagon Papers] to be brought up until after the election. I mean, just let—convict the son of a bitch *in the press. That's the way it's done*. . . . Nobody ever reads any of this in my biographies. Go back and read the chapter on the Hiss case [in which Nixon accused Alger Hiss in 1948 of being a communist spy] in *Six Crises* and you'll see how it was done. It wasn't done waiting for the Goddamn courts or the attorney general or the FBI."

Conversations such as this one are convincing instances of candor: Nixon speaking unguardedly, off the record, venting strong feelings. Although he knew—at one level—he was being recorded in the Oval Office, it was impossible to carry on the press of business, day in, day out, with half an ear constantly cocked for the long view of history. Furthermore, Nixon never suspected he might one day lose control of the tapes. Still, there were times when his awareness of the recorder must have put the president on his guard. Consider the following exchange in the midst of the Watergate crisis:

### MAY 16, 1973: THE PRESIDENT AND KISSINGER, 9:07–9:25 A.M., OVAL OFFICE

PRESIDENT NIXON: Yeah. Christ, there's something new every day, you know. Now it's the CIA wanting to do this shit.

KISSINGER: And then they—Haig and I went on the offensive yesterday on these—

PRESIDENT NIXON: Which you should.

KISSINGER: —National Security wiretaps.

PRESIDENT NIXON: Those are totally legal.

KISSINGER: We said they were legal. We had the duty to do it. What is wrong with the National Security?

PRESIDENT NIXON: Well, the point is—I think—the next thing you can say we had—I mean, the leaks the least as it was, seriously impaired some of our negotiations and that they be allowed to continue, the great initiatives might not have come up.

KISSINGER: That's what I am saying.

[Withdrawn item. National security.]

PRESIDENT NIXON: Let's not worry about it. We didn't—the idea that it was ever used. Some jackass Senator said that perhaps—what he was saying is that it was used politically.

KISSINGER: Never.

PRESIDENT NIXON: Those taps never saw the light of—I never saw them, you know. I didn't even know what the Christ was in those damn things. The only one I ever saw was the first one on [journalist Henry] Brandon and it was certainly much of nothing. Do you know what I mean? Hell, they didn't have anything on Brandon.

KISSINGER: They have none. But Brandon wasn't ours anyway. It was J. Edgar Hoover's.

PRESIDENT NIXON: I know. Well, nevertheless, he did a lot of taps.

[Withdrawn item. National security.]

PRESIDENT NIXON: They were legal, but Henry, it's a rough time, I know. A rough time for all of us around here. . . .

Several potentially key elements have been removed by archivists for reasons of national security. As a result, the information about whose phones were being tapped and why remains tantalizingly vague. But a more puzzling problem remains. The tone of this conversation is more stilted than the previous conversation with Haldeman. Why are Nixon and Kissinger going to such lengths to justify to each other their reasons for ordering phone taps on reporters? They seem, almost, to be pleading their case to some unknown audience. Nixon assures Kissinger that the taps were legal, and both agree they were used for national security reasons. Leaks, Nixon claims, had "seriously impaired some of our negotiations," and had they not sought to close the leaks, "the great initiatives might not have come up." Notice also the attempt to shift some responsibility to J. Edgar Hoover and his FBI.

We must suspect the possibility that Nixon (and perhaps Kissinger as well) was speaking to the tapes. If so, the two men held this conversation less to persuade each other than to influence the way history would judge their actions. In writing his memoirs or answering hostile critics, Nixon could cite this conversation to demonstrate that he had always acted from within the law and with the nation's security interests in mind. Historians should thus treat this piece of evidence with caution.

*Nixon regularly blamed others for those actions that history was likely to condemn.*

On the other hand, no matter what Nixon intended, the conversation provides useful clues about his behavior. Nixon regularly blamed others for those actions that history was likely to condemn. In this instance, he asserts that he was forced to tap phones because other people leaked sensitive information. Nor was he alone in doing such bugging, he insists; J. Edgar Hoover had also tapped reporters' phones. Rather than conclude that Nixon was acting out of principle or to protect national security, historians may deduce from the perceived lack of candor that Nixon is rationalizing his breaking of the law.

So the tapes are not valuable merely because they show unguarded moments. Candor is not that simple. In fact, even if we assume that all the people being recorded are oblivious of the tape recorder, it remains unavoidable that whenever two or more people talk with one another, they present different public selves, depending on who is in the room. It is too simple to contrast a public versus a private Nixon. Almost unconsciously Nixon will behave one way when Henry Kissinger is with him and another way when only Bob Haldeman is in the room. In this regard Nixon is no different from any of us. We fine-tune the presentation of our outward selves depending on whether we are in the company of a mentor, a parent, a pastor, or a lover.

But the dynamic of Watergate, as it unfolded, ensured that conversations recorded by the tapes became increasingly strained and less candid. As more lower-level officials began cooperating with prosecutors and implicating those closer to the White House, higher officials such as Mitchell, Dean, Haldeman, and Ehrlichman saw their own peril increasing. For this reason John Dean, the president's lawyer, steeled himself on March 21, 1973, to tell the president that the cover-up was unraveling and that Nixon needed to act to contain the crisis. "We have a cancer—within, close to the president, that's growing," he began, and laid out in his lawyerly way the perils they faced in order "to figure out how this [growing scandal] can be carved away from you, so it does not damage you or the Presidency. 'Cause it just can't. It's . . . not something you are involved in."

"That's true," replied the president.

"I know, sir, it is," replied Dean. "Well, I can just tell from our conversations that, you know, these are things that you have no knowledge of." Yet in truth, there is little candor in this exchange on the part of either man. Far from having no knowledge of the Watergate burglary, Nixon consistently attempted to cover it up over the previous nine months. And Dean relates in his memoirs that during this very conversation, he was constantly being surprised at how much the president knew about the burglars and the hush money they were demanding. With everyone exposed increasingly to the threat of criminal prosecution, it was difficult to be frank. Nixon himself confided to his diary that night: "It will be each man for himself, and one will not be afraid to rat on the other."

By the end of April, Nixon was certainly following his own advice. After forcing Haldeman to resign, he was protesting his own innocence to Alexander Haig, Haldeman's replacement as chief of staff: "Let me say this, Al. I am not concerned myself about anything incriminating in anything that I've done. I mean, I know what I've done. I mean, I've told you everything I did. You know what I mean. I frankly—I was not informed and I don't blame people for not informing me." Haldeman, who from the very start had conspired with Nixon to limit the FBI's investigation, departed the administration declaring to the president, within range of the microphones, "I did not know, and you did not know, and I don't know today, and I don't believe you do really, *what happened* in the Watergate case." Yet as Haldeman and Ehrlichman left the White House, they worried with the president whether Dean might convict them with his own evidence. "I just wonder if the son-of-a-bitch had a recorder on him," Nixon speculated.

It is the ultimate irony. Far from being "candid" records of unvarnished feelings, the White House tapes ended up bearing witness to a hall of mirrors in which conspirators told lies to one another that neither the listeners nor the speaker sometimes believed, and microphones recorded the anguished speculation that someone *else* might be taping. "One of the challenges of reading the Watergate transcripts," noted Nixon biographer Stephen Ambrose, "is trying to keep up with the daily reconstruction of history. These guys could move the pea under the walnut far faster than the human eye could follow. They invented motives for themselves, or presented the most self-serving rationalizations for what they had done and could not escape, or when they could get away with it simply lied."

Novelist E. M. Forster once discussed the difference between characters in a novel and people in real life. A character in a novel is different from the rest of us, Forster proposed, because he or she "belongs to a world where the secret life is visible, to a world that is not and cannot be ours, to a world where the narrator and the creator are one." Real life, on the other hand, is quite different, haunted as it is "by a spectre. We cannot understand each other, except in a rough and ready way; we cannot reveal ourselves, even when we want to; what we call intimacy is only a makeshift; perfect knowledge is only an illusion."

Following the auditory trail of Richard Nixon, we have come somewhat to the same conclusion. It would be misleading to portray Nixon as a man neatly divided between private and public selves, just as it would be a mistake to assume that the audiotapes reveal only his secret, therefore "true" self. The tapes are only another piece of raw material against which historians must deploy all their considerable skills in order to place the conversations in context. Although the tapes do provide a window into the lives of the people whose voices they captured, they do not supply us with a clearly unobstructed view. Even now, many aspects of Nixon remain puzzling. Henry Kissinger, who knew Nixon well and who was an accomplished student of history, once confessed himself at a loss to explain his former employer. Ironically, these off-the-record comments were picked up by a microphone left on by accident in a pressroom where Kissinger had been speaking. Nixon "was very good at foreign policy," Kissinger told his hosts and—unwittingly—the world, but

> he was a very odd man. . . . He is a very unpleasant man. He was so nervous. It was such an effort for him to be on television. He was an artificial man in the sense that when he met someone he thought it out carefully so that nothing was spontaneous, and that meant he didn't enjoy people.
>
> People sensed that. What I never understood is why he became a politician. He hated to meet new people. Most politicians like crowds. He didn't.

Kissinger's praise of Nixon's skill at foreign policy suggests one final caution. Neither the excerpts of the tape recordings quoted here nor the 600 pages of transcripts released by Kutler can convey anywhere near the whole complexity of the Nixon presidency. Whereas the tapes of the Cuban missile crisis show Kennedy at his best, Watergate captures Nixon at his worst. Think what a different image we might have if, as with Kennedy and the Cuban missile crisis, the only surviving recordings covered Nixon during his triumphant trips to China and the Soviet Union. As more tapes are released, we will learn much of interest about Nixon's diplomatic achievements and about his controversial, often iconoclastic domestic policies. Viewing the man through the lens of Watergate inevitably injects a certain distortion.

Yet it must be said: this focus on presidential crimes was Richard Nixon's doing. The pattern of behavior established early on—demonstrated by the president's reaction toward Brookings—leaves no doubt that Nixon himself was the navigator who steered his administration full speed onto the shoals of Watergate. It was not unruly subordinates but the man at the top who kept repeating, "We're up against an enemy, a conspiracy. They're using any means. *We are going to use any means.* Is that clear?" And it was Nixon, in the final hours of the conspiracy, who could not resist making one last effort to retain the allegiance of Haldeman and Ehrlichman before they went to talk to the prosecutors. "Let me ask you this, to be quite candid. Is there any way you can use *cash?*"

Despite the worst of his inner demons, Nixon will be remembered for more than Watergate. But abuses of power this corrosive have only once in American history precipitated what would surely have been an unequivocal and bipartisan conviction on impeachment. For that reason alone, Nixon will never escape Watergate. Like a can tied to the tail of an offending dog, it will rattle and bang through the corridors of power for all of—one must excuse the phrase—recorded history. Historians may have tied on the can, but Nixon supplied the tail. And the tapes.

# *Additional Reading*

Stanley Kutler's *Abuse of Power: The New Nixon Tapes* (New York, 1997) is the place to begin. Readers who want to listen for themselves should go to the Web site for the National Archives in Washington. Over the past few years, the National Archives has released most of the Watergate tapes as well as additional Nixon materials. To hear them online, go to http://nixon.archives.gov. Kutler's take on the "White House horrors" is laid out in *The Wars of Watergate* (New York, 1990).

For tapes from John Kennedy and Lyndon Johnson that offer new insights into the politics of civil rights, see Jonathan Rosenberg and Zachary Karabell, *Kennedy, Johnson, and the Quest for Justice: The Civil Rights Tapes* (New York, 2003). Ernest R. May and Philip D. Zelikow, eds., *The Kennedy Tapes: Inside the White House during the Cuban Missile Crisis* (Cambridge, MA, 1997), provide excellent analysis and commentary. Michael R. Beschloss, ed., *Taking Charge: The Johnson White House Tapes* (New York, 1997), gives an invaluable running commentary on the Johnson tapes. The tapes are available in an audio version, which makes for riveting listening. Originals of the Kennedy tapes and transcripts are available from the John F. Kennedy Library in Boston, and the Johnson tapes are available through the Lyndon B. Johnson Library in Austin, Texas. For an incisive commentary on the presidential tapes, see Bruce Shulman, "Taping History," *Journal of American History* 85, 2 (September 1998): 571–578. A much fuller discussion of presidents and taping is William Doyle's *Inside the Oval Office: White House Tapes from FDR to Clinton* (New York, 1999).

Bob Woodward and Carl Bernstein describe their pursuit of the Watergate break-in and cover-up stories in *All the President's Men* (New York, 1974), which focuses primarily on events through April 1973. *The Final Days* (New York, 1976) picks up chronologically where the first book left off. One comprehensive history of Watergate is J. Anthony Lukas's *Nightmare: The Underside of the Nixon Years* (New York, 1976; rev. ed. 1988). Stephen Ambrose, in writing *Nixon: The Triumph of a Politician, 1962–1972* (New York, 1989) and *Nixon: Ruin and Recovery, 1973–1990* (New York, 1991), had less access to tape materials than Kutler did; Ambrose takes a more charitable view but still lays the blame for Watergate squarely with Nixon. For the impeachment proceedings, see the House Committee on the Judiciary's *Impeachment of Richard Nixon, President of the United States* (Washington, DC, 1974). And transcripts of the original White House tapes, prepared by the Nixon White House staff, are available either in *The Presidential Transcripts* (New York, 1974), as issued by the *Washington Post*, or in *The White House Transcripts* (New York, 1974), by the *New York Times*.

# CHAPTER 17
## *Where Trouble Comes*

*In filmmaking, where the director places the camera determines point of view—and how the story is told. But the stories told at Son My, without the cameras rolling, upended a generation of films about Vietnam.*

POV: the abbreviation sounds military. It could be part of the shorthand used so often in the Vietnam War, either to label geographic areas (LZs are landing zones), to name armies (VC stands for Viet Cong), or even to list the status of soldiers (KIAs, killed in action; WHAs, wounded in hostile action). POV, however, is not military jargon. It is a screenwriter's abbreviation for *point of view*. In films, a "POV shot" records a scene as if it were being viewed through the eyes of one of the actors. Where the director chooses to place the camera, to establish POV, determines to a large degree how the story is told.

Where should one place a camera in the Vietnamese village of Son My on March 16, 1968? When the artillery shells begin falling early Saturday morning, any camera angle would probably seem arbitrary. But for a moment, consider the question in terms of altitude: camera positions measured in feet above sea level.

*POV, ground level:* A dirt road, running past rice paddies not far from the South China Sea. Nguyen Chi, a farmer's wife, is on her way to market when she hears explosions. She turns to see billowing smoke rising a mile back, in the cluster of houses where she lives. Frantically she runs toward a hut by the road whose occupants have rushed outside. She follows them to a small underground bunker built for such occasions. The boom of artillery fades. Helicopters advance across the sky. As Nguyen Chi peers from the earthen shelter, she sees choppers land in a rice paddy not far down the road.

*POV, altitude 500 feet:* Nine large army assault helicopters sweep over the countryside. At 7:30 in the morning the sun is already heating up their gleaming black bodies. Inside, men from the 11th Brigade's Charlie Company sit nervously. They are launching a surprise attack on the Viet Cong's crack 48th Battalion, said to be holed up in the village below. Expecting heavy resistance, the men carry twice the normal load of rifle and machine-gun ammunition as well as grenades and other ordnance. As the choppers descend, their blades change pitch for the landing, making a crackling *pop-pop-pop*, almost like rifle fire. The nervous door gunners spray the surrounding fields with rockets and machine-gun fire. These last few moments of descent are the most vulnerable: with the choppers settling like clumsy ducks on the water, the men will be easy prey for an ambush. Scrambling, soldiers drop into the paddy and fan out.

*POV, altitude 1,000 feet:* Lieutenant Colonel Frank Barker hovers in a smaller chopper. Charlie Company is part of his task force, assembled to root out the Viet Cong in the area. Barker watches from his assigned air lane at 1,000 feet. After twenty minutes, he sees the second wave of helicopters flying in, unloading another fifty men. Charlie Company regroups and heads into the hamlet, where the vegetation is denser than in the open fields. At 1,000 feet, it is difficult to see what's going on. But there is smoke and, over the crackling static of the radio, the sound of small-arms fire. At 8:28 Barker radios Captain Ernest Medina, the commander on the ground. "Have you had any contact down there yet?" he asks. When Medina replies that they have killed 84 Viet Cong ("Eight-four KIAs"), Barker's chopper banks and heads home for the unit's operations center.

The POVs could continue their upward spiral. The air corridor at 2,000 feet is reserved for the American Division's commander, Major General Samuel Koster, who flies over Son My several times that morning, well above reach of ground fire. At 2,500 feet the operations commander also monitors the action. Stacked in layers of airspace, looking on from higher and higher perches, these POVs provide increasingly wider views of the terrain. Yet the perspective becomes more remote with the increase in altitude. Because these observers see more, they also see less.

The report of the morning's action becomes distorted not only by height but by distance, as it is relayed to the world at large. At the operations center, Press Officer Arthur Dunn telephones a two-page "after action" report into division headquarters, using the statistics compiled by Colonel Barker's

> *If 128 Viet Cong were killed, why were only three of their weapons captured?*

staff. The totals have risen to a final count of "128 enemy killed, 13 suspects detained and three weapons captured." The body count is the largest recorded for the task force since it began operations two months earlier. One number makes Dunn uneasy: the three weapons captured. Could the Viet Cong retreat from a fierce fight taking along virtually all their dead comrades' firearms? Unlikely. Something seems fishy.

In Saigon, even more distant, the press officer has no time for such questions. He merely provides reporters with their story, which makes no mention of the number of weapons captured. The *New York Times* front page reports that "about 150 men of the Americal Division encountered the enemy force early yesterday. . . . The operation is another American offensive to clear enemy pockets still threatening the cities."

As the *Times* recognized, this operation was neither the first nor the last of such sweeps. It amounted to one more confusing day in a war that, by 1968, was being waged with more than half a million American troops. How important was Charlie Company's assault? To journalists the picture remained unclear, and there was little time to follow up on yet another skirmish in a distant hamlet. None of the dispatches coming out of Vietnam gave any hint that the events at Son My, if told from the perspective of the men who entered the village, might send tremors across America that would change how the nation thought about the war. For the time being, their POVs went unreported.

## CINEMATIC MYTHS AND VIETNAM

During the same months that Charlie Company was conducting its search-and-destroy operations, Warner Brothers completed final work on *The Green Berets*, Hollywood's first dramatization of the war. The film's star and coproducer, John Wayne, had made a career of climbing into the boots of outsized heroes. For more than thirty years, "the Duke" had been the featured player in countless westerns, including *Stage Coach*, *Fort Apache*, and *The Alamo*. He had assaulted enemy-held islands in World War II dramas such as *Sands of Iwo Jima*, *Back to Bataan*, and *They Were Expendable*. In the midst of this new war, Wayne watched with dismay the growing domestic protest against American involvement in Southeast Asia. As a conservative patriot, he decided to fight back by directing and starring in a combat epic designed to show why Americans were at war.

The turbulent events of 1968, however, made patriotism a harder sell, even for an old hand like Wayne. In January, the Viet Cong had launched a series of surprise attacks during the Vietnamese celebration of Tet, the lunar new year. The strength of the Tet assault shocked many Americans, who began more and more to doubt the government's rosy progress reports. By the end of March (several weeks after Charlie Company's operation at Son My), the war had so divided the nation that President Johnson chose not to seek reelection. Events at home as well as abroad seemed increasingly violent and chaotic. In April, Martin Luther King Jr. was gunned down by an assassin; in June, so was Senator Robert Kennedy, the presidential candidate who seemed most likely to replace Johnson on the Democratic ticket. Both King and Kennedy had become outspoken opponents of the war.

In such tumultuous times, Warner Brothers became edgy about the prospects of its new film. Newspaper ads touting *The Green Berets* were almost defensive: "So you don't believe in glory. And heroes are out of style. And they don't blow bugles anymore. So take another look—at the Special Forces in a special kind of hell." Although antiwar demonstrators picketed the film's premiere ("John Wayne profits off G.I.'s blood," read one sign), an eager theater audience cheered as their hero, a tad paunchy at 61, led his Green Berets to a newly erected outpost "in the heart of VC country." At the end of more than two hours of action, U.S. Special Forces had tangled with mortar fire, nighttime raids, and poison punjee sticks, emerging triumphant in a fight for their embattled outpost. The movie's POVs were bold, colorful, larger than life.

*The Green Berets* was easy for the critics to dismiss. ("A film best handled from a distance and with a pair of tongs," sniffed the *New Yorker*.) But enough of Wayne's fans rallied round to make it a solid financial success. And *The Green Berets* was hardly the only feature film to use the war as its setting. Over the past forty years, at least twenty-five films have portrayed aspects of the conflict. For better or worse, far more Americans have come by their understanding of the war by viewing dramatic films than by reading scholarly histories. In that sense, historians and filmmakers have become rivals: revisiting the same battlefields, delving for significance in an ambiguous past.

> *The Green Berets was "a film best handled from a distance and with a pair of tongs," sniffed the* New Yorker.

How should we approach films that purport to portray history, especially a subject as controversial as the Vietnam War? We can, of course, give each film a scrupulous fact-checking to determine which parts are true and which are false. Are the costumes right? Did a historical figure do the things he or she is said to have done on screen? If the characters are fictional, are they representative of historical figures in similar situations? This approach—administering a kind of historical lie-detector test—can reveal a great deal. But historians routinely examine the past in more imaginative ways. If we can ferret out unspoken biases in the photographs of Jacob Riis, why not probe the cultural assumptions of *The Green Berets*? If the audiotapes of Richard Nixon can reveal nuances of personal character, why not explore the camera's points of view in a film like *Apocalypse Now*?

Still, a good deal of caution is needed in this task. The best movies have a visual immediacy more vivid than any reality evoked by the printed page. Movies about Vietnam confront viewers with the *feel* of war—the oppressive heat of a jungle trail, the explosive chaos of a firefight. Yet even the best filmic realism is false or misleading. To begin with the obvious, the soldiers tramping across a rice paddy are actors, not real combatants. The location in which they appear is almost never that of the historical event. Just as historians re-create their own versions of the past in prose narratives, so also do directors and their production crews on film.

But filmmakers and historians part company on their principles of reconstruction. A historian's first commitment is to remain faithful to the historical record. No matter how difficult it is to reconstruct the often ambiguous past, no matter how ingeniously historians tease out meaning from the evidence, our source material remains our starting point.

For filmmakers, their principles of construction involve questions of drama, not fidelity to the evidence. Does the screenplay move along quickly enough? Do the characters "develop" sufficiently? Does the plot provide enough suspense? These concerns dominate, even when that oft-repeated claim flashes across the screen: "based on a true story." If historical sources cannot supply enough material to round out a tale, directors and screenwriters will tinker with the plot and characters until the story provides them with what they need.

The kinds of changes that are routinely made can be seen in Oliver Stone's *Born on the Fourth of July* (1989). Stone based his film on the memoir of a Vietnam veteran, Ron Kovic, who became involved in the antiwar movement. Kovic's faith in the war was shaken by two traumatic events that overtook him in Vietnam: a nighttime firefight in which he accidentally killed one of his own men, and another night patrol during which his unit killed and wounded some Vietnamese women and children. According to Kovic's book, the two events took place several months apart, but the film combines them into a single incident. Similarly, Kovic describes a trip to Washington for an antiwar rally; in the film, he participates in a violent protest at Syracuse University instead, where his high school sweetheart attends college. In fact, Syracuse had no violent demonstration and Kovic's book made no mention of a high school sweetheart. The film includes many similar alterations of detail.

No doubt Stone would defend the changes he made for dramatic reasons. Consider, for example, the most crassly commercial alteration: giving Kovic a girlfriend. To justify a budget of millions, a film must make money, and audiences are attracted to plots with an element of romance. For dramatic reasons, too, the idea makes sense. Young, innocent Kovic goes off to Vietnam a patriotic marine, while his sweetheart goes off to college and becomes an antiwar demonstrator. Now Kovic's struggle to come to terms with the war is intertwined with his search for a romantic relationship. Similarly, it makes dramatic sense to distill Kovic's war traumas into one vivid sequence, to leave time for the film to focus on his growing involvement with the antiwar movement. As for the decision to invent a protest at Syracuse rather than re-create the one in Washington, one suspects that Stone simply wanted to save on production costs. Recreating a full-scale march around the monuments of the nation's capital would have been much more expensive.

Even with these changes, Stone could argue that he has remained faithful to the essence of Kovic's story. If the goal of the film is to show the long, painful road from patriotic innocence to disillusionment and finally to a new commitment to political change, do the smaller plot details really matter? This is a dramatic film, not a monograph. Like novels or plays, films strive for an artistic standard of "truth" that resides less in the particulars of the historical record than in rendering situations and characters in authentic, human ways. In aesthetic terms, Stone could argue that he respected the integrity of Kovic's story and that *Born on the Fourth of July* reveals a great deal about Americans who fought in Vietnam.

But the point remains. No matter how "true" a feature film is to the emotions of its characters, its makers place dramatic considerations above fidelity to the historical record. And this recognition leads to a more interesting series of questions. Instead of simply trying to discover which details of a film are historically true or false, why not analyze the dramatic construction of the film? Accept that producers and directors are concerned with a different kind of artistic "truth"—or even that the search for profits pushes Hollywood to distort the past. In short, why not leave behind the reconstruction of a nation's history for an exploration of its myths?

A myth, to quote one dictionary definition, is "any real or fictional story, recurring theme, or character type that appeals to the consciousness of a people by embodying its cultural ideals or by giving expression to deep, commonly felt emotions." Many prominent myths derive from the traditions of preliterate societies: tales of Thor and Zeus, or hazy historical figures such as Helen of Troy or Hiawatha. But novelists and playwrights routinely create new narratives that speak to more recent hopes or anxieties. And Hollywood, an industry that markets the fantasies and fears of popular culture, is inescapably in the myth business, creating stories and characters that embody cultural ideals and anxieties.

What sorts of myths? Consider *The Green Berets*. Audiences already knew John Wayne as the star of films that embodied two well-established mythic traditions of American cinema. The first was the western, whose central tale is a saga of white settlers crossing the prairie in order to subdue the wilderness and supplant it with a new, more vibrant civilization. Wayne, whether playing a rangy cowpoke or a dashing cavalry officer, embodied the highest ideals of that new America. He was strong, independent, honest, and fair, at once tender and tough. Equality and liberty were the watchwords of the West, contrasting sharply with the inequality of aristocratic Europe or even with the decadent, overcrowded cities of the East.

From John Wayne the hero of the West, it was only a short step to Wayne the Green Beret of Vietnam. Instead of hunting coppery-skinned Indians who menaced defenseless settlers, the Duke would now chase Asian guerrillas who lurked in the jungle. Rather than commanding a fort in Apache country, he would defend an outpost near the Laotian border—this one conveniently nicknamed Dodge City. Once again, the heroes of the West would have a chance to uproot the corruptions of the East, this time the infection of communism that had spread across Eurasia.

Wayne's previous roles reflected a second mythic tradition of American cinema: the combat epic that came of age during World War II. In the standard-issue World War II melodrama, an ethnically mixed assortment of recruits is thrown together in a frontline platoon, each soldier finding himself tested in the heat of battle. As the platoon shares the agonies and triumphs of a common experience, they are forged into a dedicated fighting unit. In effect, the story retells the classic myth of the American melting pot, in which immigrants from a multitude of ethnic backgrounds learn to live in a single nation. As the platoon unites to work for victory, it embodies the very democratic ideals that set America apart from other nations. Repeatedly, Wayne played the hero who made this myth powerful. Like many others of his generation, Ron Kovic remembered viewing as a boy one of Wayne's classic Pacific combat films:

Castiglia and I saw the *Sands of Iwo Jima* together. The Marine Corps hymn was playing in the background as we sat glued to our seats . . . watching Sergeant Stryker, played by John Wayne, charge up the hill and get killed before he reached the top. And then they showed the men raising the flag on Iwo Jima with the marines' hymn playing, and Castiglia and I cried in our seats. I loved the song so much, and every time I heard it I would think of John Wayne and the brave men who raised the flag on Iwo Jima that day.

Combat films like *Sands of Iwo Jima* and westerns like *The Alamo* and *Fort Apache* worked because their tales reinforced Americans' ideas about themselves as a people. Indeed, the mythic traditions of both the western and the World War II epic assumed that Americans were an exceptional people, set apart by their experience with democracy and liberty. This tradition of American exceptionalism could be traced back as far as John Winthrop's sermon to his fellow Puritans in 1630, that their new colony in Massachusetts would stand as "a city on a hill" and a shining example to the rest of the world. Winthrop's pride was motivated by a religious vision of the Puritans as a chosen people, but over the years that vision gained a political dimension as well, from the heritage of the American Revolution. The vision became overtly nationalistic during the nineteenth century as the "manifest destiny" of western expansion transformed the United States into a continental nation. Wayne's films were among the many dramas that drew upon such themes.

In making *The Green Berets*, Wayne was well aware of the messages he was constructing. In late 1965, knowing he would need army cooperation to film battle scenes, he wrote President Johnson, making a successful pitch for the picture:

> Some day soon a motion picture will be made about Vietnam. Let's make sure it is the kind of motion picture that will help our cause throughout the world. I believe my organization can do just that and still accomplish our purpose for being in existence—making money. We want to tell the story of our fighting men in Vietnam with reason, emotion, characterization and action. We want to do it in a manner that inspires a patriotic attitude on the part of our fellow Americans—a feeling which we have always had in this country in the past during times of stress and trouble.

Wayne also recognized his own near-mythic stature in the American cinema. "Thirty-seven years a star, I must have some small spot in more than a few million people's lives," he told the president. "You cannot stay up there that long without having identification with a great number of people."

How does *The Green Berets* establish its myths? Since film is a visual medium, examine first the images conjured up by the story's characters. Wayne himself plays Colonel Mike Kirby, a tanned, tall, laconic officer who hates the bureaucratic hassles of his rank and insists on joining his Green Berets in the field. Kirby's dramatic foil is George Beckworth (David Janssen), an antiwar newspaper columnist. The visual images confirm his status as antagonist: Beckworth is a nervous chain-smoker, generally unwilling to look anyone in the eye.

**Colonel Kirby (John Wayne)** stands with Hamchunk, an orphan aided by American forces in *The Green Berets*. Apparently the producers worried that an Asian orphan was not enough to melt the hearts of American viewers, so they provided Hamchunk with a puppy to follow him around.

At Dodge City, Colonel Kirby meets his South Vietnamese ally, Captain Nim (George Takei), an able sort, but distinctly more bloodthirsty than the Green Berets. He has "personally greased" fifty-two Viet Cong that year, one of the men informs Kirby, and Nim hopes to double the number before another year goes by. (He keeps score on the wall of his "hootch," or thatched hut.) Like all the film's Vietnamese characters, Nim speaks a Hollywood pigeon English. "My home is Hanoi," he tells Kirby. "I go home too, some-day . . . you see! . . . first kill all those stinking Cong . . . then go home."

Beckworth is upset to find Captain Nim slapping around a captured VC spy—so violently that even Kirby steps in to restrain him. When Beckworth demands an explanation, Kirby reveals that the spy has killed an American medic on a mission of mercy in a nearby Montagnard village. The doctor was found in the jungle "beheaded, mutilated," says Kirby. "His wife wouldn'ta recognized him." Such contrasts of brutality and innocence defiled become the central stuff of Wayne's mythical Vietnam. While the Green Berets provide villagers with humanitarian aid, the VC assume the role of savages, raping young girls and torturing wives in front of their husbands.

To provide viewers with a heartrending visual reminder of the war's horrors, the fort at Dodge City is also furnished with a lovable Vietnamese orphan whose parents have been killed during a VC raid. Named (of all things) Hamchunk, the orphan is followed about by a little puppy, apparently because the film's producers felt that an Asian orphan alone was not quite enough to melt the hearts of American viewers. In the climactic assault on Dodge City, the VC commit the ultimate atrocity: they grease poor Hamchunk's pooch, and the tearful orphan buries it as the bombs fall helter-skelter around him. The valiant Captain Nim perishes too. "He bought the farm, sir," one of the men informs Wayne, but adds reassuringly, "he took a lot of 'em with him."

As so often happens when dramatic needs come first, complex issues of geopolitics are reduced to intensely personal relationships and bold visual images. The can-do American colonel, the stalwart South Vietnamese ally, the hapless orphan—all reinforce the myths embraced by *The Green Berets*. The film ends with Hamchunk again at loose ends, walking with Wayne along the beaches of the South China Sea. "What will happen to me now?" he asks plaintively. Wayne sets a green beret atop the boy's head and then (as in so many earlier westerns) walks into the sunset with his pal. "You let me worry about that, Green Beret," he says. "You're what this war is all about." No matter that Vietnam's beaches face *east* (this sun would have to be rising); the message of these visual images is strong and clear. Americans have come to Vietnam to protect innocents and promote democracy, just as they had in Hollywood's previous wars.

While visual images establish mythic themes, a film's narrative structure can be equally revealing. As we have seen, filmmakers are constantly con-

*Examining the way a film's story is constructed can help reveal how a film's myths are built.*

structing their versions of history with drama in mind. When a soldier is wounded fatally in a firefight, we must ask ourselves, why at that point in the screenplay and not earlier? When a woman discovers something unsettling about the personal background of her lover, we must wonder, why now? Or why at all? For historians, questions about why events happened in a particular order can be resolved only by analyzing the primary sources. In the case of films, characters are killed off or lovers are jilted because the screenwriters, the director, or the producers wish these events to happen. Thinking about the way a story is put together, in other words, can expose the intentions of the film's creators.

In this light, the plot of *The Green Berets* is tantalizingly odd. Its various parts don't quite fit together. Most of the film focuses on Colonel Kirby's defense of his border outpost. But tacked onto this tale is a second, unrelated story. As he prepares the defenses of Dodge City, Kirby is suddenly flown from his outpost to attend dinner at "Le Club Sport," a fancy nightspot in the city of Da Nang. There, he sees an Asian beauty dining with a Vietnamese companion. Before we can learn more, a couple of Green Berets appear and yank Wayne from his dinner: the VC attack has begun.

Only after Dodge City is safely retaken do we discover that the mysterious lady is a double agent hoping to lure the Viet Cong's highest-ranking general into a trap. Wayne then leads a commando team armed with drug-tipped arrows and crossbows deep into enemy territory. Sneaking into the general's bedroom, the Green Berets drug him and pack him off in a body bag to a rendezvous where he is lofted on high by a helium balloon and whisked away by an American airplane dragging a hook. The whole concoction is sheer implausible fantasy, with no relation to the rest of the film. Worse, the extra length makes *The Green Berets* drag interminably.

Why tack on the extra plot? Any Hollywood script doctor could have seen that the way to shorten an overly long film was to eliminate it. But if the producers considered that option, they never carried it out. Why not?

Put yourself in the place of the screenwriter. Try eliminating the second plot and walk with John Wayne through what has now become the final scene of your new, shorter epic. Everything remains as before—the same dialogue, same camera angles. See how the new ending plays.

The Green Berets stand victorious outside Dodge City, thanks to an air attack that has strafed and killed nearly every VC in the fort. "We can probably move in there tomorrow," says Wayne, "God willin' and the river don't rise." Sounding like he's back in sagebrush country, Wayne does move in. The VC flag, fluttering over the outpost, is cut loose and blows away. As Wayne surveys the territory, one of his sergeants walks up hesitantly:

SERGEANT: What do we do now, sir?

KIRBY: First we get some sack time. . . . [Pause. Looks grimly around.] And then we start all over again.

*And then we start all over again?* Can this be the climax to all the tragic bloodshed, the anguished deaths, the carnage? We start all over again? When the flag went up at Iwo Jima, it stayed up. But in 1968 the course of fighting in Vietnam was different—as even Wayne recognized. American armed forces did not try to capture territory; instead, they attempted to kill as many of the enemy as possible in a war of attrition. When American search-and-destroy missions cleared an area, they usually either moved on in another sweep or returned to their base, leaving the territory once again to the enemy. In Vietnam, the victories never quite stayed won.

Suddenly, the reason for the awkward second plot becomes clearer. In 1968 the real war in Vietnam could provide no prospect of a definitive victory. Yet unlike history, an action-adventure film demands a climax in which its heroes' hardships and deaths have not been in vain. The only finale Wayne's writers could devise was a second, wholly implausible victory. *The Green Berets* clings valiantly to the cinematic myths of World War II and the Wild West, but only by abandoning even tenuous links with reality.

# SON MY: AT GROUND LEVEL

The realities of the war, however, were becoming harder to evade. John Wayne's film demonstrated that although myths might distort history, they could not ignore it entirely if they hoped to speak to audiences in lasting and satisfying ways. The tension between the ideal and the real, between what should have been and what was, made *The Green Berets* an unconvincing film for many Americans. And in the summer of 1968, the seemingly routine search-and-destroy mission at Son My was beginning to catch up with the myths in which Wayne sought to clothe American involvement in Vietnam.

Several days after Charlie Company returned from Son My in March, another helicopter from the 11th Brigade swept low over the area. Ronald Ridenhour, a door gunner, was struck by the desolation. Nobody seemed to be around. When Ridenhour spotted a body, pilot Gilbert Honda dropped down to investigate. It was a dead woman, spread-eagled on the ground. As Ridenhour recalled later,

> she had an 11th Brigade patch between her legs, as if it were some type of display, some badge of honor. We just looked; it was obviously there so people would know the 11th Brigade had been there. We just thought, "What in the hell's wrong with these guys? What's going on?"

As the chopper continued its sweep, several Vietnamese caught sight of it and ran to a bunker. Ridenhour wanted to flush the men out with a phosphorus grenade, but the pilot refused to come in low enough. Ridenhour was angry. Why hadn't Honda pursued? The pilot was evasive; all he would say was, "These people around here have had a pretty rough time the last few days."

At first Ridenhour forgot the incident. Then a friend mentioned Charlie Company's operation. According to the word going around, Charlie Company had eliminated the entire village. Astonished, Ridenhour talked throughout the next few months with a number of soldiers who had been at Son My. The more he heard, the more outraged he became.

When he returned home to Phoenix, Arizona, he could not let the matter rest. In March 1969 he summarized what he had learned in a letter and sent copies to the White House, the Pentagon, the State Department, and members of Congress. Prodded by several representatives, the army began an inquiry. By the end of August 1969, the Criminal Investigation Division had interviewed more than seventy-five witnesses. The investigators' attention centered increasingly on the leader of the first platoon, Second Lieutenant William Calley. On September 5 the army charged Calley with the premeditated murder of 109 "Oriental human beings . . . whose names and sexes are unknown, by means of shooting them with a rifle." Regulations required that the charges be filed by the commanding officer where Calley was currently stationed. That was Fort Benning, Georgia, a location used two years earlier by John Wayne to film much of *The Green Berets*.

To the surprise of some Pentagon officials, newspapers did not feature the story. But following a tip, journalist Seymour Hersh interviewed first Calley and then other Charlie Company veterans. One, Paul Meadlo, agreed to tell his story to *CBS Evening News* on November 21. His revelation sent reporters scrambling. Both *Time* and *Newsweek* ran cover stories. These new accounts referred less often to Son My, the name of the village used in the newspaper accounts of 1968. Instead, they used the name of the hamlet within the boundaries of Son My. On the army's map, that village was labeled My Lai (pronounced *mee lie*).

Inevitably, the memories that surfaced were fragmentary, imperfect. Some members of Charlie Company preferred not to talk with anyone. Others felt an aching need to speak out. In the end, there were only partial points of view: wrenching, disjointed perspectives from which to piece together what happened that March morning as the men disembarked from their helicopters.

*POV, on the ground, at hamlet's edge:* The soldiers, high-strung, advance nervously. They expect return fire at any minute—or the concussion of a booby trap exploding underfoot. A sergeant turns, sees a man near a well. "The gook was standing up shaking and waving his arms and then he was shot," recalls Paul Meadlo. Another soldier: "There was a VC. We thought it was a VC." As the platoons reach the first houses, they split up and begin pulling people out of the hamlet's red brick houses and its hootches.

*Below ground, in a bunker:* Pham Phon hears the artillery stop. When he pokes his head out, several American soldiers are 200 feet away. Telling his wife and three children to follow, he crawls out. Phon knows how to act when the Americans come. Above all, one must never make a sudden movement, running away from the soldiers or toward them—they will become suspicious and shoot. One must walk slowly, gather in small groups, and wait quietly. As Phon approaches the Americans, his children smile and call out a few words of English; "Hello! Hello! Okay! Okay!"

The Americans are not smiling. The soldiers point their rifles and order the five to walk toward a canal ditch just outside the hamlet.

*A group of infantry:* There is noise, suddenly, from behind. One of the men whirls, fires. It's only a water buffalo. But something in the group seems to snap, and everyone begins firing, round after round, until the buffalo collapses in a hail of bullets. One of the soldiers: "Once the shooting started, I guess it affected everyone. From then on it was like nobody could stop. Everyone was just shooting at everything and anything, like the ammo wouldn't ever give out."

Soldiers begin dynamiting the brick houses and setting fire to the thatched hootches. Private Michael Bernhardt: "I saw these guys doing strange things. . . . They were setting fire to the hootches and huts and waiting for the people to come out and then shooting them. They were going into the hootches and shooting them up. They were gathering people in groups and shooting them."

At the center of the hamlet, about forty-five Vietnamese are herded together. It's about 8:15 A.M. Lieutenant Calley appears and walks over to Paul Meadlo. "You know what to do with them, don't you?" Meadlo says yes. He assumes Calley wants the prisoners guarded. About fifteen minutes later Calley returns. "How come you ain't killed them yet?" he asks. "I want them dead." He steps back about fifteen feet and begins shooting. Meadlo is surprised but follows orders. "I used more than a whole clip—used four or five clips."

Ronald Haeberle follows the operation into the hamlet. Haeberle is a photographer from the Public Information Detachment. Because the army anticipates that this mission will be a major action, he is there to cover the engagement. He comes upon some infantry surrounding a group of women, children, and a young teenage girl. Two of the soldiers are trying to pull off the top of the girl's black pajamas, the traditional Vietnamese peasant garb. "Let's see what she's made of," says one. "Jesus, I'm horny," says another. An old woman throws herself on the men, trying to protect the girl. The men punch and kick her aside. One hits her with his rifle butt.

*"What should we do with 'em?" one soldier asks. "Kill 'em," says another.* Suddenly they look up: Haeberle is standing there with his camera. They stop bothering the girl and continue about their business. "What should we do with 'em?" one soldier asks. "Kill 'em," says another. Haeberle turns away as an M16, a light machine gun, is fired. The women and children collapse on the ground, dead.

As he makes his way through the hamlet, Ronald Grzesik comes upon Paul Meadlo, crouched on the ground, head in his hands. Meadlo is sobbing like a child. Grzesik stoops and asks what's the matter. "Calley made me shoot some people," Meadlo replies.

Pham Phon and his family wait nervously at the top of the canal ditch. By now perhaps a hundred villagers have been herded together. At first they stand, but soon the Americans make them sit, to prevent them from running away. Phon hears gunfire in the distance and has a horrible premonition. He tells his wife and children to slip down the bank into the ditch when the soldiers are not looking.

Lieutenant Calley orders some of the men to "push all those people in the ditch." Calley begins shooting and orders Meadlo to follow his lead. Meadlo: "And so I began shooting them all. . . . I guess I shot maybe twenty-five or twenty people in the ditch . . . men, women, and children. And babies." Another GI, Robert Maples, refuses to use his machine gun on the crowd. But other soldiers fire, reload, and fire again, until the villagers in the ditch have stopped moving.

Underneath the mass of bodies, Phon and his family lie terrified. They are unhurt, except for one daughter, wounded in the shoulder. As the hours pass, Phon says nothing, praying his daughter will not moan too loudly from the pain; praying the soldiers will move on.

By 11:00 the guns have fallen quiet. At his command post west of the hamlet, Captain Medina has lunch with his crew and several platoon leaders, including Lieutenant Calley. Two girls, about ten and eleven, appear from out of nowhere. Apparently they have waited out the siege in one of the rice paddies. The men give the girls cookies and crackers. After lunch, Charlie Company blows up a few underground tunnels it has discovered, demolishes the remaining houses, and moves out of My Lai.

Or more precisely, it moves out of what on army maps is labeled "My Lai (4)." Actually, the map gives the name My Lai to six different locations

**Army photographer Ron Haeberle's searing photographs** of the events at My Lai, published in *Life* magazine in December 1969, provided shocking counterimages to those in *The Green Berets.* The older woman is being restrained by other villagers after she attacked soldiers who had been molesting a younger woman (*right rear*, buttoning her blouse). "Guys were about to shoot these people," Haeberle recalled. "I yelled, 'Hold it,' and shot my picture. As I walked away, I heard M16s open up. From the corner of my eye I saw bodies falling but I didn't turn to look."

in the area. To outsiders, Vietnamese place names can be confusing. "Villages" such as Son My are really more like American counties or townships. Many hamlets exist within each village, and even these are divided into sub-hamlets, each with its own name. The Army has not successfully transferred all the names onto their maps. Thus when friendly Vietnamese informants tell Army Intelligence that the Viet Cong's 48th Battalion is based, say, at My Lai, they do not realize that the army shows six My Lais on their maps. On this morning of March 16, Americans have attacked the wrong hamlet, one approximately two miles away from the reported stronghold of the 48th Battalion.

The people who live in this settlement do not call it My Lai. Its official name is Xom Lang—merely, "the hamlet." For years, though, residents have also referred to their home by a more poetic name, Thuan Yen; a rough English translation is "peace," or "the place where trouble does not come."

## DENIAL

By the time the facts about My Lai became known, the wider debate over the war had forced Lyndon Johnson from office. Richard Nixon began a lurching four-year course of scaling back the conflict. Antiwar protests flared when Nixon sent American troops into neighboring Cambodia, but tapered off again as the president carried out his policy of "Vietnamization," steadily withdrawing American troops, leaving South Vietnamese forces to absorb the brunt of the fighting. By 1973 American and North Vietnamese negotiators had hammered out a treaty that allowed Nixon to claim "peace with honor." But this treaty was largely a face-saving gesture. Despite all pretenses, the war's outcome was a defeat for the United States. Few knowledgeable observers were surprised to see the North Vietnamese complete their conquest of South Vietnam two years later.

As the war wound down by fits and starts, so did the controversy over My Lai. The details of the attack had been so repellent, many Americans at first found them hard to accept. A poll taken by the *Minneapolis Tribune* revealed that nearly half of the 600 persons interviewed believed that the reports of mass murder were false. Other citizens angrily defended the accused. "It sounds terrible to say we ought to kill kids," said a woman in Cleveland, "but many of our boys being killed over there are just kids, too." At the end of a lengthy military trial, Lieutenant Calley was found guilty of "at least twenty-two murders" and sentenced in 1971 to life imprisonment. Following appeals and a forty-month stay in federal custody, Calley was paroled in 1976. Four other soldiers were court-martialed, but none convicted.

Supporters of the war resented the publicity given My Lai. They pointed out that only months before, communist forces had massacred several thousand civilians at the provincial capital of Hue. They noted, too, that since the late 1950s, the Viet Cong had engaged in a campaign of political terror, assassinating village officials appointed by the American-backed South Vietnamese regimes. In contrast, they portrayed My Lai as an aberration in American policy: "the actions of a pitiful few," in the words of General William Westmoreland. President Nixon admitted that there "was certainly a massacre" but believed it to be "an isolated incident."

In one sense, historians have confirmed that judgment. The available records for the war reveal no other mass executions of similar magnitude. At the same time, congressional hearings as well as conferences sponsored by Vietnam Veterans Against the War produced testimony of other GIs who had on many occasions subjected civilians or suspected Viet Cong to harsh treatment, torture to extract information, or indiscriminate killing. Those opposing the war pointed out that even in the case of My Lai, where misconduct occurred on a large scale, the story had not come to light until a soldier entirely outside the army's chain of command had prodded high officials to push for an investigation. How many other, lesser incidents went unreported?

Although the ultimate significance of My Lai remains unclear, the encounter became a defining moment in the public perception of the war. It did so, a historian might suggest, because it left shaken the long-cherished myth of American exceptionalism. As defenders of a democratic culture, Americans were supposed to behave differently from the rest of the corrupt world. They were not the sort, *The Green Berets* suggested, who would rape young girls or execute innocent civilians. Furthermore, My Lai attracted so much attention because it made the issue concrete and personal, in just the way that film dramas strive to do. John Wayne had reduced complex political and economic issues to visual, intensely personal images ("You're what this war's all about," Kirby tells little Hamchunk). Similarly, Ron Haeberle's searing photographs, reproduced in *Life* magazine, served as counterimages that shattered the mythic stereotypes of *The Green Berets*. Henceforth it would be impossible to take the plot and themes of a western or a World War II epic and re-create them in Vietnam.

For nearly a decade, Vietnam remained a subject too hot to handle in feature films. Hollywood dared approach the war only indirectly, as in the irreverent comedy *M\*A\*S\*H* (1970), set during the Korean War. By 1978, however, attitudes were changing. A new wave of Vietnam movies were scheduled for release, encouraged by reports of Francis Ford Coppola's epic under way, *Apocalypse Now*. "When I started," Coppola recalled, "basically people said, 'Are you crazy? You can't make a movie on Vietnam, the American public does not want it.'"

Before Coppola could fulfill his lofty ambitions, however, Michael Cimino beat him in the race to capture Vietnam's mythic high ground. "Ready for Vietnam?" asked the *New York Times*, as *The Deer Hunter* opened in December 1978. Cimino told the *Times* that he had joined the army about the time of the Tet offensive. "For me, it's a very personal film. I was attached to a Green Beret medical unit. My characters are portraits of people whom I knew." Judging from the first reviews, Americans were indeed ready to confront Vietnam head-on. "The film dares to say that things have come down to life versus death, and it's time someone said this big and strong without fear," enthused *Newsweek*. "What really counts is authenticity, which this movie has by the ton," raved *New York* magazine.

But what was meant by "authentic"? To a historian, the characters do seem less stereotyped than those in *The Green Berets*. The dialogue is more natural, less stilted. Yet the film's story and images seem just as mythic. The first third of the drama takes place not in Vietnam but in Clairton, a steel town nestled in the foothills of the Alleghenies. Michael (Robert De Niro), Nick (Christopher Walken), and Steven (John Savage) are leaving their mill jobs in this Russian American community, off to serve in Vietnam. Steven is married after his last day at work; then he and his buddies head into

**Images of the "one-shot kill"** are central to *The Deer Hunter*. Michael (Robert De Niro, *left*) embodies the frontier ideals of America. For him, the encounter with a buck on the mountainside is a defining, purifying moment. In contrast, the Viet Cong are depicted as inhuman torturers who pervert the idea of a "one-shot kill" into Russian roulette, which Michael and Steven (John Savage, *right*) are forced to play.

the mountains for one last deer hunt together. Michael, the leader of the group, regards the hunt as a defining, purifying moment. One must do the job right, he tells Nick: bring down a buck with only one shot. Like Natty Bumppo, James Fenimore Cooper's nineteenth-century hero of *The Deerslayer*, Michael embodies America's noble ideals. The film's images emphasize the deep ties binding these men: at work, the fiery flames of the blast furnace; after hours, the enveloping dark of the neighborhood bar; at the wedding, the glittering icons of the Russian Orthodox church; out hunting, the misty, otherworldly peaks where Michael seeks his buck.

Moving and bold—yes. But authentic? The answer to that question is less clear. Cimino went to extreme lengths shooting these sequences, to obtain the proper "look" for his myths. Clairton is an imaginary town, created by shooting in eight different locations spread over four states. Its imposing Russian Orthodox church is from Cleveland and is twice the size of anything a town like Clairton might afford. The hunting scenes were shot not in the Alleghenies but on the other side of the continent, in the Cascades of Washington. When the deer proved too small for Cimino's taste, he airlifted in larger animals from a New Jersey preserve. "We needed big deer," he said. "I told them there would be a revolution in the theaters if we killed Bambi." Audiences expect big deer and overwhelming mountain peaks. And because myth deals with expectations rather than reality, Cimino obliged.

The first third of the film ends with the men sitting quietly in an empty bar, one of them rather implausibly playing a melancholy bit of Chopin on a piano. Still in semidarkness, we hear the first faint *whump whump whump* of helicopter blades. In a flash we are in Vietnam—the lush vegetation, the smoke, choppers bearing down on a hamlet. Things now happen quickly, confusingly. A Viet Cong guerrilla throws a grenade down a bunker, wounding the peasant inside. We see Michael lying, perhaps stunned, in the grass nearby. Suddenly he springs up and incinerates the VC soldier with a flame-thrower. Reinforcements appear, among them Steven and Nick.

After a firefight, the scene shifts abruptly to a Viet Cong camp where Steven, Nick, and Michael are held with other prisoners. Sadistic guards force them to join a hideous game of Russian roulette, in which a prisoner places against his temple a pistol loaded with a single bullet, spins the cylinder, and fires. The losers die; the winners play the next challenger. Nick is nearly unmanned by the experience but survives. Michael one-ups his tormentors by daring to play with not one bullet but three. When he wins, he uses the bullets to kill the guards and then escapes with Nick and Steven.

The three men manage to reach American lines, but Steven loses both legs, while Nick, his sanity shaken, disappears into the underworld of Saigon, where casinos offer the same ghastly game of roulette. The final third of the film follows Michael back to Clairton, where he attempts to reconstruct the lost world of loyalty and community that the war has shattered. Finally he returns to Vietnam in a last attempt to rescue Nick, now a dazed, drug-addicted professional on the roulette circuit. The two face each other over the table—Michael, hoping that one final game will jolt Nick into returning home. But in his haze Nick plays on, and this time loses. Back in Clairton, his friends gather after the funeral. As the film ends, they sing "God Bless America"—tentatively at first, then with feeling.

The roulette scenes "act as a central metaphor of this film," noted Jean Vallely, a writer who interviewed Cimino for *Esquire* magazine. Certainly, the scenes are emotionally wrenching, impressively acted, and vividly shot—far more powerful than anything in *The Green Berets*. "I wanted people to feel what it was like to be there, to be in jeopardy every moment," Cimino explained. "How do you get people to pay attention, to sustain twenty minutes of war without doing a whole story about the war?" For Cimino, authenticity seems to revolve around dramatic feelings, constructing an emotionally arresting moment rather than a re-creation of the war's historical context. When Vallely probed for more information about the roulette scenes, Cimino seemed reluctant to talk, admitting only that he had read about such games "in a newspaper report."

Journalists who covered the war were less reticent. None of them had read any reports of Viet Cong forcing prisoners to play roulette, to say nothing of Saigon casinos practicing the sport. The best *Time* magazine could dig up was one or two unnamed "old hands" who were said to have recalled "a few episodes" from the 1920s and 1930s. Peter Arnett, a journalist awarded a Pulitzer for his reporting from Vietnam, complained, "I am

*Journalist Peter Arnett complained,
"I am now discovering that increasing
numbers of Americans believe the last
act of the war took place in a sinister
back room somewhere in Saigon,
where greedy Oriental gamblers were
exhorting a glazed-eyed American
G.I. to blow his head off."*
now discovering that increasing numbers of Americans believe the last act of the war took place in a sinister back room somewhere in Saigon, where greedy Oriental gamblers were exhorting a glazed-eyed American G.I. to blow his head off." Seymour Hersh, who had helped bring the crimes at My Lai to light, walked out of a screening of *The Deer Hunter* in disgust.*

But if *The Deer Hunter* is not authentic in its historical details, do the film's myths reflect a kind of emotional truth about the war? The answer requires consideration of the emotions called forth by the film's plot. As we did with *The Green Berets*, we need to ask what can be deduced from the way that the film is constructed.

*The Deer Hunter* is an even longer film than *The Green Berets*. It runs a full three hours and four minutes, to be exact. Yet how much of it portrays the actual experiences of American GIs in Vietnam? If we eliminate the scenes about the games of roulette—events that bear no relation to the real Vietnam—the answer is, *less than four minutes*. In that brief interval we see a Viet Cong guerrilla drop a grenade into a bunker; we see Michael retaliate; and we see Michael, Nick, and Steven become prisoners. The structure of the film, in other words, suggests that very little of *The Deer Hunter* had anything to do with Vietnam. Yet of course it does. We need only imagine our Hollywood script doctor rewriting the plot to eliminate the war entirely. In the new version, Michael, Nick, and Steven are leaving Clairton to dig for gold in the jungles of Venezuela. Once there, they are captured (in about four minutes) by rival prospectors, who force them to play roulette . . . and so on, until Nick tragically blows his brains out in a backroom in Caracas. The structure of this new plot is precisely the same as the old one. The dramatic tension should be every bit as gripping. Yet would such a film receive the attention lavished on *The Deer Hunter*? Probably not.

Clearly Cimino intended for audiences to come away believing they had experienced something of the war's agonies: the haunting trauma of shattered communities, friendships, and lives. But in suggesting how that trauma came about, the film's plot amounts to a comforting, even racist fantasy. By spending only four minutes considering American actions in Vietnam, *The Deer Hunter* deflects attention away from the real traumatic events of the war and onto stereotyped villains. *They* did it to us, the film suggests: we were

---

* Apparently, Cimino's mythmaking was not limited to the movies. Reporter Tom Buckley discovered that the filmmaker had fudged his age in the *Times* interview, claiming he was thirty-five instead of forty. He had never been a Green Beret and had spent most of his six months of active duty at Fort Lee, New Jersey, with about a month thrown in for medical training in Texas, where he might have met a few of the Special Forces. This active duty occurred not in 1968 but 1962—well before the heaviest American involvement in Vietnam.

shattered by swarthy, inhuman tormentors. In their evil hands, the holiest myth of the West—the ritual of the one-shot kill—was perverted into an evil game of torture. Filmgoers who didn't want to "feel guilty" about the war could now leave the theater singing "God Bless America," believing that the myths at the center of Michael's world (and theirs) remained intact. Not surprisingly, *The Deer Hunter* received the Academy Award for Best Picture in April 1979. As Michael Cimino bounded to the podium to collect his Oscar, the man who handed it to him, gaunt from a recent bout with cancer, was John Wayne.

And in one final irony, the realities of Vietnam again stood cinematic myth on its head. For there was at least one documented case of roulette that remained unnoticed by *The Deer Hunter*'s critics. The day after My Lai, Captain Ernest Medina flushed out another Viet Cong suspect as Charlie Company continued south. When the man refused to talk, Medina took his thirty-eight-caliber revolver, placed it at the man's temple, and spun the barrel. Medina later insisted the gun was empty, but several of his men disagreed. When the villager still refused to talk, Medina "grabbed him by the hair and threw him up against a tree," said one eyewitness. "He fired two shots with a rifle, closer and closer to the guy's head, and then aimed straight at him." The suspect broke down and began babbling; he was a communist province chief. Pleased, Medina posed for a picture. Drinking from a coconut held in one hand, he held in his other hand a large knife at the prisoner's throat.

## THE SEARCH FOR NEW MYTHS

Clearly the anguished experiences of Vietnam made it impossible for *The Deer Hunter* to follow the older, patriotic myths of the western or the combat dramas of World War II. Cimino's film won acclaim because it acknowledged the pain of Vietnam. Yet it still refused to come to grips with the circumstances of the war. In 1979 director Francis Ford Coppola's *Apocalypse Now* provided a rival portrait that faced the realities of Vietnam more squarely.

Although the central plot of *Apocalypse Now* was as fictional and almost as far-fetched as *The Deer Hunter*'s, it did portray the kind of stresses laid bare at My Lai. Coppola's audience could never confuse his soldiers with the fresh-faced GIs who followed John Wayne or with Cimino's injured innocents abroad. In a sequence some critics hailed as the most thrilling battle scene ever filmed, Robert Duvall's character, Colonel Kilgore (whose name reflects his temperament), leads a helicopter assault nearly as ruthless as the one at My Lai. Although harrowing, the assault seems almost surreal because the choppers descend on their target hamlet blasting Wagnerian opera from huge loudspeakers. (This move is to "scare the shit out of the slopes," Kilgore explains, reflecting the casual racism so often a part of the war.)

Just as the troops at My Lai left an 11th Brigade patch between the legs of a prominently displayed corpse, so Kilgore deals out playing cards of death on the bodies of his slain villagers, to serve as both boast and warning to the VC. Just as Charlie Company set up camp after the massacre and went swimming along the beaches of the South China Sea, Kilgore eagerly unpacks a surfboard to ride the waves offshore. The resonances with My Lai are unmistakable. Yet audiences may have been so swept away by the sheer bravado of the chopper assault that they failed to realize how much the scene undermined the cherished myth that Americans preserved their humanity in the heat of battle. Many viewers embraced the scene's affirmation of America's technological supremacy. In a chilling example of life imitating art, some American assault helicopters in the Gulf War of 1991 attacked Iraqi positions as loudspeakers aboard boomed out recordings of Wagner.

Colonel Kilgore's excesses, however, are only a prelude to a more metaphysical confrontation with the realities of My Lai. Captain Willard (Martin Sheen) has been sent on a mission to eliminate a Green Beret colonel named Kurtz, who has deserted and is operating independently just across the Laotian border. As Willard journeys farther into the jungle, he himself becomes more ruthless, more like Kurtz. When the boat taking him upriver is sidetracked by a needless attack on a peasant sampan (the jittery crew opens fire prematurely), Willard shocks the other soldiers by coldbloodedly killing a wounded woman so that his mission will not be delayed while they take her downriver for medical attention. He then pushes deeper into the jungle toward the amoral Kurtz. He is descending, it seems, toward the same elemental savagery that characterized My Lai.

But in the end, *Apocalypse Now* is defeated by its own literary pretensions. In trying to make the film more than just another war picture, Coppola modeled his story on Joseph Conrad's literary classic *Heart of Darkness* (1902). Set along Africa's Congo River at the height of European imperialism, Conrad's tale concerns a man sent to investigate a colonial ruler gone "native"—also named Kurtz. Coppola's implication—that Vietnam is America's own imperialist nightmare—was an intriguing notion. But as played by an overweight, eccentric Marlon Brando, Kurtz only distracts from the grittier horrors of the real war. His lunacy is so otherworldly that it has no connection to the experiences of ordinary American GIs in Vietnam or to the earlier scenes in *Apocalypse Now* that gave the film its mythic power.

Meanwhile, many Americans remained reluctant to examine the causes or context of the brutality demonstrated at My Lai. It was simpler to embrace again the traditional myths of American valor, honor, and decency. The most prominent advocate of this approach was Ronald Reagan, a Hollywood actor turned politician who understood well how cinematic myths were made. As a presidential candidate in 1980, a year after the release of *Apocalypse Now*, Reagan called on Americans to "stand tall" and praised the war in Vietnam as a "noble cause."

Hollywood, too, burnished its views of the war. Two of the most popular films of the Reagan years starred Sylvester Stallone as the smoldering, half-Indian, half-German, entirely muscle-bound John Rambo, a Vietnam vet with vengeance on his mind. In *First Blood* (1982), Rambo takes his

**Mythical images of the West** are twisted in Francis Ford Coppola's *Apocalypse Now*. In place of the can-do Colonel Kirby of *The Green Berets*, Colonel Kilgore, played by Robert Duvall, conducts a harrowing raid on a Vietnamese village. Duvall's cavalry hat draws the connection with the cinematic genre of the western, but the tragedy at My Lai has given this gleeful colonel a grim undertone: "I love the smell of napalm in the morning," says Kilgore after his conquest is complete.

frustrations out on the sadistic sheriff and the establishment of a corrupt town in the Pacific Northwest, leaving Main Street in ruins. But the sequel three years later (*First Blood, Part 2*) finds him back in Vietnam on a secret mission to discover whether Americans listed during the war as MIAs (missing in action) are still being held as prisoners. In the film's entirely fictional plot, Rambo locates an MIA prison camp with the help of an Asian beauty he encounters deep in enemy territory. ("Too much death—death everywhere—maybe go America—live the quiet life," she remarks hopefully to the one American who has proved himself utterly incapable of settling down peacefully anywhere.) But when Rambo radios in the camp's location, the "stinking bureaucrat" from Special Operations calls back the rescue helicopter. He has assumed Rambo will fail, thus allowing the controversy over MIAs to disappear. Needless to say, Rambo manages to fight off entire detachments of Vietnamese and their Russian allies, rescuing the American prisoners and piloting them safely home.

Once again, the film's dramatic structure reveals the same unwillingness to confront the real war in Vietnam. Although the producers clearly supported the notion that Vietnam was a "noble cause," the plot is not about the war itself. Why? In an escapist adventure, Rambo must be allowed to win. By focusing on the issue of MIAs, "victory" was defined in terms of the far simpler task of rescuing a dozen prisoners. And like *The Deer Hunter*, the film's motivation centers on what they did to us, rather than on the more ambiguous question of American involvement in Vietnam.

Furthermore, the mythical Green Beret of the 1960s has been transformed. In 1968, when real lives were being lost and real atrocities committed, *The Green Berets* was careful to show John Wayne restraining his bloodthirsty South Vietnamese allies. By the 1980s—a generation distant from the real horrors of the war—Rambo's version of valor was a muscular body that had become a finely tuned killing machine. (During the years when the war was actually fought, Stallone himself was spending his draft-age years teaching at a private girl's school in Switzerland, studying drama in Miami, and acting in a soft-core porn film titled *The Party at Kitty and Stud's*.)

In part, the passage of time and fading memories made it possible for a wide audience to accept Rambo's fantastic myths. Americans no longer had to face the war every night on the news. But greater distance had also drained the political debate of its old divisiveness. That opened the door, by 1986, to a very different film about Vietnam. The director of *Platoon*, Oliver Stone, had served in Vietnam for fifteen months and had been wounded twice. Returning home, he wrote a screenplay about the war, but in 1976 no one would produce it. A decade later, producers were willing to take the risk.

*Platoon* became one of the first commercially successful films to look at the war itself; to see Vietnam as history. As the opening credits roll, Chris Taylor (Charlie Sheen) steps out of the giant maw of a cargo plane into the oppressive heat of Vietnam. But the sounds of jet engines, jeeps, and airport clatter are muted. Over them, a serenely sad melody fills the soundtrack, a technique that distances us from what we are seeing. The music is Samuel Barber's *Adagio for Strings*, a composition that first received widespread attention in 1945, when it was broadcast following the announcement of Franklin Roosevelt's death. In *Platoon*, its elegiac melody mourns men and times past, a feeling reinforced by an epigraph on the screen: "Rejoice, O young men in thy youth." Taken from the Bible's book of Ecclesiastes, the words are not those of celebration but of warning, spoken by one whose youth has long vanished. ("I have seen everything that is done under the sun, and behold, all is vanity and a striving after wind.") As Taylor and other GIs cross the runway, they see the body bags of dead servicemen being loaded into the plane, heading home—those who have striven, perhaps, in vain.

At first, *Platoon*'s format seems much like the old World War II dramas, with their ethnic mix of soldiers learning the hard lessons of war. But this is Vietnam, and *Platoon* recognizes the differences. We meet Bunny, the violent redneck who takes bites out of beer cans; Rhah, the tough-minded Puerto Rican; King, a black draftee from the rural hills of Tennessee; Lerner, a naïve white recruit; Junior, a street-smart black soldier from the urban north; and Chris Taylor—the observer, newcomer, and college-educated odd man out who has volunteered for service. Because of the war's duty rotation system, recruits stayed in Vietnam for only one year. Thus the composition of fighting units was constantly changing, as each "grunt" in the field served out his 365 days and departed. Under such a system, morale was difficult to maintain, since newcomers were treated as greenhorns whose mistakes were likely to get the old hands killed. And the old hands had every incentive to duck tough assignments that might send them home in a body bag.

*Platoon* also dramatizes the anguish of fighting in Vietnam. Taylor is tormented by ants that crawl over him; he faints from the heat and humidity of a hard march; he stares anxiously into a rainy, impenetrable dark, trying to spot the invisible enemy. Then on New Year's Day 1968, the platoon comes upon an enemy bunker complex. At the center of the jungle camp a fire still burns—evidently the VC have fled only moments earlier. Sergeant Elias (Willem Dafoe) probes a tunnel complex, inching along in the dark, hoping not to be blown away by a waiting guerrilla. Others in the platoon are spread out along the camp's perimeter, each nervous about being isolated. Suddenly a booby trap explodes, killing a soldier.

From out of the jungle the men march to a village. The VC have retreated here, haven't they? Along the way, another soldier is found brutally murdered, leaving the platoon in a dangerous mood. The villagers go placidly about their farmwork; yet the Americans realize that at the very least the hamlet's residents have been helping the guerrillas, and perhaps are VC themselves. The scar-faced Sergeant Barnes (Tom Berenger) stalks angrily through the settlement, finding concealed ammunition, herding some of the women into a pigpen. Taylor flushes one man from a bunker and, temporarily enraged, shoots at the feet of a peasant, making him dance in fear. Then Bunny crushes the man's skull with his rifle butt. Outside, other women and children are crying as Barnes questions the village's headman. The hysteria, the fear, and the rage clearly upset the men, who are on the verge of opening fire indiscriminately. Sergeant Barnes shoots one woman who has been yelling at him, then points his rifle at the headman's daughter and is about to execute her when Elias physically attacks him and tells him to stop. Barnes backs off, but fixes Elias with a steely eye. "You're dead," he says. The platoon's lieutenant gives the order to torch the village, and then the soldiers move out.

What makes this sequence remarkable is that unlike *The Green Berets, The Deer Hunter*, or Rambo's fantasies—even unlike *Apocalypse Now*—it provides an answer to a question that is at bottom historical rather than mythical. What we see unfolding before us is My Lai—or rather, a My Lai in the making, averted only because Sergeant Elias steps in. But because the film has followed the platoon's mission over the course of several months, we are seeing the incident in context—a context that closely mirrored the Vietnam experience of many American GIs. The trauma of Vietnam becomes not merely a question of what they did to us. Nor is it even a question of what we did to them, which is the equally distorted reverse-angle perspective. *Platoon* makes it easier to see that in a civil war, where the civilian population is divided, war becomes an ambiguous, dangerous occupation, especially for foreigners who understand little of Vietnamese culture. The women who protest "No VC! No VC!" may be cooking enough rice to feed an entire unit hiding nearby, and the children who accept candy from GIs and call out "Okay! Okay!" may turn around and lob a grenade. "I used to like kids," said Herbert Carter, one of the soldiers at My Lai, "but I can't stand them any more."

In a war in which territory was never gained permanently, how could victory be measured? Body counts were one way. "Anything that's dead and isn't white is a VC," went one Army joke making the rounds. A member of Charlie Company recalled being shocked, shortly after he arrived in Vietnam, to see a troop carrier drive by with "about twenty human ears tied to the antenna." Even Lyndon Johnson could not resist exhorting troops in Vietnam to "come home with the coonskin on the wall." When GIs began to measure victory in terms of bodies counted, when friend and foe looked alike, and when more than a half dozen men in Charlie Company had been killed by exploding booby traps, the ingredients for trouble simmered. "It just started building," recalled Ronald Grzesik. "I don't know why. Everybody reached the point where they were frustrated. . . . I remember writing a letter home saying that I once had sympathy for these people, but now I didn't care." Two days before My Lai, Gregory Olsen, a devout Mormon in Charlie Company, wrote his father about what happened after another booby trap incident:

It all turned out a bad day made even worse. On their way back to "Dotti" [other members of the company] saw a woman working in the fields. They shot and wounded her. Then they kicked her to death and emptied their magazines in her head. They slugged every little kid they came across.

Why in God's name does this have to happen? These are all seemingly normal guys; some were friends of mine. For a while they were like wild animals.

It was murder, and I'm ashamed of myself for not trying to do anything about it.

This isn't the first time, Dad. I've seen it many times before. I don't know why I'm telling you all this; I guess I just want to get it off my chest.

To its credit, *Platoon* reflects these realities. Yet it reaches no hard conclusions about the issues it raises. Having made reference to My Lai, the scene in the hamlet ends with an image of American innocence. Against the backdrop of burning huts, the platoon escorts frightened villagers to safety. GIs who moments earlier were ready to murder and rape now cradle children in their arms—just as, at the real My Lai, Colonel Medina and Lieutenant Calley shared cookies and crackers with two girls from the village. Repeatedly, *Platoon* returns to this tension between good and evil. During another mission, the violent Barnes makes good his threat to kill the saintly Elias. The mythical overtones are strong: with a church in the background, Elias dies like Christ, his arms stretched out as if in crucifixion. But here, good and evil do not boil down to us versus them. The good Elias is every bit as much

**The amoral Sergeant Barnes (Tom Berenger)** threatens to kill a young villager in *Platoon*. Contrast this scene with the one of John Wayne in *The Green Berets* on page 427. The events at My Lai have obviously altered dramatically the cinematic images of Americans at war in an ambiguous conflict.

a soldier as the evil Barnes. The experience of My Lai has forced *Platoon* to give up the myth of American exceptionalism—that Americans are more virtuous, thanks to their special circumstances. Americans must wrestle with the evil within themselves, as all people do.

Elias as a Christ figure, Barnes as an amoral realist . . . these are mythological and dramatic—rather than historical—concepts. But they reflect the circumstances of the war in far different ways than do the myths of *The Green Berets* or *Sands of Iwo Jima*. *Platoon*'s ambiguities reveal the difficulty of imposing traditional myths on Vietnam, a war that demanded myths of its own.

In the end, it will not do to say that *Platoon* is better history than *The Green Berets*—although most historians might conclude that it more accurately portrays the conditions of the war. Myths of the cinema will always reflect the needs of drama more than the requirements of historical evidence. For their part, historians must remain faithful to their own creed: to examine the images of the silver screen rationally and with the same skepticism they bring to any primary or secondary source.

But is a rational, skeptical approach enough? If truth be told, people do not often make love or die for their country on rational grounds alone. The best history recognizes those deep-seated emotions that myths address. For that reason we have examined not only the facts of My Lai but the more intangible effects the event has had on our self-image as a nation. In their eagerness to become mythmakers for the millions, the magicians of Hollywood have offered us not one but many myths with which to shape our lives. The power of history to undertake a reasoned analysis of the past offers hope—and perhaps a method by which we may come to appreciate the authentic truths that the best myths reveal.

Return one last time to Son My. As historians, we cannot expunge the painful record of what took place, but it may be worth repeating that My Lai stood as an extreme of the American experience in Vietnam. If the booby traps, the ambushes, the frustrations of an unseen enemy worked on all soldiers, not all chose to behave in the same way, even at My Lai.

*POV, above the hamlet in an observation helicopter:* Chief Warrant Officer Hugh Thompson, of Decatur, Georgia, is sweeping the area. He spots a wounded girl by the side of a rice paddy and decides to mark her location with a smoke grenade so that the men on the ground can provide medical help. Thompson is astonished to see a captain walk over to the girl and shoot her. Turning north, Thompson sees a small boy bleeding along a trench and marks his location with smoke. Casually, a lieutenant walks up and empties a clip into the child.

Beside himself with anger, Thompson tries to contact ground forces. When he cannot get through, he radios a loud protest to brigade headquarters. Then, circling over the hamlet's outskirts, he sees a canal ditch with "a bunch of bodies in it." A pilot nearby is reminded of "the old Biblical story of Jesus turning water into wine. The trench had a grey color to it, with the red blood of the individuals." Thompson spots some children still alive among the mass of bodies. Nearly frantic, he lands his small chopper and picks up a child about two years old, dazed with shock. He calls in another gunship for a dozen more youngsters. In the air once again, he sights the same lieutenant who shot the child he had marked earlier. The lieutenant—Thompson later identifies him as Calley—is in the process of destroying a bunker in which women and children are huddled.

This time Thompson lands, gets out of the chopper, stalks over to Calley, and tells him to remove the civilians. The only way to get them out, responds Calley, is to use hand grenades. "You just hold your men right here," Thompson retorts angrily, "and I will get the women and kids out." Thompson orders one of the waist gunners in his chopper to aim his machine gun "at that officer" and shoot if he tries to interfere. Then Thompson walks back and places himself physically between Calley's troops and the women and children, until a chopper arrives to evacuate them.

For his actions, Thompson was belatedly awarded the Distinguished Flying Cross. The curious historian may consult the citation in army records; it is less than direct in describing the conditions under which Thompson had been "disregarding his own safety." It notes only that he found the children "between Viet Cong positions and advancing friendly forces." As usual, the raw material of the past is neither as clear-cut nor as comforting as the larger-than-life deeds of the cinema. It remains for historians, sifting through such telltales, to fashion narratives that are worth not only dying for, but living with.

# *Additional Reading*

All the films we discuss are available on videocassette and DVD. For broader coverage of the films of Vietnam, see Albert Auster and Leonard Quart, *How the War Was Remembered: Hollywood and Vietnam* (New York, 1988); Linda Dittmar and Gene Michaud, eds., *From Hanoi to Hollywood: The Vietnam War in American Film* (New Brunswick, NJ, 1990); and Pat Aufflerheide, "Vietnam: Good Soldiers," in Mark Crispin Miller, ed., *Seeing through Movies* (New York, 1990). A number of compelling documentary films about Vietnam are worth viewing. *Hearts and Minds* (1974) illustrates how the format can convey a highly interpretive message; *Vietnam: A Television History* (1983) is a thorough thirteen-part series originally aired on the Public Broadcasting System (PBS). Both pay far more attention to the Vietnamese side of the war than most American accounts do. Another PBS series, *Frontline*, has examined the My Lai incident in *Remember My Lai* (WGBH Television, 1989). Two edited collections allow readers to engage for themselves the issues raised by My Lai and the Vietnam War. David Anderson, ed., *Facing My Lai: Moving Beyond the Massacre* (Lawrence, KS, 1998), gathered a distinguished group of historians, military people, veterans, and journalists for a conference on My Lai; this book contains their perspectives on the massacre and its meaning. James S. Olson and Randy Roberts, eds., *My Lai: A Brief History with Documents* (New York, 1999), gathered primary materials about the event.

The number of books on the war itself is vast. Robert Schulzinger, *A Time for War: The United States in Vietnam, 1941–1975* (New York, 1997), covers the American side, while Marilyn B. Young, *The Vietnam Wars, 1945–1990* (New York, 1991), pays more attention to the Vietnamese context. A judicious introduction is George Herring's *America's Longest War: The United States in Vietnam, 1950–1975*, 4th ed. (New York, 2001). Michael Lind, *Vietnam: The Necessary War: A Reinterpretation of America's Most Disastrous Military Conflict* (New York, 2002), rejects both liberal and conservative interpretations of the war. Finally, Robert Brigham, *Is Iraq Another Vietnam?* 2d ed. (New York, 2009), explores a much debated question.

# Credits

**Prologue**
p. xix: Library of Congress, Prints and Photographs Division; p. xxviii: The Art Archive/Bibliothèque des Arts Décoratifs Paris/Gianni Dagli Orti.

**Chapter 8**
p. 172: Library of Congress, Prints and Photographs Division; p. 174: John Jacob Omenhausser, "Guard Challenging Prisoner," 1864. © Collection of the New York Historical Society. (ae00045); p. 176: Library of Congress, Prints and Photographs Division; p. 182: National Archives; p. 191: National Archives; p. 197: Public Domain; p. 201: American Folklife Center, Library of Congress; p. 202: © TRBfoto/Getty Images/PhotoDisc.

**Chapter 9**
p. 208: Library of Congress, Prints and Photographs Division; p. 210: Library of Congress, Prints and Photographs Division; p. 211: Public Domain; p. 213: Library of Congress, Prints and Photographs Division; p. 215: William Henry Jackson, "Teton Range," 1872. National Archives; p. 217: Library of Congress, Prints and Photographs Division; p. 219: Museum of the City of New York, The Jacob A. Riis Collection;

p. 221: Museum of the City of New York, The Jacob A. Riis Collection; p. 222: Museum of the City of New York, The Jacob A. Riis Collection; p. 223: Museum of the City of New York, The Jacob A. Riis Collection; p. 224: Museum of the City of New York, The Jacob A. Riis Collection.

**Chapter 10**
p. 230: Library of Congress, Prints and Photographs Division; p. 231: Library of Congress, Prints and Photographs Division; p. 233L: Library of Congress, Prints and Photographs Division; p. 233R: Library of Congress, Prints and Photographs Division; p. 235: Library of Congress, Prints and Photographs Division; p. 237: Library of Congress, Prints and Photographs Division; p. 239: Library of Congress, Prints and Photographs Division; p. 240: Scientific American, November 7, 1891/ Yale University, Sterling Memorial Library; p. 245: Library of Congress, Prints and Photographs Division.

**Chapter 11**
p. 257: Library of Congress, Prints and Photographs Division; p. 265: Library of Congress, Prints and Photographs Division; p. 266: National

# Index

Note: Page references followed by "n" refer to footnotes.